C000193195

Legless but Smiling

Norman Croucher

Legless but Smiling

An Autobiography

'Legless but Smiling' is a slogan of Callestock Cider Farm, Cornwall.
It is used here by their kind permission.

Legless but Smiling
An Autobiography
©Norman Croucher

All photographs ©Norman Croucher
Except:
The White Edge ©Gordon Stainforth
John o'Groats to Land's End ©Oxfam
Mount Assiniboine ©Barry Needle
Near the top on Masherbrum II ©Graham Lipp
Harry Hakomaki approaches the North Col ©Harry Hakomaki
Frostbite ©Nick Kekus
Hard Ice on Cho Oyu ©Craig John
The individual contributors of photographs and quoted texts
retain all rights to their original material.

Cover Photograph: *Hound Tor, Dartmoor* by ©Jude Croucher

Design & Imagesetting by Toni Carver

Printed and Published by:
The St. Ives Printing & Publishing Company.
High Street, St. Ives, Cornwall TR26 1RS, UK.

ISBN 0 948385 34 0

Distributed to the book trade by:
Cordee, 3a DeMontfort Street, Leicester LE1 7HD

CONTENTS

CONVERSION TABLE

Note on conversions

FOR those who are irritated by the unstoppable trend towards the use of metric measures it may help to remember that 1 metre = 1.09 yards. So what is in any case probably an approximation of a cliff height, rope length or overland distance is so very nearly the same in yards as in metres as to make no difference. If you prefer thinking in feet, multiplying metres by three is a useful 'rule of thumb' if you remember to use it only for shorter lengths since the error is accumulative.

Fourteen Mountains in the world exceed
8,000 metres = 26,250 feet

The Conversions

1 METRE = 3.28 FEET OR 1.09 YARDS
2.54 CENTIMETRES = 1 INCH
1 KILOMETRE = 0.62 MILE
1 KILOGRAM = 2.2 POUNDS

Metres	Feet (Approx.)
10	33
20	66
30	98
40	130
50	165
100	330
200	660
300	1,000
500	1,650
1,000	3,300
2,500	8,200
3,000	9,800
4,000	13,120
5,000	16,400
6,000	19,700
7,000	23,000
8,000	26,250

CHAPTER 1

The Early Days

THE most unusual question I have been asked at a ladies' luncheon club was, 'I know your legs are artificial, but are they still your own feet?' And a local radio programme reported, 'Norman Croucher, a double leg amputee, has recently returned from Peru, where he climbed a mountain of twenty-two feet.' They were wrong by a factor of one thousand.

So let's start with what is accurate, and at the beginning, and no, they are not my own feet.

The year was 1960. I was nineteen years old and wanted to climb but had lost my legs below the knees in a railway accident. People said it was a crazy idea, to think about climbing with artificial legs, but that hope was cherished throughout a convalescence of six months.

''E's gone bonkers,' was my mother's reaction, but two days on a rock climbing course before I lost my legs had planted the indestructible seeds of enthusiasm. 'The Cornwall Youth Committee has kindly agreed to subsidise the cost of the course, the charge for those attending will therefore be 12/6d,' said the pink leaflet, which I still have. That course was months before, as if in another life, when legs were real.

Since the accident, always, always on my mind was climbing, so one day I scrambled awkwardly on rough grey rock on a beach cliff, only a few metres high. Yes, climbing was on, so I wrote to a climbing instructor, Jim Smith, and we arranged to meet. He was thin, agile, in his forties. As we sat in his car, ready to drive the few miles from his home to the sea cliffs, I mentioned my legs for the first time and said I would like to climb.

'Legs can be very handy when you're climbing,' he remarked, 'but we can soon find out what you can do.' Then away we went to the cliffs of Cornwall. It seemed that the question of saying no had not entered his head. Many others have not reacted so positively over the years, and there has been rejection in one form or another from the secretaries of two climbing clubs, a president of the Zermatt Guides, the receptionists at two other Guides Association offices, leaders of two expeditions, a doctor who was prominent in athletics for disabled people, and several individual climbers. Mount 'Closed Mind' is a hard one when you encounter it, but is all the more rewarding for the magnitude of the overcoming. And for every obstructive person there was an open-minded and encouraging counterpart, a Jim. He was patient, thoughtful, and above all sufficiently skilled to be confident that he would choose relatively safe situations for my experimental attempts; to go with an expert was the way to find out without too much danger, so we started on little bits of rock of twenty or thirty metres. Where the faces were steep, they were easy because of plentiful holds for the hands and feet in the form of ledges, cracks and jutting knobs of grey granite. I was a real beginner; two days on a rock climbing course before I lost my legs helped me to decide that I could still climb, but when it came to performing the movements I had to start almost from scratch.

It was essential to look down frequently at my boots to make sure that they had not moved, as they were inclined to slip from small holds. Another problem was that if I raised a foot to a hold only as high as a chair seat I lacked the leg strength to step up. Arms had to provide so much of the power, whereas the usual climber gains most power from the legs. In consequence, I spent much time grunting like a gorilla as I fought to gain height. A further difficulty was the limited bend of the knees, not much over ninety degrees. Most frustrating of all was my inability to move the feet from the ankles to left or right, up or down, to fit nicely on holds. The feet just stuck out rigidly at attention, pointing straight forward. In addition, I lost several inches in reach through not being able to stand on tiptoe. So there were several hindrances which could have been used as excuses if I did not want to climb, but none which truly precluded the sport. Rather than prevent participation, my physical condition only set limits on the difficulty of the routes which I could manage, and obviously progress would be very strenuous by comparison with other climbers. I was very grateful to Jim, for largely because of him the adventure had begun.

Over the next few years I was drawn to several cliffs in Britain. In those early, tentative years on rock it seemed that while many cliffs and outcrops were accessible, mountains put up barriers which might forever exclude me. It was not that the climbing was hard on mountains, for often the reverse was true; but the journeys were long. The combination of a march from the nearest road followed by a lengthy climb seemed too ambitious to contemplate. Early on Jim had invited me on a mountaineering trip to Scotland, which I turned down because the distances and altitudes involved would be too great; at the time that may well have been the case, though it is ironic that I imposed my own limits and would later contemplate tackling mountains which were about ten times as high. So nine years of rock climbing went by with hardly a thought about mountains, except for nagging regrets that they were not for me. Then, one day, in 1969, on a sketch map of Snowdonia, the name and position of a mountain caught my eye. The peak, Tryfan, was marked as about nine hundred metres high and from the roughly drawn map I judged the summit to be within a mile and a half of the nearest road. There was one fact in my favour at that time: the month was February, snow lay deep on the mountain, and cold conditions suited me because the stumps of the legs were less inclined to injury when cool and free of perspiration. If I attempted Tryfan I could decide as I went along whether I should climb the mountain or merely see how far I could go. Ambition had to be tempered generously with caution in those early days of exploration.

A colleague called Peter agreed to give it a try. We slept in his mini-van in a lay-by at the foot of Tryfan on a night so cold that our sandwiches froze hard, but the next day was fine, and with my heart full of hope and trepidation, we set off. To start with there was half an hour's easy trudge through ankle-deep snow on the lower slopes. We each had an ice-axe; they would be our brakes if we slipped. In places we crossed gaps where a slip would have sent us tumbling a long way, but the chances of such a fall were remote. Still, with a novice like me around we could not afford to take risks, and I felt the need for us to be roped together when we passed exposed spots. At such times Peter positioned himself so he could hold me on a rope if I fell. We call it 'belaying', which means to attach yourself to the rock and hold the rope for anyone who takes a tumble.

Each hour was punctuated by two short rests and six hours flew by. Near the top I was so exhausted I could do no more than crawl on all fours through the snow for a few metres. While I rested, Pete scouted ahead, and soon shouted down, 'It's only a couple of hundred feet to the top from where I'm standing. Just a walk!'

We hurried on to stand within five minutes besides Adam and Eve, the two big rocks which crown the summit. It was a small mountain, but at least it was a mountain. I felt an elation which I was to be moved to seek again at the top of many peaks. It was then that Peter revealed that the secretary of a London climbing club had tried to talk him out of climbing with me, though she had shown a different and false face to me. I cursed her name; I think I was entitled.

The whole descent took about two hours, in good weather all the way. What a day!

I could hardly believe I had climbed a real mountain. Suddenly, a whole new world opened up, though at the time I did not realise how much influence the mountains would have. This was a distinct watershed in life. Higher mountains beckoned, but it seemed advisable first to undergo some form of endurance training to improve my stamina on long treks. A few weeks later I made up my mind to walk the length of Britain, the eight hundred and seventy miles from John o' Groats in the north of Scotland to Land's End in Cornwall, raising money for Oxfam. A doctor friend said Oxfam should refuse to encourage my walk, but though I appreciated her concern such a cotton wool attitude suffocated rather than protected me. The walk was a critical stage in what was to become of me, and I needed to make it both physically and psychologically.

Unlike many people who had undertaken the same walk, I travelled alone, without a support group, and with only £160 of my savings in a Post Office account for expenses. If I had carried camping equipment the weight would have been more than I wanted to take, so I would have to search for cheap meals and accommodation wherever I went.

September 18th, 1969. A sunny, windless morning at John o' Groats. I started to walk and eagerness led me to cover sixteen miles, causing my stumps to split open and bleed in half a dozen places by the end of the day, so I was very sore when I arrived at the town of Wick, looking for a place to stay for the night. As it transpired, almost half of my accommodation was provided free of charge, by people who took me into their hotels, guest houses and homes and refused to accept any money because I was making the walk. In addition, at several places I was undercharged.

The second day was very hot. Within six miles the pain became almost unbearable and I had to call a halt. I felt sick with pain, and disappointed that it had taken more than five hours to move six miles. For someone who planned to walk eight hundred and seventy miles it was not an impressive performance.

The next day was no better; the state of my stumps was deteriorating and I was in a dazed condition all day long with exertion and pain. The first two weeks of walking were filled with pain and the smell of antiseptic ointment. Then my stumps toughened to the punishment they received, though still they broke open now and then. The stumps set the limits. With the walking spread over daylight hours I maintained an average of ten miles a day and to make life easier I put my rucksack on a golf caddy-cart.

After 170 miles on the road my stumps were still very sore by the time I had walked all morning, but the raw patches of flesh had benefited from daily application of antiseptic ointment, and were healed, or nearly so.

With the rucksack mounted on a golf caddy-cart I received much bewildered scrutiny while trundling up high streets and along lonely country roads.

Inevitably, one question recurred.

'I hope you don't mind me asking, but how did you lose your legs?'

In the planning stage of the walk I had anticipated that this would happen often, and I did not look forward to being asked.

'I was drunk when I was nineteen, and was run over by a train which cut off my legs.'

'Oh!'

The question had to be faced repeatedly, because, naturally enough, people were curious. The alternative was to retreat, to hide, to miss a large part of life itself, for the long walk proved to be a link in a chain which led to some delightful climbing experiences, so it had to be put into words, that the fault was mine. How ashamed I was to say that at first, but it was a comfort that as the fault was mine there was no reason for bitterness against any man. To come to terms with the physical and psychological consequences was up to me. The blame was mine and I just had to get on with living. What I would have given for it to have been the result of a respectable industrial accident or a sporting injury but, no, it had to be lived with. Adjustment, acceptance, were based partly on the thought that in a way it was fortunate that no one else was to blame, for bitterness would have been a great hindrance. I had my fair share of depression, but I simply could not feel bitter or self-pitying because my mind rejected these feelings and put the blame fairly and squarely with me. Before long I recognised I would have to come to terms with how it happened; that it had happened was not so difficult to accept. There are a number of similarities between reactions to death and to acquiring a handicap, including amputation, but these are neither identifiable nor quantifiable. A paraplegic friend of mine will tell you how he was as good as told off by a counsellor for missing out the denial stage, and not grieving to the desired extent after his disabling accident. I have never met a man more adjusted to his handicap than him, and if anyone maintains that the denial and grief will out in a traumatic way, well, they have not in thirty years. Of course I had deep regrets about getting drunk and neglecting my own safety, but I did not grieve greatly about what could not be changed, and I did not deny because it seemed so odd to ignore what was plainly the truth. Having said that, denial is understandable, partly because some people need healing time. The stages of adjustment oft quoted by disability and bereavement counsellors are at times useful guidelines, but they are not rules. The human psyche is too complicated to be thus easily analysed and categorised. What is common, what is most likely, is not necessarily true where the human being is concerned; there are exceptions, enigmas and barely believable truths.

One phrase the press sometimes use of me is 'triumphed over physical disability', but that is only part of the story. At the age of nineteen I came home not as the wounded hero, but as the fool. The option was there to hide under the rock rather than to climb it. Getting about on artificial legs was the easy bit; overcoming shame and getting on with life, and circumventing negative attitudes towards my climbing, were the hard parts. The challenge, psychologically, was greater because of the circumstances of the accident, and someone helped me a great deal by saying, 'No one can make you feel inferior without your consent.' That took a long time to sink in, and I can't even remember who said it, but those words were a shield carried from John o' Groats towards Land's End, and quite soon I had no more need of a shield. I had experienced a small bit of limelight and survived. And above all, mine is a relatively minor handicap; that is a blessing.

On the day of the accident I had intended sleeping rough, partly because I liked the idea and partly because I did not have much money. During the day I found a suitable sleeping place for the night among some trees. When I returned there at night in my drunken stupor I must have walked too far in the darkness through the trees. An awful pain in my chest was probably accounted for by my falling down the embankment of the railway line which, unknown to me, ran through the trees. At some stage I came to, dazed, confused, but somehow not frightened.

My legs were severed, although I did not know it at the time. I realised, without any sense of horror, that something was wrong with me. The pain was no worse than if I had been lightly kicked on my ankle bones, but I felt helpless.

I called for help, and a schoolboy who was out late saved my life by telephoning the police. He had, for the first time in his fourteen years, been allowed to go to the cinema on his own. The film had broken for a few minutes, so he was later on his way home than he would have been; otherwise he would not have heard me and telephoned the police.

There were vague patches of consciousness. I saw a white-coated, bearded man leaning over me and I heard him say, 'You'll be all right, son.' He had a glass syringe in his hand, and we were in an ambulance. Later I was wheeled, lying on my back on a trolley, through an archway of red bricks. I felt cold. Then I was in a brightly lit room, embarrassed when a nurse took off my trousers and underpants. She cut the material with scissors to make it easier to remove them. Snip, snip, snip, snip, and my lower half was naked.

It was confusing. Something was surely wrong, yet I could not understand what it was. People seemed to be concentrating their attention on my legs. When I tried to sit up they gently eased me back. There was pain, and that was the only connection this distant and dreamlike scene had with reality. Drugs reduced the ache in my legs to a bearable level.

Of the operation, naturally, I know only what I was told. The surgeon, Mr. Shields, had to set to work immediately as I had lost a lot of blood. While the operation was proceeding someone by mistake fetched a trolley from the mortuary to take me away. He was told not to be premature, and I was stitched up and taken to a ward.

After the operation my misty consciousness came back for only a few seconds at a time. A nurse sat at the bedside, watching. I was glad of her company. I vomited gently, as if I was full to overflowing. She held a bowl to my lips to catch the black liquid which ran out. My chest ached badly. The ache reminded me of the time I had indigestion after eating huge chunks of coconut one Christmas when I was about ten years old. I was not aware of much pain in my legs.

Every few minutes I woke up and noticed more of my surroundings. There were screens around the bed and I knew I was in a hospital ward. The nurse gave me a few sips of water from what looked like a small teapot, white, with the spout attached to one side instead of the front.

At the bottom of the bed the blankets were supported by a tubular metal framework, like a miniature rigid tent frame, to keep them from resting on my legs.

Once I woke up vomiting a green liquid; the next time it was yellow. In this period of drifting into and out of sleep I gradually learned what was wrong with me. There was no definite point at which the fact became obvious, no sudden mental shock, only a slow piecing together of bits of information in such a way that I was fairly aware of the nature of my injury long before I actually knew what it was. By the time breakfast was brought round, I knew for sure that my legs had been cut off below the knees.

The nurse announced that it was eight o'clock in the morning. The operation had been completed six hours earlier and we were in the Amesbury ward of the Odstock Hospital near Salisbury, Wiltshire.

Quite soon the nurse took the screens away from the bed and left me. Even though I wanted company I had been waiting to be alone for a few minutes. The patients close to me seemed to be asleep, and I raised the bedclothes and peeped under. There, neatly bandaged, were the two stumps, the strangers with whom I would have to learn to live. Lifting first the right one, then the left, I examined each more closely. It was fortunate that I had come to understand how bad the injury was before I saw the stumps. Although the shock at seeing them was unpleasant it was not as bad as it would have been had I not been prepared. I stared for a few moments until, exhausted, I lay back on the pillows and fell asleep.

Visitors came quite often during my weeks at the hospital. Some of my family drove 180 miles from Cornwall each weekend. Many of my visitors, particularly the older ones, were embarrassed at seeing me, but I was grateful that they took the trouble to visit, and I did my best to make them feel at ease. It is difficult enough for some people to visit a patient who has been seriously injured, but the fact that the majority of my relations were teetotallers made them feel even more awkward with someone who had nearly died as a result of being drunk.

As my body adjusted itself to its changed circumstances the stumps became quite painful. The blood had to find new pathways through which to circulate, since the routes it had taken for many years had been cut off. A feeling rather like intense 'pins and needles' stayed with me all day and night.

The strangest of all the new sensations to which I had to grow accustomed were the 'phantom' pains. I often felt dull pain in my ankles, although I had no ankles, and it seemed as if the second toe on my right foot was curled underneath the big toe. I would lie in bed for long periods trying to straighten it. Yet I must say I am fortunate in not suffering badly from phantom pains, which make a misery of some amputees' lives.

After several weeks at the Odstock Hospital I was transferred to a convalescent home at Perranporth, on the Cornish coast. The home, which consisted of two houses, was set on a hill overlooking the town. There were generally thirty or more patients, over half of them confined to bed.

A few days later my mind was occupied with an important event. I was to be fitted with pylons, which would enable me to begin to walk long before I was fitted with artificial legs. The pylons were each to consist of a plaster cast fitted round the stump, and a metal extension rather like a peg leg. The opportunity to start to walk again could not come too soon, and it would be many weeks before my stumps were in a state to be fitted with artificial limbs.

My first attempt at walking down a ward at the convalescent home on crutches was a wobbly business after ten weeks in bed, but day by day the increase in the distance I could walk was noticeable. It was satisfying to find that it was impossible not to improve steadily with practice. Rather like cycling, the skill could not be unlearned.

It took two or three days of walking practice before I felt confident to tackle the stairs. Concentration was important in walking, and was even more so in climbing or descending stairs. This was the time when I felt most like a mechanical man, ascending and descending with precise, considered movements. Again, continued practice helped, and being able to go up and down stairs brought the outside world within reach.

'You can go into town with the others today,' the nursing sister said. I was surprised, having been practising on pylons for only a week. Four or five hundred metres each way was an exciting prospect. Two hours later I set off on my mini marathon, with half a dozen patients who could walk quite well. A hobbling procession of men, some with walking sticks, wended its way down the road. Like several hens they clustered protectively around their one crutch-assisted chick. The march to the park took roughly ten minutes, and we sat by the boating lake on a fine August day for an hour, before retracing our steps.

That trip was easier than I expected and was the first of many excursions to the park. For two weeks we all went to the boating lake to hire rowing boats, and soon, instead of going to the park, we walked an extra two hundred metres to the sea front.

One afternoon, on the way back from the beach, we passed a tree which looked inviting to climb. I scrambled over a small wire fence to reach the tree, and began. I had to do most of the work with my arms and place my pylons carefully, very carefully. After a great struggle I rose only three metres or so above ground level, but an important idea was reinforced; when I had artificial legs I would climb.

Now, back to the long walk. Day after day the ribbon of road stretched relentlessly away into the distance. When I had walked about 250 miles I met a man who had run from John o' Groats to Land's End, starting a few days before me. He had taken nineteen days and was hitch-hiking home when we met; he came up and introduced himself because he had heard that someone was pushing a caddy-cart to Land's End. Sitting on a windowsill of a derelict house, we had a long talk. His name was Eric Beard, and he was a mountaineer. We exchanged addresses in order to keep in touch and climb together in the Alps; he jotted my name and address in the front of his diary. Several days later he was killed in a motor accident and at the scene of the tragedy the

9

police found his diary – with my name and address on the front page. My wife, Judy, was informed I was believed to be dead. Fortunately, she knew where I was staying the night and was able to ring me.

I preferred to travel without publicity over the majority of the walk because I could move more quickly. It was encouraging to be recognised by well-wishers, but I succumbed too easily to the temptation of offers of cups of tea, pints of beer and meals, and lost time as a result. On one day I accepted twelve cups of tea for the sake of being sociable, at houses and cottages along the way, and spent a long time behind bushes relieving myself. So I was content to be the anonymous stranger who was stared at as he wheeled his little cart down the road, and that was how it was over most of the walk.

Through Kendal, Lancaster, Preston and Wigan. On the way out of Wigan the right stump began to swell. After a mile I had to rest, then again after half a mile. Before long there were stops every fifty metres as the throbbing pain grew worse. On that day I managed only four miles, and had to rest the whole of the next day.

With two-thirds of the journey completed my stumps still split and bled at times, but less often than at the beginning of the walk. Through Tewkesbury, Gloucester, Bristol and Taunton I plodded at an old man's pace. The average daily distance remained at a little more than ten miles, although at times I pushed on for fourteen. Sometimes for a week or more there was no escape from the rain or from water splashed up by traffic.

On entering the county of Cornwall there were fewer than one hundred miles to go. I ambled through the little village where my father was born and from where he was taken to live in the local workhouse as a boy, and soon I approached mid-Cornwall, where I had grown up.

Mount Hawke, St. Agnes, Cornwall is a pleasant country area close to the sea. Memory does not produce many details about the neat little whitewashed Meadow Cottage where I was born. The cottage was at the end of a rough hundred-metre farm lane, and I know you could pick oak-apples from a tree in the lane.

My mother used to take my elder sister's dinner to her at the nearby school. Once she made some stew which she put in a basin. We got ready to go out in the rain to the school, but mother knocked the basin from the stove on to the floor. She cried as she knelt and cleaned up the mess. We took another bowl to the school. When we got there the teacher said I could ride on the rocking horse, and I did. We had a tame rabbit which ran about in the garden. One afternoon a man came to the door holding it, limp and still. He told my mother that, thinking it to be a wild rabbit, he had shot it. We were all very sad, even though we soon acquired an Alsatian dog, kept in a kennel which had corner posts stuck nearly a metre into the ground. When guns sounded during the war that dog could drag the kennel on a chain to our back door.

I remember my elder sister and I were throwing stones down a mine shaft near our cottage when an air raid siren sounded. We ran home very fast because the Germans might shoot us or drop bombs on us from their aeroplanes. The Germans did bomb our village, my parents said, though they had been aiming for an aerodrome three or four miles away. The bombs fell in a line up a road and none exploded except the last which landed in a field and killed a cow.

There is no chronological order to these memories, which are almost the only ones I have of the years up till 1944, when we moved to live eight miles away at Truro, a city at that time of 10,000 inhabitants. I was approaching four years then.

My father, who was a driver in the Royal Army Service Corps when I was born, had bought a butcher's shop at Truro, some time after he was invalided out of the army, with extremely bad varicose veins. We lived behind the shop in Lemon Street. It surprises me that I can remember so little of the seven years I lived in the city. I know that with my mackintosh draped over my shoulders and buttoned at the top like a cape I was Batman on some of the streets near home when it was dark. We were cowboys tracking Indians along River Street towards the playing fields at Hendra, where the battle would take place. We became aeroplanes to fly down Lemon Street, and trains to 'puff-puff' up.

We moved to another butcher's shop (recently demolished to make way for a multistorey car park) and our little back garden was home to many pets. I could take my tortoise from there for walks down Back Lane. Once we walked at least a hundred metres together on a hot summer day.

I started with two mice. They did as nature dictated and soon I had dozens. I sold them for threepence each, then sixpence, but eventually tired of feeding and marketing the tiny things, and gave away the whole business to a friend.

A young crow with a damaged wing became my prized companion, partly because I had found and nursed it, but largely because when I took it into a field as soon as it had recovered it followed me home instead of flying away. It would sit on my shoulder. Probably it looked on me as some sort of mother, but unlike its real mother I did not know how to feed it properly, so it died.

The only lizard I ever kept had been rescued, tailless and bitten, from our cat. I gave it a home in a big biscuit tin in the wash house. It flitted from twig to twig and darted through the fresh grass and earth I put in the tin. One night it escaped, and I was lucky to find a slowworm to take over its old quarters. Unfortunately, the cat, after many attempts, caught and killed the slowworm. I came upon the body bitten in two on the wash house floor.

A circus put a show on for a week in the Moorfield, a rough field at the bottom of our garden (and now the site of that car park). We children went to the circus and for many days after we had seen the animals, the talk was of circuses, lion taming and performing dogs. I set about forming my own circus. Worms were useless; there was no trick which they could perform. Woodlice were not easy to handle and were uncooperative and flies always escaped. Caterpillars, however, had potential as performers. They could walk the tightrope, and rear on end on a tiny platform dangerously high above the sawdust ring. Ladybirds were agile and pretty, but were inclined to open their wings and desert their jobs. After a week I lost interest in the circus and set free the performers, even including Sybil, the fortune telling spider.

Life was enriched by an ample supply of relations, particularly aunts and uncles. Dad had a car in which we took frequent trips to visit them and friends, and we often travelled around Cornwall. Living in a small city meant that we had people around us all day, and that suited me. There were adventurous companions close at hand with whom to go down to the river or to the park or through the woods.

The 11-plus examinations were not the ordeal I expected, and I gained a scholarship to the local public school, Truro School, where my first term began in September 1952. The place frightened me from the start. The tradition was unfamiliar, the staff and most of the pupils seemed to come from social backgrounds distant from mine, and at the age of twelve I lacked the confidence and experience to handle the situation. I took the path of least resistance by conforming and working fairly hard. At the end of my first year at Truro School my father decided to buy a farm, something he had wanted for a long time. He purchased one on Carn Brea, a two hundred metres high hill near Redruth in Cornwall. The tiny farm consisted of thirty-three acres of land, on which my father kept dairy cattle, pigs and chickens. Carn Brea itself was an interesting hill, with granite outcrops rising from ferns and gorse, with a view of the sea, Stone Age circles, old tin mine workings and even a small imitation castle, used now as a restaurant but deserted most of the time we lived at Carn Brea. It was a place where the imagination of an embryo explorer could run riot, and I explored every inch of the hill, climbing the outcrops, none higher than a two storey house, but mountains in my mind. An affection for weather-sculpted rock began there.

My scholarship to Truro School was for a pupil resident at Truro, so I forfeited the scholarship when we moved to Carn Brea, and entered the second year at the Redruth Grammar School. I sometimes wonder what different path life would have taken if I had remained at Truro School; I believe I would have settled in, whereas I found the move to the Grammar School unwelcome at first.

Throughout my teenage years I grew more restless and those days of oil lamps, rock and roll, muddy lanes, pigs, manure and hay were clouded with loneliness which I attempted to forget in school books. I was often torn between staying at school to pass examinations, and leaving to begin a job. The advice I received on this matter from teachers was undoubtedly correct: it was better to stay. I knew this was true, but still I was impatient to get my years of study behind me so I could join the adult world. I liked Cornwall, but I yearned to travel to other places. The county was a pleasant backwater, which I wished to leave for a few years.

Studious year followed studious year at school and I usually came in the first three in the top stream in the annual exams. My pursuit of knowledge was aimed at gaining higher marks at school and this approach rendered most of the subjects tasteless, and my father was disdainful of education; he had worked his way up in manual jobs from the workhouse.

Scholastic achievements went almost unnoticed at home, and my father would have been content for me to have laboured as he always had. It was natural I was expected to work on the farm for what little pocket money there was, but this meant that while my two sisters were taken out by horny males I could not afford to take girls out often. Morally I was bound to work on the farm instead of undertaking work which would have brought in extra money.

Our family atmosphere was loving and my parents were not particularly strict, though my father quite often struck me, in the way no one thought twice about in those days. He was short but very strong, and had been a successful amateur boxer as a young man. As far as I know he won all his fights bar two; one when someone broke his jaw in a boxing match and the other two weeks later, when he fought with the undiagnosed broken jaw. Family and schools taught good, old fashioned values, and I am sure the mores of Methodism rubbed off on me to an extent, though I do not belong to any man-made Church, and did not follow the Temperance path. Nor, in my later years, did my parents, who used to finish their daily routine by drinking copious quantities of brandy and Ribena as a night-cap – all very medicinal, of course.

Their language was Cornish colloquial, smattered with 'Well, I'm blowed', 'bloomin' great', 'proper job', ''tidn so', 'dreckly' and so on. Mother was blunt to the point of occasional unintentional rudeness; in the same way a friend described his mother as 'having a heart of gold and the gob of a dragon'. If you had a pimple on your face Mother would most likely remark on it, and early on in life I identified 'pimple-pointers', those who point out things which cannot be rectified and are best left unmentioned. Mother was a pimple-pointer, and spontaneous.

'You got a cat?' she asked when we visited a neighbour who had no pets. 'Smells like it'.

More recently, to a male TV reporter with whom I would have liked to establish a rapport before our interview, Mother came out, on first acquaintance on the doorstep, with, 'Oh, you're some small.'

Of one of her sisters, who was considering attending a slide lecture I was giving, Mother said, "She might like the slides even if she don't want to listen to you".

'I tell 'em flat and plain', she would say, 'specially if they get on my tripe'.

But despite such big talk, and perhaps because of their humble beginnings – workhouse and farm labouring for Father and domestic service for Mother – they were in awe of 'nobs', 'boss-men' and 'yer higher ups'.

''Tis all done for show an' the bulk of 'em is hand-shakers'', was Father's view of the Council. Hand-shakers were Freemasons, whom he had hated ever since being black-balled for membership. In the presence of doctors and teachers, for instance, they both became deferential, though this wore off by the time they were middle-aged; and how!

Father disliked trade unions, and was almost equally dismissive of management.

'They work together like two pairs of gloves, idiots on both sides.'

My parents' sayings were colourful, like the one for someone who was blinking, which was 'winkin' and blinkin' like a louse in ashes". If you had a good appetite you might 'eat like a stag and become 'full as an egg', and if you overdid it you might be 'sick as a shag' (cormorant). An upset stomach was 'trouble with yer pots'. A noisy person was 'old 'ollow guts', an angry one was 'some ugly' and could be 'teasy as a snake'. Strangers were to Father 'Pard' or 'Pardner' or 'Boy', but never 'My ansum'. Those of lesser intelligence 'couldn't tell A from the track of a duck' and if they were tired they looked like a 'stewed owl'. Goods could be 'dear as saffron' but I don't recall hearing the opposite 'cheap as chips'. Mother's unwitting best was "'E was like a spare pick at a wedding'. Yes, pick, and of one relation in particular she used to say, 'Course, she never think before she open her trap'.

When she met them, Judy was as much bemused as amused. For instance, in a restaurant where Father stared at the raisins in the salad he had been served and asked 'Has a rabbit been here?' His statement that 'You never see chickens all the same height' puzzled her, and still does. On the occasion on which he fixed a new lock on the Men's Institute door and locked himself out, he described his method of getting in as, 'I jiggled yer doin's an' bent the other bit an' that gave me purchase on yer whasaname'.

'I see', said Judy, who always tolerated him.

When she found Mother kept her feather duster in the deep-freeze Judy thought this odd, but there was a rational explanation, which was that the cat would go wild to get at it and attack the duster if he could smell it in a cupboard.

Passing by a cemetery, Father commented, 'Lovely view for them in there', and if that was not enough to make Judy wet herself, Mother added, 'If they're looking east they're in cock-eyed'.

Like any family we had our skeletons in the cupboard, and we seemed to have a whole built-in wardrobe suite full of them. Father's father had been idle, and had fiddled a war-related pension for an injury which had nothing to do with the war. Mother's mother did not cry when her husband died, but wept and wept when her very friendly doctor passed away. Grandad had once tipped a bucket of pigswill over her, and she had fired a shotgun at him, and missed. This incident accounted for there being a small replacement panel of wood in their back door, where the pellets had blown a hole. One of my mother's brothers married a Methodist preacher who soon deserted the marital bed, so he bought two cows and a field a mile away from his farm, established a mistress in a cottage there, and visited his cows every day for the rest of his life. My father's sister entered into a bigamous marriage while her husband was in a psychiatric hospital. Father's mother, deaf and about 140 cm tall, was pretty normal until later in life, when she wandered around in the nude; Mother's father did the same. One great-uncle did time for embezzlement, an uncle narrowly escaped a similar penalty for theft, and another was an occasional petty thief who stole on impulse for fun; he was the sort of man who would steal a barrel of tar and then think, but what shall I do with it? A great many of my relations were to the best of my knowledge honest and ordinary, but there were usually three or four who were not being spoken to, and several who were not on the exclusion list were pulled to pieces behind their backs for being toffee-nosed, smarmy, in debt to my father, or a scrounger.

'How you came out of that family I'll never know,' Jude often says.

Outside the classroom were activities which I found healthier. For instance, the P. E. teacher ran a gymnastic club in his spare time. On two evenings a week about twenty of us practised and put on displays in the district. I captained the team for a while, but I did not like taking any position of responsibility, because I was very shy.

The activities of the school's Air Training Corps squadron were broad and interesting, despite the fact that there was a tendency for the emphasis to be placed on the size of the squadron rather than the quality of the cadets. We fired guns, flew quite often, went to R.A.F. stations for two-week camps and a small number of us went on a gliding training course where we gained badges, entitling us to fly solo. My instructor's words after my first kamikaze-style landing are embedded in my mind.

'Son, if you make another landing like that, you'll be sitting on your arse in the grass, in the middle of a pile of firewood,' he said. But I did improve, and his report said, 'Worked hard'.

In the summer of 1956 I sat and passed eight ordinary level GCEs and stayed on at school to study 'A' levels. The majority, in my opinion far too great a majority, of pupils took science subjects at 'A' level. The trouble was that several people who were not very good at science were persuaded to take maths, physics and chemistry instead of subjects they were better at and enjoyed more. My preference was for English, French, history and geography, but I listened to the propaganda from some of the staff about science being the key to a secure and worthwhile career, and swallowed the bait. I half-heartedly joined the science course, and it was months before I finally accepted that I had made the wrong decision.

Cross-country running and rugby were two enjoyable outlets for pent-up energy. Our school cross-country teams achieved good results and I particularly liked running. I was even presented with my county colours for a mediocre, no, poor performance in the South Western Counties cross-country championship.

The best thing about this period was that I began to climb on a Youth Service course, and alone on the granite outcrops of Carn Brea, and at a flooded quarry near the farm. Going back to the quarry not long ago I was pleased to see that the steep brown wall above the green water looked quite hard. So, there really had been a budding climber inside me. The wall was at the same time a harsh reminder of the agility, the physical ability, which was gone forever, snatched by drunkenness.

The school was restricting me when in the manner of most men I wanted to kill a lion, or win my spurs, or defend the tribe or shoot the rapids. I could not put up with being trapped at a desk or in laboratory. I had no need of an intellectual challenge; I needed a challenge which would stretch me near my limits to help me to grow up. My years at school had softened me, and made me too dependent on people and places that I knew. I had rarely been away from home and did not know how to look after myself.

Not long after I passed physics and failed mathematics and chemistry at 'A' level, I made a big decision. Ignoring any advice to the contrary, I left school and worked on a farm for a few weeks to make some money.Then, with a few pounds in my pocket and a small suitcase of clothing I left home for a 'gap' year before the term had been coined.

I had no plans about where I would go except that I intended spending some time in London and some time abroad. To start with I worked as a labourer in a market garden in Exmouth and lived in lodgings, then after a few weeks moved on to work in a piston ring factory at Salisbury, in Wiltshire; I felt that the experience of factory work would broaden my outlook. I had no friends in Salisbury as I was there for only four days, but I found plenty of company in the pubs. As it was summertime, I slept out. I was looking for a lion to kill. In a way I suppose I found one, and it nearly ate me.

Judy and I met four times for weekends during the walk from John o' Groats to Land's End, and she took two weeks off from her job to accompany me through Cornwall. Each evening we were driven back to stay with my parents.

Finally, at Land's End. Fifty or sixty people waited, and as I took the last few paces over granite rocks to the cliff top by the hotel, their clapping and cheering signalled the end of the ordeal, which had lasted ninety days. The walk was finished and my stumps were toughened sufficiently for me to contemplate climbing in the Alps, but before we move on to my Alpine climbing, which began in 1970, I should tell you briefly what happened to me in the intervening ten years since I lost my legs.

Life came to a lull after I left the convalescent home at Perranporth and went home to wait for my artificial legs to be fitted. For two months the days were occupied with making a model aeroplane, reading, occasional trips around the locality by car or bus, and marquetry.

Nowadays, artificial limbs would be made available much sooner, but eventually the day came when I was summoned to the artificial limb centre at Plymouth to be measured for my limbs. On 20th December 1959, came the best Christmas present I have ever had, for that is the day on which my limbs were fitted, six months after the accident. I spent the evening struggling from one piece of furniture to the next, tottering from a chair to the table three paces away, turning carefully, launching myself at the sideboard and so on, till I was quite exhausted and sore. Gradually, I could take longer and longer journeys between the furniture, measured first in paces, three, four, five, and then tens of paces. In a day or two I made short expeditions out of doors with crutches. A few more days passed before I could launch myself away from the security of a wall or a door handle to totter without sticks or crutches along the rough lane which ran beside our house. I fell occasionally but came to no harm.

I was helped at Truro hospital by a physiotherapist, but after two sessions he decided I was getting plenty of practice on my own, and cancelled all further hospital appointments.

The light metal strap-on legs were uncomfortable to wear for long periods at first, so I took them off when I rested. As day followed day, walking became easier. I was fortunate in having a good sense of balance, and youth enabled me to adapt to the physical problems of learning to walk. When my stumps became damaged through too much walking they healed quickly.

Despite difficulty in finding anyone prepared to insure me – in the end I paid a double premium – I bought a motor scooter. That little green machine greatly increased my independence, but I still walked quite a lot for practice.

I took two temporary jobs, one as a laboratory assistant, the other as a clerk in a slaughterhouse, while I waited to see if I had been accepted on a teacher training course. The first of those jobs, started eight weeks after my legs were delivered, took me away from home into digs in another Cornish town. The move to digs was deliberate, forcing me to manage without people fetching and carrying all the time.

I had found the first job after an unsuccessful try at the local Labour Exchange.

'As a disabled person,' the man there had told me, 'you could be a lift operator, a car park attendant, a tailor or a watchmaker.'

It must have been obvious that the limited choice offered was not received with enthusiasm, and I think the man took offence. Whether by mistake or in retaliation I don't know (I suspect the latter), but a week later a green card from the Labour Exchange came by post. It informed me that there was a vacancy I might be interested in, quite close to home – as a hod carrier on a building site! It was a rather ambitious prospect for one so recently disabled, and I did not apply.

Shortly after I had ceased to use walking sticks I contacted Jim Smith and undoubtedly the highlights of that period were weekends with Jim and other friends on Cornwall's glorious sea cliffs, in fair weather and foul, on solid grey granite.

Soon after my interview with the principal at the Borough Road Teacher Training College at Isleworth, Middlesex, I was informed that I had been accepted for a three-year course commencing in September, 1961.

Part way through the first term we were sent on a teaching practice. I spent three weeks in a junior school and found it difficult to cope with the standing and walking involved, and picking my way between the tiny desks and chairs and little feet was very tiring. At the end of the day I used invariably to get back to college, fall asleep in a chair and miss tea. Whenever I am asked to talk to leg amputees I remember those days; it takes time to become accustomed to artificial limbs.

I joined the college climbing club but was discouraged from taking part in their activities, so I climbed only when I went back home at weekends once or twice a term; several years later the secretary of the club contacted me to apologise abjectly for his attitude. How times have changed! Similarly I was refused permission to use the college gymnasium; it will be too dangerous, I was told. Weight-training exercises – dangerous? Then came a fifty-mile walk during rag week. I can walk a few miles a day and cover the distance, I thought, but the organising committee rejected my entry. Since you already know of my subsequent long walk you will appreciate the irony of that little story. I mention these incidents not as a complaint but to illustrate how attitudes, including mine, have changed in a few years; I did not press my case.

One fellow student, John, asked if I would like to go to a party at Berridge House, a domestic science college at West Hampstead, where his girlfriend, Sue, was a student. I said yes. Sue was waiting with a friend called Judy. While John and Sue chatted, Judy and I went through the usual routine of polite questions like, 'What subjects are you studying?' and 'Did you enjoy your last teaching practice?' and 'What do you think of London?' Why she didn't faint with boredom, I don't know.

At the party, Judy wanted to dance. I told her to go ahead if she wanted to, but I would sit as I had slightly hurt my leg in an accident. We sat and talked all evening.

When Sue rang John at college they arranged to invite Judy and me out for the evening. Judy was rather upset at first because one of the students at her college told her about my legs in a very tactless manner. A sentence something like 'Imagine a little legless trunk rolling around' disturbed Judy more than learning of the nature of my disability. However, we had a nice evening, and over the next few days John's car could be seen nightly tearing along the North Circular Road bearing us to and from Berridge House.

At the end of the first year at college Judy went to her parents' home in Staffordshire and I went to Cornwall for the summer holiday. We wrote to each other regularly and arranged for her to spend two weeks in Cornwall at the end of the holiday.

In the meantime I found a holiday job selling home-made ice-cream in a shop near the beach at Perranporth. It was a pleasant labour selling cornets and lollies from two o'clock each afternoon till eight o'clock.

Judy arrived for her holiday. We had a grand time, travelling around Cornwall on my scooter, and at the end of her two-week stay we were both looking forward to returning to London so we could be near to each other again.

After my second teaching practice, in a secondary school at Northolt, I decided I had made a mistake in choosing to teach. Hours of standing and walking created a very wearing pain in my right leg. Nowadays when I am tired I am reminded of the strain of my first two or three years of walking with artificial legs. I am glad that time is behind me, but I should point out that part of the trouble was that I was very active, and generally speaking anyone with a sedentary job will manage. As well as that, things get easier as the years go by, as you will see if you read on; and I know now that I could cope with the standing and walking which teaching would have required. On top of that, the pain in my right stump was not normal and could probably have been corrected surgically if I had not adopted a 'grin and bear it' attitude, and complained.

Near the end if my second year at the college the principal and I talked over the situation. He was considerate, and we agreed it would be best for me to leave college. A fellow student turned up after one of my talks recently to complain that I should not have been allowed to leave without repaying my grant, but the silly man did not realise that the John o' Groats to Land's End walk had changed my abilities dramatically. I soon secured an interim job as a clerk in a slaughterhouse in Cornwall, and stayed at my parents' home. Getting the job pleased my father greatly, as I had steady employment and was no longer a student.

'You'll soon be on ten pounds a week', he said. 'Job for life'.

I wished he had not said that about this dead end position, and when he heard a few months later that it was time to move on, he said that if that was the case he wanted me out of his house.

Being homeless and with very little money in my pocket, prospects looked a bit bleak for a while, partly because there were several forms of employment, such as labouring, which I could not fall back on, but I sold my scooter and set off to find work; it did not take long. After a brief stay with friends in Herefordshire and a few days with Judy's parents, I saw a newspaper advertisement which interested me, and applied for a job.

I was soon embarked on an entirely different course in life, as a social worker at St. Martin-in-the-Fields church in Trafalgar Square. It is tempting to cite examples of people who evoke a ready sympathy, for those were many, but the truth is that most of the smelly, inadequate, demanding, manipulative, insane, drunk, aggressive, violent, dis-organised, confused people we dealt with would rapidly evaporate the sympathy of most who met them. Though men and women often came just for a meal voucher or an item of second-hand clothing, we tried, whenever it was appropriate, to connect them with bodies such as hospitals, sheltered homes and specialist welfare organisations which had time for them, and expertise. Some were on the run from the police, many were mentally ill, a proportion were mentally handicapped, and a large number suffered from severe personality disorders. Many slept out all year long, under Charing Cross railway bridge, in parks, in doorways and in unoccupied buildings. They preferred such places rather than the dormitories where coughing, groaning, mumbling, screaming, snoring sleepers disturbed the night, and some just did not like being close to others in hostel dining rooms and dormitories. A few had been thrown out of the hostels because they were incontinent, and those who were on the run sought the anonymity they believed came from having no address.

Judy and I married in Staffordshire in 1967 and lived in the vicarage of St. Martin's. We enjoyed being in such a central position and our windows at the top of the building gave a view of the meetings, demonstrations and celebrations which took place in the Square. Judy taught domestic science for a few months, then joined the Office of Population Censuses and Surveys, where she remained for over twenty years, until voluntary redundancy gave her a happy release.

After a couple of years at St. Martin-in-the-Fields I began to work more and more with young people who drifted around the West End, particularly with hippies and heroin and cocaine addicts. Many of the latter were obtaining their drug supplies, at least in part, on prescription from a few general practitioners who prescribed indiscriminately for profit by making a charge for writing a prescription. By selling a proportion of the drugs so obtained, and in many cases through homosexual and heterosexual prostitution, by mugging (at that time referred to as 'rolling', but the same nasty crime) and sometimes by work, they raised sufficient for the next prescription charge. Soft drugs, as they were called, were widely taken as well.

I worked around Soho, Piccadilly Circus, Trafalgar Square, Covent Garden and adjacent areas by day and by night, with a small band of co-workers who mostly worked for six months in the West End. In any week in summer we were asked by parents, hospital staff and social workers to trace four or five young people who had gone missing. We made contact with about half of those we were looking for, which is as much as can be expected considering the circumstances we worked in, and remembering that many of the people we wished to find never in fact came to London. Though we were instrumental in reuniting scores of children with their parents, happy endings were not inevitable, but this was an important facet of our work. As well as that we generally tried to counsel young men and women about the hazards of the West End. Sometimes we found them employment or accommodation, and we made arrangements for them to receive various forms of social and health care. Homeless young people often came to congregate or sleep in the church, but they were not the sort of congregation other churchgoers welcomed, so part of the crypt was opened during the day as an alternative venue. Inadequately staffed, inadequately ventilated and lacking toilets, resulting in a deep, stinking pool at the entrance, the place was inevitably a focus of the drug scene. The philosophy of the church was that it was wrong to turn these people away to a more hostile environment, but I was never comfortable about the crypt in the two years I was responsible for running it.

In one month three young people I knew died of drug overdoses. Two of them, both women, were buried in adjacent graves; I had escorted the mother of one of them to a mortuary for her to identify the body of her twenty-year-old daughter. From a sheltered life in Cornwall, work in London had made me grow up. I had seen too much of the ugly side of life, had witnessed much suffering, and at the end of four-and-a-half years at the church I was exhausted, partly physically, because of the often peripatetic nature of my work, but mostly because of the emotional demands.

Running the crypt bothered me more than I recognised. After years of emotionally challenging work at the church, with no distinctly definable objectives, in a well-intentioned but amateurish atmosphere, with no real training or certain knowledge that we achieved much, with no measure of whether what we did was ineffective or beneficial or even harmful overall to those we hoped to serve, I found faith alone was insufficient. That baptism of fire at the church shaped me more that anything else in my life; it humiliated and injured my spirit, but that came back stronger for the battering it had taken. School, family and other influences somehow amalgamated to shape a perhaps uncolourful man who toed the line and tried hard. That was already my nature, probably influenced by stirring tales and good examples from the wars and their aftermaths. The punching-at-clouds, uncertain world of lunacy, disorder, violence and confusion into which I had stepped was too tough in the long term, and I had to get out, bowed but not quite broken; I was burnt out. From then on I needed campaigns whose success could be measured; not just physical challenges, but they would do to start with. Compared with what I had been through, all would now be relatively easy; give me something I could fight. I was depressed, but something good came of that, because depression spurred me into making a big change in my life. Judy was concerned, and patient, and needed to be, to go along with my next project, which was that walk from John o' Groats to Land's End.

While at the church I had climbed occasionally on rock outcrops near Tunbridge Wells, and with Peter, a colleague from St. Martin-in-the-Fields, had climbed Tryfan. That ascent led me towards the thought that a long walk would be good preparation for more mountaineering, so when I felt the time to leave the church had come, the prospect of the John o' Groats to Land's End walk seemed more than just attractive, it seemed part of my destiny. The long walk served its purpose. It toughened my stumps sufficiently to allow me to contemplate some lengthy mountain treks. If ever there was a time when alpine climbing was physically within my ability it was after my stumps had survived the harsh treatment they received over eight hundred and seventy miles; so I had to go to the Alps.

CHAPTER 2

To the Alps

THOUGH his parents were against the idea, I talked a Cornish climbing friend, Mike, into coming to the Swiss Alps with me in the summer of 1970. We drove there in his mini-van.

A mountain railway carried us one morning up the steep track and through tunnels carved from mountain rock to the Jungfraujoch, a pass of over 3,400 metres, between the Jungfrau and the Mönch (Joch means pass). The train clattered up a steep track where the gradient reached twenty-five degrees. Rhododendron bushes and pine slipped by the windows, then there were no more trees or bushes. Rich green alpine pastures on both sides of the line were speckled with flowers of yellow, pink, red, purple, and blue which matched the sky. Cows nodded and their bells rang while they munched, ignoring the train; familiarity breeds contempt, even of the iron monster.

Kleine Scheidegg, 2,061 metres, is the crowded interchange where you take another train for Jungfraujoch, arriving in less than three quarters of an hour. You're in a tunnel almost all the way. Emerging from the tunnel into the Jungfraujoch station is like drawing up in a long, rough-hewn cave about twenty metres wide. Thirty paces from the platform is the mountainside, which you can reach by walking through a lobby. An observation balcony overlooks the fourteen-mile-long Aletsch glacier, where two glacial moraines make dirty lines, perhaps 300 metres apart, down the centre.

'Must be wheel marks from a truck,' an American told his wife. Some truck! (If you don't know what a moraine is, have a look in the Glossary.)

The hotel hung from the steep mountainside in the way that a fortress might: much of the building was inside the rock. For the visitor there was a man-made ice cave carved beneath the Jungfraujoch plateau, a souvenir kiosk, a post office, a summer ski school, husky dogs fighting each other and occasionally obliging by giving sleigh rides, and a 112 metre ride to a prominent observation terrace at the top of a small peak.

All the climbers we met were equipped with skis, and they explained that the snow was remaining soft later than in most years. Attempting to reach the Jungfrau on foot was out of the question, but we were told that the Mönch was accessible, so we settled for that mountain. Allowing a full day to acclimatise to the rarer atmosphere, next day we did no more than walk a little way to inspect the glacier approach to the bottom of the route we hoped to take; the next day we would climb.

When that day arrived we had breakfast at 3.30 a.m. and began to trudge to the Mönch at 4 a.m. Mist intermittently swirled around the mountain tops which could be seen easily in the bright dawn light. In thirty-five minutes we were at the foot of the south-east ridge, up which we intended to climb. How nervous, how excited I felt as we began to plod up the forty-degree snow slope at the foot of the ridge; after rising about 60 metres we crossed stretches of rock separated by snow.

A rope was unnecessary on the easy lower part of the mountain. The rocks were covered with good footholds and handholds, and until the sun had been shining on the snow for an hour or two our boots crunched reassuringly with each step upward on the white carpet. As the morning wore on the snow softened and our soles sank deeper.

After three hours of steady progress we estimated that we were over half way up the mountain and there we tied our rope on for safety, and moved one at a time while the stationary climber remained still, tied to his ice-axe rammed deep in the snow. The comments of some climbers came back to me: the Mönch is not difficult to climb, but it is a little dangerous; if you fall you will fall a long way. In some places a slip, if not halted by rope or ice-axe, would have sent us tumbling and slithering two or three hundred metres.

Ahead of us on the mountain stretched the tracks of a party of three which took six hours the day before to reach the summit and return to the bunkhouse, and they had moved speedily on the lowest snow on skis. I estimated that their performance indicated that I would need twelve hours for the return journey, and that was rather long for me to keep going in those days.

At about 9.15 a.m. we struggled up a snow ridge which flattened out into a broad shoulder. We had been climbing and walking for five hours.

The slight mist cleared and the summit was suddenly visible, separated from us by a gently rising snow ridge. We slowly made our way in the direction of the top of the Mönch, a matter of a few minutes' walk away. We were within about a hundred metres of the summit when we halted. The ridge was corniced all the way, and I began to feel uneasy. The sun had been beating on the snow for several hours, and we were concerned that it was insecure. A painful decision faced us. The summit was about a hundred metres away and no more than fifteen metres above us. The way was easy, but dangerous, and despite our intense desire to reach the summit, we felt unsure about going on.

Ambition and enthusiasm tugged us upwards while caution and a feeling of risk pulled us downwards. We did what was sensible; we turned back. The Mönch is 4,099 metres high. We reached about fifteen metres short of that, so we failed. But it was a successful failure, to climb almost all the way at a time of year when the snow was not in its best state. I was not greatly disappointed, for though we had not quite made the summit I had done enough to know that Alpine peaks were achievable. Eleven hours after leaving we were back in the bunkhouse.

'In three or four weeks the snow will be good,' several climbers told me. I could not stay that long because of the expense, and anyway Mike wanted to return to England immediately.

At home I felt very relaxed at first with my 'near' ascent. My left stump took ten days to heal where the skin was broken, but that was a very small sacrifice for the thrill of the climb.

Within two or three days of arriving home Judy and I were planning another jaunt to Switzerland in August. For the first week of our holiday we intended to stay in the bunkhouse at Jungfraujoch while I climbed, and for the second week Judy could take the reins and lead wherever she wanted to go. No experienced climber I knew wanted to go to the Bernese Oberland in August, so I had to be prepared to pay for a guide if I could not find anyone else to climb with at Jungfraujoch.

Judy and I travelled overnight by train, arriving on 26th July at Grindelwald. I went straight to the mountain guides' office there that morning and asked about hiring a guide for the Jungfrau.

'The snow is still bad on the Jungfrau,' the woman in the office said. 'The bad winter has left a lot of snow and the hot weather has made it softer than usual. The guides are not taking people up there often this summer. It is too dangerous. The risk of avalanches is great.'

I was not sure she was being straight with me. There was a sinking feeling in my stomach; one I was to experience many a time in my mountain career. It seemed a waste of time to ask if she could find me a guide. However, I pressed on, explaining about my legs and asking her to try to secure a guide who would take someone whose climbing would be very slow. A man she contacted was prepared to take me up a small local mountain and no further. Though his desire to take this unknown quantity on a test run was understandable, we could not afford it.

Judy and I dejectedly left the office and went for a cup of tea while we thought the situation over and tried to resuscitate my shrivelled expectations. It seemed that I would have to wait for another year, but we decided to go to the bunkhouse at Jungfraujoch for a few days in case the snow improved.

When we reached the bunkhouse several people said they had climbed the Jungfrau that day, and they had taken up to seven hours to complete the wearying journey on the very soft snow. Guides were taking clients up, and the woman in the guides' office had not been entirely honest with us.

The following three days we spent in walking through the snow and over those three days we gleaned information from other climbers, piecing together opinions and impressions to form a picture of the state of the surrounding mountains. The Mönch return trip was as short as four-and-a-half hours for the speediest men, and that meant I had a good chance of climbing it right to the top. Even if I could not go up the Jungfrau I could attempt the mountain which just beat me a month before.

On Thursday, I asked the hotel manageress, Frau Sommer, if she knew any guides. Fortunately her husband, Ueli Sommer, the hotel owner, was prepared to act as a guide for me on the Mönch, and we arranged to climb early on Friday morning.

Friday came. I had breakfast at four o'clock and fifty minutes later the muscular and sun-tanned Ueli Sommer and I stepped out into the light snow. I suppose Ueli was about thirty-five years old. He was chief of the local ski patrol at Kleine Scheidegg and knew the local mountains intimately.

The going was good over the gently sloping snow and while we took a brief rest at the foot of the ridge we were to ascend I thanked him for not refusing to climb with me.

'I have a friend with an artificial leg and he goes all over the place around here,' he said.

'But I thought you might be a bit worried about guiding someone with two artificial legs.'

He raised his eyebrows and stared at me briefly.

'Two?'

'Yes, two.'

'Oh, I didn't know. I thought it was one. Anyway, we had better be on our way. Tie the rope on.'

The gently falling snow shower ceased, but the mist remained to hide the peaks. I was not interested in the view anyway as we toiled upwards over patches of snow and rock. Two or three times Ueli cut steps in the ice, but generally there was only rock or firm snow to climb.

By 6.30 a.m. it was warm enough for me to remove my jacket. We were making, for me, good progress and were about half way up the mountain. Ueli went ahead, up short steps of rock, and we reached the shoulder where the final long snow ridge started. Mike and I had stood there wondering whether or not we should continue, but this time there was no need to argue, for Ueli continued in his easy strides in the direction of the summit.

The final two hundred metres to the top now looked firm, safe and innocent. We reached the spot where Mike and I decided to turn back, and Ueli and I passed by.

I was carefully watching where I placed my feet and long ice-axe when we came to a level patch of snow about the size of the floor of a large room. It looked like the summit.

Ueli stopped and slipped his rucksack from his shoulders.

'Is this it?' I asked, hardly daring to hope that it was.

'This is it. Congratulations.'

The mist was patchy and obscured the view, apart from occasional glimpses of the Mönch's snow-covered neighbours; but the future was bright and rosy in my mind. It was twenty minutes past eight, so in all we took three and a half hours. Not bad.

The next two days I rested. Climbers returned from the Jungfrau much more quickly than a few days previously. The weather remained good. My stumps were in fine condition. After climbing the Mönch I was acclimatised to the altitude. Everything had slotted into place to give me an opportunity to attempt the Jungfrau.

Ueli could not go because he had already been engaged by another climber, but he contacted an older guide, called Hans Almer. Hans, looking weather-beaten as an old seaman, was a man of few words, but the words he said were sweet music for me.

'Yes, I can go up the Jungfrau with you. Start at two o'clock tomorrow morning.'

I awoke at one o'clock and dressed in darkness. Hans and I had breakfast and at two o'clock we were standing on the snow near the bunkhouse. In the flickering, yellow light thrown by Hans's candle lantern we looked around us. The sky was cloudy and it was raining. I was keyed up for action but the weather conditions were not good.

'We must wait two hours and see what the weather is like,' Hans said before going back to his bed in the hotel. Perhaps I would have to wait till next year after all.

Hans left me in the hotel lounge, where I could get some sleep, then sleepy-eyed and silent, he reappeared to tie on the rope and lead me out into the weak daylight at 4.15 a.m. The weather was good.

We descended a steep slope of thirty metres of snow, crossed a narrow crevasse by stepping over it, and started out on the hour-long walk south-westwards across the glacier, before strapping our crampons to our boots as several groups of climbers caught up with us. At the bottom of the thirty to forty-degree snow slope were congregated about thirty quiet climbers in all.

For the next three hundred metres in height we heaved our bodies up inclined snow. Two ice-axes helped me. A bergschrund, the name given to the large crevasse which forms between the mountaintop snowfield and the glacier it feeds, gave us no trouble because many people had already found a safe and easy way over its jumbled, broken chunks of ice. My hands began to ache with the effort of tightly gripping two ice-axes, but soon we were able to rest at the Rottal Sattel, a saddle between the Jungfrau and a nearby peak, the Rottalhorn. We were then nearly three thousand, nine hundred metres high.

Turning north-westwards from the Rottal Sattel, we walked along fairly level snow to the easiest ridge of the Jungfrau. There at a stretch of brown rock curving upward into the distance, I grew excited. People had told me that there was a sixty-metre length of gently sloping rock to climb just before the summit. I was panting, sweating and tired, and reluctant to ask Hans if we were on the last bit of rock because of the mental setback to be borne if we were not. I kept my eyes down on the rock immediately in front of me and pulled myself gradually higher.

I heard voices above me, and looked in their direction. Nearly thirty people sat in a group on the rocks fifteen metres away. They were relaxed, eating, drinking and chatting, so I knew they were at the top.

Two minutes later I was beside them. I had climbed the Jungfrau, 4,158 metres high, and had taken four hours and five minutes to get there. Hans seriously shook my hand and congratulated me.

It took nearly six and a half hours to descend carefully to the bunkhouse, underlining what I already knew, that I could not skip easily back down as others did. I was touched to find that three holidaymakers from the north of England had waited, shivering in the cold air for a long time just to shake my hand.

From the first rock climb with Jim Smith in Cornwall to reaching the summit of the Jungfrau, nearly a decade had gone by. It took that long to turn a disabled man into a mountaineer, and then only into a beginner. I thought at the time that I had reached a target and a terminus. But the call of the mountains is strong, and far from being at a terminus I was only a short way along the journey. I had dabbled with the peaks and now I found it hard to manage without them. My mountaineering life was just beginning.

Climbing became increasingly important and soon Judy and I agreed that my career would have to take second place for a while to two ambitions; at the same time as progressing as a climber I hoped, particularly through writing, to do something towards creating opportunities for other disabled people in outdoor pursuits. I wanted them to have the chance to find the enjoyment I had found, not necessarily in climbing but in any outdoor activity they chose, like camping, rambling, angling, gliding or canoeing. Competitive sports for people with certain handicaps had been promoted for several years, but, with few exceptions, non-competitive sports had been neglected. It was time for suitable non-competitive sports to be promoted too; not instead of, but as well as competitive games.

Judy remained in her civil service job while for a few years I was employed in the Post Office, at an accommodation agency, as a social worker, in the civil service, washing up in a hotel, at any work which would fit in with the timetable. Often I felt uncomfortable about this way of life but Judy rarely wavered in her conviction that for a few years, climbing and the creation of opportunities for other disabled people should take precedence. She was patient with her restless husband over several uncertain years. A prime consideration was to allow sufficient free time in summer to train and if necessary to wait for the right weather conditions; the latter proved to be a key factor in the events that followed.

Looking back I can see that greater attention paid to earnings, career and security could have lost me the dearest ambitions, but it was not always easy to see that at the time. Similarly if Judy had been more materialistic I might have failed in those ambitions. Now, periods of low wages meant that we had little money, but we saved what we could towards climbing trips. Our home was a bedsitter in Ealing, London. Perhaps we were materially poor at times, but only by comparison with our consumer society. Judy was happy with our arrangements, whereas many times I questioned whether I should place more importance on regular employment and career prospects. But mostly we felt as if we had no choice, that it was inevitable that our lives would take a certain course.

At the beginning of my climbing life rock climbs were graded according to their difficulty: Easy, Moderate, Difficult, Very Difficult, Severe, Very Severe. Modern equipment and techniques have led to the introduction in recent years of higher grades, so my efforts while climbing Severe and occasionally Very Severe routes would nowadays be seen as rather tame to hard climbers; but I do not mind if my efforts fail to impress them. I climbed what I could manage, not what they can, and with increasing age I have to stick even more to that philosophy. I climb what I enjoy.

In the winter of 1970-1, Peter, with whom I climbed Tryfan, and I, tried to decide on a satisfying alpine route, which we could manage in the summer. By December the target was vaguely fixed; we would attempt a long, high alpine route involving at least two days of climbing. The Jungfrau was a high route, but it was not entirely satisfying because the climbing started at a high altitude. We believed that a long route, tackled slowly, could be undertaken by adapting normal climbing methods to my limitations. Many alpine climbs require a full day's activity for an able-bodied climber if he wishes to avoid spending a night in the open at high altitude. Generally, the mountaineer will, in a day, climb from a hut or some other shelter to the summit of his choice and back again to a bed. Some climbers plan to camp or bivouac at high altitudes so they have time to complete longer and harder routes. Bivouacking differs from camping because a normal tent is not used. Bivouac equipment could bring many mountain routes within my range and ensure that I never went too far in one day. The idea was to climb just enough in one day, without injury to the stumps, so climbing could be spread over consecutive days. Whenever the skin on the stumps split, further climbing brought very rapid deterioration. Bivouacs would change all that.

The mountain that eventually came to mind is well known: the Eiger. I had seen it many times when waiting to climb the Mönch and the Jungfrau. The three mountains stand together, and I had often felt a little disappointed that I could climb two of them, but not the third. The local story is that the Mönch, or Monk, protects the Jungfrau, the Virgin, from the Eiger, or Ogre. Now it looked as if that third mountain could be within reach. I could acclimatise at the Jungfraujoch, and we could start the climb from the Eiger Glacier station without a hot trek up through the alpine pastures from the valley. Also, I knew some guides in the area and felt that one or more of them might be prepared to climb with me. I thought two days would be sufficient to scale the Eiger by an easy route in reasonable conditions. The route we had in mind was known as the west flank, a highway by comparison with its north face.

We bought bivi-bags, polythene sacks large enough to accommodate a person, for protection against wind and rain. Used in conjunction with warm clothing or a sleeping bag, a bivi-bag is adequate for quite harsh conditions. Bivouac experience was the next necessity, we decided, so in February we charged off to North Wales. Two days before there were radio announcements about roads blocked with snow in the area. We planned to tramp about the snowy mountains for hours and bivouac at night, but it was not to be. I had 'flu and spent two nights shivering in the bivi-bag under a rock, and one day sitting either on a rock in weak winter sunshine, or in a café. Hard-man aspirations thwarted, we returned home. One piece of equipment seemed to be mocking us on the drive back: sticking out from under a jumble of rucksacks, rope and clothing was an implement we had commandeered to speed up digging a shelter in the snow – my mother-in-law's coal shovel.

I had been puzzled by some wildly inaccurate compass bearings I had taken while sitting on a rock in North Wales. The bearings just did not correspond with the map, and differed by as much as twenty degrees. It was some time before I realised the cause – the map was set on my knees and whenever I held the compass near the map the metal in my legs made the needle deviate!

Peter was about to be engaged and it seemed to me that his girlfriend was very nervous about him accompanying me on the Eiger. Reluctance seeped slowly into his attitude, eroding his former enthusiasm, though he said nothing directly to me. His girlfriend did not climb, and I could understand that she might regard mountaineering as a pointless and dangerous pastime, and if so she was more than justified in hoping that he would not risk his life on a mountain, particularly with me. So one day I asked him if he really wanted to go, and he confessed that he had changed his mind. As well as the girlfriend, a friend whom Peter regarded as an uncle figure had dissuaded him from going. The man told me so himself some weeks later, adding that he was sure I realised he was correct. I refrained from pointing out that he had probably done Peter a great disservice by advising him on a subject about which he was ignorant, since Peter was an unconfident man who needed success.

I wrote to Ueli Sommer, whose reply arrived in May. He said he could go, and suggested taking a porter as well. So, if I didn't find another partner in time, I could go to Switzerland and climb with Ueli.

Although the legs were kept in a good state of repair by the fitters at Roehampton, I could not ignore the fact that breakages could occur on the mountain. I examined each artificial limb closely before and during each long climb, and to add strength I bound the metal legs with strong insulation tape around their weakest points, at the tops of the shins. They would stand up to any amount of walking but climbing put abnormal strains on the metal. By wrapping the insulation tape around in much the same way as you might to strengthen a pick handle, the effect was to protect the metal from cracks, and to slow the growth of any cracks which might form.

What other differences were there between me and an able-bodied climber? Well each step would cost me more in energy, much more. I would be slower than an able-bodied man and my stumps would be injured if I went too far in one day – in a way the stumps were my Achilles heel. By planning to bivouac I was bringing the route within my personal limits. At least, that's what I thought.

*   *   *

Proceeding by train to Grindelwald, I then took a ticket on the local mountain railway, which has the Jungfraujoch Hotel at its terminus.

Ueli came to the dormitory the next morning. I had been expecting to bump into him soon because he divided his time between the Eiger Glacier Station Hotel and the Jungfraujoch Hotel.

'Ah, Norman, I was not expecting you for a few days. I am busy now, but we must talk soon.'

'There's no hurry. I'd like a day or two to acclimatise.'

Despite my eagerness to get on with the climbing, there was no sense in rushing into the headache, nausea and weakness which could result through attempting an exacting climb without being acclimatised. Two or three days would be enough to get reasonably used to the lower level of oxygen, one-third less at Jungfraujoch than at sea level.

It was two days later that we had an opportunity to talk, in the restaurant.

'I think round about Tuesday it might be all right, if the weather is good,' Ueli said. That was five days away.' On Tuesday there will be a good moon so we can start early. I will look for someone to go with us. I believe you should have two people with you. I think you might reach the summit in one day. Then we can come down and bivouac. Of course, we must wait for perfect weather.'

He left for a few minutes, then came back and introduced a young man in his mid-twenties.

'This is Treas Schlunegger. He can go with us. So it is all settled, if the weather is good.'

The days crept by, and hardly a cloud passed over Jungfraujoch without me glaring at it. On the whole the weather was good. Monday came, and at midday I began to pack my kit to take it by train down to the Eiger Glacier Station Hotel, from where we would start climbing the next day at about one a.m. Then Ueli came into the dormitory.

'I have just been on a rescue on the Eiger, on the west flank,' he told me. 'We had to bring down four people who were caught in a storm. I know them and they are good climbers. There is too much ice on the rocks at the top and it is very dangerous. I think we should not go now. Maybe if we have a week or two of good weather the west flank will be all right, but now it is too difficult. Even these good climbers had to be helped down. Luckily they were not hurt.'

I had been expecting bad news because the weather did not look good but all the same it was a great disappointment; coping with disappointment can be a frequent feature of any ambition, and you just have to get on with it.

'I must go now, and we can talk later,' Ueli said.

About four hours later, in the afternoon, I saw him again. He was wrapped in a down jacket and was on his way out of the hotel.

'I have to go to the Eiger again, to the west flank. Someone has been killed. We are going by helicopter.'

Next day Ueli told me about the rescue.

'An Englishman was killed and his three companions have been rescued. Conditions were terrible there. One of the men is in hospital in a very serious state. They were well equipped and I think they were good climbers.'

Back at home Judy had heard a news broadcast, which said that an Englishman had been killed on the west flank of the Eiger. She knew that I was about to climb and she couldn't help thinking that the dead man might be me. The announcer gave details of the accident, weather conditions, etcetera, while she listened. It was only at the end of the news item that the victim's name was given.

'Now we must decide what you will do,' Ueli said.

'You think it will be a week or more before the west flank is in good condition?'

'Yes. Or perhaps more. It will take a long time for the ice to melt. You must decide what you want to do. It will be a long wait. Or you could try the Matterhorn.'

'I'd like to stay here.'

'All right. Stay as my guest. One person more or less won't make any difference. You can wash some glasses, and if you do that you can eat and live with the staff.'

That was very considerate of him, and work would help to pass the time. The routine of putting glasses through the glass-washing machine and drying them, slicing bread and washing spoons and dessert cups, kept me busy for about five hours a day. Time dragged by. It was all mist and long faces. The weather improved a little over a few days.

'But we must still wait until conditions are very good,' Ueli said. 'We must be careful.'

More glasses to wash, more bread to slice, more clouds to fill the sky, day after day. Wait, wait, wait. Improvements in the weather were short lived. All I could do was wait. The only perseverance I needed had nothing to do with climbing, but with waiting. It was simple – if I did not wait I would not have the chance to attempt the climb that year. Nearly four weeks went by, and I waited. Four weeks! It would have made sense to go to some lower ranges I know about now, but I was a real mountain innocent then. Often it rained or snowed or hailed. I waited still. Then the weather began to improve, and was fine for long enough for hopes to rise. Was this the time, at last?

'We must talk to Treas.' Ueli said one Monday. 'If he is available we can go to the Eiger Glacier station soon. If he is not free I will find somebody else.'

The weather remained good. Later that day I saw Ueli again.

'While the weather is good you must take the opportunity,' he said. 'I have seen Treas and he can go on Wednesday. Unfortunately I cannot go myself on that day, but Treas will find another guide.'

Treas and I sat in the restaurant to make plans the same day.

'We go to the Eiger glacier station tomorrow,' he said. 'I will contact another guide to go with us.'

'He will have to understand that we will need to bivouac.'

'We will see. I have to go to the army the next day.'

'We climb on Wednesday and you go to the army on Thursday?'

'Yes.'

'But I can't get up and down in one day.'

'We will see. Maybe you will go very fast and go up and down in a day.'

'No. It will take me at least two days. It will be dangerous if I try to go too far in a day.'

'Perhaps the other guide can stay with you.'

'It's no good me rushing,' I emphasised. 'I can only do this if I take at least one and a half days, and a bivouac for one night.'

'We will see what happens,' he said evasively.

It was possible that we could reach the top in a day and Treas could descend to the Eiger Glacier station while the other guide and I bivouacked. The two of us could then descend the next day. I wanted to pin down Treas and the other guide to more definite arrangements, but it turned out there would be no opportunity to meet the other guide until an hour or two before beginning to climb. The plans were not satisfactory because they were indefinite, but they were not sufficiently vague to cancel the arrangements. We planned to start climbing shortly after midnight on Wednesday, 25th August.

On Tuesday I packed my equipment and went down by train to the Eiger Glacier Station Hotel. It turned misty during the afternoon and I doubted we would climb. Another delay looked likely so I didn't feel very excited. Still, I went to bed very early in the evening in case the weather improved.

Treas woke me at two a.m. The sky was clear and starlit.

'We can go,' he said.

I hurriedly put on my legs, hoisted my rucksack and went to join Treas and the other guide, Robert, for breakfast. Robert was about the same age as Treas, in his mid-twenties. He was bearded, softly spoken and smaller than Treas. He didn't speak much English, but anyway at that time of the morning we were mostly silent. Who wants to talk at two in the morning, when sober?

We sat around a coffee table in their hotel room and drank tea. Knowing that later I would be glad I had eaten, I forced down a few slices of bread and jam, for energy. Ugh! Fifteen or twenty minutes went by before we pulled on warm outer clothing, slipped our rucksacks on and tramped to the front door of the hotel. The air outside didn't feel very cold. There was no wind and hardly any cloud.

'We put the rope on here in the light,' Treas instructed, and we tied on to the rope, me in the middle and Robert at the rear, with three or four metres of rope between Treas and me. He lit a candle lantern and Robert produced an electric torch.

'Ready?' Treas asked me.

'Yes.'

So, here at last was the chance to see if I could get up the third of the great trio. It was nearing three o'clock. He led off up the rocky track that ran for a few metres beside the railway, then it went to the right of the tunnel. I found once more that walking in dark surroundings was difficult. People with feet can keep their balance in the dark partly because of leg and foot muscles telling them which way the ground is sloping. My dead feet told me nothing, so my eyes became more important for giving information about any alteration in the slope and nature of the land. My eyes could glimpse the stars, a few clouds and the dark, looming outline of the Eiger, but mostly they had to remain on the mobile patches of light cast on the uneven track by the candle lantern and the torch. In an hour or so it would get lighter and as the mountain steepened I would be able to use my hands as well – then there would be no balance problem.

The track continued along a moraine, the broken rubble that collects on the edge of a glacier. An avalanche crashed and rumbled down the mountain to our right, a long way away. We came to natural steps of black rock that was wet and slippery. There were easy ways to choose through this section but it was not simple to pick the route in the dark; straying to the left or the right would have made the going much harder. Robert and Treas engaged in much discussion about the route as we picked our line up the rock, and now and then we retraced our steps to find an easier way. In daylight there would have been a fairly obvious route to follow.

Slowly the mountain silhouettes took form, to become three dimensional as light fell on faces, snowfields, ridges. Eyes, fixed on rock, on snow, on anything still, were like a long visual arm stretched out to help balance. Wherever possible I kept both hands on the rock, for steadiness and power. Sometimes when Treas and Robert walked upright it was better for me to scramble on all fours, like a chimpanzee, especially on loose plates of rock that clinked like chunks of cast iron as we walked over them. Within an hour of leaving the Eiger Glacier station, Treas extinguished the candle. The sky was light in the east, still dark in the west. There were a few steep steps of two or three metres but the climbing was easy.

Half past four. The absence of cloud was encouraging. Thick mist masked the valleys, but that was nothing to worry about. We carried on over a long slope of small stones to the base of a snowfield, which looked as if it had a gradient of about thirty degrees. Here was crampon territory, so we sat to strap the spikes on our boots. Treas, being in the lead on the rope, cut steps in the snow and ice to make it easier and safer. The ice was very hard in parts and required several strokes of the ice-axe to make a reasonable step, big enough to take nearly half a boot. Chop, chop, chop, chop. This was a restful period for me because there were a few seconds between each pace upwards. Plates and chips of ice slithered down as Treas chopped.

A beautiful pink glow spread over the white snows of the Jungfrau, backed by a sky of light blue. It was one of those superb moments that may suddenly strike a mountaineer as soon as he has a chance to take notice of his surroundings, when he reaches a summit and relaxes, or strolls on an easy path, or stops to put on an extra sweater. When there is time to look around, the mountains can in a moment remind you that just being among them is part of the fun.

The snowfield was about two hundred metres long and it took half an hour to climb. We continued up more rock as soon as our crampons were off. The limestone here was fairly steep and we traversed to left and to right along ledges to choose the best route, rather than taking a direct line up the tiers. As we moved on we came upon verglas, a thin coating of clear ice making the rock look as if someone had attempted to preserve it under a layer of glass. There was no way to avoid the verglas so caution was needed with every move, whether when walking along a ledge or climbing upwards.

How would I regard the climb if I had legs? The viewpoint of any route was coloured very much by disability. Embarked on a serious expedition and four hours away from civilisation, the trip was not undertaken lightly. Yet a fit mountaineer could trot up to where I was in an hour and a half. He could have set out at the same time, climbed to the same height, returned to the Eiger Glacier Station Hotel and been in bed for an hour or more. For him, a bit of exercise before breakfast; for me, a journey which was exploring my limits. Anyone who is blasé about the danger on even the easiest of high mountain routes is foolish or inexperienced or ill informed, but the fact remains that the able-bodied man does not need to approach a route with quite the same serious consideration – he would not take two guides on the Eiger west flank, for instance. (Nor would I, now.)

We arrived at the Fruhstuckplatze (Breakfast Place), a level area of rock where climbers often stop to rest and eat, about seven hundred and fifty metres above the Eiger Glacier station. About nine hundred metres of height to be gained. I felt fine. We sat down and looked across at the precipitous North Wall.

'I think you should not bivouac,' Treas said. He pointed to the summit of the Jungfrau. 'See how the snow is blowing. The wind is too strong.'

I had noticed the plume of wind-blown snow which streamed from the head of the Jungfrau. Obviously the wind was quite strong high up, even though the sun shone in a clear sky and we were in only a light wind.

'I have been on this mountain before and there is nowhere to bivouac,' Treas added. Either he was lying, or he required a palatial place to bivouac.

'People bivouac quite often on the west flank,' I said. Especially the English, I thought ruefully, many of whom were slow, once a year alpinists, laughed at by experienced French, Swiss, Germans and Austrians, who could visit the Alps for weekends.

'It is not good with this wind. On the ridge up there we could be blown away,' Treas countered, changing tack.

'We will not be on the summit ridge today.'

Robert sat in silence. I wasn't sure that he understood what was happening. I had climbed slowly but even so at the rate I was going we had a good chance of getting two thirds of the way up the mountain in another two hours. Even though the climbing might be a little more difficult, I could keep up the same speed. In daylight and with plenty of time we could find a good bivouac site, I felt sure, and from two-thirds of the way up the mountain I should reach the summit the next day, or even on this day.

'We must not waste our lives,' Treas remarked. 'You have no feet and you don't want to lose your hands as well.'

Cheeky monkey, I thought.

For several seconds I said nothing and stared at the rock at my feet. I was angry and extremely disappointed, and I considered going on alone, but that would have been stupid. There was no alternative but to follow Treas's advice. Without companions the climb would have been too dangerous, and it was obvious that it was useless to argue with Treas. He had been reluctant from the start to talk about bivouacking.

'We can go a bit further so you can take some photographs of the North Wall,' Treas said. 'There is a good view from a bit further up. Then we must go down.'

Thanks for nothing, turd. He had little or no idea what this climb meant to me. I was merely a source of income.

How about going up further and then saying I was too tired to descend? No, they would start to talk about a rescue party, or Robert could flatly refuse to go any higher the next day.

'Damn it! Damn it! Damn it!' I said in a murmur to myself. There was no point in making a fuss.

'If we're not going up to the top we might as well go down now,' I said.

Treas took a radio from his rucksack and spoke into it to let someone at Kleine Scheidegg know that we were returning. A few words in acknowledgement came back.

We started down at once. All the way I was wondering if the next year I could find two companions who would be prepared to bivouac on the Eiger west flank.

As we approached the Eiger Glacier station Treas said, 'It was good today. You are a strong man.' In the circumstances such a statement gave me no pleasure. I felt drained of energy, not because of the effort, but through disappointment.

From the hotel I rang Judy and promised to head for home so we could go on holiday together. We talked about going to Scotland to walk and climb. I was at a turning point where I could accept that the lengthy routes were too much for me, then I could spend my time on short, less exhausting routes. This feeling stayed with me for less than a day, until I was on the way back to England. Then I knew that I would continue to pursue other mountains because failure was a bitter food. I would not be satisfied until I had climbed a few long routes or proved to myself that I could not manage them. If able-bodied mountaineers could tackle extremely hazardous routes involving several bivouacs then there was no reason why I should not bivouac on routes which were within my limits.

Within minutes of arriving home I was persuading Judy that she would enjoy a mountain walking holiday in Switzerland. She liked the idea.

'Then I can try the Matterhorn,' I explained. 'There's a hut part way up so I wouldn't have to bivouac. Ueli thought it might suit me for that reason.' I could think of no other mountain with a hut so conveniently placed from my point of view; there are many, but I did not know about them.

A week later we were in Switzerland. As soon as we reached Zermatt I went to the guides' office. The man in charge refused to find me a guide because he considered the climb to be too much for me.

Judy was waiting outside the office.

'Laughing boy in there says I might find a guide at the Hörnli hut, but I'm not very optimistic about finding one up there if he can't or won't find one in Zermatt.'

Next I rang Felix Julen, the President of the guides, who was at the Hörnli hut at the time. It was from this hut that the Matterhorn was usually climbed.

'Well, come up to the Hörnli hut so a guide can give you a test to see how you can manage. If you can climb all right two guides could go with you on the Matterhorn at the weekend or early next week.'

The idea of a climbing test was sensible, and the suggestion meant that Felix Julen was at least prepared to give me a chance to show what I could do, rather than turn me down right away.

We took a cable car to Schwarzee, 2,582 metres, and then there was a rough trail to walk for a couple of hours to the Hörnli hut at 3,260 metres. At first, the stony trail weaved up like any well used path on a British moor or mountain. The final bit of track zig zagged up the Hörnli Buttress to the hut. It was cold enough for small patches of ice and snow to remain there in the shadows. How many times we zigged and zagged, I don't know. Thirty, thirty-five, forty? The sharp turns to left and right went on and on, bringing us at last to the hut.

When I met Felix Julen he had changed his mind and suggested I should go to the guides' office again.

'The man there said he would not find a guide,' I explained. 'You will remember, that is why I rang you. But there is plenty of rock around here for the test.'

'Well, I think the weather may turn bad,' Herr Julen said.

It did not, but it is not always easy to tell. However, impending bad weather was no reason for going down to the valley. There was rock to be climbed within a couple of hundred metres, and a hut and hotel to retreat to if the weather did turn bad. It was obvious that the embarrassed Felix Julen had had second thoughts, perhaps after talking with other guides. That a guide was cautious about climbing with me was understandable because I was an unfamiliar type of problem, but I was far from pleased that I had been invited up to the Hörnli hut for a test which did not take place. Yet I knew so little in those early days, and did not have a basis on which to press my case. What annoyed me most was that Julen had not been open minded and honest.

'Poor thing. You haven't had much luck,' Judy remarked later. 'And it was his suggestion that you should come up here.'

'If I met some other guides perhaps they would go. I don't know.'

Felix Julen was well respected in the valley and on the mountains. Without his backing it was unlikely that I would find a guide. I felt like some kind of mountain leper, but I was not going to leave it at that.

'Do you remember I told you about Eric Beard, the man who was killed while I was walking to Land's End?' I said to Judy.

'The man the police thought was you?'

'Yes, well, he wanted to climb Mont Blanc with me. He thought that as I couldn't go far in a day it would be a good idea to go hut to hut, doing a little bit at a time. There are three huts I can use on the way up. Might even miss one out on the way down.'

'It's worth a try.'

If I met me now, I would counsel against attempting such a big mountain at this early stage, but I knew no better.

So we caught a train to Chamonix-Mont Blanc. The hyphenated name, linking the famous mountain with the town that thrives because of it, is officially used nowadays. Altitude: about 1,000 metres. Population: about 8,000. A clean French mountain valley resort where dozens of hotels and restaurants await the tourist.

We booked in at a cheap dormitory and I went to the guides' office as soon as possible. There's just a chance, I told myself, that they'll help. Just a chance. I explained my circumstances and somewhat to my

42

surprise the woman behind the counter said she would find me a guide, and asked me to return the following day. I'll believe it when I see it, I thought.

An hour later Judy and I were having a meal in a café when two young Americans, a man and a woman, came in to eat. We got into conversation and they, Kevin and Barbara, said they hoped to climb Mont Blanc too. They were experienced rock climbers, and Kevin had some mountaineering experience, including having climbed Mont Blanc once before.

At the guides' office the next day the woman didn't duck behind the counter or put on a false beard and glasses. She beckoned to a middle-aged man.

'Francis Bozon, Monsieur Croucher,' she said.

The man and I shook hands. He was about 170 centimetres tall and strongly built. His dark hair, trimmed short, was turning grey at the back and the temples. He was serious looking, and obviously a quiet man. Chris Bonington has skied with him and once described him as a 'good tempered sheep dog'. Even as we shook hands he was weighing me up. He spoke hardly any English so we struggled along in French.

'The lady has explained?' I asked.

'Yes.'

'It may take me six days.'

'I understand. You have climbed with crampons before?'

'Yes, quite often.'

'Where have you climbed?'

'Mönch, Jungfrau, some snow climbs in Britain, a little way up the Eiger west flank, rock climbing in many places for ten years. I've acclimatised for a month at over 3,000 metres.'

'Have you a stove?'

'No.'

'I have one. Gloves and something to cover the face?'

'Yes.'

I didn't want to assume prematurely that he had made up his mind to go, but judging from his questions about equipment, I was almost certain he had.

'When you buy the food, I would like plenty of soup and when you get cheese, ask for 'fromage de la montagne'. I like dried fruit too,' Francis said.

No doubt at all. He would go. He was a Jim.

'What's the weather like?' I asked.

'I think it will be all right tomorrow.'

'I have bivouac equipment for the Vallot hut.'

'There is an old observatory near the Vallot hut. I will get the key and we can stay there. It will be more comfortable.'

We wrote down a food list.

'I can't carry much weight,' I explained. (Nowadays I would carry my share.)

'I will take all the food.'

'That's good. It will help a lot.'

'Have you a car?'

'No.'

'We can use mine. We go along the valley and board a train at Le Fayet to Nid d'Aigle. Normally we would go from Les Houches but at this time of year the cable railway is closed. Tomorrow we'll walk from Nid d'Aigle to the Tete Rousse hut.'

Judy could tell from the look on my face when I left the office that the arrangements had been made. She was waiting with Barbara and Kevin.

'We go tomorrow,' I said.

'Great!' Kevin said, and Judy beamed.

'I'd better go home. I've had twelve days of my holiday already and I want to save a few days so we can go climbing in Wales and Scotland,' she said.

We all went for a meal. On the way Kevin explained that he was interested in my climbing because his father had an artificial leg. He and Barbara decided that they would not take the train up to Nid d'Aigle but would make the three-hour journey on foot from Chamonix, a trip which hardly any climbers bother with nowadays.

The sky was overcast when Judy and I got up the next day. We headed for the Co-op, which was open by half past seven. We were hunting through the shelves for light food when Francis Bozon appeared and helped fill the wire basket to the top with provisions before disappearing in a hurry. He had selected enough food for at least six days.

'He really does intend getting to the summit,' Judy remarked. 'I'm not judging just from the food but from the way he behaves as well.'

Judy and I had breakfast together, and after that things happened quickly. Francis Bozon arrived at the guides' office with his son, a cheerful young man who was training to be a pilot. Francis managed to pack all the food in his rucksack, Judy and I hastily made our farewells, and the trainee pilot attempted to get his car airborne on the road to Le Fayet. From Le Fayet the Tramway du Mont Blanc trundled up to the terminus at Nid d'Aigle (2,377 metres) where we arrived at eleven thirty a.m. The sky was clear and the sun quite hot. We stepped from the train. Ahead of us, seven hundred and fifty metres to rise over an easy trail to the Tete Rousse hut.

'I prefer that you walk in front,' Francis said, indicating the rough path we would take southwards. I began to walk and could picture him watching each step, weighing up whether we should go or not. With an ice-axe to steady me on boulders, I moved slowly and all the time watched where I was placing my boots. It became unpleasantly hot after a few minutes of exercise, but at least I didn't stumble. A bad performance at that stage could have meant an end to the trip.

Our route took us through rocky country, devoid of pretty colours but starkly impressive, where vegetation begins to give up the struggle to live. Not far above was the line where the snow remained all year round, and only a few species of hardy plants survived. We stepped over tough grass and small plants clinging where they could in the shelter of boulders and stones. No trees or bushes could live at that altitude. The view was far from exotically beautiful or lush, but was imposing and rugged. Here beauty was represented by wilderness in simple form and limited colours.

Words passed infrequently. Language difficulties restricted us and I was concentrating too much on walking to have time to chatter or take much notice of the scenery. On a popular hiking trail to Mont Blanc I was having to work hard where an able-bodied person could amble along.

My stumps felt slightly painful in much the same way as your feet may feel uncomfortable if you walk ten miles on a hot day. This unpleasant sensation would worsen until I stopped walking and climbing, but it would be a long time before it became distressing. There was cool mist only a hundred metres higher.

Odd patches of snow lay in dips in the ground and in the shade. We approached a huge rib of rock, part of the Aiguille du Goûter. The trail zig zagged up in an easy gradient over gritty mud at first, then over fractured brown rocks. The only noises were those we made: the sound of breathing, the scrape of an ice-axe, the crunch of a boot. Thin mist came down around us and the air cooled. Turning now this way, now that, we followed the track. About an hour was enough to take us to the top of the rib, where we sat by the edge of the Tete Rousse glacier. From there on only steep rock would be free of snow and ice.

I knew we had to cross the glacier but I had no idea how far it was to the Tete Rousse hut. We had taken just under two and a half hours. The guide book mentioned that two and a half hours to three hours was a normal time from Nid d'Aigle to the Tete Rousse hut. It seemed reasonable to reckon that it would take me another hour to reach it.

'Five minutes to the hut,' Francis said.

'Ah, good.'

It was a surprise. Time spent at the Hörnli hut had helped me to acclimatise well enough not to suffer from lack of oxygen. We were over 3,000 metres high and although the lower level of oxygen is not very serious at that height, one can rapidly become tired with exercise before acclimatisation.

There remained only two or three hundred metres to go, slightly upwards across the glacier. The mist rose, and there was the wooden hut at 3,167 metres. The snow covering the glacial ice was firm and no crevasses could be seen near us. We followed footprints which went towards the hut. A guide with a young lady client came down the glacier in our direction and stopped; they had come up on the same train. We shook hands all round and the guide explained that the young lady was suffering from altitude sickness. The guide chatted with Francis for a while before leading his client back towards the valley.

The Tete Rousse hut was not unlike a wooden army barrack hut, with room for sixty people. The climbing season was drawing to a close, so the summertime guardian had departed. During the winter the hut would remain unlocked and there would be plenty of blankets for the few people who went there.

Kevin and Barbara arrived, tired after the trek from the valley. It was cold in the hut, as there was no heating. We sat on benches with our elbows on wooden tables and talked as we sank mug after mug of tea, until the light began to fail. By then there were four other climbers in the hut. Everyone pottered about with torches, packing kit for an early start in the morning, and we all turned in by eight o'clock. The weather was good and Francis thought it would be fine the next day. Because of the cold we all wore plenty of clothes as we all slept on the long, communal mattresses.

Under a blanket, I took my legs off, switched on a torch and examined my stumps. There was no damage on the left but the skin was rubbed away in two small patches on the right. If the slight injuries got worse they could prevent me from climbing far. Already there was a very real threat to success. I washed the stumps in icy water, put antiseptic ointment on the injured spots, and went to sleep, deeply at first but later in the night I awoke for brief periods, to lie wondering if my stumps would manage the journey. Through a small gap between the window shutters the sky remained clear and starlit.

Morning. On with the legs, and I joined Francis in the dining room, which was faintly illuminated by the blue gas flame of his stove. He was making tea.

'The weather is good now,' he said. 'But the barometer has fallen a little.' He knew this because he carried a small altimeter. If the altimeter reading crept up when we weren't climbing, the barometer was falling.

We drank tea and ate in silence. I finished a couple of slices of bread and butter, forced down, then we carried our rucksacks outside and sat on the front step of the hut to strap on crampons. The light grey sky gave no hint of the way the weather would turn. The wind was light.

Francis passed me one end of the climbing rope and I tied it around my waist. Although it was not a dangerous glacier route, it was comforting to have a rope as a security measure while we crossed the edge of the Tete Rousse glacier.

Francis stepped forward, ahead by a few metres. There were indistinct bootprints from the day before and we followed their line. The snow was firm but not icy, and sometimes under our boots it let out a distinct squeal like a flock of geese, or creaked with the noise of an old wooden chair. These sounds are so much a part of the scene that you might not notice that each of the many forms of snow has its own slight but definite sound under a boot, the geese sound resulting from the fracture of tiny snow crystals.

The trail curved a little to the left, then to the right, in a steady pull upward over snow inclined at twenty degrees or less. Up the left bank of the glacier; the words left and right are applied to a glacier as if you were looking at it from the source. Soon the glacier had been left behind as we began to scale the Aiguille du Goûter, at the top of which was visible our next proposed stopping point, the Aiguille du Goûter hut. The hut stood 3,817 metres high at the top of a cliff. We had six hundred metres to climb up that cliff, via an easy rock rib. The angle of the rib, varying between thirty-five and fifty degrees, suited me because I could use my hands most of the time. The place is notorious for stonefall and many people have been killed or injured there. I was concentrating too much on where I was putting my boots to think much about falling stones, although my ears did pick up the sound of a few rocks clattering down in the distance. The guide book suggested up to three hours for this section from the Tete Rousse hut to the hut above, so I expected to take four hours or more.

The rock was quite broken but offered plenty of safe holds. Parts to be taken with extra care were the many snow and ice covered rocks. We kept our crampons on all the time and alternately grated over rock or crunched across ice and snow. There were cracks which gave good holds, plus little natural steps of rock and small slabs so chipped and rough that hands or boots would grip anywhere.

'Wait here,' Francis said at one point early on. He went ahead to a spot from which he could belay me across ten metres of fairly steep snow and rock. He watched closely as I crossed; I was still being auditioned for the part.

The right stump hurt a little but the cold helped. The cliff faced west so was shaded from the early morning sun when it broke through the cloud.

The risk of stones falling would have been greater if there had been people above us to dislodge them, but apart from four figures descending far above there was no one to be seen. Francis kept a few paces ahead; he was picking the best places to stand in case I slipped. He remained silent and vigilant, always expecting the unexpected. At times he could walk up steps of rock where I had to climb, but it was pointless to envy him his powerful legs. If I had legs I would have to climb much more difficult routes to gain the same satisfaction as I would if I reached this summit... if, if, if.

At eight o'clock we stopped for a rest.

'This is a bad place to be after a storm,' Francis remarked. 'Ice covers the rocks. If the weather turned bad we would have to go down. But it looks good. Perhaps we can go as far as the Vallot observatory today if you feel all right. We must take advantage of the weather.'

'Perhaps.'

I didn't sound enthusiastic because the prospect of going from the Tete Rousse hut to the Vallot observatory (4362 metres) in one day, missing out the Aiguille du Goûter hut, had seemed out of the question. The guide-book suggested it would take an able-bodied mountaineer six hours in reasonable conditions so it would take me at least eight hours, and possibly as many as ten hours. That was too long for the stumps if I wanted to continue to climb to the summit the next day. No, better to be prudent than too eager. Four hours to the Aiguille du Goûter hut would be a comfortable amount of climbing for one day. Caution could prevent me getting to the summit, but it would keep me out of trouble. After all, I was a learner.

I did not miss the significance of the proposal Francis made: it meant that after watching me like a hawk he was satisfied that it was all right to aim for the summit.

By nine a.m. the hut perched on a ledge above us looked strangely close. If I needed four hours to get from the Tete Rousse hut to the Aiguille du Goûter hut, it would take an hour and a half to reach that ledge. Distances can be deceptive on mountains, but I was almost certain that the hut was only half an hour's climb away. Our pace remained constant and soon there was no doubt that the hut was close. In half an hour we were there. It was a wooden building, covered in sheet metal outside. Some of the windows were round, like portholes, and the long, low building looked like the hull of a stranded ship.

'Good. Three hours,' Francis said, grinning. 'Now you can rest and this afternoon we go on to the Vallot.'

'I think so.'

This was not what I had planned. What I had had in mind was to leave the Aiguille du Goûter hut only if the weather forecast was favourable. I didn't mind being caught in that hut in bad weather, but the Vallot observatory was rather high to be stranded in. However, we had plenty of food and could stay warm in the observatory, so if the weather turned bad we could sit it out and descend at the first opportunity.

Outside the hut we sat down to unstrap our crampons. In this hut, as in many alpine huts, it was usual to remove boots and stack them in racks in the entrance, and people wore rubber shoes provided by the hut guardian. Francis soon had his boots off and went in to order tea for us. I sat on a step and unlaced a boot, but when I came to slide it off it wouldn't budge. It was frozen to my wooden foot. After a good deal of time spent banging the foot on the ground, tapping the boot with my ice-axe and levering up the leather, I got one boot off. I was hard at work on the second one, thumping it with my ice-axe, when I looked up. A climber, walking past, was staring at me. I smiled at him and carried on with the job in hand. He moved away, open-mouthed. When I went into the hut I sat near him at a table. Giving me a funny look, he got up and went to a table at the far end of the hut. When you think about it, I don't suppose many people would want to sit close to someone who belts his feet with an ice-axe!

Inside the hut was room for about seventy people on the mattresses. The dining room was large, like a village hall, and there were half a dozen other climbers there. Delicate Jack Frost leaves decorated the windows but it was warm inside the building. We sat at a table and drank tea from large bowls, and our talk centred at first around the weather.

'It may change soon,' Francis explained. 'The barometer is still falling.'

'The wind looks strong above here now.'

This was clear from the streamers of snow being blown from crests.

'It is, but not too strong for us to go on. I have spoken to the guardian and we can rest here now.'

'That's good.'

'And at midday we start for the Vallot?'

It was a question, not a statement.

'Yes.'

'We will rest here then, for two hours,' Francis said.

We made our way to a dormitory where I took my legs off. The right stump was bleeding from the end, where the bone finished. The wound was no bigger than a 2p piece but the small area of damage was surrounded by swollen flesh. I was tempted to stay at the hut until the next day.

Two hours of dozing sped by. Back in the dining-room we had a bowl of soup each. Kevin and Barbara were there, having arrived about half an hour after us. They decided that their four-hour stint up to the Aiguille du Goûter hut was enough for a day.

'See you tomorrow at the summit,' Kevin said, as Francis and I prepared to leave.

Boots on, crampons strapped under boots, glacier cream and lip salve smeared over skin, goggles on, rope tied, gloves on. Without goggles, the dazzling sunlight reflected from the snow could be unpleasantly bright and could even cause snow blindness. Crevasse danger was small the way we were going. The hut guardian provided a spare ice-axe to help me long. It would be snow and ice all the way from the Aiguille du Goûter hut at 3,817 metres to the Vallot observatory at 4,362 metres and from there to the summit.

It was one o'clock when we started. The sun beat down on a fairly steep snow slope, which rose for thirty metres behind the Aiguille du Goûter hut. We turned to follow the ridge at the top of the slope towards the south, trending south-eastwards. On the right side the rocks of the Aiguille du Goûter fell away steeply – six hundred metres of cliff is quite a sight when you walk along the top. A well-trodden trail led across the ridge, which was an extended mound of snow like a huge long-barrow curving along the clifftop. It was a spectacular, yet not dangerous, place to be.

Our boots sank perhaps a dozen centimetres in the snow. I walked in Francis's footprints because his weight had compacted the snow there. While sorting out equipment and rejecting all but the essential articles, I had decided against taking ski baskets for the ends of the ice-axes, and I soon regretted leaving them behind, for the ungainly craft, me, needed outriggers on soft snow. With great effort, muscles were forced to correct balance; two ice-axes with ski-baskets could have done the same job with almost no effort, like ski sticks.

An hour passed and I began to find it hard going. The right stump hurt a lot. I struggled to inhale sufficient oxygen to fuel a straining body. The gradual incline, fifteen to twenty degrees, dragged on and on up the snow; a hundred metres, two hundred metres, three hundred metres, five hundred, eight hundred. Ice-axes sank alternately in the snow to the left and right and provided hardly any support. Boots, after being raised clear of the snow, would be thrust forward to sink fifteen centimetres, fifteen centimetres through which they had to be raised at the next step.

Two hours after leaving the hut I was very tired.

'I must rest,' I called out to Francis.

'All right.'

Dropping slowly to my knees, I stayed where I was, kneeling. It was as relaxed a position as any other in the circumstances.

'We are going slowly,' Francis remarked.

'Yes, but Vallot today,' I said between gasps, 'and perhaps the summit tomorrow.'

'Perhaps'

By three o'clock the sun was much less hot than when we left the hut. The biting wind precluded an extended rest and in two or three minutes we toiled on. The gradient lessened, for we were nearing the top of a huge dome of snow, the Dôme du Goûter, a hump with a width of about seven hundred metres. Gradually, almost imperceptibly, the snow levelled out and became firmer. Though bathed in sunlight, the snow was frozen by the wind racing across it. We trudged over the top of the Dôme. It had taken over two and a half hours from the hut by the time we reached the top of the Dôme. I wondered if twenty-four hours later I would look on the summit with contentment and satisfaction, or with disappointment. Hope was so strong it was uncomfortable.

The Vallot hut and observatory, half a mile away, came into sight. To reach the observatory it was plain to see we had to descend from the top of the Dôme du Goûter to a saddle called the Col du Dôme, and from there climb a slope of snow and ice at about thirty-five degrees. Had I been fresh it would have been easy. But I was struggling to keep going.

On the descent of the Dôme the sun no longer shone. Whether this was because it was behind the Dôme du Goûter or clouded over I did not notice, but the air turned bitterly cold. Without the warming rays of the sun the wind could have chilled the body and sapped the strength to a dangerous extreme in a short time. I was glad there was not far to go. It was like being forced to run for hours on end; I would have been relieved to stop at any moment. There was no chance of any more than a brief halt, though, until we reached the hut, because it would have been unwise to have lingered for long in that wind.

Icicles formed on my beard and my gloves froze stiff. The cold affected me more than usual because of the fatigue brought on by between six and seven hours of climbing. Despite the freezing wind, I had to stop to catch my breath when we reached the Col du Dôme. The wind buffeted from the left side in gusts, which made it difficult to keep balance. It was like walking in a crowd with people shoving you around. I felt close to exhaustion as we began the two or three hundred metre climb up to the observatory. Normally it would have taken about ten minutes but I was stopping every fifty metres to catch my breath. Each time we halted Francis stood a few metres above me and now and then I thought he looked a bit concerned. I hoped he was not deciding that we should go down the next day.

At last we reached the observatory, a wooden hut built in 1890 on a tiny, isolated outcrop of rock. The hut was about eight metres long and three metres wide, and the windows overlooked the Dôme du Goûter. A few metres away was the Vallot emergency hut, a life-saver in bad weather. We were using the observatory because there was a big stove and wood there, and it was more comfortable.

Francis produced a key and unlocked the door. There were a couple of tables and two chairs, rows of shelves along the walls and two beds with blankets piled on them. The shelves were crammed with pots, pans and crockery. A small stove stood near the door. The place had an atmosphere of passing time: enamel pans stacked by plastic bowls, candles and new electric torches, Polaroid sunglasses on a shelf near some seaside postcards which were forty or more years old, and Francis's portable gas stove on a table above a box of firewood.

'How tired are you now?' Francis asked.

'Tired and a bit ill, but happy.'

'You have climbed seven hours today. That is quite a lot at this altitude.'

'Yes. I don't like soft snow. I made a mistake not bringing the snow baskets to fix on the ice-axes.'

Soon, that would not be a problem, but at that stage in my climbing, I was still working on basic aids to mobility. And seven hours would come to be considered a short day.

'Four hours is a long time from the Aiguille du Goûter hut to here,' he said.

'Much too long.'

Francis soon had the wood stove going and we drank soup and tea. Icicles from my beard plopped into the tea as I sipped. The sky grew dim and we lit a candle while the hut groaned and shook with the force of the wind which roared outside. Even with the fire blazing it was quite cold, so we sat close to the stove.

'The wind is bad,' Francis remarked. 'If it stays like this we will not be able to go up.'

We turned in early, each wrapped in a huge pile of blankets. My right stump was swollen and bruised and blood had caked at the end. If we continued to climb the next day it would get worse. The normal time from the observatory to the summit was about two hours. If the weather was good the next day the only thing to do would be to carry on. It wasn't working out at all like the reasonably east, injury-free trip I had in mind. I was learning about my limits the hard way.

The wind howled and tugged at the hut all night, making it creak and shudder. By four a.m. it had not eased, nor at six o'clock, nor seven. Francis got up and lit the fire. He stood for a while at the window. From my heap of blankets I called out; I knew the answer already.

'Can we climb?'

'No. The wind is too strong.'

I settled back and fell asleep again, to be woken a few minutes later by Francis, with a cup of tea. I drank it, then with a feeling of dread reached for my legs and put them on. It would be obvious right away if the overnight rest had been enough, I told myself, as I stood up. My heart sank. The stump was still very swollen and tender, in which case further movement would increase the damage. If the weather cleared up, which was unlikely, there would be a painful journey ahead. Outside, the sun was shining, but white whirlwinds of snow scurrying across the Col du Dôme were further evidence of the raging wind.

We drank soup and ate ham and bread. Francis was like a caged animal. On the other hand I sat as much as I could. I hoped he didn't realise this was because I found it painful to stand. He made no complaint when left to do all the odd jobs.

At about half-past five that same morning Kevin and Barbara set out to try for the summit from the Aiguille du Goûter hut. Six more people left the hut at the same time. The wind was so strong that two people soon headed back. Before long, two more returned to the hut. Kevin and Barbara kept going as far as the Vallot hut and observatory, where they came to the conclusion that it would be silly to go any farther. A short distance ahead of them two German brothers had a disagreement about whether they should continue. One detached himself from the rope and walked towards the top. The way to the summit was clearly visible, as were the huge streamers of snow being torn from the summit ridge by the wind. The other brother, and Kevin and Barbara when they arrived at the hut, watched and waited. The longer they sheltered in the hut, the more they became convinced that Francis and I had headed for the summit, and come to grief. What they didn't know was that they were in the emergency hut while we were safe close by in the observatory.

The lone German eventually reached the summit, began the descent, and rejoined his brother. Together they started back to the Aiguille du Goûter hut, followed closely by the two Americans.

At about half-past ten Francis noticed two people descending the slope near the observatory and we went out to watch them. Barbara and Kevin waved excitedly when they saw us.

'We thought you were dead!' Kevin bawled above the noise of the wind. 'You going to try tomorrow?'

'If the weather is all right. You be coming back tomorrow?'

'No. We've had enough today. We're frozen. But good luck to you.'

Francis stood looking out of the window for long periods, or paced the room. At three o'clock he was standing at the window when he said, 'I think it is finished for you.'

Probably true, I thought, but I hated to hear the words.

'It's in the hands of God now,' I said. I couldn't decide whether God would be interested in getting anyone up a mountain. Despite the misery I felt, I tried to remain outwardly optimistic so we would not make definite plans to descend the next day.

'It would be bad to be caught here in a storm,' Francis said, 'We could be stranded for days. Tomorrow, probably we should go down.'

'How's the altimeter?'

'It's dropping.'

'That's good.'

'Perhaps.'

Success hung by a thread, a thin, thin thread. The chance of reaching the summit could fall away and be lost. Even the descent would be difficult if snow conditions were bad.

In the afternoon the sun began to sink into a hummocked sea of cloud above which only a few of the highest mountains, including the one we were on, peeked out. The red sun, big and round, slid from a sky of gold and yellow into the cloud in a display which in itself might have made the journey to the observatory worthwhile for a mountaineer who had no summit ambitions.

'The sun was watery when it went down,' Francis said, 'It's a pity.'

We lit a candle and had more soup, tea, cheese, bread, ham and dried fruit. The wind hammered away at the observatory. There was none of the usual excitement and preparation in anticipation of a day's climbing; we just went to bed and fell asleep.

A number of times during the night I woke up. The wind continued unabated. Forlorn thoughts seem worse at night and I was glad to spend most of the time in sleep rather than thought.

I didn't see the dawn break. In the early daylight I looked at my watch. Half-past six. It was cold and quiet in the building. There was no noise. No noise at all. Then I realised why: no wind! The wind had died down!

Francis started to shuffle about. He looked at his watch too, then sprang out of bed. Hurriedly pulling on his boots, he called out to me at the same time.

'The wind has gone! We can climb!'

It was evident as soon as I stood that thirty-six hours of rest had reduced the swelling on the right stump. The pain was slight. We gulped tea and gobbled bread and ham before packing a minimum of equipment into our rucksacks.

Francis locked the hut. It took only seconds to rope up. It was about seven o'clock. The sun was bright in a clear sky, with hardly any wind. Two hours to the summit. What if the weather turned bad, forcing us to retreat? That would be extremely unlikely in such a short time. Stonefall? No danger. Avalanches and crevasses? Hardly any risk at all. Mechanical failure of legs? A bare possibility. Me giving up? Not a chance of that.

He led the way. The wind had stripped the slope behind the observatory of much of its snow. We cramponed upwards across hard ice and snow for a few metres, then swung along, left, right, left, right, at a smart pace up a gradually rising snowfield. Four people, in two parties, were ahead of us by two or three hundred metres. They had started out early from the Aiguille du Goûter hut. We could see no one below.

The slope narrowed, became steeper, and joined the Bosses ridge. Apart from the difference in colour it looked like a desert sand-dune. We charged along the crest, breathing like stags pursued by hounds, and Francis coughed frequently.

The pace didn't slacken across two snow humps, the Grande Bosse and the Petite Bosse. The top of the Petite Bosse is less than three hundred metres below the summit. A few metres to the right was the border with Italy; we may have walked right on the border in some places.

The route descended into a slight dip after the Petite Bosse. Two of the other climbers were only twenty or thirty metres ahead, and the other pair not far in front of them. We were not racing, but it was clear that two nights spent above four thousand metres had aided acclimatisation.

'Rest for a minute, please, Francis.'

'All right.'

The observatory was already an hour's march behind us. Time had flown. The weather showed no sign of changing for the worse.

I caught my breath and we began the trudge up snow past some rocks called the Rochers de la Tournette. That left one hundred and twenty metres to rise. The ridge to the summit stood out unmistakably. From a broad slope it grew up at an easy angle to the top of the mountain. This was the most exposed place above the observatory; the top of the ridge narrowed until it was about as wide as two bootprints, side by side.

On the broader section of the ridge, low down, we kept up a good pace. The two men in front decided to belay right away; whenever one of them moved forward the other stood still with the rope passed around an ice-axe which was rammed deep into the snow. The theory is that if someone falls the ice-axe will remain in the snow as an anchor; snow conditions are rarely suitable for holding more than a very short fall that way. Francis considered that we did not need to belay on the lower part of the ridge so we tramped past the two men by walking below them on the slope to our left.

'The suffering is almost over,' the leader of the pair said to us in French.

Soon after, Francis went thirty or forty metres ahead while I remained stationary. As soon as he had his ice-axe firmly planted in the snow and the rope around it, he called for me to advance. When I reached him he moved ahead again on his own. Four or five times he belayed in this way. The pair a few metres in front, two Italians, were belaying as well. They belayed several times, then they just walked on because the ridge broadened. We followed them, a few metres behind. They stopped, took off their rucksacks and started taking photographs. They were at the summit. Within seconds we were beside them, 4,807 metres high on the top of Mont Blanc, western Europe's highest mountain.

Francis and I shook hands.

'Thank you,' I said. 'You have been a patient guide.'

Weeks and months of tension simply disappeared, as if washed away. I was ecstatic just to be there, without fully knowing why I had gone. But wow, I was there! There was a sensation of such excitement, as if I felt good music without hearing any. Sometimes a glimmer of that summit feeling comes back at an odd moment and I know why I went. The ascent, once over, never dies. It has happened many times since, that golden feeling, on many a mountain top.

The date, 18th September 1971, was exactly two years after I walked out of John o' Groats. The one was the prelude to the other.

The settled weather allowed a good view across the Pennine Alps, to the Matterhorn and Monte Rosa. Between them and Mont Blanc stood mile after mile of snowy peaks, a gigantic mountaineers' playground. I hoped to explore it all one day, and should perhaps have started on the lesser peaks there.

We had taken an hour and three-quarters from the observatory to the summit. After about fifteen minutes we were on the way down. Back at the observatory, Francis started to peer at the sky again.

'Now we can rest, but we ought to go down to the Aiguille du Goûter hut this afternoon. This would not be a good place to be stranded.' Right matey!

We continued slowly down over the soft snow. My right stump became swollen and painful again. If only I had stopped at the Aiguille du Goûter hut on the way up, instead of pressing on to the observatory, the stump would have been all right. But if I had stopped at that hut Francis might have decided against heading for the observatory in high winds the next day. We might not have reached the summit at all. No, the discomfort was a small price to pay.

The descent was not easy for Francis as my snail's pace prevented him taking rhythmic strides. For the first time he became impatient and his voice was sharp.

'No, move to your right! The snow is firmer there!' he barked. Even a good-tempered sheepdog may snap now and then. Few people could have remained patient when fatigue made my movements progressively more slow and sloppy. On top of that, he had risked his reputation as a guide by accompanying me. If any mishap had occurred on the mountain he would have been criticised heavily. He was entitled to be a bit tense.

We took three and a half hours to struggle from the Vallot observatory to the Aiguille du Goûter hut. An able-bodied party could have managed in half the time, or less. The slushy snow yielded underfoot and occasionally we sank almost up to our knees. Once more I learned that it was all I could do to keep going in such warm conditions on snow.

At the Aiguille du Goûter hut I went straight to the dormitory and flopped on the bunk. As soon as I lay down I was seized with violent coughing fits. My overworked back muscles felt as if I'd been carrying a cow around all day, nausea came on, the right stump was in very poor shape, my head ached with pulsing pain, I shivered and my nose started to bleed. Did I feel it was worth it? Without a doubt.

I slept deeply and the next day we flew down from the hut by helicopter. Really I wanted to climb down but one stump needed a day's rest, a day which Francis did not want to waste in inactivity. He was afraid that the weather would turn bad and leave us stranded in the hut for days and cause him to lose lucrative guiding time. I suggested that if he wanted to go down I would find someone to descend with the next day, or whenever the weather allowed, but he would not hear of this. In fact we argued for some time for I felt that while it was stupid to damage my stump further, flying was taking too easy a course. It was appropriate to my circumstances to make good use of the hut. It seems strange, looking back, because the stumps would take three times as much punishment nowadays. But these were early days and I was still finding out how the leg amputee could best manage in the mountains. With mixed feelings I agreed to fly, rather than to climb, but there was one temptation: the chance of my first helicopter ride was difficult to resist. It was superb!

The next morning the guides presented me with a certificate, signed by the chief guide and Francis. A few reporters came to the guides' office and I made a radio recording in hesitant, inaccurate French. Francis was recorded too, and although I didn't understand all that he said, I was pleased to hear some of his comments.

'We took about four hours from the Vallot to the summit and back. That is a good time,' he said. 'And he walks better on crampons than many normal people.'

A short celebration with some guides was followed by lunch with a press photographer, his girlfriend and two young guides who had completed an extremely hard ascent. The same day I flew home from Geneva. Perhaps it was really September, but I was a little boy, it was Christmas and Mont Blanc was mine.

CHAPTER 3

The Eiger and the Matterhorn

LIFE was busy after Mont Blanc. Following a few television and radio broadcasts I was picked as one of the thirteen 'Men of the Year' who attended a luncheon at the Savoy Hotel in London. It was interesting to meet the other 'Men of the Year': the world motor-racing champion, Jackie Stewart; the English cricket captain, Ray Illingworth; John Dawes, who captained the British Lions rugby team; Sir Geoffrey Jackson, a former British Ambassador in Montevideo who spent months as a prisoner of guerrillas; Chay Blyth, the round-the-world yachtsman. As well as these famous personalities, a soldier, a policeman, an RAF pilot, a lifeboat coxswain, a fireman and a submarine captain were presented with certificates for bravery or achievement. It was sobering to meet men who accepted danger as a part of jobs they felt they ought to do. The sportsmen may have looked more dashing but we were humbled by the presence of men who risked their lives for others.

The Eiger was on my mind so I kept in training by climbing and walking. All the time I hoped to meet two or three good climbers who would leap at the chance of going up the west flank of the Eiger but for a long time no one turned up.

The tedious wait for good conditions on the west flank in 1971 was engrained on my mind; for this reason I made sure I would be free to climb for several weeks in the summer. Mountaineering dictated my life pattern and I took a temporary job. The job lasted until midsummer, which meant I would be free to spend as long as I could afford in the Alps then. It may seem irresponsible to count mountaineering before a career, but I was not going to lose out on the wonders of the mountains because I chose regular pay or job security instead. Age, family responsibilities, a minor permanent injury to hip or back, lack of money or short holidays – each could rob me of the mountains if I delayed too long. Thirty-one is not old for a mountaineer, but as the years creep by opportunity can suddenly or slowly disappear it you don't take it when the time is ripe.

Eventually two companions for an attempt on the Eiger west flank attempt contacted me; they were Dave Parsons and Len Dacey. Dave was bearded, bespectacled and jovial, and had the Welshman's tendency to talk in a high-pitched voice when excited. At the time he weighed a bit more than twelve stones, which looked heavy for a man of 173 centimetres. This was his sixth visit to the Alps and he had wide climbing experience in Britain. He was twenty-eight years old and had just abandoned the career to which his degree in ceramic technology had led him. He was a 'life and soul of the party' sort of person, who, having once made up his mind on any topic, stuck firmly to his point of view. Len Dacey was about thirty years old, quite slim and around 165 centimetres tall. He, like Dave, was bearded. On the mountains he could move with great speed when he wished, and he had climbed in the Alps five times. He worked as a design engineer.

Eiger Glacier Station. Five o'clock was not many minutes away when we left. Daylight had come by then. It was warm enough with a shirt and a thin sweater on. The sky graduated from bright blue in the east to dark blue in the west. It took an hour and a half to reach the bottom of the first snowfield that we had to climb. A year before I had estimated it sloped at thirty degrees but looking at it again I reckoned the angle was a little less. We roped up with me last. Len had a cigarette while we put on crampons. He was a heavy smoker.

The firm snow was just right for Dave to kick steps, and we followed in his footprints. The snowfield presented no problems and in forty minutes we were on rock again. To our right was a wide gully, or couloir. Frozen streams snaked down the mountain; between them there was no ice. Occasionally we would spot a cairn that marked the way but we would be unable to reach it easily; thick ice coated the rock on the way. The normal route weaved up, traversing frequently to the left and right to avoid the hardest or most dangerous, broken rock. Time and time again we had to abandon what would have been an easy way if there had been less ice.

As we would on a rock climb in Britain, we belayed frequently. The usual way of tackling a route like the west flank, with everyone moving at the same time while roped together, did not seem appropriate in such conditions.

We kept to rock as far as possible, following little ribs, surmounting small, easy cliffs and scrambling up slabs of loose rock which fractured under our boots. Mostly it was not steep or difficult, but in places we felt uncomfortable.

'This is the sort of place where you get the chop if you're clumsy,' Dave said.

It was plain to see that in good conditions the climbing was not hard, but the ice made a tremendous difference. In every direction were ferns of frost, displayed over rock like the most delicate of silver jewellery.

Snow lay in cracks and places shielded from the sun, and occasionally we climbed for a few metres in a narrow gully filled with snow. Wherever possible it was better to avoid the snow because it had become soft. Avalanches thundered down neighbouring mountains but we encountered none.

One place where we stood was familiar. It was there that we had turned back on my first attempt on the west flank. Treas had called this place Fruhstuckplatze, but another guide told me that Fruhstuckplatze was the name given to an area lower on the mountain. The first time it had taken four and a half hours to get that far; this time it had taken six and a half hours. Heavy rucksacks had slowed us, but most of all the ice had been our enemy, forcing us several times to leave the route.

'We must be over half way now,' one of them remarked.

'No. Not yet,' I said. 'This is where we turned back last year.'

When we talked of half way we were trying to judge the height. Some mountains rise irregularly and the difficulties may be concentrated in one short section, not necessarily near the top. The Eiger west flank rises fairly regularly and the climbing is roughly consistent throughout, so height gained was a guide to our progress.

We climbed for two more hours. In hindsight I can see that a better knowledge of the route would have helped us over this section; the steep rock we climbed could have been avoided. Belaying as much as possible we headed slowly upwards until at half past one we reached a broad, snow-covered ledge.

'Great bivi spot,' Dave said. 'And it's about two-thirds of the way up.'

Len thought we were about two-thirds of the way up too.

'I don't think we're much above half way,' I said. It was meant as a comment but it sounded like a moan.

The ledge was about three metres wide and seven metres long. At one end the north face fell away vertically. We were pleased to find such a big step in the ridge because there was room to put up our tent.

By 8 p.m. the light was fading rapidly and we settled down for the night. Fine weather tempted us to believe that we could reach the summit the next day. The night was not cold.

Cough, cough, cough, cough. The morning sounds of Len and Dave getting up were as unpleasant as an alarm clock. Five o'clock. Clear sky. At six o'clock we moved off. Frozen streams hung down the mountain and restricted our choice of route once more. We were soon on rock that we thought would be graded as Difficult. It was harder than we should have encountered on that part of the route. Some days later I discovered that the rock was much easier to climb on our right, on the far side of a broad, frozen stream.

The angle was probably less than fifty degrees but we were uncomfortable again. Sometimes, strung out at the full forty-five metres of the rope, we couldn't find one good belay anchor between us. Thin splinters of rock scraped and crackled underfoot.

'I'm not coming down this bit,' Len remarked definitely.

Weaving through snow-cloaked boulders, we arrived at the bottom of a snowfield. In three and a half hours we had not risen more than two hundred metres. We sat to put on gloves and crampons, and two German speaking climbers caught up with us. They waited for us to climb.

Len took the lead because he had more snow and ice experience. There was a step of nearly vertical ice, four or five metres high, in front. I suggested we should look around for a better way on to the snowfield but we could not see one.

Len chipped out a couple of footholds with his ice hammer, a tool with a long pick for cutting into ice. His crampons bit in the holds he had made. He moved up a short way and embedded his ice hammer in the ice as a handhold, then found on icy hold for his left hand and used the front points of his right crampon. The ice hammer dug in higher up and his left crampon came up and bit home. With one or two more movements he was standing on the snowfield.

Dave and I got up with less effort than I expected.

The German-speaking pair watched us and wandered off below the snowfield, presumably hoping to find an easier way on to it, or around it.

'Must be quite close to the top now,' Dave said

'Yes. Not far now,' Len agreed.

I could not share their optimism but did not voice my opinion.

Estimating the angle of a snowfield is not easy but I think this one was about forty degrees. I suppose it was one hundred metres from top to bottom. We plodded steadily up. Part way up the snowfield we could probably have moved to the rock on our right, but we were not sure. We kept to the snow. For security, I would have preferred the rock. Above the snowfield was a cliff. To avoid it we went to the right. I knew Dave and Len thought we were quite close to the summit. It looked as if we would soon see how close when we skirted around the cliff and gained a little height.

We rounded a corner and our hearts must have sunk simultaneously. We were not even as high as the ridge that ran between the Mönch and the Eiger. At the lowest point that ridge was more than three hundred metres below the Eiger. At a rough guess I put us four hundred and fifty metres below the summit of the Eiger.

'Oh, hell!' Dave said.

For a minute or two we stood and looked around before tramping up a forty-five degree slope of snow. The slope had been exposed to the sun for several hours and had lost its firmness. Each minute seemed long as we struggled on.

Midday was near. Dave stopped.

'It's time we talked about what we're going to do,' he said. 'I'm not saying we should turn back but we ought to take stock now.'

'We should go down,' I said. I had had my doubts about reaching the summit so I was not suddenly disappointed.

The snow was noticeably worse as we descended but the ice was quickly melting to make the rocks easy to climb. If we had been able to start two days later the rock would have been almost free of ice. Taking our time, we were back at the tent in four hours.

I had hoped to climb the Eiger with friends rather than guides, and whether I went with friends or guides the mechanical effort required of me would be the same. However, there was one advantage of taking a guide: we would not be slowed by route-finding problems.

'There's beer down there,' Len said. 'When I'm in the valley all I want to do is get up here, and when I'm up here I want to get down there. It's crazy.'

On the last bit of the descent next day, much to our annoyance we found that the ice had melted away to leave a route which we could have climbed in half the time. Higher up it was probably still quite icy but not as bad as when we were there. Time and time again we recognised places that were so slippery on the ascent that we could climb them only with great difficulty. Now we could saunter down.

Our wives met us near the Eiger Glacier station. They were surprised and sorry to hear our news.

'Pity you have to go home,' I said to Len and Dave. 'I'll try again.'

They were both tempted to stay but had to go back to work.

Judy looked as if I was about to play football in a minefield. She was not usually so anxious when I climbed.

'You could be home in five or six days,' she said. 'All you need is good weather and a couple of guides.'

*   *   *

Good weather and a couple of guides. It started to rain just after I reached Grindelwald. At the guides' office I explained to the woman in charge about hiring two guides who would bivouac for at least one night. On a postcard, I showed her where Len, Dave and I turned back. The woman asked me to contact a guide, Hans Kaufmann, by telephone.

He asked how long the various stages had taken me on Mont Blanc and I told him.

'How long can you climb?'

'Last time I climbed for nine hours on one day and ten hours the next day. I could go on for longer but I think that would be unwise in normal circumstances.'

'We could take bivouac equipment with us and if you are going well on the first day we can leave that equipment part way up the mountain and go on to the summit.'

'Maybe. But we'll have to bivouac once.'

I did not want him to think I could manage without bivouacking. He was silent for a few seconds. Had I put him off by insisting that we would bivouac?

'I will find another guide for when the weather is very good,' he said.

The weather was bad at the time so I decided to go to the hotel at the Jungfraujoch to wash glasses and acclimatise. If it were not for that job I would have been unable to afford to wait for long.

Four weeks after leaving England I was waiting for good weather while a blizzard raged outside. That meant the west flank would take a few more days to come into condition. The news was not all bad: Herr Kaufmann had found another guide to accompany us.

I met Hans Kaufmann one day at Jungfraujoch. He was thirty-five years old, younger than I had judged from his voice on the telephone. He was broad, ruddy complexioned and heavy featured, a farmer, I was told, who guided during the summer.

'We could go in three or four days if the weather is good,' he told me. But it did not improve, except for short periods.

September came. Six weeks had elapsed since I left home. Six weeks and still I hadn't got up one mountain! But that was my own fault for not changing my objective. Sunday, 3rd September, was not a happy day. In the morning I saw that it had been snowing quite heavily. I had to face it – my chances of making another attempt on the Eiger in 1972 were small. The season was drawing to a close. The Eiger Glacier Station Hotel was due to shut down in a few days until the ski season. And it would take several days for the recent snow to clear. How I wanted to be rid of this ambition, so I could climb for fun.

One Sunday evening, the television weather forecast was good. Within ten minutes Hans Kaufmann rang.

'The forecast is good,' I told him.

'I know. I will ring the other guide. We need two or three days of good weather. If it is all right we can go to the Eiger Glacier Station Hotel on Wednesday and climb on Thursday.'

Monday was hot and the fresh snow melted quickly from rocks in front of the hotel. Tuesday was hot as well. Early on Wednesday morning it was snowing lightly but the shower was brief. Once more I rang Hans Kaufmann, who suggested we should wait until noon to see how the weather turned out. If it was fine we could go to the Eiger Glacier Station Hotel the same day.

The glass washing machine droned away in the little room where I worked. At a quarter past twelve the phone rang. It was Hans Balmer, the second guide.

'What do you think about the weather, Hans?'

'Well, I think the weather will be good. We can start at two o'clock tomorrow morning.'

The train ride down through the tunnel felt like the beginning of an adventure. The tension of waiting subsided. I found it difficult to believe that the weather could get worse again in a few hours.

In the early evening someone said the last train had come up from Kleine Scheidegg. The guides had not arrived. Anxious minutes dragged by. Much to my relief, there was another train and they were on it. Hans Balmer was twenty-six years old and looked more like a fit, blond German than a Swiss of the Bernese Oberland. He was often silent, unlike his older friend, Hans Kaufmann. They were both farmers and had more sense of humour than most of their neighbours.

A waitress at the Eiger Glacier Hotel, Birgit, asked if I thought I could manage the climb without a bivouac and I told her I was certain I could not. Within twelve hours I would learn the significance of her question.

The guides and I went up to our room to sort out equipment. I kept an eye open for articles of bivouac equipment and they had plenty. They brought torches, stoves, matches, fuel, food and ample warm clothing. We each had a nylon bivi-bag, which is a waterproof cover for a sleeping bag.

I went to bed and fell asleep before the guides turned in.

The light flashed on in the room shortly after one a.m.

'Time to get up!' Birgit called to the three of us.

We all dressed quickly and, taking our rucksacks, went downstairs to the restaurant. The usual breakfast was a flask of coffee with bread, butter and jam, but we were in for a surprise. Birgit was serving bacon and eggs. Soon the unexpected breakfast party grew to a dozen people, including several of the railway workers, a two-man television team and two journalists. The railway staff had been drinking until then and were in high spirits, in contrast to my mood of quiet nervousness. While we ate, people laughed, talked loudly in German, and tottered about. This was the noisiest early morning start I could remember.

Torches were switched on and several people accompanied us over the first two or three hundred metres of track. The TV crew set up some powerful lights and a journalist took still photographs before recording a short interview.

'We will make another interview when you come down,' he said. It crossed my mind that I would not look forward to the interview if I failed once more to reach the summit. What a miserable occasion such an interview would be!

After the special breakfast and the recording, we did not set off until nearly three o'clock. Hans Kaufmann led the way and Hans Balmer followed me. Like a pair of cinema usherettes they shone their torches where I put my boots. They did that job well.

My two companions conversed in German.

'I hope you don't mind us talking in German,' Hans Kaufmann said. 'We are deciding which way to go. It is not easy to find in the dark.'

I suspected that as well as discussing the route they were weighing up my chances of reaching the summit. If they were not it was surprising, because they had not seen me climb before.

Snow and ice avalanches and rockfalls that we heard were all a along way off. A stream gushed down to our right. The night was full of the noises of rock, snow, ice and water heading relentlessly downhill.

The rock steps were familiar: up two metres, almost level for three metres, up a metre, straight ahead for two metres, up three metres, level for seven, and so on. Even though near-vertical in places, each step had sufficient holds to give easy climbing. We neared the top of the steps when Hans Balmer stopped to pass me one end of a five-metre piece of rope.

'It is better if you put a rope on now,' he said. 'In the dark it is not easy.'

I tried to keep my thoughts on the climbing of the moment, rather than thinking ahead to the summit. Somehow the time would pass and in four or five hours I would have a good idea of the chances of success; by then we could be aiming to reach the summit the same day. Or would we have decided to turn back because I moved too slowly? I concentrated on going at a reasonably fast pace in the hope that we would be in a good position in a few hours. Contrary to my expectations I did not bring up the egg and bacon. Because of the extreme effort of climbing, a feeling of nausea was often with me.

The torches were switched off. We crunched ahead, crossing an icy, three-metre wide channel left by an avalanche slipping down, probably days earlier. The avalanche chute presented no danger and we found an easy place to step over the gap between the top of a snowfield and the rock. The two hours we had taken was twenty minutes less than on the previous attempt.

In a minute or two our crampons were off and we were scrambling upwards to the lift of a wide and deep gully. Daylight strengthened rapidly. We walked with little effort along ledges that had given trouble to Dave, Len and me. Now we stepped over little streams that trickled quietly and spread themselves to a width of less than a metre. A month before they had been metres wide, and frozen in the morning.

In an hour and a quarter we climbed from the top of the snowfield to the place Treas Schlunegger had called Fruhstuckplatze. The same section had taken over four hours with Len and Dave. What had been quite hard climbing turned out to be an easy scramble when there was no ice.

'Fruhstuckplatze,' I said.

'This is not Fruhstuckplatze,' Hans Kaufmann said. He pointed the way we had come. 'Fruhstuckplatze is down there. Can you keep going like you have done?'

'I think so, or nearly as fast.'

'That is good.'

With a remarkable view across the north face, this was a natural place to rest. We then took no more than half an hour to reach the spot where I bivouacked with Len and Dave. In three and three-quarter hours from the Eiger Glacier Station we covered the section of the route which had taken eight hours and forty minutes the time before. The difference was due mostly to ice.

'This is about half way,' Hans Kaufmann said soon after we passed the former bivi site. That meant we were about 3200 metres high.

A little later he said, 'We will leave your rucksack. We can reach the top today and come down here to bivouac. If you do not want to get down this far Hans and I will come and carry your rucksack up to you.'

'Sounds all right. I may not be able to descend as far as this today if we do get to the summit. All the way up and half the way down in one day is pushing it for me.'

I lodged the rucksack under a big boulder. Several other boulders in the vicinity were large enough to provide weather protection if we chose to bivouac under them.

'How are you feeling?' Hans Kaufmann asked.

'I feel in great form.'

'And your legs?'

'The stumps seem to be undamaged.'

Hans Balmer grinned and made a remark in German. The only word I understood was 'champagne'.

Having left the rucksack behind I could keep up a good pace. We scrambled between boulders where Len, Dave and I chose to climb a snowfield: it was possible to pick an easy route over rock beside the snow.

'Many people say we are crazy to climb with you, but they say we are crazy anyway,' Hans Kaufmann said.

'What did the other guides say?'

'Mostly they say you cannot climb the Eiger. They say it is not possible.'

'Why did you and Hans think it was possible?'

'Well, I talked to you about what you have done before so I thought you could do it. We have even bet a bottle of champagne that you will go up and down in one day.'

'With Birgit?'

'Yes.'

She's won, I thought, and it disturbed me a little to think that after all my explanations the two guides still believed I could manage the Eiger without bivouacking once. It was a long way to the summit, let alone back to the hotel.

'I think I will have to bivouac on the way down,' I stressed.

'We will see.'

'It is not possible,' Hans Kaufmann said in German. Then he said in English, 'He cannot climb the Eiger,' and laughed.

'It is not possible,' I echoed in German.

'Champagne!' Hans Balmer called out.

'Champagne!' the other Hans shouted.

It crossed my mind that it was a bit early for such confidence, but it must have been a relief for them to see we were progressing as fast as I had said we might. I reminded myself that there was quite a long way to go and slackened the pace a little.

At the Eiger Glacier station some of the railway and hotel staff were taking turns to watch through a big telescope. Clear weather allowed them a perfect view. Almost the whole route could be seen.

68

White scratch marks showed us where people had climbed the rock with crampons when it was icy. The angle varied a few degrees above and below forty. It was easy, as there was hardly any ice. The rock rose monotonously for fifty metres, a hundred metres, two hundred metres.

'It is not possible,' we all said many times, in German.

The route trended again towards the north face. We climbed on the very edge of a mile of rock, which approached the vertical. On our left the drop was exciting and awesome at the same time.

Hans Balmer went ahead in a small, steep gully. As he ascended, stones clattered around him every second or two, but fortunately none of them was large. He climbed ten metres up the right bank of the gully as we looked at it.

The summit was in sight, separated from us by a hundred metres of rock ridge and then a ridge of snow. An hour to go, I thought.

Surely we could not fail? The weather was right, and I was not tired. What could stop us? Dangerously soft conditions on the final snowfield, stonefall, or injury from a fall. The risks from stonefall or a fall were remote. So, it depended on the snowfield. 'It's a bit too warm,' Hans Kaufmann had said on leaving the hotel. Yes, it depended on the snowfield.

'It is not possible!' Hans Kaufmann sang.

'Champagne!' his friend yelled. 'Champagne!'

We followed the rock ridge. No ice. Easy climbing. Plenty of holds. Ledges and steps of a metre or so and rock sloping gently. Soon all the rock was behind, apart from a small mound visible at the summit. Ahead, a snow ridge at forty degrees or less. It looked a hundred metres long. We started to climb. Hans Balmer took the lead. I kept my eyes down on the snow, watching every step. Right axe, left leg, left axe, right leg, right axe. The snow was far from firm.

'It will be dangerous here in an hour or two,' Hans Kaufmann said. 'The snow is getting soft. If you fell you would be finished. You could not stop.'

Right leg, right axe, left leg, left axe. Minutes went by. I took a peep at the summit. It seemed as far away as it had five minutes before. A trail of bootprints behind proved we had risen a long way, but the summit seemed to argue with that.

Left leg, left axe, right, right, left, left, right, right. I drew breath easily. We moved fast, eagerly. My head still down. The angle of the slope was constant, then it lessened quite suddenly. I noticed there were some rocks at the same height as us on the right, three metres away, and then saw that we could not go any farther. We were on the summit. In front, the south-east face plunged. From the right and left, sharp ridges of rock and snow met the summit, 3,970 metres high. Was I dreaming or was I really there? For a moment it was difficult to appreciate the reality.

The guides shook hands with me.

'Thank you both,' I said. 'I'm delighted to be here.'

They deserved more thanks than I put into words.

It was half past eleven. A number of guides had told me they reckoned to take six or six and a half hours with a client, so I was not dissatisfied at reaching the summit in eight and a half hours.

There was great excitement amongst onlookers at the Eiger Glacier station. I was glad they could witness the event because some of them had given me a great deal of encouragement.

The deteriorating snow dictated that we should descend quickly so we rested only briefly. To the south and east, fluffy white clouds added soft lines to a mountain wilderness, and I would have liked more time to sit and stare.

'How do you feel? Hans Kaufmann enquired.

'Not bad. A bit tired but in three or four hours we can stop where we can bivouac.'

'I think you will get back to the hotel today.'

'We'll see. It will be more sensible for me to bivouac, I expect.'

My stumps were sore but I felt as if they were not bleeding.

'We must leave here now,' Hans Kaufmann said.

After an easy descent of four hours we could bivouac at least half way down the route. I was sure that until then I could maintain reasonable concentration. However, things did not work out as I thought.

The sun had been relentlessly at work; the snow towards the bottom of the ridge was noticeably softer less than an hour after we had passed over it on the ascent. It was dangerous and I was not at ease until we left the snowfield behind.

There was no need to hurry. Hans Kaufmann led the way down the rock. Heat made the descent tedious but I was too contented to take much notice of physical discomfort.

'It is not possible,' we joked. 'Champagne!'

We drew level with two ascending climbers. From their speech I took them to be English. They asked where the summit was and Hans Kaufmann pointed it out. As they plodded on I wondered how they would manage on that final ridge, which they would reach nearly two hours later than us.

Quite soon we passed the place where Dave, Len and I turned back. We had made the right decision in not carrying on to the summit on that occasion, without a doubt.

As we continued a rock crunched down the mountain thirty metres from us. Like an under inflated football it bounced in shallow arcs, and was soon out of sight. For several seconds we heard it thudding on. Now that we were descending, gravity was more in our favour, but could still cause a fall, or send down an avalanche, or rocks.

A few minutes later Hans Balmer shouted from behind.

'Achtung!'

I turned to see something flying through the air towards me. I ducked behind a rock and was showered by small particles of ice. The ice had smashed on the rock and the pieces were too small to do any harm. For an instant as they fell they had looked menacing.

We carried on.

'When we reach your rucksack we will rest and have something to eat. Then we can go down to the hotel,' Hans Kaufmann said.

'That will not be wise,' I told him. 'I think I should not climb much more today.'

'We should not bivouac up here if we can get back to the hotel.'

The last hour before we arrived at the boulder where we had left my rucksack was a wearying trudge. In the heat my stumps began to feel very painful. It was four o'clock so we had climbed for thirteen hours. That was the longest I had climbed and I could not expect the stumps to take much more punishment without serious damage. I estimated that it would take four to six hours to reach the hotel. To climb for such a length of time would far exceed my reasonable limits.

When we had rested for a few minutes Hans Kaufmann said, 'Now we must go down.'

'I think we should stay here,' I objected.

'If it snows we could be in trouble,' he added.

'It's a bit late to remember that it sometimes snows up here. The weather is good!'

Hans Balmer picked up my rucksack and was busy tying it on the top of his own. The extra few pounds would not make much difference to him.

Certainly, if we went well below half way we would be safer in the event of a storm. The weather was fine but it was possible it would change.

'I'll go on for an hour or two and see how I feel,' I said.

Needless to say, I moved slowly. Fatigue was partly responsible and I could not put my heart into a descent that I regarded as unnecessary. From experience I knew that once the stumps had had enough their condition would deteriorate rapidly.

The fourteenth hour of climbing went by. I moved as an unwilling slave. I could keep going but I wondered if I should.

'How heavy are you?' Hans Kaufmann asked.

I told him.

'If you become very tired we could carry you when it is dark,' he said.

'No you bloody well won't!'

'No one would know.'

'I would know.'

Hans Balmer joined in, saying, 'You are very hard-headed. Just because you have no legs you don't want to be carried, but sometimes men who have whole legs have to be carried. Some people like to say they have bivouacked on many mountains.'

'It doesn't take much sense to see that this is a special case. We knew I would need to bivouac.'

'You have climbed down all right so far,' Hans Kaufmann said.

There was no rhythm to my climbing; each movement had become a separate mental and physical effort in a disjointed labour.

The fifteenth hour passed – a whole, long hour of great exertion and failing concentration. We took a rest. Lying back on a rock, I tried to muster my thoughts. I had climbed to the summit and descended to a safe height to bivouac and it was not sensible to go on. I was worried about causing serious physical damage to my stumps. I vomited, through sheer overwork, and perhaps through dehydration, too.

'Come on,' Hans Balmer said after three or four minutes.

Hans Kaufmann tugged at the rope to get me to stand. Rude bastard.

'Hang on a minute!' I said. 'I want time to think.'

Thoughts came slowly and were hard to grasp. Feelings flooded my mind: exhaustion, pain, elation, indecision, anxiety about my physical limits. I could have sat down at any time and refused to move, so why didn't I? The truth was that although I believed it was stupid to continue, half of me wanted to complete the climb in a day. It felt so wrong to go on for more than fifteen hours; I battled with my own better judgement. I would have liked half an hour in which to sort out my jumbled thoughts.

'Come on!' Hans Balmer said. 'You can do it.'

I stood and began to climb down again. The sixteenth hour crept by. By half past seven it was getting dark. We were at the top of the lowest snowfield. The two English mountaineers we had seen earlier passed by. Poor snow had forced them to give up not far from the summit, on the final snowfield, and I realised how lucky we had been. In the whole day they were the only climbers we saw.

'You can sleep in a good bed when we get to the hotel,' Hans Kaufmann remarked to me.

'I could sleep in a good sleeping bag now if you bandits would stop,' I said. 'Anyway, I want some of that champagne if we get down tonight.'

'Of course,' he said. He smiled. 'You know, you will be happy if you can climb the Eiger in one day.'

'I hoped to climb the Eiger but I did not want to be a stupid sort of mountaineer. I would never have set out to climb it in one day.'

On the descent of the snowfield my knee joints ached and the flesh at the back of the knees was tender. That worried me because knees do not put up well with bad treatment. I wondered how long I could go on without suffering serious effects from exhaustion and excessive exercise. One thought frequently entered my mind, that I was not cold. It was a good sign.

The seventeenth hour passed. After the first six hours of climbing I was, understandably, quite tired. Six more hours had taken me to what I considered to be the extreme of my reasonable limits. Five hours of discomfort and fatigue followed and we still had to descend a long way over rock. We needed torches on the lower part of the snowfield and I did not relish descending the rock by torchlight. But I did not stage a sit-down strike. I knew if I insisted on bivouacking the guides would stay with me; they could not risk abandoning me on the mountain. I wondered why they were so keen to reach the hotel. Was the attraction the thought of proving the other guides wrong? All the time I wondered why I did not stop, and the only reason I could find was that I wanted to complete the route in one day. My cautious self had to be content that we were approaching safety. Obviously, determination and sense were not to be completely and simultaneously satisfied on this occasion.

I appreciated that it was a big mental strain for guides to undertake the responsibility of leading a disabled client on a long route. The pair with me were among the very small number of Grindelwald guides prepared to take the job on, and I was grateful to them.

Our torches probed through the darkness, seeking the way. It was not easy to find. Hans Balmer went ahead, searching for a route down the rock steps. He wandered to the left and right, finding the route and losing it every few minutes. I took advantage of every delay to rest. We meandered down for an hour, the eighteenth hour. I had passed through hardship into joy, then back deeper and deeper into hardship; but the joy was still complete.

Someone with a powerful torch left the hotel and came towards us.

From a hundred metres or so above them we could see that they were waving the torch around. It was Birgit and Barry, an English chef, swinging the torch about in greeting and encouragement. They signalled for several minutes before returning to the hotel. It was nice to know someone was thinking of us.

Every step down, every reach for a handhold, was like the movement of someone who has just woken in the middle of the night. My feet might have been made of lead, not wood.

The nineteenth hour came to an end. Slowly, we neared the lights of the Eiger Glacier station. At last we reached the track through the glacial moraine. Nearly there. We passed by the railway lines and overhead cables, the houses and huts. We were a few metres from the hotel when I saw a table supporting glasses and bottles of champagne. A dozen or fifteen people waited to welcome us. As we reached the hotel entrance the television crew started to film. Suddenly it came to me that I was feeling cold. It was a strange sort of feeling which I could not understand. It was like nothing I had felt before. Then I put my hand down and found that there was no seat at all left in my trousers! From then on I made sure I was facing the camera.

The time was half past ten and the climb had lasted nineteen and a half hours.

Everyone seemed thrilled. Someone started pouring champagne, the journalist conducted another interview, then we had a celebration meal and wine. While several people drank, laughed and talked loudly in the restaurant I fell asleep sitting upright. The guest of honour, asleep at his celebration party!

The next day I heard that Hans Kaufmann had said in advance that he had no intention of bivouacking unless it was absolutely necessary. I was angry about that, but the guides had carried out the job and I liked the pair of rogues. And I could have insisted on stopping. By carrying on I had been taught something new about my limits: sense was likely to stop me long before fatigue.

Frau Sommer arranged a champagne breakfast for the morning after the climb. She, the guides, Barry and I sat on the hotel balcony for a meal of eggs and bacon, assorted meats and pickles, tea and champagne. The next day I went to Berne for a radio recording, and a Scotsman at the studio provided more champagne. I flew home the same day and at our local pub there was more champagne as soon as Judy and I walked through the doorway. 'Congratulations on your feat,' someone said, and from somebody else came, 'He hasn't got any'. For a few days life revolved around newspapers, radio and television broadcasts, and celebrations with friends. Then it all went back to normal.

*   *   *

'How about doing the Matterhorn this summer?' Dave Parsons asked.

'I've thought about it. I'm not too sure. The normal route is crowded. I like quieter routes. But I'm tempted.'

'Out of all the peaks it's always the Thing that stands out,' Dave said. The Thing was the Matterhorn. Steep on all sides and wildly beautiful, the remarkable pyramid demanded attention, and it was easy to see why it tempted climbers to the top. It stood there, seemingly aloof, yet accessible at the same time, in the eyes of our group, gathered in Zermatt.

Shortly after our arrival, we witnessed a very sad scene. Next to ours stood two tiny tents, temporary homes for four young Japanese men. We didn't see much of them because they spent most of their time climbing. One afternoon word filtered down to the valley that two Japanese had fallen to their deaths on the normal route on the Matterhorn. It did not occur to us that it might have been two of the men from the neighbouring tents because there were hordes of Japanese climbers in the Alps. But on the morning following the announcement of the accident two of the men turned up, obviously shocked, to pack up both tents and all the equipment. They did so quietly and one sight really brought home the sadness of the occasion – when the two small men left the camp site each was burdened with two large rucksacks, one tied on top of the other.

The Belvedere Hotel on the Hörnli ridge of the Matterhorn was much improved since my previous visit and the kitchen, particularly, was no longer filthy. We stayed in the hut next door and were away by half past three the next morning, along with about sixty other alpinists; yes, sixty.

The moon was just bright enough to manage without a torch, although most people used head torches. We followed a long line of lights up a rocky path. A fixed rope of six or seven metres hung down the first bit of climbable rock and everyone went up quickly, hand over hand, with feet walking up. Without that rope there would have been a bottleneck close to the hut.

An easy track climbed and dipped, and several lights in front veered a little to the right into dark shadow. We followed the torches up a crumbly rock face, nearly vertical in places but very easy. At the top a party of three seemed to be having trouble. We had to wait quite a long

75

time while the leader descended into darkness over a cliff. In a minute recurred several times in the next few minutes. The leader called up; he sounded anxious. The man feeding the rope down to him found a spike of rock and passed the rope around it.

'I don't remember this bit,' Dave remarked. He had been on the route before, once when he climbed up and down that way and once when descending after climbing the Zmutt ridge of the mountain.

Time crept by and the leader's rope was fed out slowly.

'Wrong way.' Dave said. 'Must be. There's nothing difficult about this part of the route.'

We retraced our way down the rock face. As the light improved we saw that we had been on the top of a rock tower which stuck up on the ridge. In all we must have wasted a large part of an hour by following the wrong people. They passed us again an hour later. We pressed on over slopes of broken rock.

'What a heap of rubbish,' Dave remarked. At close quarters the mountain lost much of its beauty.

People above were dislodging lots of stones and in the half light it was not easy to see them coming. We were worried, with good reason as it happened. As one shower of Mother Nature's cannonballs bounced down we froze, ready to duck or dodge. The stones thudded down to our right and stopped not far below as they met a large ledge. A minute or two later another rock barrage began to fall from a hundred metres above. They came nearer and nearer but we could not see them. Judging from the noise it gradually became more and more evident that they were coming our way. We pressed ourselves against the rock. Clunk, clunk, clunk. Fist-sized stones sped by and there was a loud thump on my helmet. It was probably a glancing blow because the helmet was not split.

'Christ!' my companion muttered.

'You all right, Dave?'

He was about four metres away.

'Yes. They missed me. You all right?'

'Yes. Got a smack on the helmet. I think one hit my ice-axe too.'

The axe was passed through a shoulder strap of my rucksack, between the rucksack and my back. On this occasion the axe had a wooden shaft, and when I came to examine it in daylight there was a chip of wood missing. I was lucky not to have been struck on the back of the neck.

'What a heap of rubbish!' Dave said again.

Snow patches were only a few square metres in area. The rock was poor in many places. Difficulty in route-finding slowed us. It was not that we went the wrong way often, but time was lost as we talked over which way looked best. We lacked the confidence of being sure we were on the route. Instead of thrusting ahead, as one can on some obvious routes, we had to pick the way, to fret at it. Or to hire a guide.

Other parties had route-finding problems and after four hours' climbing several people were only a few minutes ahead. A man with a bandaged head descended with two companions.

Nowhere was the rock climbing above Difficult standard. In six hours we were at the Solvay hut, 4,000 metres.That was a very long time – four hours would have been satisfactory for me.

The hut was perched right on the sharp ridge. Five or six disconsolate people hung around, waiting for friends who had carried on. Most were tired, probably because of the altitude, and one had injured his knee in a fall. He felt that he would be unable to descend so a message was taken to the Hörnli hut to summon a helicopter.

'What shall we do tomorrow?' Dave asked me. 'To tell the truth, I'm not too happy to go on when there are only two of us.'

'I was thinking about that. We usually would have someone else on a route like this.'

'So we go down tomorrow?'

'I think so. Anyway, this has been good reconnaissance.'

'Yes. You wouldn't have any trouble with the rest of the route.'

At six a.m. the next day we abseiled down a couple of steep pitches and climbed down the mountain. (In simple terms, abseiling means sliding down a rope.)

I failed to climb the Thing and as it was a rubbishy route I was not disappointed. Or was I? It was strange. I had felt little ambition to stand on the summit, but it was as if the mountain had control and could make me want to climb. Where was my former indifference about that peak? It was gone for sure, for ever; the lure of that lovely mountain was just too strong now I had seen it.

The mountains had given me so much pleasure and I wondered how many other disabled people took part in outdoor pursuits. There was a lack of information available, and after a talk with Lady Hamilton, Chairman of the Disabled Living Foundation, I was given the job of compiling a guide on outdoor pursuits for disabled people.

Although I was in favour of competitive sports for disabled people, I felt that the emphasis had been so much on that side that non-competitive activities had been neglected, partly because of the often unfounded assumptions on the part of some organisers of sports for disabled people that such activities were beyond the abilities of those they dealt with. There was a tendency to expect disabled people to take part only in a limited number of sports and mostly in a segregated situation. Total integration within the community was clearly not always possible but it did seem desirable to lean towards integration wherever this was realistic. With very few exceptions, only the more obvious and easiest sports had been tackled on a large scale; the most notable exception was the Riding for the Disabled Association, which brought riding to thousands of disabled young people and adults. From the start the 'father' of sport for disabled people, Sir Ludwig Guttmann, made clear his opposition to much that several of us were trying to achieve, and a politically naïve (then) young man like me was hurt by the venom of this powerful, authoritarian old man. But other disabled individuals gave support and helped to create the demand, and now adventure sports for people with disabilities are well established, even commonplace. While such activities can never be entirely risk free, neither is driving a group in a minibus to Stoke Mandeville to play table tennis. We followed the right and careful path between foolhardiness and overprotection. Though I am not certain who put my name forward, I suspect that I was recommended for an OBE "for services to disabled people", for withstanding the flak which came my way because of challenging the rigid and constricting views of established disability sport bureaucrats.

The Matterhorn had been on my mind all year. After climbing to the Solvay hut I had asked at the Zermatt guides' office if a guide could be found for the following year and the man there said it would be all right. However, when I wrote to the office to confirm this I received no reply.

The London editor of a Swiss news agency contacted me to see what I had planned for the summer.

'The Matterhorn. But I don't know if any guides will go, and even if they do I can't afford to pay them. And none of my friends are going to Zermatt this year.'

Because of a way of life which left enough time to do the things I very much wanted to do, climb and write the outdoor pursuits guide, my annual earnings were only £500.

A couple of years before I had written half a dozen letters to large business organisations to request funds for a climbing trip. I was always rather uncertain about writing these letters because I couldn't really believe that anyone would be prepared to take the responsibility of being associated with one of my climbs, and I couldn't see why someone else should pay for my excitement and pleasure. The response from the firms was three dozen cans of beer and the offer of a free tin of antiseptic ointment.

The Swiss editor of the agency was sufficiently interested in the proposed climb to be prepared to pay the guide fees. Unfortunately the President of Zermatt guides then decided that the ascent was too dangerous for me. True, like anyone else attempting the Matterhorn I could be killed or injured, but I did not consider the risk to be any greater for me. In fact it was less for me than for some of the unfit and inexperienced people who paid to be taken up.

Eventually contact was made with Hans Kaufmann, with whom I had climbed the Eiger; he would go.

Less than twenty-four hours after leaving Victoria Station I was nearly three thousand metres above sea level at the Gandegg hut, reached easily in twenty minutes' walk from a cable car out of Zermatt. August was not quite half way through.

Training at altitude was essential, so I joined five Germans who invited me to climb with them on the Breithorn, 4165 metres. Though I had explained, it was only when we returned from the summit that they understood about my legs; they just thought I was a bit slow.

Back in Zermatt I booked in at a dormitory at the top of the Bahnhoff Hotel, and rang Herr Perll, the Swiss editor of the news agency. He was a mountaineer and intended taking pictures on the climb, but he was away for three days, I learned.

I mooched around Zermatt. The weather stayed fine and the climbing boomed. For three or four days the Matterhorn was thronged with mountaineers, and then the weather turned nasty. I had missed my chance. Damn, damn, damn.

On ringing Herr Perll again I was told he was still away on holiday, so I moved to a dormitory in a mountain hotel at Gornergrat and spent three says walking about at around the three thousand-metre contour.

Down to Zermatt again. On the telephone to Herr Perll.

'I will come to Zermatt on Wednesday,' he said.

Three more days to wait, to wander about.

In the basement of the hotel was a kitchen where you could cook for yourself, and it was there that one day a very distinguished visitor appeared: Lord Hunt. In the company of his wife and a friend he was planning to travel over to Chamonix across the mountains. As a result of our meeting there Lord Hunt later came to the press launch of the outdoor pursuits guide. Sir Roger Bannister, at that time Chairman of the Sports Council, was at the launch too. So with the leader of the successful British Everest expedition and the first man to run a mile in four minutes at the same event we were not short of famous personalities. And it was very appropriate that the foreword to the guide was written by Sir Jack Longland, who used to climb with one-legged Geoffrey Winthrop Young.

It was tempting to go and do some more high peaks, but I had to stay around and be ready to climb the Matterhorn. I could not risk doing too much in training for fear of damage to the stumps. Instead of going up the high peaks I made do with easy ascents in the area: twice I went up the Ober Rothorn, 3,415 metres, and twice up the Unter Rothorn, 3,103 metres. Mostly I went alone because these were safe, busy trails, and once with Jon Ryder, an exceptionally fit American who became so fond of Zermatt that he stayed on to work on the Gornergrat railway for the winter.

Days crept by. In the brief spells when the weather was fine Hans Kaufmann considered that conditions on the Matterhorn were not good enough for me. The weather was never stable for long, and then there was another setback: Hans Kaufmann said he was busy for several days so could not go even if the weather was suitable. The Zermatt guide who would have gone with him was busy too. Whether they were really busy or had had second thoughts I could not say, but I had to start looking for guides again. I'm not superstitious but the day on which this news came was Friday, 13th September.

I had been in Switzerland five weeks and was still waiting. I was always bloody well waiting, it seemed, but again, it was my choice.

A few phone calls led me to get in touch with Eddy Petrig, a guide. He had heard that I was in the village so there was no need for long explanations.

'When do you want to go?' he asked.

'As soon as possible.'

'I would like to go,' Eddy said at last. 'I will contact another guide to be with us.'

'That's fine.'

'And I will ring you when it is time to go.'

Eddy was influenced, I believe, by the fact that he felt that the guides had not behaved properly, in failing to reply to my letter.

Frau Biner, who usually ran the Bahnhof Hotel, was convalescing after breaking a thigh, so two of her relations, Kathy and Miriam, looked after the place. Being among the longest staying guests that year, Jon and I were treated with special kindness, and the friendliness of many people is one of the things I remember most about the trip to Zermatt.

'If you climb the Matterhorn you will be very happy,' Miriam said one day. 'And if you cannot it will make me very sad.'

The weather forecast gave no cause for optimism for a couple of days. 17th September arrived and my sixth week in Switzerland began.

'What's the matter with you?' Eddy's wife asked him with irritation. 'You're out looking at the weather every fifteen minutes!'

He admitted to me later that he had been very anxious while waiting. I was under a strain too.

'I feel like my stomach's connected to the barometer,' I told Jon. 'Every time I see it go up or down my guts do too.'

'You'll do it if the weather gives you a chance,' Jon insisted.

Still the weather would not let me go, and waiting was getting me down. Anyone who has set their heart on a dear goal and has been frustrated day after day, week after week, will understand what I mean.

'allo! Telephone!'

It was the Spanish housekeeper, a large, friendly lady, calling me. Eddy was on the line.

'The weather is not really settled but we should go,' he said. 'You should ring Herr Perll and get him to come to Zermatt now. Otherwise you will not get a chance this year.'

Götz Perll arrived the same day. Bearded, dark, of average build, thirty-four years old. Gradually scraps of information built up a picture of the man: independent, determined, married five years with one baby of nine months, originally from Germany, fond of skiing, but not greatly experienced as a mountaineer.

The next day was 20th September. At eight a.m. thick mist cut off the sky. By half past nine the same morning it was raining lightly. Eddy rang at ten a.m.

'We will wait until the forecast at half past twelve. There has been some snow at the Hörnli hut.'

'If not this year, then next year,' I said. Like the grains of sand in an egg timer, minutes were running out. If they ran out completely it would be next year before the timer could be turned over to start again.

Eddy was definite: 'I want you to do it this year now you are trained.'

The barometer fell a little. Oh dear! And by noon it was raining again. At one o'clock the phone rang and Götz picked it up. He talked seriously for a minute or two, and as he talked he raised one thumb in the air.

'We go to the Belvedere Hotel this afternoon,' he said. 'Eddy is very confident that you can do it but it depends on the weather.'

In haste we bought food for the trip, had a good meal and hurried off to the cable car, where Eddy waited with Richard Biner, an aspirant guide who was to climb with Götz. Richard did not speak much English and was a quiet man.

Eddy stared at my boots. They were light, ideal for me but too light for a mountaineer with real feet.

'Don't your feet get cold with those boots?'

'I suppose so. But it doesn't matter.'

'Of course. I am stupid.'

He was an amazingly young-looking man. At first I thought he was in his mid-forties but in fact he was fifty-seven years old. He was not the type who bulged with muscle; this lean, agile person moved in a deliberate, cat-like way and it was difficult to believe that in most societies he would be only a few years from retirement. Eddy had travelled to several countries and had lived some years in Canada. He has been married a few years, and perhaps his young children helped him to remain as young in mind as he looked in body. He seemed to belong more to my generation than to his own.

The cable car whisked us up through light rain, up more than a thousand metres in minutes to Schwarzee, at 2,582 metres. A thick mist blanket hung greyly over the area.

'It's no good. We must go down,' Eddy said, but he was not serious and led the way up the trail.

'You can go in front and make the pace if you like, Norman. Go as slowly as you like,' he suggested, and within five minutes said, 'Don't go so fast. I don't want you pooped for tomorrow.'

'Going too slowly makes it more difficult. It's like doing press-ups: the slow ones are harder.'

'All right. You know what is best for you.'

Down in Zermatt a chimney sweep called at the Bahnhof Hotel.

'That is good luck,' Miriam told Jon. 'Now I know Norman will succeed. The chimney sweep is always a sign of good luck.'

For an hour we tramped on in single file. The mist thinned. It was wonderfully cool for walking. Snow and ice lay on the zig-zags of the Hörnli buttress.

'The wind is from the north,' Eddy announced. 'The weather will be good tomorrow. That is because you are an angel without wings. You are lucky. And you did not say you could do more than you can when I talked to you. Now I am excited. As long as the weather is all right you will do it.'

The weather. Always the weather. If one heavy snow shower came the route would probably not be in condition again that year.

We were at the Belvedere Hotel in one and a half hours. The manager and his wife had kindly promised to keep the hotel open for an extra night the following day, the day on which, if all went well, we should either get back or be staying in the Solvay hut. This brought home to me just how close we were to the end of the season.

A man arrived at the hotel.

'Norman, this is Leo Imesch,' Eddy said. 'He will be going with us.'

Leo was broad, tall, fair, about twenty-five years old, a kind and cheerful man with a big moustache. He hoped to qualify as a guide the next year. So there we were: Eddy, Götz, who had made the event possible, the cheerful and enthusiastic Leo, quiet Richard, and me. The hotel manager kept offering me wine but I drank tea instead. His wife prepared a very substantial meal. Suitably fed, we went to look at the weather again. Stars stood out sharply over mist-filled valleys.

'It will be good,' Eddy said once more.

I turned in early, and while I slept Eddy and the hotel manager argued violently about my chances. Eddy was confident, the manager was not, but still gave Leo a bottle of strong spirit for us to share in celebration if we reached the summit. We would learn the irony of that argument the next day.

The sound of someone laughing quietly woke me in the morning; my legs, still wearing trousers, leaned against the bottom of my bunk as if resting too, and caused much amusement among my companions.

Now the real climbing would begin. Up the jagged Hörnli ridge, keeping mostly to the left side, at other times moving on the very crest of the ridge. This was roughly the route of the first ascent more than a hundred years before, when four of the party of seven fell to their deaths on the way down.

Three people left the hotel in front of us; the manager and two friends. Five a.m. Not light, but not black. Eddy led, with me and then Leo behind. Richard led Götz. The weather refused to let us know for sure that it would remain good, but the signs were reasonably favourable.

Thick snow had accumulated on the normal way near the hotel. Throughout the usual climbing season the rock there would have been clear but now we crunched over a firm, white covering.

'Numerous short pitches of 2', the guide book said. Two is equivalent to something between Moderate and Difficult, and we started up the first of those pitches. I saw little of the surroundings apart from the rock, ice and snow under my boots and hands, and I remember the mountain only in bits and pieces. There was a near vertical pitch, short and not hard, there was a bit of track through broken rock, there were stretches of snow covered, sloping rock and more steep rock with good holds.

Eddy had climbed one ridge of the Matterhorn, the Zmutt, fifty-two times, and had often used the Hörnli ridge for descent. With one companion he made the first winter ascent of the Zmutt ridge in 1948.

Head torches were soon extinguished. Unlike on my previous trek that way there had been no long line of lights ahead of us, and the absence of other climbers meant there was little need to wear helmets as a protection against stonefall.

I had to push myself to keep up a reasonable pace. After half an hour, an hour, an hour and a half, two hours, it would have been too easy to drop back to a more comfortable pace, but it was essential to press on so we would be as high as possible as quickly as was sensible.

'Go as you like,' Eddy emphasised. 'You know what you are able to do,' and soon after he said, 'I think that you should go a little more slowly. It is a long way.'

'You are doing well,' Leo added in encouragement.

Götz did not request any hesitation for photographs. Sometimes he and Richard were ahead and sometimes they were behind.

Another pitch of Moderate rock, and another, until we were directly below the Solvay hut. The three men who had been ahead turned back because the hotel manager was feeling unwell. He looked very sheepish, as well as sick.

Ahead was the Moseley Slab, at the top of which, the route description said, was a near-vertical corner to climb. All went well for us and we were soon seated inside the wooden Solvay hut, 4,000 metres high. Three and a half hours from the bottom of the ridge. Not bad. We sipped hot tea from flasks and ate little bits: cheese, dried fruit, meat.

There was mist higher up. For the time being, at least, the weather was satisfactory. How lucky we were that there were no other climbers around: no stonefall and we had the peak to ourselves, without delays on the harder sections. It felt right. My major disappointment with the route, that it was crowded, did not apply that day.

In a few minutes we were on our way again, up the Upper Moseley Slab, twenty metres, steep and graded Moderate. Then there was one of the few exposed, narrow rock ridges to walk and scramble over. More scrambling and easy climbing brought us in half an hour to the Shoulder, a large snow and ice slope at forty-five degrees. Time for crampons. At intervals of forty metres or so large metal stanchions had been driven in as belay anchors. Eddy went ahead from stanchion to stanchion and I followed only when he had the rope around one of them.

Down in Zermatt, two thousand, seven hundred metres below, Miriam was watching through a telescope. She picked us out against the white backcloth of the Shoulder, and was even able to see that the second man on the first rope was hunched over and moving quite slowly. She knew who that was.

On the Shoulder a familiar feeling of nausea began to bother me. I think this was caused by physical effort because six hours of any exertion that really makes you puff is quite a strain. So there was the nausea barrier to be faced again.

Firm snow held reassuringly at each step. It took perhaps fifteen minutes to get up the Shoulder. More climbing on rock brought us abruptly to the edge of the north face, plunging down on our right, but we hardly hesitated to look.

Leo and Eddy were talking to each other cheerfully in German; obviously they were optimistic. Now I was confident too.

Next to overcome was a section with fixed ropes. I knew that afterwards there was only a steep rock and snow slope to the summit. The ropes hung permanently down the steep rock and were ice-coated in places. Without crampons it would have been difficult to keep our feet firmly on the icy rock as we hauled ourselves up hand over hand. I felt that the route would have been more enjoyable without those ropes, although in icy conditions I was pleased the use them.

'My mother worries when I am here,' Leo remarked. 'My uncle was killed on the Matterhorn when a fixed rope broke. On the Italian side.'

Up a rope, heave, heave, heave with gloved hands, up another and another. There was a last very steep pitch to pull up at the top of that section and then we were on the slope known as the Roof.

Only the Roof to go. I would make it! I would make it!

From then on it was a scramble over rock and snow. Loose rock and snow moved under our feet.

We were moving quickly. My ambition was almost at rest, but not quite. Another glance up at the top, a rapid, triumphant scramble and there we were, on the summit of the Matterhorn, 4,477 metres. The sharp summit ridge was almost horizontal and approached a hundred metres in length, with flanks falling away steeply for hundreds of metres on either side. Seven and a quarter hours from the hotel was slightly less than I had expected in those conditions.

Everyone was grinning.

'I know this sounds silly but I don't know whether to laugh or cry,' I said.

'You do what you like. We understand. It is a very happy day for us too,' Eddy told me.

Leo added, 'This is one of the best days I have ever had in the mountains.'

Götz looked thrilled and declared that this was one of the happiest days of his life. It was his first time on the Matterhorn.

I laughed quietly, frequently, like someone with a secret. I was released and had no need to return next year.

As we shook hands all round Götz clicked away with his camera. Moving a few metres below the summit to escape the bitter wind we sat on rock to nibble at food and drink tea. The bottle of spirit supplied by the hotel manager was forgotten.

No one else reached the summit that day. We had met three men who turned back and later saw two more who got to the Shoulder before going down again.

Cloud blocked our view of Zermatt but we could see Mont Blanc. A red helicopter chattered by, quite close, and people inside waved. We waved back and I thought how pleasant it would have been to tell them how contented we were. The aircraft flew down and was soon out of sight behind cloud. Before long we followed the same general direction, downwards.

'Can you get back to the hotel today and miss the Solvay hut?' Eddy wanted to know. And clearly he wanted a positive reply.

'I think so.'

Our elation was understandable but we had done only half of the job. Now we had to get down safely. We descended the Roof and the fixed ropes with reasonable speed. On narrow ridges we tried a new method: Leo would walk while I lightly rested a hand on his rucksack to help balance. In this way we moved quite rapidly on airy ridges, but I now have reservations about that method from a safety point of view.

We passed the two climbers who had reached the Shoulder. Difficulties in route finding had slowed this pair, and they failed to get back to the hotel that night.

Eddy and Leo remained patient, vigilant, good-humoured. The Solvay hut was reached in what for me was a sprint time, two hours. We sat there having a snack and sipping at the hotel manager's spirit. There was no question of spending the night in the hut; we felt we could reach the hotel before dark, and in any case we had torches.

The steepness of the mountain suited me as I found it easy to descend by lowering myself with my arms. After ten hours of climbing I was beginning to tire and Eddy twice called a halt for a rest.

'There is no hurry,' he advised. 'Just concentrate.'

While we sat and admired the view he said, 'You should not push yourself so hard. You enjoy the mountains and perhaps ten hours is enough for you in a day.'

Down again, down, down, steady, down, steady, concentrate. We drew close to the hotel, where a small group of climbers waited to congratulate our party. Night did not overtake us: we were back in the hotel at six-thirty p.m., twenty minutes before darkness. The round trip had taken thirteen and a half hours.

Soon only a dim outline of the mountain remained. I watched it for a long time. Had I really climbed up that shadow?

I felt guilty at not being able to touch the special meal which the manager's wife cooked for us, but I could not keep anything down. I must be one of the few people in the world to have celebrated a climb with a glass of hot water. There I sat, quite tired, rather sick, and above all, delighted. Of the manager, there was no sign; he had gone down to Zermatt to avoid meeting us.

Miriam, Frau Biner and Jon rang to congratulate us all. Before long I went to bed. The only damage to my stumps was one abrasion about the size of the nail of my small finger.

By half past six the next day we were up and breakfasting. The two men who had been caught out by darkness had bivouacked above the hotel and descended safely at dawn.

Richard and Leo hurried down to the valley while Eddy, Götz and I went more slowly. What followed then? A welcome bath at the Bahnhof Hotel, half a dozen cups of tea with Miriam and Jon in the kitchen, the warmth of their sincere congratulations, some wine with Eddy and Jon, plenty of big meals, a telephone call to Judy, who was delighted. Now I could go home.

Miriam and Jon saw me off at Zermatt station. It was growing dark as the train trundled down the valley but I could still see the fresh snow that lay in a continuous carpet down to 2000 metres. The following day I would be thirty-four years old, and I felt more like eighteen. I was overwhelmed with feeling, with the wonderful taste of success. The ambitions were behind and I could go and climb without such single-mindedness. Trail walks, glacier treks, beautiful mountains: all were waiting. Yet despite feeling so young it was as if I had already lived one life, in a hurry. Any more would be a bonus.

The Mönch, the Jungfrau, the Breithorn, Mont Blanc, the Eiger, the Matterhorn: they are my dear friends who have let me taste life at its sweetest. I have memories which cannot be taken away, and what better treasures could I hope for? I am indeed a rich man.

CHAPTER 4

Plans for Peru

ON lush Swiss mountain pastures and silvery glaciers we wandered contentedly above Saas Fee, a delightful village of timber chalets and bright flower boxes and jingling, clip-clopping, horse drawn carriages, all sheltered in a broad valley. In every direction, fields and forests and pastures lifted from the valley floor, gently at first, then more steeply until they met the white hems of peaks where the snows always lay. A fat glacier snout poked down the head of the valley and in some lights threatened to thrust its way right into the village and crush it all. Judy found complete enjoyment in walking but I burned to climb, so I talked with a mountain guide, a local man, who agreed to do the south-south-west ridge of the Egginer. Though short, the ridge was supposedly quite hard, and it was wise to be with an expert. Camillo, big limbed, heavy featured, ruddy faced, about 180 centimetres tall, could get along quite well in English so it was easy to explain what was on my mind. His pleasure at learning this prospective client was a fairly experienced climber was in no way diminished when a shortage of legs was mentioned, so I began to wonder if his command of my language was as good as we had mutually and tacitly accepted from the start. It seemed better not to labour the point too far. He would find out soon enough and perhaps by then it would not matter.

'I'll take the cable car with you when you go tomorrow and wait at the bottom of the mountain,' Judy announced. Hopes of training my wife as a climber had never borne fruit, though for a while she had tied the rope on and I had dragged her around, an unwilling puppy on a lead. She managed a thin semblance of enthusiasm over some years but there was no point in trying to fool ourselves. It's simple enough to understand what was wrong: she carried the burden of reluctance all the time. She wanted to climb because she did not want to be left behind but she had no love for the sport itself. There's no shame in that; maybe she had too much sense. Sometimes we walked together on the easier slopes, so mountains were half bond, half wedge between us, though not strongly so in either sense. She was not so fast uphill, but on the way down and headed for home she moved like a camel that has smelt water.

From the way he bubbled full of cheer on the fine, fresh morning of our climb, and chatted amiably to total strangers on the path to the cable car, it was clear the prospect of a shortish climb with a mountaineer of some experience appealed to Camillo. Poor Camillo. While we sat to wait for the first car of the day, the unusual outline of my trouser legs caught his eye; straps and metal created unnatural bulges at the knees. His brow folded into two vertical furrows above his nose and a finger pointed.

'Vat is this?'

So he had not understood. What on earth had he thought I was saying when he nodded and said, 'Yes, yes,' the day before?

'The leg is artificial, Camillo.'

From Camillo there came a long, uncomfortable pause, then he made a statement just to end the awful silence.

'You must be very careful.'

'That took the bounce out of him,' was Judy's observation afterwards. Camillo's bounce had deserted him right enough, and his already long face seemed stretched another five centimetres by jaw-dropping misery. Battling with indecision, he teetered uneasily on the very brink of changing his mind about going until, like a delivering angel's chariot from my point of view, a hearse in Camillo's eyes, the cable car drifted quietly down and I got in, fast. Camillo followed, leaden-footed.

Fifteen awkward minutes of silent ascent crawled by and from the isolated upper cable car terminus we headed for the mountain. I could have done with a straightforward walk on even, compacted snow, but nature had decided shortly before that it was time to have an avalanche there, so we had to pick a way through a jumble of ice chunks up to tea chest size sprawled in our path. A long ice axe helped me balance in a walking stick manner, but this was tough going and Camillo saw me waddling along at my worst even before we had reached the ridge. Once at the ridge's bouldery foot I squatted on a rock to tuck my trouser legs out of the way in socks, and in order that Camillo should realise properly what he was taking on, and to give him some encouragement, I bared one beige painted metal leg, hairless, of course, with an ankle sufficiently slim to be coveted by the ladies.

'Strong enough for climbing,' I said, hammering the limb, clunk, clunk, with a fist. Camillo brightened a little and I deceived myself into believing, because I wanted to, that I had won his confidence, until his next question arrived.

'But zee other one is all right?'

It had the ring of a prayer.

'No. It is the same.'

'Ah.'

Poor devil. I felt for the miserable man who stood before me, but found myself unable to generate sufficient compassion to let him off the hook.

'They're off below the knees so it's not so bad. I climb a lot,' came out in a rush. Might just as well have said, 'I don't fall off every day.'

'I've done much longer routes, Camillo.'

That was better. Despite his grey gloom a retreat was not suggested. For a while Camillo seemed prepared to accept me rather like an iron ball on a chain that would follow him everywhere if it could and pay the fee at the end of the day. It's not quite the relationship you expect between guide and client, but it would do.

So we got on with it. The south-south-west ridge rose at first as an intimidating jut of cliff, though one could assume from its grade of 3, (1 being easiest and 6 hardest) that it could not be as hard as appearances suggested.

Having roped ourselves together we called goodbye to Judy and set off through higgledy-piggledy boulders strewn about the base of the ridge. Judging from the look on Camillo's face we might never meet again; he possessed a kind of 'We're going to die with our boots on' expression and held his head high.

First the ridge presented a short chimney as high as a two-storey house; a chimney is simply a crack wide enough to get your body in. This was an easy one. Subsequent rock sections had helpful holds just where I would have asked: sharp ledges as wide as a thumb for the toes, or large as widow sills, prows of rock big as a fist to grasp or stand on, cracks that would take fingers or a hand, a deep hole which admitted the toe of a boot, and a thin flake with a tombstone resemblance over which a hand could be hooked.

So good and so numerous were the cracks and protrusions that we could move quickly, and quite soon we passed the only others out to enjoy the route that day, three in all. It was rare for me to pass anyone. My word yes, rare. Camillo's face was easily read, and radiated growing surprise and relief. Was he relieved! Misery had evaporated with the humpy white morning mist of the valleys below. Camillo smiled again; some of the bounce had come back. Perhaps the Englishman was not mad after all.

'I am happy now I have seen how you can climb,' he informed me.

He would go ahead and find a ledge to stand on so he could hold me on the rope if I fell, and from twenty-five metres or so above he would call, 'Coming now', and when I caught up he would say, 'Stopping now'. Ahead again, he would order, 'Coming now', once more.

'Always we must make the safe,' he repeated many times as he flicked the rope behind a rounded spike of rock, a bollard against which the rope would run and buzz if I tumbled.

On that day, on the Egginer's firm rock, rust-red and lichenous, even the steepest parts felt safe, though very occasionally with a tentative touch, like a cat pawing its way carefully around a strange room, I found a loose hold and rejected it. So, steadily we gained scores of metres up the cliff and within an hour and a half were ploughing ankle deep across a clean, level, fresh snow plateau, a distinct step in the sharp angle of the ridge. Camillo's happy yodels darted and echoed around. His bounce was definitely back to normal and he said, 'We will make all the difficult pieces on the way. There are some steep pieces we can go around but we will go over. There is more snow than sometimes and that makes it harder but we will make them.'

A thin cloak of snow masked the holds here and there and had to be brushed away with a hand, but mostly the climbing was agreeably straightforward. Camillo bellowed down to three people far off on the easy route to tell them the way, but for some reason we could not fathom they retreated when no great distance from the top.

The summit came in sight sooner than I expected. A couple of pitches on rock, a short scramble, and there we were, after three hours on the go. The climbers behind conferred sincere congratulations when they arrived, for Camillo explained my circumstances.

'We have done everything, all the hard pieces, and I am happy,' he told them.

The descent of the easy way, a monotonous clamber down loose stones, was tolerated rather than enjoyed. At the bottom where Judy waited, Camillo stopped hikers on the trail to tell them proudly of his unusual client. Each would listen for a while, nodding Germanically, seriously, very slowly, and saying something like, 'Is that so?' and then they would ask the whereabouts of this man. The image they had could not have matched the real thing, for each time Camillo pointed me out I was leaning limply against a boulder and retching noisily, like an unhappy donkey braying. It lasted three hours or more; sometimes I could not eat for twenty-four hours. On some alpine climbs I felt as if I had volunteered for a bad dose of flu; continuing to climb while in this condition could be a terrible hardship. What I did not realise in those early days was just how much each climb was taking out of me.

I greedily wanted more, and chose the Jagihorn, 3,206 metres, above Saas Grund. Jon Ryder needed no persuasion to go. Our journey was broken conveniently for the night at the Weissmies hut at 2,720 metres. After three hours on the mule trail at my plodding pace we drew near the wood-shuttered building and there was the mule itself, chewing at short grass. A doleful St Bernard lay outside, then padded up to be patted. Not far away the pale terracotta Jagihorn, a cathedral arch in outline, rose sharply to a humpy summit. It was only slightly snowy, where isolated specks of white had survived the sun.

On a short, sound and snowless route there was no need for the usual sleepy, zombie walk into the biting cold at three or four o'clock on the morning, so we waited until seven o'clock before emerging from the hut. A faint scratch of rarely trodden path took a direct way across moraine and two shallow streams towards our mountain. The steep pull up the lower grass and earth flank took perhaps twenty puffy minutes before we scrambled over broken rock to the foot of the south rib.

'Looks like where we join the rib and the real climbing starts,' Jon remarked.

On rock lying back a little from vertical, a horizontal ledge, at its narrowest half the width of a boot sole, invited us along a wall without difficulty to the rib. Jon muscled up the steep first pitch. He had left his home in America and slogged all winter clearing snow on a Swiss mountain railway, saving his pay and reserving the whole summer for a climbing holiday. His age I put at about twenty-five years and his muscular physique and short-cropped hair gave him the appearance of a typical fit and strong American sportsman. Apart from climbing, fanatically keeping fit and playing chess, he would explain with a mock Noel Coward accent he 'took a certain interest in the popsies, too.' With the same accent English friends were addressed as 'You bloody rotter.'

The mood was right and I threw myself at the rock, savouring each sight, smell, sound and touch. There was a delightful pitch of 3 (about Very Difficult in the British grading system) and we moved together rather than one at a time; only rarely did either of us feel the need to stop alternately to belay. We relied instead on slipping the rope behind natural gateposts or spikes of rock as we went, 'making the safe', as Camillo would say. The mountain gave us more rock of about grade 3: a short wall rising almost straight up but with an abundance of holds.

A steep corner, like two walls meeting in the corner of a big room, bulged where we would have preferred not on the right and forced me to hug the rock close like someone scared, to press past the bulge. I had to be extremely cautious and avoid that dreaded fall which, even if of only two or three metres, was too dangerous to risk, almost too frightening to contemplate, for someone who would land on metal legs. What would the impact do to my spine or hips? And, my mind kept asking, if I landed from a greater height, would my knee caps be torn away as I sank into the metal legs? Falling and not striking the rock below was a different matter; I'd had one or two falls of three metres or so in circumstances where the stretch of the rope merely cushioned the fall and prevented me hitting the ground. In reality the thin red rope offered great security against death, and serious permanent injury was improbable as long as we took the trouble to climb as we should. However, I could never forget that one bad fall could mean the end of climbing, perhaps of walking too. Buckled legs could be hammered back into shape but real bones might not mend so easily. Perhaps I was over concerned and overcautious, but I remembered an acquaintance who fell from a horse, landing on her one artificial leg; she had severe, long term problems through damage to the stump.

The route followed the crest of the rib more or less, with air on either side.

'Want to keep goin' fairly fast so we don't get stormed on. Would be tricky if it got wet,' Jon said as he moved on.

There was angry weather headed our way but we expected to be up and down well before it caught us. Where Jon skipped nimbly across like a competent tightrope walker, I straddled a short, sharp horizontal ridge and worked across in little bumps. À cheval the French say: on horseback. On either side the rib fell away, precipitous and exciting, inducing the enjoyable state of mind in which alertness was not spoiled by too much fear.

Jon started up a vertical wall. Soon the rope hung straight down from his waist, clear of the rock for six metres, and I wondered why I wanted to follow. Why did I enjoy all this? No answer came but I realised what in important place climbing had seized in my life. The restless urge to be in the mountains surged through me with increasing strength as years went by.

'Mountains are dangerous. You could waste your life if you go on climbing,' a friend once advised, but I could not agree with that. Life could be wasted by climbing carelessly and it could be wasted in another sense by not climbing at all.

The rib gave almost continuous climbing connected by short bits of scrambling. An hour and a half winged by.

'Wait until you see what's ahead,' Jon shouted down.

'What is it?'

'I don't like to tell you, you bloody rotter.'

'What?'

'I think it's the summit.'

'There must be more.'

'No, there's a big stone man here.'

I'd never heard that expression for a cairn. But he was right, and in a couple of minutes we ambled over the last bit of easy scramble to the jagged summit, where twenty people could have stood at once. We were the only ones there.

It had been easier than expected. Formerly I had had extreme trouble walking on soft snow. On that same holiday I had started practising on snowshoes; it required care to avoid stepping with the giant feet on the rope to the man ahead and the resemblance of my gait to that of an elderly cowboy was remarked upon, but hours of snow-muffled steps confirmed that my old mountain enemy, soft snow, could be defeated with these ancient weapons. Once more the mists of confusion rolled back and the way ahead was clear: where necessary I could avoid floundering in soft snow by wearing snowshoes. However, provided they were not too long, some harder rock routes were more attractive than easy snow routes. Though there was still much to be learned the harsh days of mountain initiation were at an end. Now I was on the right track. And if I could go on some slightly harder routes, how about some really big mountains, with a few bivouacs? It was worth thinking about.

We wandered down the easy way and Jon headed straight back to the valley. I took some time off at the hut because I liked it there, and the afternoon was whiled away in dozy contemplation of the peaks.

That evening, dim gaslamps left dark shadows untouched in corners of the warm hut and under tables and benches. Hammering rain, with us at last, made the building more cosy. I ate a meal which had the fantastic flavour only a hard earned appetite can impart, and dreamed of future climbs. That was the nice thing about climbing: there was always something to look forward to as well as something to look back on.

Frequent visits to the Roehampton limb centre were necessary when I climbed, and this was one of many reasons that pushed me towards being self employed, so I could go as often as was required. Everyone at the centre was helpful, particularly my doctors, Doctors Tiwari and Fletcher, and my prosthetist, Brian Campbell. We often discussed possible adaptations to my legs for climbing, and for a while we even contemplated using some form of cloven foot; mountain goats manage well enough, was the basis of the argument. However, Judy was not impressed.

'I know you're a bit of a devil but that's going too far.'

From a practical point of view, as yearnings turned more and more towards mountaineering rather than rock climbing, the idea was not so good because it would mean carrying yet more weight in the form of a pair of feet and a spanner or two, but I regret a little the lost opportunity of leaving a very interesting set of tracks in the snow. Or getting on a bus to go climbing would have been amusing.

1976 saw a big breakthrough, when I took a pair of crutches to Chamonix, and set out on a high walk. For the first time since losing my legs I felt as if I could run. In reality, on level or downhill stretches the pace was no better than a fast walk, but what a joy that was! No longer did I have to take every step with care on the rough path, for with two sturdy outriggers it was possible to make long strides or short, to pick and choose where my boots landed, to drop lightly on movable stones and pass by so quickly that it did not matter if they rolled over. Now I had become a four legged animal, there was no need to concentrate on keeping in balance all the time or to use back and stomach muscles to correct a lean this way or that. A slight stumble of one leg or crutch was of no consequence because there were always three other legs around to keep me under control. Immediately, and delightfully, it was apparent that approaching mountains would be not only less tiring but safer because I was steadier. The walk from John o' Groats to Land's End toughened the stumps a good deal but still they were vulnerable in the heat. Hiking from a valley for five or six hours to a high alpine hut could be a terrible slog when the sun was up; now, with the new-found freedom, the magic carpet, those walks could become another part of the fun. Crutches could even help on snow sometimes, I felt sure. Snow had always been my worst foe when the sun turned it soft, and to battle along in midday heat, sinking up to the knees or further, made me hate snow. But sometimes, bad snow had to be tolerated. In an attempt to keep the stumps cool and less sweaty at one time I used to wear long socks and fill them up with snow when the sun grew hot. The theory was that by keeping the metal legs cold the stumps would stay cooler. While sitting on my rucksack and scooping handfuls of snow into the socks you can imagine I was the object of many a questioning glance, and people who came my way chose a wider than necessary detour to get past! If the method had any effect it was slight, and I had soggy socks all the time. Now with crutches adapted like ski poles the snow problems could be reduced. There was another advantage that I did not realise at the time: crutches took so much of the effort out of balancing that the 'nausea barrier' had to be broken through less often.

The wretched random rubble of a glacial moraine gave a lot of trouble and I floundered there almost as badly as I always had, but everywhere else easy movement and the freedom to gaze all around were mine. I saw the forests and pastures as never before; the need to watch every step, head bent down, like a man looking for mushrooms was gone. We were out for twelve hours that day, and though the balls of my thumbs looked red as ripe strawberries through taking the weight, I was overjoyed to have discovered the best way to get about on the lower mountain slopes. The trails seemed suddenly to have become prettier and to have shrunk to a third of their former length, so without even trying to reach a summit a great feeling of satisfaction was mine. And I started to think more seriously about longer ascents on bigger mountains. That was how much difference the crutches made.

Mooching about in the Lake District beneath a crag to pick a route I slipped on a stone and twisted one leg. A purple swelling, half a hen's egg, rose up immediately on one stump and a large area was bruised.

'Your stump's like a giant plum,' Judy said. 'Moby plum.'

After all the time spent climbing without much in the way of injury it seemed incongruous to be hurt on a path. Walking was very painful and the crutches came to my aid. The stump swelled so much I could not get the artificial leg back on, but with one leg and crutches it was possible to get about. So I learned something more, that if a leg failed mechanically or if a stump was injured, crutches really would enable me to move over rough country. Practice bore out the theory, and greater independence was a proven fact. So how about those bigger peaks?

All at once in me was a real yearning to go to the Andes. The Andes. The Andes. The name conjures up a feeling of excitement, of greatness, of seriousness, of adventure, of challenge, of peaks around 6,000 metres. But where, in the huge Andes? Little bits of information, whether correct or not, coupled with impressions and assumptions, nudged me this way, then that. A couple of visits to the Alpine Club in London to browse through books and journals led further towards the Peruvian Andes and gradually I homed in on one region: the pretty Cordillera Blanca.

Invitations to go on other people's expeditions do not pour in when you lack the lower parts of your legs so it soon became clear that if I wanted to go there I would have to do the organising myself, and in all probability lead the expedition as well. It must be emphasised that if it were not for the greater independence that resulted from using my crutches, I would not seriously have considered going. After experiments in different types of terrain it was obvious that metal spikes on the ends would be an advantage sometimes, and I had some made.

To get an expedition going several hurdles had to be cleared, not the least of these being the fact that I did not know anyone else who wanted to go. An expedition of one. It was hard to decide where to start, except that it was clear other expedition members had to be found. Nowadays I could organise an expedition quite quickly, but those were dilettante days, and I had no expedition track record.

Early on I contacted Julie and Terry Tullis, climbing instructors who also ran a climbing equipment shop. They said they would go and suggested that a globetrotting friend of theirs, Dennis Kemp, might like to as well. He soon wrote from New Zealand to say yes. As well as having built up wide experience in the Alps, Himalayas, USA and antipodes, he had climbed in Peru. His appearance was that of an ageing hippy, and he was tougher than first impressions might suggest. Another member, Harry Curtis, was invited as much for his good nature as for anything else. He wrote back saying he was excited by the prospect and was getting himself fit 'doing three push-ups a day and jogging the hundred yards to the pub.' Then someone who was prepared to help with the organisation of the expedition, and put in some funds too, turned up. His name was Mike Welham and he worked as a diver. Mike's experience included alpine climbing and an expedition to arctic Norway in winter. Most of the work of an expedition goes by unseen and this was where Mike's help with the organisation was extremely valuable. His wife, Jackie, enthusiastically joined in the work too, and few expedition organisers can have been as fortunate as I in coming across so much assistance. One of Mike Welham's friends, Mike O'Shea, was taken on more to look after base camp than as a climber; he was so keen to go he even gave up his draughtman's job and became self-employed so he could have time off. So when Terry and Julie finally sold their shop and committed themselves to the venture, we had seven members: the two Mikes, Harry, Julie, Terry, Dennis and me.

I applied for a Winston Churchill Travelling Fellowship and got to the stage of being shortlisted for an interview. In the year before, 1976, over three thousand applications were received and just over a hundred awards were made, so I did not overestimate my chances. However, shortly after the interview by a very distinguished panel, I was awarded a generous grant of £1,400. Considering that mountaineering can be a very risky activity, I felt their decision to back me was enlightened.

A host of details required attention: injections, travel arrangements, visas, equipment, currency, elusive sponsors still to be found. With expedition members living in Wolverhampton, Norwich, North Wales, Kent and London, communication was not always easy, particularly as two people were not on the telephone. But slowly, detail by detail, things came together.

Denny Moorhouse, founder and managing director of Clogwyn

climbing equipment manufacturers, readily promised us a lot of equipment, and some weeks later he showed an interest in going himself. I said yes, and that made us eight.

A bus, with every seat filled by a local or a foreign visitor, droned out of early morning Lima, past plush hotels and big statues and monuments, past single-storey hovels half-hidden behind bamboo fences, past buildings with crumbling faces. Over all there was a greyness, which came partly from thick fog, the 'garua', sitting on the city for months each year. The city had a population of almost three million people, many of whom lived in slums, or in shanty towns hung on dry dust hills or planted on dismal flat land.

By no means everyone was poor; in some parts of Lima the grand Spanish style houses and squares were well kept. In ten minutes you could leave a slum and be drinking tea in a bit of old England, out of time, out of place, in the Lima Cricket Club, or eating in an expensive restaurant in the Miraflores district. Towards the city's outskirts the road verges deteriorated into dust and rubbish tips, and the smell of rotting matter took over.

In simple terms we had to head north and a bit westwards on a road hugging the desert coast, with the sea on our left. At about the halfway point a hundred miles up the coast we turned right to zig zag roughly north-east through rapidly rising country, and then left to go a bit west of north again. Houses and shacks thinned out as we went further up the desert road, until there were no dwellings and hardly a speck of growth to break up the sandy monotony.

We slipped gradually into the sort of Peru that was to fascinate us all for the next six weeks. Flashing by like a quick taster of a way of life we would get a little closer to, went cacti of highly individual species, barefoot children, women with babies in colourful blankets slung on their backs, bright home-woven clothing, dark skins of smiling Indian faces, small scavenging dogs, roadside cafés, and drinks stalls, dirt roads and donkeys, and hairy little pigs wandering free and quite tame. Nearly everyone wore a hat of straw or a trilby or bowler, against the sun.

We had followed our right-hand turn and the road was soon a real mountain twister, taking its time to get up to the high country. Now almost always on one side or the other was a gigantic drop but the driver hammered on. In Peru, driving seemed to involve faith as much as it required petrol; some taxis had on their dashboards little shrines in which bulbs lit up each time the brakes were applied.

Ladies spinning wool while they walked along, cows, pigs, goats, horses, lambs, potato and maize crops and thatched adobe houses sped by the bus windows, and as we topped a hill a surge of excitement ran through the gringos, for there ahead were the fantastic sharp peaks with their gleaming white coverings of snow. Between us and the mountains, light browny yellow, almost golden, plains intervened and the sky above was bright blue and clear. It was unbelievably beautiful.

Huaras. We had arrived. There around us was the town, population 50,000 people, 3,050 metres high. Only a slight shortage of breath told us we were that far above sea level.

Denny and Dennis found us a dormitory in the Hotel Barcelona, and a couple of tricycle baggage transporters were quickly bargained for to carry our equipment there. On the fifth floor of the square concrete hotel we dumped our rucksacks on some of the mattresses and hurried upstairs to the flat roof just above. Being the tallest building around, the hotel made a fine viewpoint; the countryside rolled away and away in humps to a superb array of peaks dominating the skyline.

How can Huaras be captured in words? Any attempt must be inadequate but, first, think of straight concreted streets, some of them recently built after earthquake and alluvion damage. An alluvion is a rapidly moving mixture of rock, sand, mud and water spilled by collapse of a lake's morainal dam, or by massive ice avalanches falling into a lake and displacing the water. Earthquake hazard influences the height of buildings, which mostly have no more than two or three floors. Away from the main streets the majority are single storey, while larger structures of reinforced concrete have been put up in the centre. Roofs are made of red tiles or corrugated iron. Some of the living creatures that crowd into the town centre I have already mentioned: barefoot children, women carrying babies in blankets, donkeys, little pigs and street traders. Shoeshine boys and newspaper boys wander everywhere, and ice cream or drinks vendors pedal their three-wheeled barrows slowly around. In all of the several markets, squatting women sell vegetables, eggs and fruit, spread out for display on blankets. There are stalls, too, for meat, ironmongery, clothes, wool and herbs. Higher up the scale are bookshops, shoeshops, chemists, dress shops, like anywhere else. So it is a spectrum, from the lady squatted beside a single cake sold slice by slice, through small tattered stalls, through big and well kept and well stocked stalls, through small shops, to some large ones. Eating out is characterised by a similar spectrum of style and price. You can buy a slice of that cake or some bread from a barrowboy or a stallholder, then there are scruffy cafés and better ones, and a few good restaurants. Wide-eyed adults and children stare in through restaurant windows like they were watching TV. Grubby stalls, grubby feet, grubby children, grubby streets. Banknotes are tatty, begging by children is commonplace, buses are crammed full, fares are cheap, the police are armed, there are lots of rickety, ramshackle cars and gaily painted trucks coming and going. The air is more of activity than bustle, with people going about their business but not rushing. The hills and mountains stand all around but not too close; Huaras does not feel closed in. And usually the sky is clear and bright blue. As you leave the centre you come across adobe huts and shacks on rough and dusty stone roads, amongst cacti and glossy eucalyptus and other trees. Patchwork farming, corn and other crops and grazing for cows and pigs, creeps into the edges of town. By day the parp, parp, parp of horns on the tricycles of ice-cream vendors, and tinny South American music from cassette and record stalls, and the traffic noise, are constant. At night the street lighting is good because the surrounding mountains give the town hydroelectricity.

We soon made the acquaintance of Pepe, the young man who with his family looked after the Hotel Barcelona and its guests. Dark, smooth-haired, demonstrative in a Spanish way, friendly, shrewd-eyed Pepe had the 'never-still' nature of a small bird. It was to him that we turned if anything needed arranging.

'Ees possible,' and, 'Ees no problem,' were his usual responses. First, he fixed up a storage space for our food and equipment, and then when we wanted to transport it to our first base camp he got his truck out and drove us up an exceptional track bulldozed out of steep mountain flanks.

Our tents were erected at about 4,400 metres and while the rest of us lazed around for a day, waiting for acclimatisation to put a bit more life in our steps, Dennis scouted ahead up the valley. At fifty-six years he was our senior member by far, a most experienced expeditioner, and somewhat intolerant of our inexperience.

All at once one of my legs began to rattle loudly with each movement. My heart sank; this was even before the climbing had started! Julie and Harry were about to descend on foot to Huaras to replace two defective paraffin stoves, and they volunteered to run a spare leg delivery service at the same time by collecting the reserve limb from storage at Pepe's. A feeling of guilt crept over me as I watched them hurry down the hill and out of sight, because as soon as they disappeared the rattling stopped. They arrived back in darkness the next evening, having had a difficult time because Harry had twisted a knee. To ease the pain on the way up that afternoon he had taken to bathing the poorly joint in streams, and in order to do this he had to slip his climbing breeches down to his ankles. As they passed close to a village Julie decided nothing was to be lost by trying to hire a donkey and she succeeded in persuading a teenage girl with such an animal to come to a stream and pick up Harry. The intention was that Harry would be transported a considerable way up the hill, but Harry had chosen that moment to cool his knee. The girl arrived to find him kneeling in a stream with his trousers down, and she may have noticed a leg lying on the bank, too. Whether she did or not, the scene can have done nothing to convince her that gringos are civilised or sensible, so she turned her donkey around immediately and went straight back to the village! Harry shouldered my leg and soldiered on to arrive at camp just after dark. My rattling noise had not returned, its cause remains unknown, and the replacement limb was not required; but thank you Harry, all the same.

Among other things, acclimatisation to the altitude we were at resulted in a sixty per cent increase in red corpuscles. After a couple of days at base camp three people emerged as getting on best with the altitude: Julie, Dennis and me. Dennis set off and took a tent up to about 4,900 metres and returned to base camp.

Julie and I headed for the tent and the next day brought steep walking for a short way, then a scramble over boulders to the foot of a ridge. I led a short pitch up a steep step, and was amazed at how I puffed on the relatively easy rock. Fresh snow during the night had made it harder, but to an extent you could not grade technically; here and there it was slippery, and you could not say much more than that. We alternated the lead, with Julie doing the hardest bits first: a short, vertical crack and a rather unstable snow slope to the summit, reached two and a half hours after leaving our tent.

Within just over a week of arriving in Peru the expedition was successful, though not wildly so. This 5,120 metre mountain was modest by Andean standards. It had been a cautious and gentle introduction. We were overjoyed, for this was the highest either of us had been.

The night of the following day was spent by several of us in a hut below our base camp. We cooked a meal and shared it with the guardian of a nearby dam, guardian in the sense of keeping an eye on the water level. Language was a problem because our Spanish was thin and the guardian had no English. One of the few things Terry could say in Spanish was 'a dog with fleas', which was best left unsaid as the guardian had a dog and gave Terry a dirty look when the phrase was used. Then Terry got into a real tangle trying to extract the Spanish for 'aristocrat'. Things like doors, windows and tables we could get by pointing, but try explaining 'aristocrat' in sign language. Egg; that was another word we needed, so I demonstrated with an orange which, after due clucking noises, was laid on the floor. We pointed at the orange and asked its name.

'Orange,' the guardian said in Spanish, and gave me a look that seemed to say, 'Stupid gringo. Everyone knows oranges grow on trees.'

Eating good food and drinking rum and honey by candlelight was only the first of many celebrations we would enjoy.

We slept on the floor that night. In the faint dawn light Harry was woken by a movement and found a rat nuzzling his arm, so for half an hour he played smash the rat with a ski stick whenever the persistent little creature returned. The rat did not lose, but retired when good light came.

The next two days were spent returning to Huaras, bathing in a natural spring bath, eating, drinking, wandering about the town, writing postcards, talking to anyone and everyone who liked to chat to gringos, dancing in a disco and having an interview with a reporter who wanted to know if I had been carried up. Some of the newspaper reports were hilariously inaccurate: they had us up the wrong mountain, with a mother called Julia Turbiens (Julie Tullis) and I had broken two legs on the way.

Because the next camp could be approached from a reasonably close track up which a truck could be driven, we were able to take fresh fruit and vegetables. With the food bought, it was off for thirty miles (fifty km) along the beautiful Rio Santa valley, a deep river cleft of rich green and yellow plenty growing on red earth, topped higher up the sides by the more mellow colours of drier country. Our truck took us to Yungay, the tragic scene of one of the worst alluvions in history. In 1970 earthquake tremors set off the alluvion which became airborne and smothered the town, killing an estimated 17,000 people. The total of deaths in Huaras at the same time was put at 16,000.

We continued by truck up a bulldozed track. Eucalyptus trees, bulbous cacti, yellowing grain crops and adobe houses blended and pleased the eye. Exchanging waves with colourfully dressed people, particularly with the children, was like giving gifts equally; they appreciated having notice taken and shouted 'Gringo' in a friendly way as we went past. Delays occurred in a couple of places where bulldozers cleared rocks and earth which had tumbled on to the track; on the running board was a man whose job it was to leap off every so often and trundle boulders aside. We climbed for an hour or more up through a gorge whose steep walls were staggering to see.

'Heads!' someone cried every so often as we drove under low branches of gnarled and twisted papery-barked trees into the broad Llanganuco valley, and past two beautiful copper sulphate blue-green lakes. After unloading our gear a mile or more above the lakes we transported it on our backs to a pretty, flat bottomed, grassy valley. There we set up base camp on the edge of trees beside a river washing quickly over smooth white stones like huge eggs.

Having established a higher camp, six of us set out for the top of Pisco, 5,760 metres. Mugs of tea, and away at 5.20 a.m. in faint moonlight, up steep ice. Some of us wore head torches, some managed without.

We tramped on for an hour in our brightening crystal world, watching out closely for crevasses but still taking the time to look around as the sun turned the high peaks pink, then gilded them splendidly.

There was a big crevasse in the way, one with the far lip higher than the near one, a blue-green grotto of thirty metres' depth. From a metre wide at the surface it widened to three metres half way down, and then the walls came slowly together. Fall down there, and the likelihood was that the victim would hang free and have trouble getting out, or be wedged in the narrowing bottom, injured by the hard ice walls. In the past I might not have got across but the crutches allowed a kind of double pole vault and the gaping hole was left behind. We weaved a way through hummocks of snow, giving a wide berth to more lurking crevasses, nothing unless you fell in, awful if you did.

Crossing a white plateau we took on an ice slope with a few centimetres of hard snow cover. At forty degrees at the steepest the slope was not really hard but high up to the right was an ice cliff draped with gigantic icicles; if any of them broke off several score kilos of clear ice would torpedo our way. We might just as well be walloped by a telegraph pole. There was an additional hazard: at the bottom of the slope in the line a sliding body would take was a broad snow chute, which would channel everything, everyone, over the top of a huge ice cliff.

Mike Wellham began to lag behind, but kept going. The slope lessened and the snow got more powdery; we sank to our ankles, then to our knees, and Denny and Dennis found their alternated work as trail breakers growing harder. At the worst we were up to mid thigh as we ploughed along in a line. The altitude had an effect and though there was little or no conversation a curse burst out from one or other of us every so often. The route was technically easy but powder snow at five and a half thousand metres is no joke. That's a feature of big mountains: a slog may be technically easy but exhausting all the same. Already I was planning that if we did not get there this time we would try again next day when the sun had chased some of the fluff from the snow.

Particularly in view of the recent snowfall, there was some danger of avalanche. To have eliminated the hazard completely would have meant staying off the mountain; the small risk just had to be accepted if we wanted to climb. Experience can help, but you can still get killed. We had to like the mountains enough to put up with the risks.

The wind picked up, whipping snow into our faces, and we pulled across face masks stitched to our fibre-pile jackets. Inside the masks, breath roared in and out.

'Much harder than when I did it before,' Dennis said. 'Much harder.'

The weather remained good, as it did much of the time in the Cordillera Blanca. We toiled up a massive snow mound to be relieved by a steadily easing gradient. Denny and Dennis continued to break the trail, then stood aside for Julie and me; we were close to the summit and they were letting us get there first. The order in which we arrived was of no concern to me, but it was thoughtful of them. Julie and I were on the summit at eleven o'clock, then Denny and Dennis, with Harry approaching soon after, swearing at himself to keep going, and then dropping to his knees every forty paces.

'Every time I looked up there was some rat on crutches still going so I had to do it,' he said of the easy but long final stretch. He lay down on the snow and hit it repeatedly with his ice axe, all the time shouting, 'I hate you! You're going to melt! I hate you! You're going to melt!' Climbing was never dull with Harry around.

Like a man with concrete legs, Mike got there eventually. He was on fairly safe ground so was not roped to anyone.

Feasting on Christmas pudding and oranges, we stayed on the summit for three-quarters of an hour or so. With the ascent of the first peak nine days earlier we had no reason to go home feeling we had made fools of ourselves; and now, at 5,760 metres, we had even less reason to be ashamed. The expedition was a success and the faith of a great many people had been rewarded.

We packed up camp next day, and as we passed the flat area where we had put up our first camp above base, two porters looking after someone else's camp called us over for some tea, which was taken gratefully. Their names were Manuel and Pedro; some of us were to meet Manuel again and share some important days with him.

Within three weeks of arriving in Peru, and in two weeks of

climbing, we had done what we came to do. And we had over three weeks left. From the start I had planned that the team would split up once we had achieved our rather vague objective because it seemed wrong that people should be held back by me all the time on what might be their only visit to Peru. Not only that, if we had to stay together for the full expedition period I would have been more fussy about the composition of the team. For three or four weeks our little idiosyncrasies were not serious as long as we were achieving our objectives, but over a longer period they might have created problems. There were bound to be a few differences of opinion and complaints, but disagreements all stayed within reasonable bounds, and everyone made a predominantly positive contribution. I was more than a little fortunate in having a team that functioned so well.

Over two days we rested in Huaras, ate, cleaned ourselves in the warm natural spring water at the Hotel Monterray near the town, and danced and drank in the local disco. We sampled the local firewater, a brandy called pisco as it happens; it is said the mountain got that name because after a French ascent in 1951 two porters consumed two litres of the stuff.

Unlike most expeditions, we had not selected definite objectives before arriving in Peru because my performance at high altitude was an unknown; we had to plan as we went along. One thing we had decided before leaving England, though, was that the real big ones of the Andes, 6,000 metres and more, were too much for me. The others might do one or two like that, but not me, so Peru's highest mountain, Huascaran (pronounced Was-ca-ran) was out because it was about 6,700 metres high. However, Julie changed all that.

'Why don't we do Huascaran?' she asked.

'Too big,' I said.

'But you're getting on very well. Let's do Huascaran. Harry, you'd like to wouldn't you?'

'Yes.'

'Come on, Norman,' Julie coaxed. 'Please.'

I knew someone who wouldn't take no for my answer. When I said all right, Julie and Harry were delighted, but not Denny, who thought we were mad to go when the weather was, to say the least, inclement. But the bad weather was higher up, and it would take us a couple of days to reach it. If we did not leave Huaras until the weather on Huascaran was favourable we could waste part of a fine period. It was a simple view, not something founded on any special knowledge of meteorology, and it had a great bearing on subsequent events for "we three gringos".

We bumped into Manuel on the street. Yes, he had been to Huascaran before. Yes, it would be wise to take a porter to help carry lower down, and to look after base camp; we could hardly have expected him to say otherwise. Yes, he was free and could go tomorrow. He jumped at the chance. Back at the hotel Pepe refereed as a deal was struck: Manuel would receive 1,000 soles a day and his food. At 300 soles to the pound it would not cost us a fortune and by local standards Manuel Fabian Oropeza, married, aged thirty-two, would be earning well.

Two days had passed since our return from Pisco, so we had not wasted much time in relaxing after one climb and getting ready for the next. We selected and packed our equipment, bought fresh food and ate a lot, and waited for the next day.

'Pepe, can you get us a pickup to Musho tomorrow, please?'

'Ees no problem, my friends.'

We climbed into the back of the pickup belonging to Pepe, who had found five girls to share the cab with him. Terry was coming along for the first part of the walk to base camp.

Pepe roared his vehicle up the road, which followed the river valley northwards and a little to the west until five miles (eight km) short of Yungay we came into the little village of Mancos. Within three minutes he had bargained for another truck for the last leg of the journey on wheels to Musho. Quite a few vehicles stood around in most villages and you just went up and asked how much, beat the driver down a bit because it was expected, and there you were. Equipment was soon transferred and away we went up a road that was hardly horrifying at all. Rough, bumpy, dusty, yes, but not much of a horror. Straight ahead lay our destination, and already the unwanted weather had slipped away and we could see it all gleaming, bright as silver.

The tree-lined village of Musho, where lived the poor local farmers, was about 3,000 metres high. There the truck driver pulled up in front of a little café and we unloaded. Harry paid for the truck hire; he was keeper-of-the-purse for communal expenses like that and he handled the job very well. The top left pocket of his jacket was known as 'the bank'. There always seemed to be someone who was behind with his contribution, but Harry kept it all straight with great patience. Meanwhile, Manuel was bargaining with someone in the café for two donkeys; the café seemed to be the centre for such deals. Within minutes two donkeys and a tiny girl, about ten years old, appeared, and Manuel loaded the beasts. With four rucksacks and two kit bags as well as two tents we had more than was necessary, but we had allowed for the fact that the weather could keep us waiting at base camp or the next one, and we could get extra food to those camps with little trouble. In other words, extra time could be bought with food. I had played the waiting game with many a mountain, and won sometimes more through patience than great effort. It's not that I am by nature especially patient, but I can wait when there is no other way where mountains are concerned.

The two donkeys may have been in excellent health but to us they looked like the sort of creature for which old ladies set up sanctuaries in this country. The laden beasts, looking ready to buckle at the knees at any moment, moved slowly forward, breaking wind, sounding like wrestlers who had been at the beans.

For half an hour Terry was with us under a boiling sun, then he shook Harry and me by the hand, kissed his wife, and turned back down the trail with a quiet, 'G'luck.'

At one point on the trail a large group of very well-dressed Austrian climbers looked aghast at Harry's untidy appearance, which included trailing boot laces and a face smeared white, clown-like, with ointment because of sunburn. Blobs of white toothpaste on his clothing, from a tube that had burst in his rucksack, did not help. They looked even more aghast when Julie appeared in view. A woman! 'We do not climb with women!' one of them had announced. Imagine their reaction when around the corner appeared the third member of this small band, with his crutches quietly clicking at each movement.

'That's our leader,' Harry said.

'But where is your expedition?' they asked me.

'This is my expedition,' I said, and they stared in amazement at our tiny group.

The biggest part of an afternoon disappeared in a nice walk between stonewalled fields, over open grazing land, up through a giant honeysuckle forest, and finally amongst twisted trees to a flat area with a cascading stream nearby. We had gained over a thousand metres. Already in place were two tents belonging to a large American expedition whose members were higher up the mountain. Two porters and a doctor sat around. The latter was conducting research into cerebral oedema, a fairly common sickness at high altitude, when fluid collects on the brain.

I saw the dawn come but couldn't really pick just when; it was so slowed down by waiting. We had a twenty metre rock step to start, then steep walking up a moraine. Taking a gamble, we carried everything to an advance base camp only 450 metres higher, rather than taking less and going on to a higher camp. I was glad of another day for us all to acclimatise instead of rushing at it, and I favoured increasing our chances of success from a higher base even though it meant we did not make full use of a good weather day.

4,570 metres. Several crestfallen Americans passed by in small groups on the way down. Two were descending because of breathing problems, three had not reached the summit because of high winds, and another four failed for the same reason. Quite a few people climbed Huascaran in any year, and quite a few failed. Three died on the route while we were in Peru. So were we biting off more than we could chew? Perhaps not; we would take it nibble by nibble.

When the time came we all put on crampons and roped up to begin threading a way up a huge glacier, between high ice blocks here, up four metres of steep ice there, along a narrow ice bridge between deep, open crevasses, stepping over gaps, mostly up, occasionally down, on slopes of all angles. Anything steeper than seventy degrees was only a matter of two or three metres high. Once a way had been found through the worst jumbled area of ice, in about half an hour, it was uphill snow all the way, for hours. Manuel went better than any of us, dumped the load he had been carrying at the next camp, and went back down to base camp with another porter descending from that high camp. Packing, snailing up the glacier and pitching the tent took about seven hours that day. It may not seem long, but we felt it was enough at that altitude, 5,300 metres.

At high altitude the need for liquid increases; serious dehydration is a risk. So we guzzled tea, soup, meat extract, hot chocolate and orange drinks, all made from melted snow. Porridge, a rice meal cooked in a pressure cooker at base camp and reheated, fruity Christmas pudding, egg powder and some very good dehydrated meals made up our solid food.

We seemed to have picked the busy season. Sharing the level snow patch were three Americans and about nine Austrians. Some of the Austrians had reached the summit that day and the Americans were aiming for it the next day.

The sunset was the best of many in the Andes. The breast-shaped sugar bun that was our target blushed salmon pink while golden clouds surrounded a sun as red as a ripe Peruvian tomato. Gradually, wide blackberry juice stains spread through as the clouds turned to pale custard.

Sunday morning came and the fine weather held. There was no rush. We knew four hours or so would be enough for the next stage, a rise of seven hundred and fifty metres. Snow slopes of only forty degrees were a hard pull at that altitude and then came a snow step of ten metres, which was at about eighty degrees. At that altitude even short stretches of steep climbing really take it out of you. That particular step had a yellow fixed rope hanging down. Harry went first, relying a lot on the rope lower down and less and less as he gained height in case it gave way. A bulbous lip at the top soon hid him from view.

'It's attached to an aluminium stake,' he shouted. 'Bit wonky but it seems all right. OK Norm.'

Half way up was a ledge as wide as a chair seat. Hanging on to the rope I waited for my panting to subside before resuming the movements which won a foot at a time to join Harry. Julie came up; no problem.

We found ourselves on a narrow horizontal ice spine with the wall we had climbed falling away on the left and a big crevasse on the right. It was not hard but 'For God's sake be careful' country. And careful we were as we balanced across for fifteen metres.

Soon we were heaving ourselves up another fixed rope of thirty metres, and another, on steep and very tiring slopes of snow. We belayed quite frequently in other places and then the hardest ground for that day was left behind.

The sun's heat hit not only from above but also by reflection from the snowfield we were on. We were about 5,800 metres up and heavily laden; the altitude punished Harry most.

'You'd better go on. I'm going to take hours,' he said.

The gradient was not too bad and, though there were a few crevasses around, the area held no special dangers. However, Julie and I preferred us to stick together. Every few minutes as we ploughed through the soft crystals, Harry flopped down for a rest, then forced himself to march on, grunting and swearing at his pack, the snow or the ski stick he carried.

A massive ice avalanche had crushed down a slope, which we had to traverse, leaving in its wake ice chunks, some as big as cars, over a width of three hundred metres. The biggest chunks were avoidable so the way was not so bad as it might have been, but the ice cliff which had spawned the avalanche, looked ready to send down others, large and small. One day it would send down ton upon ton of grinding, charging, concrete-hard ice.

'We had to give up on Huascaran because three or four large avalanches wiped out the route just above Camp 1,' a friend wrote to me the next year.

Having crossed quickly beneath the hanging menace, Julie was moving best and went ahead up a stiff snow ramp. At the foot of the ramp was a flat area surrounded on three of its four sides by high mounds of snow.

Harry soon puffed up.

'Camp here, Harry?' I asked.

'Yes. Not going any further.'

Shelter, food and drink were foremost in our minds, along with some thoughts about how the next day might go. The tent was soon up, and snow was heaped on a pan to melt over the stove. I was obnoxiously cheerful, the others were quieter; I'd have to watch it or I'd get on their nerves.

The three Americans passed by at dusk, having made a successful ascent, and a fast descent mostly on skis. We zipped up the tent and got into our sleeping bags; night-time temperatures above the snow line could drop to minus 20C.

Six o'clock in cold morning daylight. I had been awake and lying still on my back for a while. At first the hammering wind had made getting up seem pointless. Now it had fallen a bit so I took a look outside.

'How is it?' came from one or other of my companions, with just the tops of heads and faces peeping from their sleeping bags and looking like shy tortoises.

'It's all right. We should go.'

The words sunk in and as if someone had thrown the switches on two robots they suddenly got into action. All at once the tent felt very cramped with three moving bodies in it. Thick breeches and fibre-pile jackets were donned hastily in the cold. We had slept in thermal underwear. I left breeches, legs and boots till later because they had crampons on; when I did come to put them on a lot of time and effort was saved doing it all in one go. So I did have some advantages.

Breakfast went down because we knew it should. The porridge seemed more like a medicine we had to take than a meal we wanted to eat, but the tea was enjoyed. Ah, liquid!

Harry had trouble putting on his gaiters.

'Take mine instead,' I offered. 'I don't really need them.' I wore them to reduce the likelihood of a crampon point catching in a sock but I could manage without, so it was no real sacrifice.

'No, it's all right thanks, Norm,' he said, continuing the struggle with his own. I thought no more about it; later I would wish I had.

The wind had almost died away. Balaclavas, mitts, windproofs on. Rucksacks hoisted. Glacier cream and lip salve smeared on. Rope on. We were ready and it had taken nearly two hours; much of that time had elapsed while we melted snow.

Leaving the tent and all but essentials behind, we crawled out into the sharp bite of the cold. Julie led off up a snow ramp we had selected as our route the day before. A right turn at the top took us along a crest above a huge crevasse. Trying to find a way around either end would have involved going into very badly crevassed areas. So instead, we had to descend a steep slope of twelve metres, drop straight down two metres of vertical hard snow directly on to a little platform, and step or jump from there across the horrible hole. The top of the vertical bit was in fact one lip of the crevasse, that much higher than its partner. It was only a wide stretching step to the other side. One by one we made the step, each time hoping that the snow on the far side would not collapse. Julie, me, Harry. Nothing went wrong. Getting back was going to be a bigger problem.

Crossing that crevasse put us in a long, wide snow trough. Turning left, we walked the length of the trough, parallel with the crevasse, then took a level ridge with gaping holes running its thirty-metre length on either side. Another giant crevasse barred the way; no, it was spanned by a snow bridge. We would have preferred a more substantial one but there was no choice. We crossed.

At first the slope remained at a few degrees above or below thirty-five. Julie kept up a steady pace but every so often I was brought to a halt as the rope pulled tight behind; Harry was having trouble with the altitude.

'The pace on Pisco was all right,' he said.

After an hour of stop, start, stop, start I remarked to Julie, 'We're not going to make it at this rate. I'll be slow on the descent so I must get up there reasonably early in the afternoon. We're stopping too often, for too long, and going too slowly in between. The longer we take the softer the snow is so the longer we take, and so on.'

Going slower than the pace which feels right can be very tiring. We had to face it: one or all of us would have to turn back. We could try again tomorrow, I thought, not liking the idea. Nothing more was said for a while because I hoped Harry would feel better. Half a minute after we had restarted following a rest the rope went tight, dragging me to a halt again. I tried, only partly successfully, to suppress pointless anger by reminding myself that Harry was a friend who was prepared to attempt a big mountain with me, and he had always been patient with me.

'My crampon's come off,' he shouted from a kneeling position. Then he called, 'I think you'd better go on without me.'

It was natural enough to feel disappointment for him because he had put in as much work as anyone to get us that far, but I must admit that the predominant feeling was one of relief.

'What a shame,' Julie said, as Harry untied from the rope. 'But I think he ought to go down.'

We had spotted two men descending from Huascaran's south summit after a bivouac. They would have to cross the worst crevasses so Harry could join them to get back to the tent.

The two of us started uphill again, swinging along at a good pace. I lost track of time but probably an hour had passed before I noticed how frequently we were stopping to rest.

'You'd better take the lead,' Julie said. 'You're going so well.'

In good snow, leading was only marginally harder. The firm south-west slope of the north summit was getting steeper. For very short stretches of a few metres at a time the angle may have gone over fifty degrees but that was not common.

'Just a minute,' Julie called a couple of times, but I tried to anticipate her halts so she would not have to. It was better that she should not; better that the rat ahead should stop first.

Another hour elapsed. Julie had been standing catching her breath for a while when she said, 'I think I may not make it. My leg's hurting.'

She would not have mentioned it unless it was really troubling her.

A lot of time had been wasted already and it really would have been sticking our necks out to hit the summit in the late afternoon. I couldn't skip back down nearly as fast as other people. The weather was good but the thought of moving in the dark amongst the crevasses, in a strong wind and with tiredness upon us, seemed too big a risk to take.

An idea crept into my head: if I soloed on quickly that would give us a reasonable chance of one person reaching the top and the expedition would be an enormous success. But I could not leave Julie on her own, especially with a bad leg. We were finished for this day, and I was not optimistic about the weather for the next.

Below us, far, far below, a lone figure climbed up slowly. It looked like Harry. It was Harry! He would not reach where we were for a long time but he was on the way up again and here was a solution: Julie could join Harry.

I never had to worry about climbing being futile because mountaineering often had beneficial effects on my work with disabled people. Always there seemed an added sense of purpose which could not be divorced even if I had wanted it so. But was that really me being swayed by a non-mountaineering reason? To some extent, yes; but I wanted this one for me too. The ambition dragon was back again, big and fiery. And with only two hundred and fifty metres to go I did not want to let down all those people who had helped put us that high. Every reason pushed me up. There might be a small risk from crevasses but the angle of the snow was going to ease before long. Solo was the only way. Unless we turned back. I would have to put it directly; try it and see what she says.

'One of us has got to get there, Julie.'

'Yes.'

'Better unrope, then. I'll solo.'

'Yes.'

It would not have come as any surprise if she had said no. When you earn your living through climbing instruction your work might well be affected if you did nothing to discourage a double leg amputee from soloing a big mountain, particularly if he got hurt or killed. People would not understand if anything went wrong; a few might, but most would condemn. What they would fail to understand is that those who have climbed with me, or helped me in other ways to go climbing, have led me along a path to the finest experiences of a lifetime. The mountains had already given more joy than a man could expect in three lifetimes. Sometimes I am troubled by what might be said of companions who may one day survive on a mountain when I do not. In some ways, more than those who would try to overprotect, they have given me life; if they are in at my death they should not be censured. They deserve no blame, only praise for their understanding, for not backing away when they could so easily have done that. Perhaps I might live longer if I did not climb, but that is arguable, and life must be measured more by quality than by length alone. Certainly, a long hollow life has no appeal to me.

Julie coiled the rope.

'See you at the top,' I said tritely; who the hell stops to make up a good speech at a time like that anyway?

Almost immediately I was faced with a wall of hard snow, three metres high. A mere garden wall, when you think about it, but running along the bottom was a body-width crevasse. Stepping across and climbing up made me sweat a bit.

I have already said that Huascaran's north summit resembled a white breast, and it even had a snow cone nipple on the top. It was a deceiver, though, for behind the nipple the mountain still rose for quite a long way; I had been warned that this was the case. The gradient eased, eased, eased back to thirty degrees, then less, getting more pleasant all the time, and I topped the false summit, slightly on its right side. Behind the phoney nipple summit, which looked so like the real one from lower down, the mountain stretched back and back for a distance I could not judge. Now steepness was not a problem, though it was slightly tiring, uphill all the way; distance and soft snow were all that stood between me and the summit. I wondered how many people had turned back through disappointment and fatigue at that point. My body wanted to go up, but at the same time did not. It was such hard work, such an awful, awful slog, like climbing in a suit of armour on a hot day.

Though distance was difficult to estimate, shortly after passing the false summit I thought forty minutes would see me up this soft, lumpy mattress laid thick on the mountain. Many times I stopped to catch breath; I did not want to stop, but had to. Before long I was down to a hundred paces between unwilling halts for gasps of thin air. On slightly steeper slopes only fifty paces separated stops, then it was back to eighty or a hundred. At each stop I would wait a few seconds before saying to myself, 'Stopped isn't going,' and it was strange how much that sea-level silly sentence helped me keep moving up there. Another helped even more: I kept approaching mounds, which I hoped would be the summit but they never were and each time I avoided disappointment by saying, 'It is what it is.' What I meant was that these things were essential, for I needed the mounds one after another as a steady stairway to the final one, so there was no sense getting angry and wasting energy. They were there to be accepted as elements of the game I had chosen to play and wanted very much to play. Over mound after mound I went, looking for a summit which seemed to be running away and hiding. But I knew it could not hide for ever, and gradually I leaned less and less on my sentences as a different strength which required no willpower took over; almost nothing could stop me now, even if I had to crawl, and a feverish elation began to fuel me for the finish. Shouts and giggles and laughs came from my mouth like it was someone else making them.

'Hey! Hey! Hey! You're going to do it! You're going to do it! You're going to do it!'

Now we were on a big mountain and not a British rock climb, the fact that part of my legs were artificial was creeping more and more into the background. I had found where fulfilment lay.

I shouted loudly, happily, mad with joy, and turned to look back at the ground that had been covered. And there, twenty minutes or so away, was the tiny figure of Julie, still going.

'Hey! Hey! Hey! We're going to make it!'

She was too far away to hear.

Five more minutes pushing on and I turned again to see how she was getting along. There was another figure close behind Julie. Harry! The more distant figure fell down in the snow, got up a minute later, slumped again within another minute and lay there. He rose again, managing no more than fifteen or twenty paces between halts.

'Hey! We're all going to do it! Two of us at least and probably three!'

Where was the nausea barrier? Dismissed because of the crutches. Formerly I had been ill purely through trying too hard; I had vomited long and often through effort alone.

Every muscle was tired but eager. And then I spotted it, the fairly level area of slightly ruffled snow that was the top. A rush of emotion came over me, a weepy feeling that is not uncommon in such circumstances, and my eyes were wet out of sheer euphoria.

Could it be done in fifty paces, in one go? No. After fifty it was still a long way away. Snow seems to stretch like elastic as soon as you set foot on it, and so often slopes turn out to be twice as long as first impressions convey. Another forty paces and a pause was inevitable. But now it was within reach. The summit had one last steepish bit, a mere twenty-five degrees but exhausting all the same. Then I was there. In front, the mountain plunged away.

'You've done it,' I said to myself.

I had indeed! It was 2.15 p.m. so it had taken six hours. Six thousand, six hundred and fifty-four metres. Over four miles up. Nineteen years of effort had led here by stages and it was fantastic! Ten years of rock climbing, John o' Groats to Land's End, eight summers in the Alps, finding out all the while, the toil of expedition organisation, and now this. Through my blood surged that wonderful sensation, which no words can properly describe – sweet as love, warm as friendship, and overwhelming. All the effort was repaid.

Julie arrived fifteen minutes later, bright-eyed with the thrill of success.

'Well, we've done it, Julie.'

'Yep!'

The people who made the first ascent could not have been happier than us. It was a moving moment, particularly as Harry was still on the way up, half an hour behind Julie. Eventually his head and shoulders approached the final steepish bit.

'It's here, Harry. We're standing on it,' we called.

The head and shoulders dropped instantly from sight as Harry crumpled in the snow, down for a count of sixty. He was up again, to stumble-step nearer before buckling knees let him down again. Flop. He dragged himself up once more, managing twenty paces before going down. But he was on the summit this time. His determination had received a just reward, and I had learned a lot about Harry: next time he stopped on an ascent I would be more inclined to spend time encouraging him to go on.

To discover something you burn to do, and to do it, is one of life's greatest rewards, and a privilege which does not come often. The discovery can be as elusive as the success; we had been lucky on both counts.

'Seems daft, though,' I said.

'What?'

'Our most important ascent is the only one we said we wouldn't do.'

We nibbled at chocolate and took photographs, some of them with Harry's camera, which, along with the film, was stolen later. Of our seven cameras three more went wrong and Mike Welham, the main expedition photographer, made only one ascent. So the pictures were rather disappointing.

There was little time for Harry to rest before we started back, but he moved downhill with no trouble. About half way back to the false summit we met the first of five Austrians (whom we had seen on the march) who toiled to the top the same day. Now gravity was in our favour their laborious movements looked strange by contrast.

Where snow was steep we belayed; a slip was more likely on the way down. At one place where I went down first I hammered an aluminium tube, the lower piece of a crutch, into the snow, and wound the rope around it a couple of turns as a belay. Julie descended towards me. She came near and then level on my left, when something frightening happened in an instant. Suddenly she cried out and her body sank in the snow.

'I'm in a crevasse!'

I held on to the rope and prayed the crutch tube would not pull out. She dropped up to the top of her thighs into the snow-covered hole and went no further.

'I've got you.'

It is impossible to say whether she might have fallen far. Perhaps she would have, perhaps she would not. Such minor falls without serious consequences are not uncommon. Some crevasses widen as you go deeper and it can be a real problem to get someone out, but we didn't go poking around to see what shape this one was, I can assure you.

'That's all I need,' was Julie's only comment after she had climbed out, and then she carried on with the job. Her leg was hurting still, so she took a painkiller.

My stumps started to get very sore after ten hours out and I had to push myself quite hard. Now we were in the most dangerous part of the day, with sun-softened snow bridges and tiredness against us. Another hour, and we approached the biggest crevasses in near darkness. An ice axe and a crutch were arranged as belays and Harry stepped across from rather soft snow to the other, higher side where he hooked in his ice axe and got himself tight up against the two-metre wall. He stood on a small bulge of ice with Lord knows what sort of hole below and behind him. We heard bits of dislodged hard snow clump clumping down the crevasse and suddenly Harry let out a sharp squeal of fright and said, 'Oh, God! Oh, God!' Whether he felt he was toppling back into the black hole or thought his feet were going to give way I do not know, but for a couple of seconds he whimpered, a very frightened man; most of us get like that now and then. Reaching rapidly over the top lip of the wall he got his ice axe deeply and comfortingly into the hard snow, and pulled up, while his crampons ran up the wall. A relieved man stood at the top and moved back several metres to set up a belay. Me next.

'Keep your belay on too, Julie,' I said. 'Please.'

After a quick step across I whammed my hammer into the wall. Now I knew something of what Harry had felt. I didn't like it. Though not hard, there was an indefinite, unreliable character to the problem. What I stood on could have broken off, and the top of the wall arched gradually in a soft and untrustworthy snow hump to join the slope above, rather than providing a distinct and firm junction. I moved up far enough to hammer my ice axe into the slope, and pulled up. A mere metre of height was gained but the danger of falling into the crevasse was over. Julie followed with no bother.

The gas stove's hissing purr and faint blue light said welcome home. This was a wonderfully secure and warm shelter to us now. Harry had assumed the role of fetching snow for melting, without anyone asking. Jobs were done, with no more than an occasional suggestion by one or other of us that they needed doing. And when the food or drink was ready the light aluminium plates or plastic mugs were handed out almost reverently, with utmost care; food and drink were comfort, fuel, and life in the end.

'Let's have something else,' one of us would say, and another pan of snow would be stuck on the burner. The white cone would sink slowly and shrink, we'd pile more snow on, that would go down, and we would make up our minds what to have next - tasty oxtail soup, tangy hot orange, meaty Oxo, good old tea?

Harry had trouble getting his boots off but managed in the end. He felt his feet for a while and was quiet. Then he said, 'Frostbite.'

We both turned towards him.

'I think my toes are a bit frost-bitten, 'he said, and Julie softly said, 'Oh, Harry.'

'My own fault,' he murmured. 'Should have put my gaiters on. The snow got between the inner and outer boot.'

Everyone but me on the expedition wore a pair of double boots, a soft leather inner like a plush red slipper that laced high up the ankle, and an outer like any big brown mountain boot.

On Harry's toes white patches and angry red blisters had formed. He wrapped his feet in his sleeping bag. Julie's leg was sore, and my stumps were a bit hurt, but she and I had not paid dearly for what we had had. What it would cost Harry in the end we could only guess. In a period of six months I heard of three climbers who lost their feet through frostbite. So it was a rather subdued trio that settled down for another night. Our down sleeping bags smelled familiar and gave us some reassurance.

During the night the wind started. Harry slept almost without a break, but many, many times Julie and I woke up, took a few sips of cold orange juice and lay there listening to the devil wind blasting at our tent. The fabric flapped fiercely with a noise like someone hammering an iron roof.

At eight o'clock we still cuddled our sleeping bags and downed hot tea, while the tent shook just as badly as during the night. At nine o'clock it was as unrelenting as ever.

'I think we had better go anyway,' I said. 'We should be sheltered lower down. Don't want to get caught up here in a storm.'

We had all been approaching the same conclusion. The contents of three rucksacks do not take long to pack, and when this had been done we crawled out to get the tent down. After kneeling and sitting on the writhing brown monster to prevent it flying away once it was down, we finished up with a lumpy bundle.

The sun shone in an almost cloudless sky, yet after quitting our hollow we entered an even worse wind, which picked up white crystals and blasted them at us; it was choking to breathe. Face masks on our fibre-pile jackets solved the problem again. Thin clouds of snow were drawn up and chased hither and thither, now in a curve, now a whirling vortex, as the wind left a clue to its path, marking its way as in a fog. It buffeted unevenly from different directions. Julie moved up a slope on to a sharp horizontal snow ridge, with crevasses on either side. The bully wind blew even worse and Julie dropped to one knee, head down, her body rocked by violent gusts. She moved forward a short way on one knee and both hands, stopped on both knees, moved a little further and halted once more. We had to watch it here because of the crevasses. If the wind had been from a constant direction we could have crossed the ridge on the sheltered side, but it kept changing and pushing us all ways. I crawled for a short way behind Julie.

One thing was certain: a day later, and we would not have reached the summit.

Descent into a downhill snow trough brought some relief from the wind, and I felt a little more relaxed. However, a sudden cry from behind soon changed that: Harry was sliding down the snow towards a crevasse. Face down and feet first, he gathered speed very rapidly, then stopped himself with his ice axe.

The wind still pushed us around as we crossed the big avalanche track.

'That fixed rope's gone,' Julie said as we reached the first steep snow slope. 'But we don't really need it. Just have to go down carefully.'

It was worth belaying, which we did. The next fixed rope had been removed as well, but that did not matter much either. We would really miss having a fixed rope on the near vertical section, though. We approached the top of that step. A glimpse of yellow, yes, it was still there, and it helped us down in turn. In that small height loss the shelter turned the wind to a mere whisper; even the thin white fringes of blown snow swirling from the heights could not convey the force of the monster still roaming up there. The sun's warmth forced us to take off our windproofs right away.

Only the glacier trudge to go. There rarely seemed to be a right way, a best way; it was just a matter of picking a route every few minutes out of many options. Time and time again two, three, four or five possible ways lay before us.

Julie was a constant optimist, always seeing a 'right' way, whether it was there or not.

'To the left a bit I think, Harry,' Julie would say.

'Where?'

In his voice now was a faint edge, a barely perceptible trace of sharpness, but he was well controlled. Everyone was a bit edgy because as the afternoon wore on it began to look as if night's rapid approach would catch us out on the glacier. Harry's feet, Julie's leg and my stumps were all giving pain, our packs were heavy, and we were tired. I have climbed with people who in those circumstances would have been at each other's throats, but we had no rows.

We bivouacked near the end of the glacier, then set off early next day for the base camp.

'Congratulations, Norm,' Harry said. 'I didn't want to say it before, but we've finished it now.'

As we approached base Manuel rushed up easily.

'Cumbre?' he asked. ('Summit?')

'Si, Manuel.'

The mountain was left behind, the snows and intricate ice patterns constantly changing shape through sun-melt and wind-blow and gravity's downhill tug. It remained for others to enjoy, if they were lucky. We left nothing there, and took away nothing but happiness; and now the cloud of gloom which had hung over us and dulled that happiness was dispersed. 'Leave nothing but footprints, take nothing but pictures,' is an old saying which almost sums it up, but I would add 'and happy memories' to what we should take. Our hearts were free of anxiety and we began to feel the lightness, which came with the realisation of a dream. Even our concern about Harry's feet was reduced, and I don't think any of us expected him to suffer permanent damage.

Now base camp had a different atmosphere. The excitement of the way up was replaced by the contentment of success, and the place seemed different because we were changed in mood. We ate and drank and midday drew near. They had been a hard few days and a rest was inviting.

'How about waiting so we can get you a donkey or a horse, Harry?' I suggested. 'You could ride at least part way.'

'No. We couldn't get one until tomorrow. I want to go down and see a doctor today.' His mind was made up firmly. Soon after, our casualty shambled out of sight through the trees in short, wincing steps. Within a few hours he was back in Huaras.

The Hotel Barcelona, 6,000 miles from England, felt like home. Harry was limping but thought his feet would be all right; the blisters seemed to be the main problem. Terry, Julie and I went with him to Huaras hospital. Rest, the doctor said, so he and I stayed at the Hotel Barcelona. Everyone else went touring various parts of Peru. We were due to meet one week later in Lima.

'I think I'll fly home for treatment, to be on the safe side,' Harry said. 'Get close to some nurses, the little darlings.'

Two seats to Lima were soon booked on a colectivo, which is a cheap communal taxi. For about £5 each five passengers travelled 200 miles (330 km). Lima Tours responded very quickly to arrange an immediate flight home for Harry. A representative picked him up in a huge, black, hearse-like car, and that was the last I saw of him for a long time.

Harry. What happened to Harry? Well, in the end he suffered the loss of just two toenails, removed because of an infection underneath. It was a tremendous relief to learn that success had not cost him more, and we were amused at his account of his visit to hospital. Picture him, an untidy man who has no need of the fripperies of fashion to prop up his confidence, scruffy after two days of flying and considerable delays, and tired through pain. Of all the hospitals Harry could pick in London he chose one which sees a large number of vagrants and alcoholics. On a hot day in August he wandered into the casualty department and announced, 'I've got frostbite!' As you might imagine, there was a certain amount of scepticism on the part of the nursing staff.

A radio broadcast centred partly around the expedition brought in several thousand pounds for the Calvert Trust Adventure Centre for Disabled People in the Lake District, so from that point of view, too, the trip was a success.

We had to go back home and 'settle down'. Many people expected, suggested and advised the same thing: settling down. Damned settling down. Awful settling down. Horrible settling down. Maybe they were right, but I could not believe it. The settling down could only be temporary; there would be other mountains, other adventures. I had found a slice of life as good as any I had ever tasted, I had the recipe and I wanted to make it again.

There is a sad sequel to this story. Julie was so enchanted by her first exciting relationship with big mountains that in order to climb frequently she became a sound recordist working on documentary films of high altitude expeditions. In 1986, having climbed higher than any British woman, to the summit of K2, the world's second highest mountain, she died peacefully, trapped in a tent by bad weather on the descent. She had had many fulfilling years on the mountains, and perhaps one should not ask for more. Though many might think she had sacrificed her life pointlessly at the age of forty-eight, she had always said she would not mind dying upon a mountain; I'm sure she meant it. Dennis, too, was killed in a rock climbing accident, having enjoyed great fulfilment from his rich mountain life.

Norman on Tocllaraju, Peru; at the crux

Norman aged six.

Aged seventeen.

John O' Groats to Land's End 1969

CORNWALL YOUTH SERVICE

ROCK-
CLIMBING
COURSE

At BOSIGRAN, ZENNOR, St. IVES

★

THE COURSE is intended for Senior Members of Youth Groups who seek a more rugged type of outdoor activities.

BASE — The Climbers' Hut, Bosigran, reserved for this course by the County Youth Service.

THE COST — The Cornwall Youth Committee has kindly agreed to subsidise the cost of the course; the charge for those attending will therefore be 12/6d.

TRAVELLING — Full travel instruction will be sent to each applicant accepted for the course.

APPLICATIONS should be sent immediately to:—

J. W. WEST,
County Youth Organiser,
County Hall,
Truro.

Tel: 4282 Extn. 85.

Saturday & Sunday, 1st & 2nd Nov.
1968

An early rock climb and, above:
the rock climbing course leaflet -
where it all began.

The White Edge, South
Wales. Norman at the
bottom.

Gordon Stainforth

Judy aged twenty.

Marriage in 1966.

The Matterhorn. The Hornli Ridge is in the centre.

The Eiger. West flank in sunlight.

Francis Bozon (left) with the author and the guides' president at Chamonix-Mont Blanc.

Julie Tullis stands before Huascaran, Peru.

Judy in 1978.

Aconcagua (left) and Ameghino, Argentina.

A broken leg which caused problems in Argentina.

Nun (left) and White Needle, Kashmir

Dennis Kemp (left), Julie Tullis
and Denny Moorhouse.

Penitentes on Ameghino. Difficult to climb on one leg.

On top of Ameghino at 5115 metres

The Polish Glacier, Aconcagua.

CHAPTER 5

A Broken Leg in Argentina and a Visit to Kashmir

I CAN offer a partial explanation as to why I climb. Though I am rather lazy about any work that does not interest me, it was evident in my teens at grammar school that I was capable of great effort when I chose. Being keen to 'get on', whatever that meant, I blindly studied hard at all subjects. While in the end my academic achievements were not outstanding, I came top each year in the whole school for 'effort marks'. Under this system teachers rated each pupil according to how hard they thought he was trying, and I was rammed down the throats of peers as the goody who was 'an example to you all.' I redeemed myself in their eyes by turning down the role of head boy and being demoted from prefect twice for 'crimes' I had not committed (throwing a snowball indoors and talking in class). I did not protest my innocence too strongly, but my point is that I did put great effort into what I was doing; unfortunately what was lacking was enthusiasm. Peer pressure to 'mess about' was juvenile and easily resisted.

Concerning sport I was more enthusiastic, and I put a lot of effort into cross-country running, rugby, gymnastics and gliding. Though I ran in the school cross-country running team and captained the gymnastics team, my efforts in sport were not rewarded with shining success; no matter how hard I tried, I did not seem to have what it took physically to excel. The one exception was when I started climbing, and everything fell into place. If I tried hard, I succeeded, eventually. Lack of enthusiasm for the subjects held me back academically, and in most sports enthusiasm and effort did not seem enough on their own, but for climbing I was both physically and temperamentally suited; I was fit and strong and climbers come in all shapes and sizes, for the sport does not demand a certain ideal physique.

Promoting outdoor pursuits for disabled people was another challenge that came my way more by chance than by intention. And, since climbing was crucial to my being a spokesman, this campaign gave an added and respectable incentive to enjoy the mountains. In any case, the challenge, adventure, excitement and emotional rewards I sought were found in greater depth in climbing than in any other sport I had experienced, and in greater depth the more effort was put in. When I resumed climbing after the loss of my legs, in essence nothing had changed; trying hard brought rewards, and enthusiasm produced the necessary effort.

It was time to grab some living again; it waited there to be taken. I only had to go out and get it. There was ambrosia for the asking, trees to be plucked of their magic fruit, call it what you will, if you knew how to find them. In my case climbing was the way to reach the ambrosia and the fruit. If life became drab that would be my fault, for I had found my path and the initiative lay with me. I felt privileged to have found the way, which was now to take me to the Andes of Argentina as a member of an American expedition. Our objective was Aconcagua, nearly 7,000 metres high, the highest point of South America's Andean spine, by the Polish Glacier route.

The Argentinian authorities laid down certain medical requirements, which included having an electrocardiogram and running a kilometre at high altitude. If they insisted on the latter I would be making a wasted journey to South America. There are reliable reports of a very experienced climber being refused permission (by a non-mountaineer) to attempt Aconcagua because it was thought his trousers were too thin. Another tells of an Englishman who was given a psychological examination in Spanish, a language he did not speak; it is hardly surprising that he was turned down.

At Miami airport I met five of the team with whom I would share a month, unless I were refused permission. We flew off immediately to Mendoza, Argentina, to join the leader and deputy leader, Bruce Klepinger and Dr Peter Cummings.

Argentina. Plenty of open space. Scrub patches around us, vineyards, orchards, farms and ranches, with pampas a long way to the east. Ten times the area of the British Isles. By appearances, a fairly affluent country compared with Peru, though I was told there were quite a few poor people there and unemployment was fairly high. Inflation, inflation, worrying everyone.

Mendoza. Almost one million population. Spanish influence in the architecture. Tree lined, wide, straight boulevards. Frequent and inexpensive buses running like good blood through the city's veins, reducing the relative underprivilege of the poorer classes. Busy with traffic, bad parking problems in the centre. A clean place where people take a pride in their dress; European and American fashions. A high proportion eating out at pavement restaurants after 8 p.m. Orderly.

Concerning the medical requirements there was news of great significance. We sat in a hotel lounge for a briefing.

'The regulations have been scrapped. Everyone can climb,' Bruce announced.

There was no explanation from those who formerly enforced the regulations, but we speculated that they had reached the conclusion there was no point in applying the rules because Aconcagua still killed a lot of people.

Things got moving. Equipment was sorted and packed, and the local press came to interview us; I kept out of their way to avoid attracting attention from the authorities. In two hired trucks we drove one hundred miles and passed without incident through a military checkpoint, where our passports were retained until our return from the mountain. Aconcagua, being close to the border with Chile, is in a sensitive military zone. Four Americans whom I met had made the mistake of checking in at the wrong army post, and at 1 a.m. were taken at gunpoint from their tents by soldiers who came from the post at which they should have checked in. It was all sorted out in the end, but cocked weapons left the Americans in no doubt that the formalities were to be treated seriously.

Unloading the trucks a little further on at the end of a dirt road, we pitched camp for the night in Punta de Vaca, a valley entrance at 2,285 metres, close to tall poplar. Now it really felt that the adventure could begin; there had been a greater possibility than I had admitted to anyone that I might have been refused permission to climb.

Two valleys, carved by the Rio de Vacas and then the Rio Relincho, would allow us gradually to cover thirty miles up something over two thousand metres in three days. We walked with our water supply, a big river, on our right, (though whenever possible we would use cleaner side streams as a source) up the steep sided canyon, through shrubs and yellow flowers and grass and thistles, all the time close to smooth, buttocky boulders. At the end of day one, on a valley plain known as Pama de las Lenas, at about 2,900 metres, was an army hut with a marquee style tent nearby, and outside the hut I made the acquaintance of Lieutenant José Alberto Guglielmone and his men. It would not be the last time I met them. The green-uniformed soldiers were busy handing out bread and cheese to everyone, a kind gesture followed by the even more friendly gift of large chunks of delicious freshly cooked meat, then prunes. The lieutenant handed around whisky, and the soldiers plied us continually with mate (rhymes with paté), a strong local tea drunk through a metal straw.

Under the orders of the lieutenant, the soldiers had cheese and ham rolls and warm, sweetened milk ready for us in the morning. We were fairly sure the lieutenant would not make any attempt to persuade me not to climb, but to avoid any possibility of controversy I headed out of their encampment first and put some bushes and boulders between us before resorting to crutches again.

Steep, loose earth and stone banks just above the river were neither particularly dangerous nor to be taken for granted. Towards late afternoon the terrain turned more sandy and gently angled, in a broad valley bottom.

Tents, some equipment and food were travelling up separately on the backs of mules driven by two gauchos. We met up each evening but, being able to ford deeper and faster water than us, they often followed a different route. At eight o'clock that evening we had our first sight of Aconcagua's tip peeping down a steep V-shaped valley. Everyone was tired, and though we camped in sight of our goal and this raised our spirits, we could see too little to get very excited.

The third day's march on a loose stone bank above the river was scary, less so for the others because they could manage better. Expedition marches like this would be quite dangerous for me, it was clear, with river crossings and loose banks. A short jump from one big boulder to another in the middle of seven metres of fast river was nothing to the others, a time for a tiny bit of courage on my part. Bruce sat on the far rock ready to grab me. It was soon done.

The land turned to grey and red desert, sandy, dusty, parched. Valley walls rose in dry scree slopes to typical weather sculpted desert rock towers. Of a few hardy plants surviving, the most common was a spiky green species growing like giant macaroons a metre across and known as cushion plants; but don't sit on these cushions as they are full of spikes. A gently sloping plateau of red earth and stones took us almost to base camp; we then turned right into a boulder field, and that was it. In a wilderness of cracked rocks we found sufficient clear, dusty space to stand the tents. Though in fine mountain country, this was a desolate place at about 4,200 metres.

A day of odd jobs and relaxation followed and at 8.30 p.m. Peter and another doctor called Tom diagnosed pulmonary oedema (fluid in the lungs) in an expedition member called Henry.

Next day at dawn, with over thirty hours of rest behind us, we were eager to get moving, so with thirty-five pound packs all of us bar Pete and Henry set out to carry gear a thousand metres up. The plan was to dump it there, return, and make two more carries on subsequent days from base camp.

'We're going to go at what may seem like a ridiculously slow speed, but you all know why,' Bruce said. Yes. Altitude. It had stopped Henry already.

We were no more than twenty minutes above base when I heard a faint crack that made my heart sink; as my left leg lifted at the next step it felt strange and confirmed what was wrong. My left leg was broken. And I had no spare.

Bruce was just ahead.

'Bruce, I've got to stop. My leg's broken.'

Sitting on the stones, I lowered my trousers as the others gathered round. Just by the knee a steel bar had snapped.

'Metal fatigue,' Jan Balut said. It was his subject and he knew. Jan was fifty-six years old, a metal fatigue expert with Boeing Aircraft Corporation. He had settled in the USA after making an escape from Poland in the early fifties.

Someone suggested trying the mountain with the leg splinted and without a pack on my back.

'No. I'd just be a passenger then. It would slow everyone.'

Our two engineers, Jan and Mike, began a short discussion on whether the leg could be splinted or otherwise repaired. They thought not, and as their conversation approached this conclusion I felt increasingly dejected, and said, 'I think it's finished for me.'

Two or three people stopped and patted me on the back in genuine and touching sympathy, and said things like, 'What a bitch,' and 'Aw, hell, Norm.'

Pete came to meet me and took my pack down. I followed on crutches. He decided to take Henry to a lower altitude to assist his recovery; he was not getting worse but he was not getting better, either.

'At one point last night I thought he might die,' Pete told me.

They left base camp at 1 p.m., walking extremely slowly, and I was left alone in my disappointment. If only I had brought a spare pair of legs! But the reliability of the limbs over many years had led to complacency beyond reason; intermittent breakages were to be expected, taking into account the severe treatment to which the legs were subjected.

Disappointment. Following shortly on the relief of finding the medical requirements scrapped, this was a particularly savage blow. Yet disappointment is something which anyone operating near his or her limits must face and come to terms with. By sticking to the Alps I could expect to get up most mountains eventually if I chose routes that were not too hard and if I was prepared to wait out the weather. But the Andes and Himalayas are different, and failure is a large inherent risk on the high peaks.

What to do? Various vague plans for one-legged ascents sprang to mind but I could see no reasonable options; the stony peaks all around would lack water.

It looked as if I would be sitting alone in the desolate base camp for a couple of weeks or more before trekking out on one leg, or taking a mule. A few crumbs of comfort for the future came from Jan, when I asked him if I should give up expeditions because of the possibility of leg breakages.

'No, just replace the broken bit with a new, stronger one, don't let them get too old and fatigued, and take a spare pair.'

Henry's condition had improved so Pete planned to make the carry to camp 1 and return to base camp, then descend around three hundred metres to Henry. It occurred to me that it would be preferable for Pete to be with the main party if Henry was well enough to be left, so without giving it much thought I volunteered to look after Henry. Pete jumped at the offer, saying he would descend with me to check Henry out after the loads had been carried.

At the same base camp were four members of a Canadian expedition bound for Everest in 1982. Though described as the 'Canadians' three of them were in fact English expatriates. They were short of a plastic funnel for filling their stove and also lacked Valium tablets; I possessed both commodities and did not want either, so traded them for half a bottle of cognac and a khaki kit-bag which had burst when one of their mules fell from the trail. The latter item could be converted into some knee pads if I found it necessary to crawl, and a tough mini skirt so I could slide on my bottom with greater comfort from the extra padding.

The sun was within a few degrees of overhead when Pete descended, eager and well ahead of the others, to base camp. Together we went down easy dust, earth and small stones to the tent where Henry waited. Pete examined him, pronounced him much improved, said, 'I owe you a million dollars, Norm,' and returned to base camp. As he left I was aware that his departure reduced to little or nothing my chances of making an ascent because Henry would require care for several days. He had quite bad headaches, coughed a lot, was bringing up a little blood, and had more fluid in his left lung than his right, though this was reducing. My responsibilities were to cook and fetch water, make sure he took his drugs, and see that he did not do too much.

At 6 p.m. Lieutenant Guglielmone and a soldier arrived on mules. When I explained our circumstances he kindly offered us a ride down. Henry did not want to go, and I did not try to persuade him because his sense of balance was poor. Two mules between four would mean two to a mule or a lot of walking for someone, and it would take at least seven hours, much of it in darkness, to reach the military camp. If Henry had not been getting better, descent would have been advisable, but his condition was improving. In any case the lieutenant had come up to look for and help one or more injured Argentinians; it could be a matter of life or death for them, whereas our emergency was over. The lieutenant gave us bread and some cooked guanaco meat (from an animal related to the llama; it was with great regret that I learned later that guanaco are not as common as I had thought. 'Probably tortured it first,' one climber remarked when his friends received a similar gift.) and departed uphill. Within a few hours he passed by again, taking two Argentinians down. What had happened to their companion we would not learn for several days.

I was four nights and three days with Henry. At times he joked, 'Anybody can climb a mountain but it takes a real man to get pulmonary oedema,' and 'Why do climbers rope together? To stop the sane ones going home.'

At times he was depressed.

'Worst thing about this is when you go home and everybody says, 'Hey, show us your slides!' and, 'Three thousand bucks I've wasted on this trip,' and, 'It's all screwed up.'

He ate well, and drank plenty, and mostly seemed content lying back being looked after. If he was morose or apathetic it was easy to make allowances because he was not well, and because of his disappointment.

One mountain was framed by the tent doorway and in between trying to improve my Spanish with the aid of a book, or being housemaid to Henry, there was plenty of time to study that peak and wonder if the patient would recover so I could attempt it. I judged it to be almost certainly possible to get within two hundred and fifty metres of the summit, but the final cliffs or steep ice would quite likely be too much for anyone on one leg. The river stood in the way and each day I spent two hours searching up and down the bank for a crossing. The explorations were fruitless, and the roar and hiss of the river were inescapable, day and night, reminding me all the while that the river was in the way.

By the third day Henry was greatly improved, taking long walks, and getting restless.

'I'm getting antsy. Approaching the limit,' he said.

So on 5th February 1981, nearly two weeks after landing in Argentina, it looked as if another little adventure might come my way, and I started to make preparations. The ripped kit-bag made two knee pads for crawling, and a mini skirt. The stove and most of the food had to be left with Henry, so the choice of provisions was very limited: a small tin of tuna (7oz) and another of corned beef, some stale bread, and nuts, mostly peanuts and walnuts.

During the night I was unsure whether I could make myself go. If I had not climbed alone in the Alps the previous summer on two mountains of about 3,350 metres, I would not have considered the prospect at all. The solo climbs were a deliberate attempt to prepare myself to climb alone in case a companion or two were unable to descend, so I could seek help.

Shortly before 8 a.m. I woke, and packed: sleeping bag, insulating mat, bivouac bag, torch, jacket, waterproof jacket and trousers, mittens, crawling pads, two water bottles, spikes and an ice axe pick for my crutches, small first aid kit, knife, camera, film, a mug for soaking the hard bread, and food.

'Henry, I'll either be back in a couple of hours because I can't get across the river or I'll be gone several days.'

'Have a nice time,' he mumbled from his sleeping bag.

I had already pointed out where I was going; he could see almost the whole route from the tent. Heading westwards and uphill towards base camp, I kept close to the ravine cut by the river. In half an hour there was below me a spot where the river divided between four shingle bands. Sliding thirty metres down the stony bank I had a closer look, and felt reasonably confident that if I could just bring myself to make a few jumps with the crutches I would be across the seven metres of noisy white water. After a short hop on to the first bank I had to put my left stump on a rock submerged five or six centimetres beneath the water, and make another jump, thrusting with the right leg and crutches to roll forward on to the bank, a loose earth and stone slope of no more than thirty degrees. I began to realise what I was taking on when it took fifteen minutes to crawl a mere fifty metres.

Gently sloping ground permitted the use of crutches again. Perhaps only five per cent of the dusty earth was covered by the giant green spiky macaroons, so when it was necessary to resume crawling I could go between them. For three hours, crawling alternated with crutching; I gained height mostly through arm strength, in little jumps on the crutches. This soon brought on a very unpleasant ache in my wrists, and before long it was a relief to crawl, even though this was extremely slow.

At the time I did not know that the mountain towards whose east summit I was headed was called Ameghino, but I had a vague recollection from a map that its height was 5,116 metres; this was correct. The route to the summit of a mountain whose name I did not know was influenced by the availability of water. There was a more direct route, it seemed, but it was devoid of water. At that altitude, where the body dehydrates rapidly, I could not risk three or more days without finding water, because I had no stove to melt snow, and lacked sufficient containers to carry all that would be required. It was a relief and pleasure, therefore, to discover there was a stream where I had thought there would be one, directly below a snowfield.

Below a very steep scree slope of a hundred metres I picked out what I called my three o'clock boulder and reached it by 2.45 p.m., after an hour and a half on my knees. I felt good, and crawled on with head down. Shortly afterwards I passed close by the first snow penitentes, an unusual formation of snow like shark fins sticking out of the sea of scree, or like two-metre axe blades, or arrowheads, or dagger blades. They varied in shape and size, up to three metres or so, but all were brilliant white and thin, and clustered close. That snow could stand up in sunshine in blades so thin – perhaps thirty centimetres thick at the base, tapering fairly evenly to the top – was a surprise.

By 5 p.m. I had had enough for that day. On thirty-degree scree I settled down for the night on a body-sized level platform beneath a big, stable boulder. The precious tin of corned beef was opened, and half was saved for the next day, wrapped up in an empty soup packet brought specially for the purpose. Every spare morsel of food had to be saved, for the diet was not only dull, but frugal.

Perhaps by then I had reached a little more than 4,100 metres, having gained not much over three hundred metres in a day. It was indeed slow going.

The next day was much the same as the day before, except that as well as crutching and crawling there was rock climbing too. I followed a brown rib, at sixty degrees to start, and rapidly easing back to thirty. It would have been bad enough with both legs on because of the looseness, which meant not only were most holds likely to break away but also what holds there were had a layer of grit and small stones covering them. Cleaning the stones away and testing each hold was very time consuming, and the padded stump was cumbersome because it would not fit on anything small. However, I gained twenty-five metres more quickly than I would have on the very steep scree to the left and right.

Soon the rib was too broken to be of use so it was back to the scree, where each knee gained only twenty-five centimetres at a step and more often than not slipped back half that distance. Sometimes I crawled on all fours; sometimes I was on my knees in an upright position, digging in the spiked crutches. At 11 a.m. I took a gully crammed with snow penitentes; using a boot and a crutch spike on the right, on the strange snow formations, and the left knee on the gully's left wall, I moved more rapidly than anywhere else. After sixty metres the gully petered out. Scree again.

Lunch was bread and nuts. Then the scree got worse. Some of it was too steep for me to gain any ground at all; at each movement of a knee I slid back further than I had climbed. By aiming upwards and to the left I actually went downwards, but gained the bottom of some slabby rocks. These, too, were hard to climb because of loose stones and grit, but they gave me another ten metres. On sore knees I struggled up more scree, scree, scree, barely rising at all; it must have taken an hour to get my body sixty metres. When I chose to stop for the night at 6 p.m. I was close to 4,500 metres high, but based on an over optimistic estimate of the previous day I thought 4,800 metres to be nearer the mark.

In a few minutes I had arranged some stones around a level space to prevent me rolling off. That night's treat was the remainder of the corned beef. The hard bread had to be chipped with my knife from the round loaf, but was eatable after a couple of minutes soaking in water in my mug.

At 9 p.m., far away to the south-east a thunderstorm lit up the clouds almost every second, turning them into giant, translucent, internally illuminated mushrooms. The storm was too distant for thunder to be heard, but I awoke intermittently over hours and it was still going on. The weather had been kind to me so far.

Having over estimated my altitude, I began the third day believing this might soon see me on the summit. Once more it took ages to clear the debris to climb on loose rock, and I had to lose fifty metres to avoid a rock spur which was beyond my capabilities while on one leg. An unpleasant slope of fractured, sharp edged boulders went on for seventy metres and led to more loose rock climbing, then to a scree traverse and another scree slope as long as the boulder slope that went before. By mid-afternoon it was clear the summit would not be mine that day, if at all.

By now I was drawing close to the snow and ice field which might be the key to getting through the final steep cliffs, but it looked too steep and dangerous. Beneath an overhang of a hundred metres of cliff I chose a spot for the night, but before turning in explored along the cliff base to the right; it ended in a chasm and offered no way up.

Being at the bottom of the cliff allowed a more accurate assessment of altitude; at around 4,800 metres I was only as high as I had believed myself to be on the previous night.

Nuts and soggy bread started the next day, as soon as the sun struck me at 8 a.m. It may have been reluctance to face failure which made me unwilling to start, and I sat quietly until 9.30 a.m.

Crossing between snow penitentes and up a slope for an hour, to the bottom of the way I hoped to go, I left most of my equipment beneath a rock wall. Food, waterproof clothing, camera, water bottle, jacket, mittens and crutches were chosen to go up.

At close quarters the impression of the previous day returned, that this was too serious. The mixed snow and ice slope reached sixty or sixty-five degrees in places, and was composed of hard, unstable snow penitentes weighing up to 180 kg (400 pounds) each.

An alternative route up an ice-crammed gully to the right looked more attractive, so, traversing the lower part of thirty-five degree ice, I headed that way. The transparent gully ice went up in steps, two metres up, a metre and a half level, two metres up, a metre level, and so on. A higher section looked dangerous and added to that there was frequent stonefall. Uneasiness increased, and determination waned, after thirty minutes. One o'clock approached and, feeling very low, I turned back.

Sliding down the scree towards my equipment at the bottom of the snow and ice which had at first appeared to be the way, I found myself saying, 'Thy will be done,' over and over again. I think I did this merely for comfort but as the words came out I looked again at the snow and ice I had originally thought might be the way, and I knew I should try it.

It is impossible to think of any other configuration of snow and ice reaching sixty or seventy degrees which might be climbed on one leg and one knee. The shark fins lay in rows across the slope, and a lot were only two metres high. Some of the highest must have reached four metres or so. Where it was impossible to climb between the fins because they were closely packed I had to get over them. This was done by knocking the top from one with the crutches to form a little platform the size of a narrow tea tray, on to which I dragged myself to stand or kneel and reach across to knock off the top of the next up the slope. The crutches were long enough for the job but I had a limited stride through having only one leg.

The ice went on for one hundred and fifty metres and at 3 p.m. it had all been climbed. I was on a wide stone ridge like a huge whaleback, leading me to the left. There could be no more than a hundred metres to rise to the summit. On the broad back of the rounded ridge stood vertical rock towers of between fifty and sixty metres and I knew I could not climb them on one leg. To the left, the whaleback fell away in vertical cliffs, so that way was barred also. With the left side and the crest blocked, everything depended now on whether the ridge would let me through on its right flank, or whether that too fell away in impossible cliffs.

Though the ridge was angled gently I lacked the strength to use the crutches, so was forced on to all fours again. To the right of the towers I crawled slowly, and the slope unfolded gradually. At first I was fairly optimistic that the slope would let me through to the right of the towers and then all the way to the summit. I skirted the first big tower and could see the slope continuing ahead, and the further I crawled along beside succeeding towers the more the slope opened out, revealing itself to be gradual, and it became evident there was nothing in the way. The stone slope went right to the summit.

At 3.35 p.m. I crawled on to the east summit of Ameghino at 5,116 metres. I could not have been more pleased with an ascent of Aconcagua itself. Ahead I looked down the cliffs all the way to our lone tent, though I could only just pick it out. I waved in case Henry happened to be looking through his telephoto lens.

By 6.10 p.m. I had picked up the belongings left below the field of penitentes. What had been hard on the way up was easy on the way down, and I slid on my bottom down the scree with my one boot dug in ahead like a plough, and spiked crutches forward and ready as brakes. A couple of times I had to arrest the rapid descent for fear of tobogganing on a mass of sliding scree over a cliff, but mostly it was exhilarating and fast. The khaki mini skirt helped prevent ripped clothing to some extent, though the legs of my waterproof trousers took a battering.

In only two and a half hours from the summit I was back at the height I had been at a day and a half earlier; by 8 p.m. I was bivouacked where I wanted to be. The last of the tuna was delicious and a crescent moon came up over my peak. Excitement drove away sleep throughout almost all the night, and it didn't matter a bit.

The scree slide next day lasted until midday and it took an hour to find somewhere to cross the river. The last crawl up an earth bank was over in twenty minutes, and I crutched to our tent. Within half an hour the weather turned bad.

Henry had left a note saying he had gone up to base camp or higher, so I was alone for the fifth day. I did not mind, and started in on the food. He had left a stove, and first I cooked cream of asparagus soup, because it required the least time to cook. Vegetable soup and bread was the next choice, followed by hot chocolate. I must confess to feeling very pleased at having prompted Pete into pronouncing that Henry should not drink any alcohol, for otherwise there would have been none left. Half an inch of cognac remained, and I settled back with a drink, to savour the contentment of a climber who has made it. I had had my mountain; I had proved to myself that if a leg broke I could rescue myself under certain circumstances.

Eight centimetres of snow fell during the night. Though I would have preferred a rest day, it seemed right to go up to see where Henry was. Simultaneously, I started to heat up some soup and to stitch my badly torn waterproof trousers. In twenty minutes I had burnt cream of chicken soup and the ugliest trousers in Argentina.

Often on a mountain, or in life in general, it is what goes wrong which is the educator, and turns a dull story into an interesting drama. There is an expression 'In every adversity is the seed of something good', which is often a load of old cobblers, but on this occasion it was true. I had learned it was advisable to have my legs strengthened and through changing my objective for a sound reason, not an excuse, had had a fine, successful little adventure. Climbing solo reinforced valuable lessons too, for if I intended going up very high mountains, I would have to be self-sufficient.

I was almost at base camp when along came Lieutenant Guglielmone and half a dozen men, on mules. He was going up to base camp and offered to take a note from me for Bruce, and leave it at the camp if no one was there. It transpired that Henry had gone higher looking for the others, so I descended with the lieutenant. He shared a mule, giving up his own well-behaved animal to me; if he had not offered the ride down I would have had to have started down immediately.

At first the ride down was easy, on firm, red desert, but it was a different matter when we were on boot-width tracks traversing forty-five degree dirt slopes a hundred metres above the thrashing river. The big mules (as large as horses) plodded up steep scree, across steep scree, down steep, sliding scree on a trail I had hardly noticed on the way up. I noticed now; perched high on the animal, with only the right foot in a stirrup, I was scared. The animals waded, feeling all the while for a firm footing, hesitating, belly deep in the fast river, and walked precipitous slopes just inches from the edge of high river banks. I was aware that with a metal leg on I had no hope of floating or swimming, even with a water wing blown up inside – a method I had tried once. When the mules coped with steep dirt and boulders I had to work at balancing to stay on, and succeeded, except once; using only the right stirrup, eventually I tipped the saddle in that direction as we turned a corner on a steep zig zag track. For several seconds my brain was not clear as a dull pain registered, and I realised only slowly that I had fallen off and landed on the stump of my leg. My mule stood absolutely still beside me. For the rest of the ride I was scared quite often, and suffered on awful pain in the stump which had taken the knock, for about three weeks. The bone may have been cracked.

In the early evening we reached the army refuge, where large portions of meat, salad and mate were consumed and I was made very welcome. Clearly Lieutenant José had assumed I would stay until the others descended from Aconcagua, and I was pleased to fall in with his plans.

'This is your home,' he told me. 'If there is anything you want you say me.'

For four nights home was a stone walled, iron roofed refuge four metres square, in which five of us and José's Alsatian dog, Neger, slept on the floor. These were the quarters of the officers and NCO's; the men had a tent.

Twenty-four years old, dapper José wanted to improve his English, something he did with great persistence, and in only four days his conversation was much better. In return I learned a little Spanish, was fed generously on meat, tomato salad, cheese, onions, bread and apricots, and was plied with mate, sweetened milk and wine.

'You are the adopted son of the Argentinian army,' they said to me. 'We will shave off your beard and put you in a green uniform.' (Beards were not permitted in the army.) Unbeknown to me, of course, they were soon to be our enemies, but there was no hint of forthcoming trouble in early 1981.

Three of the 'Canadians' arrived first. They had reached Aconcagua's summit on the same day as I had climbed my mountain, 9th February. On the way they had come across the body of an Argentinian who had fallen, sustaining head injuries. Not far from his body was the wreckage of a search helicopter that had crashed while attempting his rescue, with the death of the pilot and serious injury to the co-pilot. The 'Canadians' had moved the body down three hundred metres to a flat area from which it could be lifted by helicopter.

Everyone but Henry and one other had made it to the summit. The team arrived in ones and twos on the day after the 'Canadians', and were fed generously by the soldiers.

The time came for me to descend from the army camp. José presented me with the wooden cup from which we had drunk many a mate, and a set of bolas, the three weights strung together and thrown to catch animals by entangling their legs. Not long before we quit camp I was informed that an unladen mule had fallen from the trail lower down the day before, and was dead. However, this ten-mile section was not nearly so horrifying as the twenty that had gone before. We headed for a roadside bar, where several of us congregated to thank José for his kindness.

A truck took us back to Mendoza, where we had a rest day and a huge meal in celebration. I had to get home on one leg, but as my luggage could be carried in a rucksack on my back this was no great hardship. Within three days we had scattered to Barbados, Peru, Chile, Canada, the USA and England, taking with us our disappointment or our joy, according to what we had done. I was full of joy.

When distant mountains called again I joined an expedition not as a candidate for reaching the summit, but as one of several working towards putting even one climber on that summit. The mountain in question, Nun, 7,135 metres, had had several ascents but only one success and three failures by the east ridge. Even the successful Japanese team who achieved the ascent put only two of fourteen members on the top. So, when I joined the team to climb Nun's east ridge in 1981 I was under no illusions. I could help by attracting a certain amount of sponsorship, I could carry loads and assist in other ways, but the success of the expedition would have to be placed before any personal ambitions.

'You're here to make the expedition financially viable,' Steve Berry, the leader, had said. 'It's not a 'Get Norman Croucher to the Top' expedition.'

That was fair comment and, though I more than paid my way, I did feel somewhat like a hitch-hiker at the time. When it came down to who had any prior claims to the summit I was last in the queue, because I joined late and thus evaded much of the preparatory work. I would contribute, I hoped, to a successful team effort; and the experience of a Himalayan expedition was something to build on for the future, for I had many plans.

The reason behind Steve Berry's choice of the east ridge was interesting: in 1946 his father had attempted the route. After a very long march to reach the mountain he was plagued by trouble with stoves, and was forced to retreat when his army leave of six weeks expired. Even so he succeeded in climbing an adjacent peak, White Needle, about 6,553 metres, which in face of all the difficulties was a satisfactory outcome. From the beginning I wondered if White Needle might be a reasonable target for my Himalayan initiation. So, though the main objective would have to come first, and it was not certain that there would be an opportunity to attempt White Needle, I asked Steve to obtain permission for us to climb this peak too. It was not exactly true, therefore, that I was going just to help on the expedition; a chance, however small, to attempt White Needle was a big temptation. If I had seen a good photograph of the mountain it would have been even greater.

'Will my new legs be ready before the twelfth of May?' I asked Brian Campbell, my prosthetist.

'Hope so,' he said, with mock indifference.

They were ready the day before, so I was able to join my first Himalayan expedition with reasonable confidence that the stronger legs would not let me down. I took another pair as well; Argentina had taught me what was wise.

From my point of view the venture commenced on a bad note, for on the departure date I was suffering from bronchitis, an ailment which has troubled me with decreasing frequency since my early twenties. (I was asthmatic as a child.) I took the risk of travelling, fully realising that I might get worse in consequence.

Because it was the International Year of Disabled People, Air India had given us two free tickets and sufficient excess baggage concession to take all the expedition equipment free of charge, and they treated us especially nicely on the flight. I remember equally well their free champagne, and their courtesy. There were five of us on board, and two more had gone to Delhi a week earlier to handle the paper work.

In the early morning hours next day we touched down in Delhi. In a stupor from travel and bronchitis, at first I walked off without my spare legs, which had been stowed in a forward cabin. That afternoon we went to take a train northwards to Jammu. We moved by taxi through the crowded streets to New Delhi station. In temperatures up to 41C (106F), and with a fever and a bronchial burning sensation in my chest, I saw little and remember even less. There is just a vague recollection of being in the land of pyjama-trousered men in the streets, the hungry dogs of India, searching, always searching for a morsel, thin, thin people with skinny, skinny arms, the incongruous conjunction of big bellies created by malnutrition, beggar cries of 'Sahib! Sahib!', dingy cafés with walls covered in old posters (many of religious topics), and lit at night by paraffin lamps.

Every foreign expedition in India is obliged to have with it a liaison officer, who may be very helpful in overcoming language problems, among other things; the one allotted to us by the Indian Mountaineering Foundation, Neelam Kumar, joined us at New Delhi station. On the train we found two wooden benches where we sat crushed four to a side, with equipment piled all round, for the fourteen-hour journey. Everywhere beside the track, in shanty towns or in the open, adults and children squatted by cooking fires. To a coddled European comes a wonder at where the excess of people find a continuing supply of wood fuel, food, and whether, amongst such an inevitable volume of human excrement, there is any clean water. Shelter is part of the equation of existence too, but less crucial in warm climes, and thin, grimy, dusty, sweaty rags sufficed for clothing for the poorest people, while others wore thin but spotless and bright garments. On the flat plains we passed good brick houses and straw-roofed mud huts, tents, lean-tos, hovels of sticks and mud with polythene roofs, and tarpaulins strung between trees, as we clattered along all the hot night, witnessing first hand the spectrum of India.

The transfer from train to bus at Jammu in the early morning was accompanied by protracted argument and haggling about taking our equipment on the bus roof. A crowd of onlookers gathered for the entertainment, and joined in, until money changed hands and the driver smiled again.

Meanwhile, an almost totally blind and ragged woman who might have been thirty or may have been fifty, I couldn't tell, attempted for three minutes to beg from one of our rucksacks which stood upright on the ground. I was unmoved, a sign of how unwell I felt; or was the thick skin of indifference, which you must have in India, growing already?

Through the bus windows we had a view of cacti six metres high, vultures, wild peacocks, hovels, and people in local dress. With blaring horn the bus chased fast along a good road at first, but it grew worse in the mountains, where muddy rockslides had torn away as much as half the road width in collapses over drops of hundreds of metres. The road itself is a remarkable piece of construction, clinging to cliffs in gorges of enormous proportions, and its upkeep is a tremendous and never ending task as successive winters attack. At many points slogans exhort careful driving: 'The Icy Hand of Death Grips Speed Kings,' said one, and elsewhere in India we saw, 'Sleeping While Driving is Strictly Prohibited,' and, 'Darling, Don't Nag While I Am Driving'! A certain number of serious accidents are inevitable on such a hazardous and busy road; two days after we had travelled the route an army lorry ran off into a ravine and twenty-four people were killed, and eleven seriously injured.

It took twelve hours to get to Srinagar and we would have liked to rest immediately, but first we had to argue at length with the local taxi drivers, while the police enthusiastically wielded batons to drive away touts for hotels, houseboats and various commodities. We stayed two days in Srinagar, a city in Kashmir, which is in the far north of India. Here we bought rations and made travel arrangements. I felt ill, and guilty at not being able to pull my weight, but some antibiotics began to bring improvement.

From Srinagar airport the next stage was only half an hour by Boeing 737. Forty items of baggage accompanied us to Leh. This town, at an altitude of 3,505 metres, population 8,500 people, has been influenced strongly by Tibetan culture and Buddhism, and is attractive as a result. An eight-storey palace standing upon a rock spur overlooks all. And far above that is a monastery. Buildings are of a distinctive Tibetan architecture, which helps them blend with the dry, hilly landscape, and prayer flags brighten the place. There are sufficient trees to give the air of an oasis in the middle of Ladakh's moonscape scenery.

Following lengthy negotiations we secured a truck to carry our equipment and two jeep taxis for ourselves. After a 3.30 a.m. start at loading, departure was achieved by 4.20 a.m. Past paddy fields in a hundred glinting mirror steps of the sky, and monasteries, Tibetan faces and the distinctive clothing which went with them, donkeys, horses, cattle, sheep, prayer flags, sparse poplar and willow in arid, stony hill country, we rose, gradually at first, then sharply on scores of hairpin bends and over the Fotu La, a pass at 4,094 metres. On a fine road surface most of the way we made good speed, and Kargil was reached before noon. This small town of 3,000 inhabitants had been more important by reason of it being at an intersection on old trading routes between Russia and India, and China to the west. Now Kargil has a few hotels, mostly scruffy, and markets like rows of wooden lockup garages raised above the ground and occupied by grocers, ironmongers, tailors, butchers, bakers and other traders. The population is predominantly of the Muslim faith.

The jeep drivers were paid off, and the jolting truck journey next day along a long, deep and fertile valley took us to Sanko village. We were perhaps half a day's walking short of where we had hoped we might be, when our truck became stuck in mud, but that was not important for we were not pressed for time. Having unloaded the equipment we camped where we were on a meadow at about 3,000 metres and within half an hour a deal had been struck with local villagers for eighteen ponies and nine porters for the next day. They duly arrived, and under a hot sun our caravan set out to walk eleven miles (18 km) on a rough road through beautiful rocky countryside where the last of the year's pink roses grew on high ledges. At first the valley floors were taken over by a patchwork of agriculture with poor villages of mud brick houses here and there, but both fields and human shelters grew less and less common the further we progressed. Most of our porters dwelt in these or similar buildings and worked these fields, undertaking porterage only occasionally, when the lucrative opportunity arose. They were simple men, and might have suffered considerable imperiousness from sahibs, but they set about their work readily. Without a trace of subservience, and with pride but no arrogance, they clearly wished to give fair service for their pay.

With bronchitis not over, and breaking in a new pair of legs, it was, for me, an awful struggle towards the end of the day.

'Norm took a battering,' said Barry Needle when we arrived at our camp that evening. He had walked with me all day. A thirty-eight year old engineer, who had resigned from his job to be on the expedition, he was our medical officer, and also took charge of rations. (The wisdom behind this being that if he poisoned you he was responsible for curing you.) Barry was very strong, industrious both in the preparatory stages and while on the expedition, and his judgement was good. He had broad mountaineering and rescue experience.

Steve Berry was thirty-two, and like everyone else but me, single. He had given up his job to go to the Himalayas, and had formerly been an estate agent, a profession which gives some clue to his personality; estate agents are neither known for shyness nor noted for having sleepless nights worrying what people think of them. Steve had worked extremely hard to organise the expedition, and he earned the right to lead it by initiating the project and by his hard work. He had a bad climbing fall several years before and as a result of his injuries, which were extensive and included damage to his head, he slept with one eye partly open; this had earned him the nickname 'Cyclops'. He had been on one previous Himalayan expedition, and had climbed in the Alps and the USA.

Richard Berry, Steve's younger brother, and known to Steve as 'Titch', was twenty-eight, a surveyor who also had given up his employment to be on the expedition. Good humoured (sometimes like a naughty boy) and generally constructive and buoyant in his attitude, he had a talent for mechanical repairs, which came in handy putting stoves right; at high altitude, where not only cooking but also the availability of precious drinking water depend on the stoves functioning, this skill is far more critical than might be assumed lightly. His father might have benefited from having such a man around.

Steve Monks was twenty-two, amongst the top few of Britain's rock climbers and determined to get as much as he could out of his sport; to this end he took only temporary jobs so he had plenty of time off for climbing. He had made many hard ascents in the Alps and Norway.

Damian Carroll was a twenty-five year-old teacher who had resigned his post on a remote Scottish island in order to go to Kashmir. His red hair went with the usual pale skin, which forced him to protect himself carefully against the sun's rays when high up; the method he chose with a large piece of cloth made him look from a distance like an Arab.

John Margesson, aged thirty, had been three years an army officer before becoming a land agent. He had very extensive expedition experience, which included a year in Africa, and he had trekked or climbed in Nepal, the High Atlas, Arctic Norway and Central America. He admitted he had little sense of humour and was very serious. I found him to be as he said, and also precise, physically strong, and a very hard worker.

The next stage of the trek, up the left of a steep-sided gorge and along a wide valley, was longer than the previous day's; seventeen and a half miles (28 km) was the estimate of one of the locals, though I felt his reckoning to be on the high side. Whatever the case, we arrived at the ancient camping place of Gulamantongus, having passed over rock avalanches and snow drifts which blocked the crude road to wheeled traffic. With skin rubbed off in various places by the new legs, in the groin, from both buttocks and from both stumps, and with blistered hands into the bargain, the relatively minor but simultaneous pains from several regions were wearing. The pain entered my consciousness in two ways, at different times as component parts from each area of injury and sometimes as a whole; so now and then I would recognise that a stump was sore at a particular spot, or a palm was telling me it was being rubbed, and when I was not conscious of one or other individual hurt I just felt myself to be generally in pain.

Now loomed a river crossing, by pony. Memories of Argentina flooded back as I clambered on the back of a small beast. Having both my legs on this time was a mixed blessing; it was an advantage as far as balancing on the pony was concerned, but they were bound to drag me down if I went in the water. The Suru river spread wide to about four hundred metres where we aimed to ford it, in two broad channels of sixty and one hundred metres and two smaller ones, separated by pebble banks. The water turned out to be not much over a metre at the deepest, so some waded across; Steve Berry nearly got swept over in so doing. In an hour and a quarter all equipment and personnel were across.

Springy turf, interspersed with muddy, rocky ground, then led us by early afternoon to a camp at 3,700 metres and next day the porters urged their ponies up very difficult moraine and boulder fields, and across an easy river. On a particularly steep jumble of moraine bank one pony fell and rolled over a couple of times, but still they all kept going. Another intermediate camp at about 4,100 metres was the limit for the beasts, and then the porters and we took everything on our backs for two days to base camp in a snow bowl, at about 4,880 metres.

When the porters left, saluting formally, smiling and waving to us, our liaison officer departed too. He said he would go trekking and would return in two weeks, but did not come back. Neelam felt unwelcome. There had been a certain amount of personality conflict between him and at least two expedition members; it would be difficult, if not impossible, to properly apportion blame in this, but certainly the fault was not all Neelam's.

For three days, in the manner of ants, back and forth we went, carrying to a dump at about 5,180 metres, and on to an advanced base camp at 5,486 metres, before the weather closed in and imprisoned us in a snow and wind blasted base camp for four days.

As soon as the weather released us on 3rd June we all recommenced carrying food and equipment to advance base camp, known to us simply as ABC, and for a further five days puffing people were tramping up and down, ferrying essentials to ABC and Camp 1. The latter camp had been established by Steve Monks and Damian on 6th June, at about 5,790 metres. Apart from seventy-five metres of snow at forty degrees or more, which is a stiff pull when you are heavily laden and very high, the going to ABC was fairly straightforward. Still, several hours at a time toiling in the heat on soft snow at high altitude was tough work. As Steve Berry put it, 'No words can convey the agony of high altitude exertion.' Those words we did use are best not repeated. On one occasion poor Richard made a carry from base to ABC, forgot to unload everything from his rucksack on arrival there, and gave part of his load a return trip back down to base!

Pressure on the bone at the end of the left stump gave an intermittent pain when I climbed, and I was worried that it might become so bad as to stop me.

From base camp White Needle was a long way away, but even at a great distance the mountain looked elegant. As we saw it the peak, all snow and ice, arched up on the left in a huge gracefully curved back to a corniced summit, from which it fell away steeply on the right side. White Needle had a great simplicity and purity of line. The view we had of Nun, though it was huge, was less impressive than from the west. I knew I should try to resist White Needle's charms, because we were supposedly suitors of Nun, but it was not easy. Much to my delight, it gradually became clear that it was most unlikely a safe route to Nun would be discovered except by going over White Needle. A reconnaissance was required and John and I jumped at the chance. We made our way up to ABC, in my case on snowshoes, which imparted a big-footed Donald Duck appearance.

Steve Monks and Damian had gone down to base for a rest. Richard and Barry were above Camp 1, conveying equipment and supplies part way to Camp 2, and Steve Berry was with John and me at ABC. On 8th June, Steve's first words were, 'Don't think we'll get much done today,' and we spent the morning unzipping the tent and looking out.

On the morning of 10th June the three of us were able to go up the gentle glacier between ABC and Camp 1. Though we roped up to cross a couple of crevasses, mostly it was a safe plod. Camp 1 consisted of two small tents pitched on an airy ridge, with a gigantic rock cliff on one side and a crevasse on the other, into which Steve Berry and John dropped up to their waists at different times. Being at 5,800 metres put us in a good position to try White Needle.

John and I, sharing a tent, both woke at 4 a.m. and though the wind was forceful, at 5.15 a.m. we started melting snow for water, in case the weather let us go. But no, a high wind persisted all day and even made us wonder if the tent would blow off the ridge or be torn to shreds, for the material drummed and the little shelter rattled violently and shivered and trembled in furious gusts. The tent survived, however, and we did too, thanks to that. During a brief lull Steve descended to ABC because of a headache.

The subsequent stormy night wailed and howled itself through, and shortly after 5 a.m. we again drove ourselves to prepare. Muesli and tea made up breakfast and not long after 8 a.m., though visibility was not good, the wind had dropped to an acceptable level. Having crossed a crevasse or two, we tackled a short, forty-five degree slope of soft snow, on which Steve Monks and Damian had left a fixed rope. After that rope length we were on the very crest of the narrow, snowy, south-east ridge of White Needle, with a rock cliff of three hundred metres on the left and steep ice and snow and crevasses to the right. With fresh snow everywhere, soft and insecure, it was quite dangerous, though not difficult. The ridge did steepen twice into short steps like a steep house roof, but generally we just had to walk carefully on an uphill gangplank on the long ridge leading towards White Needle. Mist hung over the white ridge most of the time and by two in the afternoon a moderately strong wind had sprung up and light snow drifted down.

'If it doesn't get better soon we should turn back,' John said.

'We could bivi.'

We said no more on the subject, both of us avoiding facing up to the unwelcome prospect of a cold bivouac, but the weather got worse and an hour later we did as suggested, digging a pit for shelter on a large snow plateau and laying out a bivouac bag. At an altitude of about 6,250 metres, we found ourselves in a good location from which either to retreat the next day if the weather remained bad, or to head for the summit if it was reasonable. In good weather we might have made the summit that day; even in the weather as it was it might have been possible to press on and get there, but time was on our side so we played it cautiously.

The night was cold, minus 20C (-4F) at ABC and more like minus 25C (-13F) where we were, but at 6.15 a.m. the weather was reasonably clear though still windy; Nun and White Needle were visible now and then. I woke John, who had suffered a fidgety, restless night through the cold, and who now proceeded to have a paddy at not being able to light the stove in the wind. It can get you that way high up, in dangerous territory, after a less than comfortable night, and I was not immune from feeling ratty either. In the end I managed to get the stove going inside my rucksack. We put some hot milk and muesli inside ourselves.

Soon Nun and White Needle had been swallowed in cloud again. As a precaution against crevasses we roped up and within five minutes John had gone to the top of his thighs in one; he went in twice more soon after.

'I'm going to be desperately slow,' he said when he got out. 'It's killingly hard.'

He was breaking trail on soft snow so had more work to do.

The weather deteriorated again quite soon. Surrounding peaks disappeared in mist and snow, and the wind picked up snow to blow hard at us.

The slope increased to a steady thirty to forty-degree slog. We would have needed half the time had the snow been firm, but we sank to the knee and cursed again and again. So it was not until just after noon that we came upon the equipment left by Barry and Richard three days before. A bivouac bag, a snow shovel, a stove and fuel were added to the little pile on the snow slope.

The elements were not with us and visibility decreased. It had been bad enough, but soon deteriorated even more to a 'whiteout', when no division can be discerned between falling snow and the slope you stand on. It is then impossible to judge angles or to see if the slope ends in a chasm, so you are close to blind.

'If it doesn't improve we'd better go down,' John said.

'I think so.'

This was an unwelcome conclusion, obviously, but we had to weigh everything up, and weigh it again if circumstances changed, and weigh it again and again. We delayed, stopping to eat a little, and in half an hour had witnessed only slight improvements in the weather. The dimly-seen slope ahead looked like it reached a tiring forty-five degrees for a short while, then dropped back to thirty-five.

'All right, let's give it a try,' John said.

He may have known that was what I tended to favour, though not strongly; I would not have argued if he had said otherwise, for we had time to try in better weather. And from our clear weather sightings we thought we had to go over White Needle to Nun because lower routes were too dangerous.

Though only a few metres ahead John was just a misty figure in the drifting feathers, but the wind did not rise sufficiently to insist that we stop. The slope eased back, and very vaguely, up and to the left, we turned left along the slightly rising ridge before reaching what we judged to be the highest point at 2.20 p.m.

Attaining the summit of this elegant white peak was all I wanted. One month to the day after leaving England, I was satisfied with the outcome of my first Himalayan venture, having reached 6,550 metres. It was a peak of modest height by Himalayan standards, but a cautious introduction suited me.

The weather cleared for a short while, sufficiently for us to conclude, on the basis of this sighting and what we had seen earlier of the slopes below White Needle, that the way to Nun's summit should be over White Needle. So as well as giving us the ascent itself the reconnaissance had been worthwhile, and a little more essential equipment had been left high up. No matter what happened next, I would not go home with an empty heart.

'White Needle, especially the steep slopes near the top – desperate,' Steve Berry wrote. 'Such a terrible struggle getting up… it was pretty scary moving along the summit ridge with massive cornices on the right and mind-bogglingly big drops on the other.' 'The last stretch up the steep slopes was very strenuous. Knackered!' was Damian's version.

In poor weather again, we did not linger on the summit, but began the descent of ground that was more dangerous on the way down, but less of an agony. Three times I went groin deep in a crevasse and John admonished me for carelessness; then he walked into one himself (giggle, giggle). By evening we were back at ABC, to find no one else had done anything that day because of the weather. Now, if we could just get someone up Nun…

Over the few days after we climbed White Needle it was verified that the route over that mountain was the way because any lower variations were too dangerous. Steve Berry and Barry had tried to cut out the tiring ascent of White Needle by keeping low, and had come back very scared, having passed beneath insecure ice pillars, on avalanche-prone slopes, on steep and rotten snow and ice, where Barry fell in a large crevasse, but managed to escape without too much difficulty.

Everyone carried towards White Needle and Damian, in company with Steve Monks, descended one hundred and twenty metres westwards from the summit to establish Camp 2 on a col there, between Nun and White Needle.

On 15th June Damian and Steve left Camp 2'… and immediately found it hard going,' Steve said. 'We were only able to take ten steps or so before having to rest and catch our breath. After several hours we had covered only four rope lengths – two hundred metres.' They climbed all day on steep, soft snow to bivouac at 6,700 metres in a bergschrund, which is a large transverse crevasse formed between two snow slopes lying one above the other, where gravity forces the lower slope to part company with the one above purely by reason of mass. Next day they crossed from the lower lip to the upper of the bergschrund, with difficulty, climbed one hundred and eighty metres of fifty degree snow ramp, and more snow, to reach the summit of Nun at 5.20 p.m. They descended the same day to their bergschrund bivouac.

'We were totally exhausted and simply crawled into our sleeping bags and went to sleep,' Steve wrote.

The next day was hard too. 'Last section up to Camp 2 is desperate,' Damian wrote. 'Steve almost out on his feet. I'm not much better. Down to five steps at a time; exhaustion, misery. Never again.'

The expedition was successful, and there was the bonus of White Needle. On 19th June, Richard and Steve Berry dragged themselves on to the summit of Nun.

Immediately after going up White Needle for the first time I had told Steve Berry, Barry and John that I was content just to carry loads for them; the appetite was sated for a while, and the left stump was still troubling me. Even so, I tagged along to camp 2 with Barry and John on my own condition, that I would turn back if the need arose.

In biting early morning cold we roped together and descended fifty-five degree snow and ice from the col for forty-five metres, crossed a bergschrund and lost one hundred metres or more while traversing forty degree snow to reach Nun's flank below the east ridge. Then began the wearying height gain on soft snow.

'I feel bloody weak as a kitten,' Barry commented at one halt.

At 11.15 a.m. we met Steve and Richard, victorious and elated on their way down.

'I was like a zombie,' Steve said. 'Titch did all the leading. Hey, Norm, didn't expect you to get this far. It's bloody hard.'

We parted company, with those who had the slope in their favour able to move three times as quickly as the unfortunates who had to go uphill on snow that collapsed underfoot and took them in thigh deep. In eight hours we covered the route to the bergschrund, which had taken Richard and Steve nine hours. So, we were not doing too badly.

Our bivouac at about 7,350 metres lay under three metre icicles hanging from the bergschrund's upper lip; the lower lip rose like a metre of parapet, giving the feeling we were on a balcony. Good weather was what we needed now.

We did not get it. However, Barry went up over the bergschrund next day and stood in heavy hail on the snow and ice slope, while I had a tremendous struggle to get over the big gap that ran like a horizontal groove gouged along the whole south face by some giant with a V-shaped chisel. I made it after expending an enormous amount of energy.

I recover quickly from exertion, and had worked out what to do next to get further up the ice; but as I rested I knew there was a decision to be faced. We were walking an extremely fine line with the weather so bad, us so high, the route so serious and retreat so difficult. We stood at the junction where daring and recklessness took different paths, it seemed. A violent inner battle took place, for in the prevailing conditions it was debatable whether two should try for the summit, let alone three – moving one at a time on ice and steep snow it was obvious that three would take half as long again as two. A party of three would be sticking their necks out and risking two bivouacs above where we were, and real problems if worse weather caught us out higher up. We knew that well enough, for even with tents and adequate food and fuel, the storm at base camp had been a reminder of what the mountains can do to a group which did not even have to go anywhere. We were out on a limb where a shortage of fuel or rations could be a real danger. The overriding argument of all was that though I was self-sufficient I was unable to carry much in the way of the extra fuel and food and equipment which were required; I did not deserve the ascent because the route was too serious. I had known all along that it would almost certainly turn out that way, and all those who had gone before had been extremely hard pressed to make it.

I must quote an outside view, to show that excuses were not creeping in but reasons were being weighed.

'I thought after his supreme effort on White Needle that he would be content with that,' Steve Berry wrote afterwards.'... His thoughts were for his companions, and his attitude throughout was that if he felt he was impairing anybody's chances he would bow out gracefully.'

By now the glimmer of hope I had nourished of reaching the summit was almost extinguished, though the ice and snow climbing ahead was likely to be less trouble than the soft snows of the previous day. With the right equipment, medium angled snow and ice gave me the best possible chance of moving quickly; time and again I was to prove this in the ensuing years.

In the end I made my decision coldly, as if someone outside was looking at it all objectively. I did what I felt I should, and accepted the responsibility as a member of a team and as the hitch-hiker of the group. Having climbed White Needle, it was easier than it might have been, to do as I should.

'I'm going back down,' I said to John, and called the same to Barry.

The two of them hesitated for some time, debating whether they should go on, even as a faster two man party. Eventually they went.

Alone on the bergschrund balcony I waited, half expecting the weather to chase them back, but they did not reappear. I began to wonder if I could have carried on if the expedition had not commenced with bronchitis, and if the left stump had been less troublesome. Would I have gone a bit better, sufficiently to make a difference?

Over twenty-four hours after I had last seen them, Barry and John puffed in, having reached the summit at 8 a.m. There they said a prayer for a climber who would have been with us but who disappeared while climbing the previous summer, in the Alps.

Six out of seven on top, and a double leg amputee to 6,700 metres; we had not done badly by comparison with the team before us.

Judy joined me in Srinagar for a holiday. The surrounding natural beauty was the main attraction, and in particular the adjacent lake area was extremely pretty; there we saw swallows and ducks and ducklings in abundance, bright kingfishers, bold hoopoes, geese and goslings and dragonflies, massed water lilies and bright pink roses, poplar and plump willow, reflected green mountains, yellow-green reeds, flat islands supporting little thatched houses a mere half metre above the clear water, floating island vegetable gardens, tourist houseboats galore, dugout boats, and shikaras, which look like brightly painted gondolas and perform the same taxi function.

I did not feel at all well, and soon Richard and I learned that we had contracted salmonella and shigella, very unpleasant and occasionally fatal forms of dysentery.

Thanks to Steve Berry most of the newspapers described the decision to turn back on Nun as 'sporting' and 'in the spirit of sacrifice'. The expedition began for me with bronchitis and ended with salmonella and shigella but no illness could lessen the pleasure of what had come about in one year: the east summit of Ameghino on one leg, taking part in a successful expedition on a hard route, getting up White Needle, and the right decision, at 6,700 metres. How much more could I expect from this splendid sport? Would not the time soon come when I would have to abandon the more ambitious projects, which brought such joy? Increasingly, friends told me that time was here. But to my mind it was far away, and time would show this to be true. There was life in the old dog yet.

CHAPTER 6

Back to Aconcagua, and Muztagh Ata, China

1982 heralded two major climbing objectives. Time was running out and the mountains had to be taken soon, I thought. I began to wonder if I could be sane, for climbing weighed so heavily on my mind and was almost all I wanted in life; mountaineering was my destiny and my delight. The prospect of more adventure was both temptation and trap, and could not be resisted. How could my response be that of a rational person? Well, though now I seemed more like an impatient, greedy gourmand than the gourmet of earlier years, this was only a continuation of the behaviour that had so far brought sublime rewards, and there was not the slightest doubt that so far my course had been proper. Nothing had changed except my limits, which had expanded with experience and, particularly, because of the crutches. If earlier climbs had been within the bounds of sanity, then so were those to come.

The first of 1982's expeditions was a return match with Aconcagua. Shortly before going to Argentina, a new set of strengthened legs awaited me at the Roehampton limb centre. They were not specially made in any way, but were just what would be given to overweight people.

'They fit very well,' I told the doctor.

'Take them off then,' he said. 'Must be someone else's'

Despite this little jest, on the whole the service received at the limb centre was good, contrary to poorly based media stories. Some people don't get on with the difficult business of coping with artificial limbs, and don't the press just love dealing with those who whinge.

At Buenos Aires airport, a customs officer was perplexed when the Englishman, on instruction, started to unpack a rucksack containing climbing equipment, but then opened a box that contained a spare pair of legs. He looked from rucksack to legs to Englishman and back again.

Pointing at the climbing equipment: 'Whose is this?'

'Mine.'

Pointing at the legs: 'Whose are these?'

'Mine.'

It did not tie up, but he waved me on.

Through contacts made a year earlier, I came across Miguel Angel Sanchez, unemployed, but not distressed by that condition, who was prepared to undertake a training climb with me. His English was little better than my Spanish, but we got by; he invented 'glug, glug' for boiling water, and I came up with 'senora pollo' or lady chicken for hen. So by bus about a hundred miles to a hostel and ski resort called Los Penitentes, run by Fernando Grajales and his wife. There we met three Americans who were training before attempting Everest by the North Ridge, a ridge that will crop up again, prominently, in this book. We all agreed we would not want risks taken to recover our bodies in the event of an accident, and six weeks later the one woman in that group fell and disappeared on Everest. She was the third person I knew to die on that mountain in a period of six weeks.

Miguel and I climbed easy Cerro Manso, 5,557 metres – Manso means mild, which characterised this mountain – in a few potter-along days, and then returned to his home.

'Miguel! Mister Norman,' his ample Mama shouted as we got out of a taxi outside their one-storey concrete house. She hugged us tight and said if you lost as much weight as I had she would go next time. However, she was adamant I should not attempt the Polish Glacier on Aconcagua.

'No Polacos,' she said many times, shaking her head and pouting, and I felt guilty for the anxiety our breed created. As a guest in their house it was always with me, not least because Miguel had once attempted that glacier with a companion who fell and was never seen again.

At the bus station, I made contact with the group I would be climbing with on Aconcagua. John Smolich was the leader.

The three day march to base camp revealed much about the characters of my nine companions. John Smolich, the soft-spoken leader, was good at seeking opinions on how the expedition should go, without giving up his responsibility for decision making. He was adamant that everyone should stay together, and though he had the usual share of early greyhounds, others whose pace varied (in two cases because of illness) and me in the party, he coped firmly and pleasantly on this issue. John had been a guide for three or four years, having abandoned a career as a surveyor.

The other John in the party, John Perone, was thin and looked older than his twenty-eight years, partly on account of his semi-bald head. He was single, a chemical engineer who lived in California.

Mary Michel was an assistant manager in a climbing equipment shop, and had been introduced to wilderness hiking at a very young age by her father. She had acquired a great deal of hiking, climbing and skiing experience, and was sensitive about doing as well as the males.

Someone who proved to be stronger than a cursory glance might have conveyed was Ramon Rodriguez Rocca, a Chilean engineering student who in addition to carrying more than his fair share of communal equipment took on board three big honeydew melons for us. He did not reach European or American average male height and lacked any obvious bulges of muscle, but that is often the way with good mountaineers. In consequence of his abilities, Ramon was a leading candidate for a Chilean expedition attempting Everest the following year.

Mr Muscle of the group was Todd Marlatt, a boisterous ex-marine who worked in the oil business in Saudi Arabia. He could easily have been taken to be too full of himself, but, though he was pretty full of himself ('What is the name of the one who talks a lot?' an Italian had asked), his anecdotes were interesting and his jokes funny.

The oldest person in the group, Ted Mayer, was forty-six, originally from Germany but now, like all but Ramon and me, living in the USA, where he owned a small printing business.

Dan Montague was a soft-drawling, easy going hospital medical technologist who also ran a raisin farm in California; 'raisin' raisins', as someone expressed it. He was less ambitious than some, and said that unlike the other 'dudes' he would be content to reach 6,400 metres as he had not previously been quite that high.

Paul Slota was a grocery store manager whose interest in photography added a good deal to his enjoyment of the trip. He was a quiet person who blended in unobtrusively.

Vladimir Kovacivic, a Yugoslav doctor, worked as an anaesthetist in Wisconsin. Apart from me, he was the only one of us who was married at the time, and he had two children. Vladimir was fast at the beginning of the expedition and emerged as the person who disliked most the constraints of being in a large group.

Ages ranged from Ramon, twenty-five, to Ted at forty-six.

The march involved a fifteen metre wide river crossing on the morning of the second day. Most of the others struggled through water up to mid belly and though none slipped the seriousness of the crossing, even with a rope, was obvious. John S. crossed with me, much to my relief. Facing upstream I entered the clutches of the water and shuffled sideways. As it became deeper I speared the crutches into mucky brown wavelets with dirty white crests, into water which tore even at those thin poles so hard it took all my strength to prevent them being pushed away. My feet conveyed no information as to the contours of the bouldery bottom, so, unlike the others, I had to chance each step and hope that I could remain in balance with the help of the crutches. If the water pulling at my crutches created a problem, what it did to my legs made the crossing the hardest I have ever attempted, for the river worked constantly to sweep me from my feet into rough water. I would sink if I went over, and the river would dash me against boulders, and if I could not get out the cold would soon finish me if drowning did not. The difficulty was reduced a little as the limbs filled with water and became heavier, but when only at knee depth I thought I would not be able to handle deeper water. A further step to the right, and the water was at mid thigh, and I fought to get the right leg moved again after its partner had joined it. The river dragged at it as soon as it came off the riverbed and I feared I would not get it down again. For second after long second I thrust as hard as I could, trying to get it on the bottom again while the river wanted to take it downstream, with or without me. I battled, and won a step, but each successive step took me further away from the bank and into deeper water. Two, three, four more short steps with the water up to my stomach brought relief in one way: I was in the middle and it was as safe to go on as to go back. John was right behind me, holding my belt. Another step seemed to take me no further. Don't look at the water; it moved so fast it would disturb any balance achieved through the eyes, and I relied more than most on my eyes for balance because my feet told me nothing. With eyes on the hills upstream, I got another step. People on the bank were shouting, 'Great man!' and 'Go for it!' The water shallowed, it became easier and easier, and I bounded out.

'We got power!' Todd shouted, raising a clenched fist, and John P. reacted more quietly with 'We's funky.'

At Plaza Argentina we stopped to rest, and talked to two people who had attempted the Polish route but had not reached the summit. Their three companions were still up there trying.

The greyhounds pulled ahead, and I stayed with John P., who had what all the Americans knew as 'the trots'. He was weakened, and had to stop frequently to drop his trousers. 'Gonna get a sunburnt butt,' he said, 'with all these trips to the bathroom.'

Three Americans whose two friends we had met at Plaza Argentina descended; two of them had succeeded, out of a total of five. It was serious, and they had passed by three bodies on the glacier, they said. As far as I could gather from various sources, one was of the Argentinian who had died when I was beneath the mountain the year before, and the other pair were Americans who had met their deaths a few weeks earlier.

Our little group had been moving only fifteen minutes up steep stony ground on the way to Camp 3 when the altitude claimed its first victim: John P. could not carry on. His speech was a little slurred and his gait unsteady, and the decision to stop was entirely his own. He descended alone to base camp, to await our return.

The more difficult part of the route started, on the steep glacier. As we sat to put on crampons the body of the Argentinian was visible two hundred metres to our left and only a few score metres up the glacier. It lay in the snow, a vague bundle, and perhaps wrapped in a sleeping bag; the distance was too great for us to tell, and no one mentioned it.

Having started up a snow slope which turned icy higher up, we were in no doubt that from now on great caution would be called for. While load carrying, even short stretches of thirty degree ice are not only tiring but dangerous too; every metre gained is one down which the fragile human could slide and bounce and tumble at an unbelievable speed, and a high proportion of accidents which occur on Aconcagua stem from slips on moderately steep ice. Two more bodies seen at a distance were evidence of this; these were the Americans.

To our relief, within two hours we were finding our way up easy angled rock and scree, and looking for somewhere to pitch the tents.

The essential plod of getting poised to climb was over; nine days from the road to the glacier had earned us an attempt at the summit. I was troubled; I had joined the expedition because Camp 3 was planned at 6,250 metres and I estimated we were a long way below that, leaving too ambitious a summit day for me. The original intention of ascending seven hundred metres had been reasonable, but we were too low by a few hundred metres. We all deserved to share the blame, for we had surrendered to that awful sluggishness of high altitude which flooded over us after not much more than four hours on the go. We would all pay for it.

It fell to Dan and me to prepare dinner that evening, and breakfast the next day, so we were obliged to start the big day much earlier than everyone else. At 3.30 a.m. the cold was intense but we had to get started on melting the snow. One stove which had been working the day before did not want to start at first, and took half an hour to coax into action; two more hours went in melting sufficient snow for nine people. Our 6.30 a.m. departure was made in the last remaining minutes of that night's darkness, and a bit too late.

Once our crampons were put on at the glacier's edge, five minutes away over steep scree, we roped ourselves together in three groups of three. I followed John and Mary and we set off in front, traversing from the right to the left across and up the glacier ice, at angles of up to forty-five degrees. To the sound of crampon rasp and ice-axe clunk and heavy breathing we made reasonably good progress, drawing gradually ahead. It would have been easier and safer climbing straight up, using two ice-axes, but we had to cross using one axe on the higher right side. (Or in my case, a crutch.) For an hour, two, three, we traversed with the icy slope to the left, a constant reminder that tragedy could be just one slip away.

Moving across steep snow John hammered in three snowstakes, to which the rope was clipped for safety. I had used spiked crutches up to that point, but found it better to use an ice-axe and one crutch on a particularly steep bulge of snow above a crevasse.

By 10 a.m. we were nearing a shoulder, which marked the beginning of a very long snow ridge to the summit, and we sat to wait for the others.

Half an hour went by as we watched them creep in funeral procession across the slope. There was a delay when someone had trouble with their crampon straps, and then someone else lost a crampon, which was recovered from further down the slope where it had come to rest fortuitously on rough ice. Somebody else came to a halt, leaning his head on his ice-axe buried to half its shaft length in the slope, and behind him a figure moved slowly with very long pauses between steps. Paul and Ramon looked like the only ones making progress without problems of one form or another. Eventually the group came together.

'It's clear not everyone in this party can make it,' John said, and we all talked over what we should do. He picked me as one who should continue, but I did not like it when he suggested that the four who were managing least well should descend together on one rope.

'You can't do that,' I said. 'This is a commercial expedition and you would be crucified if you sent down four of your least able clients without even one guide. There are bodies already at the bottom of the glacier, and a slip is more likely on the way down.'

He accepted that either he or Ramon, or preferably both of them, should descend with the clients, but he would not allow the others to ascend on our own. So we failed in one way through looking after the weaker brethren, through doing what we ought to do; but then we might have failed anyway. What with the waiting and the talking, three-quarters of an hour was irretrievably lost; the stove that worked had cost at least half an hour, and the one that failed to function had set us back a further hour. Whatever the cumulative factors to delay us had been, it was plainly late to launch out from this point. Boiling clouds higher up revealed the presence of high winds. Everything was weighed, and we descended. (Later I read an Argentinian description of the route, in which an extra, higher camp was suggested; there is something to be said for dividing the route in that way.)

John, Mary and Ramon had gone well, with Paul and me next in line. However, when it was decided back at Camp 3 that four or five people might try again next day, I agreed with John that the route was too ambitious for me from this low camp. Therefore Dan and I would cook again and get the water ready very early next day. The plan was to be awake by 3 a.m., or earlier.

No one got up that night. I shared a tent with Dan in which we melted the necessary snow, and was unaware of what went on in the other tents, but it was reasonable to assume that the weather was unfavourable. With that thought in mind I drifted back into sleep, and slept till late. Imagine my surprise when I learned that their failure to get up had nothing to do with bad weather but was a result of the lethargy of high altitude; I could hardly believe they had come all this way only to give up when the odds of success were a good deal better for a smaller party sent on its way earlier and minus the slower members. Vicissitudes were to be expected in this high and wild place, and when the mountain shunned you that need not prevent you trying again. Still, for everyone, there are days when motivation has been taxed too much; they had taken a beating, spiritually as well as physically, and some of them had been taken aback at how they managed. Yet even the 'Bambi-legged' men of the day before wanted to join in another attempt. Only Dan had decided against. He and I were melting snow a little later when John came to our tent. 'Dan, if we were to traverse over to the normal route would you come too?'

'Sure.'

Here was the answer; the antidote to disappointment was at hand, if we succeeded.

Only three and a half hours of traversing rotten scree and snow patches and a snowfield led us to the highest mountain hut in the world, the tiny Independencia, set at about 6,500 metres. (There were several different estimates of the altitude in various accounts concerning Aconcagua.) This wooden, wedge shaped building looks like a piece of cheese left there with the thin end pointing at the sky. It was nearly two metres high, and became known to us as the chicken coop, where we cooked.

Todd was soon bent over a stove and shouting, 'Come on bitch!' He and Vladimir would share the extra burden of getting breakfast next day. I was pleased the second summit attempt would not begin that way for me, but as it transpired I did not get it easy on this eve of expectation, or in the first hours of the next day; my water bottle, kept inside my sleeping bag to prevent freezing, leaked. One and a half pints (.85 litre) of water distributed itself through the down filling, resulting in frequent awakenings and a lot of shivering, huddle, huddle, all night. This was hardly the start I had hoped for to a very hard day.

Vladimir crawled into the chicken coop at 5.30 a.m. and cursed a troublesome stove. Oatmeal cereal, bland, unwelcome and unappetising, but necessary. Away at 7.30 a.m. Weather: cloudy, low wind. Up easy snow to a slightly rising crest of snow and stones. A traverse on scree, and across an easy snowfield for two hundred metres.

Soon our pace was broken by boulders, loose boulders, which made us wary that one of our number might set one rolling on to someone else, so we tried not to get in line below anyone. We were in a gully, which gave loose scrambling like some of the harder routes on British mountains, but the extra several thousand metres made any further comparison meaningless. The steepest snow was only twenty degrees; it felt more like sixty, and demanded considerable effort from us all, making every step a little battle against inertia. Effort, effort, effort, effort.

Following a fifteen-minute halt at 11 a.m., John and I went ahead, with Ramon well in advance of us. The top of the gully was not far away and it was likely that from there we would see where we had to go. I feared we might be faced with a distant and high summit, which would lead John to say we would have to turn back. Not so far away was a storm.

At 11.45 a.m. John was a few metres ahead as we weaved between boulders lying on steep ground. He stopped, and said, 'Come here and take a look.'

His voice betrayed nothing, neither elation nor dismay, but as I scrambled towards him he gave me the obvious clue by saying, 'You deserve this. You've worked hard enough for it.' Unless he turned out to be a surprise sadist, the news was going to be good.

I reached him, to discover that the gully ran at a right angle into the ridge that linked Aconcagua's twin summits, with the higher north one to our left and the south to our right as we came up. The south summit looked more interesting, snowier, and showed us a fine ridge, but it was the bigger one we were after, the highest of all the Andes. The north summit was a rock chunk that I estimated to be one hundred and fifty metres above us.

'Be there in an hour,' John said.

I felt good, with a belly full of warm hope.

'I was worried it might be further away and a lot higher and I might have to say it was too far,' John said.

Progress was slow but inexorable. Ramon was soon waving at us from the summit, while John and I waited thirty metres short vertically for the others to catch up. Paul was right behind me, Dan going well behind him, and forty minutes separated him from our tail-ender, Todd. He was just behind Ted and Vladimir. So with the exception of Ramon and John, who were in a class of their own, the early greyhounds were finding it hard. Beware of seeing that as judgement, rather than as the observation it is intended to be, but there is a lesson there for some: save yourself for the important bits.

At 1.15 p.m. we dawdled like a single file, exhausted army patrol and flopped down on the summit, a flat brown rock area bigger than a tennis court and almost free of snow, presumably because of high winds. We took photographs of each other alongside a metre high tubular alloy cross.

'Congratulations,' Ramon said to several of us in turn. 'Congratulations.'

The training ascent, three weeks to the day before, had paid off. At 6,960 metres, we were all at the highest we had reached. I felt not pride, but a splendid surge of satisfaction. That dissatisfaction which just over a day before had seemed beyond relief was now banished. I had sought inner serenity, and found it. The results of the two expeditions to Argentina added together were so precious, so much more than I could have hoped for.

If ever the summits give me only a sense of relief from suffering, and permission to go down, without some feeling also of a sense of purpose, then I shall stop climbing. It is not a question of trying to prove anything; that time is long past, if indeed it ever existed. But there must be more to it than just a cessation of the physical and mental suffering brought about by pushing my limits to such an extreme that I need no coach to goad or encourage me further. I could think of Aconcagua and other ascents again and again and again, bringing them to mind at any time to relish the thoughts, fanning embers into flame as a never-ending source of spiritual warmth.

Twenty minutes on the summit of the lofty mountain seemed like no time at all.

'Touch it and get back down,' Todd had said, but like the rest of us he could not resist a break.

The storm that had been approaching enveloped us within minutes of our leaving the summit. Loose rocks rapidly became slippery too, plastered by a couple of centimetres of snow. Now our minds turned more to survival than success; the summit was behind, courted, won, and abandoned. Reaching the uppermost snowfield we went silently down amidst the cloth sounds of a place of snow. Fortunately, the wind did not rise much; for an hour and a half snow feathered down but visibility was always satisfactory and we had all retraced our steps to the chicken coop within plus or minus fifteen minutes of 4.15 p.m. And there we slumped, again.

Dan had several fingers frostbitten, and Ted and Ramon each had one finger affected; none of their injuries was serious, as it transpired.

Todd melted a little snow for us, but everyone should have got more liquid inside them; lying inside the chicken coop I had plenty, for no one else came to get it and I drank a lot before it refroze. I called out that I would make some soup, or cook something more substantial if one person came to help, but there were no takers. That was the measure of how tired everyone was. We were at the edges of exhaustion, and those who ate made do with a few nuts and 'candies'. It would be downhill all the way now, so this was not as serious as it might have been. Yet it taught me a lesson about how unconcerned some could be for their fellows.

John was eager to get down and we did not melt any snow prior to departure next morning. During the grumbling, swearing, squabbling like starlings, muttering descent Ted had to stop to 'go to the bathroom' and Todd told him to hurry up, saying, 'This weather could kill us,' and 'Hey, man, we're all hurting.' The weather was intermittently quite bad, and everyone was tired and a bit anxious, and most of all keen to get off the mountain.

At Camp 2 Todd got the stove going in the early afternoon and we experienced the delight of quenching intense thirst simply with water. The finest wine in the world could not have given more pleasure. At Camp 1 a couple of hours down, Ramon cooked a meal, and everyone but Paul and I hurried down to base camp, where they arrived in darkness. My stumps had grown extremely painful, most likely through the cumulative effects of several days on the go. When Paul got home he had infectious hepatitis, a disease which he might already have contracted at this stage, which would account for his feeling unwell.

After a good night's rest Paul and I descended to base camp, met up with the others and went down the same day to the junction of Relinchos and Vacas valleys. My stumps felt even more painful, causing me to go slowly. Soon most of the others were just scurrying, coloured dots, mostly red and blue, and as the powerful words, going home, drew them down they became black dots and then were too far away to be seen. The two Johns waited for me and accompanied me over the steep, loose and dangerous river banks; I was grateful for that, particularly because John P. had more reason than the rest of us to want to desert the mountain as fast as he could, because he had failed. Though I wished to go home too, I did not feel like many of the others, who resembled fugitives fleeing a plague area; no, I liked just to be there, and to look back and savour it all.

Almost three days to get from Camp 1 down to the road. Pain was no stranger to me, and it was tough going, as ever when I covered long distances. This time will pass, was all I could tell myself; no, there was something else I could say, that it was worth it. Everyone felt the last stretch to be 'endless', but they could not have experienced the same enormous degree of relief that I did at the sight of the trees at the end of the valley. They waved in the wind like friends, and signalled, 'Here it all ends.'

Fernando waited with his pickup, and hugged me the way they do there, before driving the few miles back. We stank, of course, after all that time without a wash; now we were back in civilisation the shower was a great attraction. We ate beef and salad at Fernando's, and drank beer and wine. We were bound together like other parties I had seen there, and we succeeded in capturing the, sometimes elusive, joy of life.

People, places and the accomplishment of dreams. I was very, very fortunate. Life would not be frittered away on the mountains, it would be well spent; events had proved this to be so once more and would again, though I was taking the risk of meeting the devil of disappointment, because I wanted to go higher still.

An American expedition led by John Cleare, an English photographer and mountaineer, was heading for Muztagh Ata in China in July and August 1982, so I wrote to see if I could be accepted, and received a favourable reply. Muztagh Ata is 7,546 metres high. John did have some misgivings about my being on the trip, mostly because there were long distances to be covered on soft snow; we would need to ski, or accept a higher risk of failure through being on foot. Even for able-bodied people the walking option was considered gruelling; in 1947 Tilman and Shipton failed to make the summit on foot, and if two hard and proven expeditioners like them had failed what chance did I have? In Two Mountains and a River, Tilman tells of the snow's 'vile consistency' and said that long hours of cold and fatigue led to their giving up. Five earlier expeditions had failed on foot. John wanted everyone on his expedition to use skis and he was worried about my lack of experience in this respect. However, he was straight with me and was prepared to be flexible and to treat me as a special case who would work out his own best methods. For ascent, everyone else would have skins on their skis. Originally made from animal fur but nowadays artificial, skins grip the snow very effectively and prevent backward sliding, and the pile lies in such a way that the skis slide easily forward.

In order to augment my meagre skiing experience prior to the expedition, I went to the Dachstein glacier in Austria, in July 1982. Here one can ski year-round at about 2,700 metres. On a pair of hired skis I set off on the twisting cross-country track, and I learned quickly. What I learned I did not like, for it was soon evident that though on uphill slopes and on the level I could cope, going downhill was a different and wobbly procedure. Downhill skiing on one real leg, assisted by small outrigger skis fixed to crutches, is easier than most people believe, but for the double leg amputee it is another matter. The single leg amputee discards the artificial limb and relies on the good leg but obviously enough, if you have two artificial legs, you can't follow suit. It is not a question of lack of determination. I reached the conclusion that after a great deal of training over many months a double leg amputee might cope quite well, but the risk of injury from downhill skiing on high mountains would be far too great, and the consequences of injury were likely to be dire. Also, the victim might not be the only one to suffer, for companions might be forced to take extra risks and fail on their climb through having to divert their energies to a rescue. Even on the way up Muztagh Ata there would be much traversing to be done above cliffs and crevasses, perhaps on ice, and skiing competence was essential; no, I could not justify going on skis. So was this a reason why I should not join the expedition? Perhaps, but there might be a solution: how about snowshoes for ascent and a sledge made from skis and a rucksack frame for descent? I made a sledge and further strengthened the contraption with a crutch tied across as a strut and footrest, and from a hundred metres up a slope, which was beyond my skiing ability, I launched myself off. I picked up speed very rapidly and dug my ice-axe in the snow as an effective brake. It seemed a better method for me, but I knew the proof of the pudding could only be in the eating, on the mountain, under expedition conditions.

Nearly twenty-four hours of air travel took us to China's capital, Beijing. The concrete buildings of the airport might have been any modern airport anywhere in the world, and we went through the typical sausage-machine of baggage reclaim carousels, immigration and customs. Then John held up a card bearing characters saying Chinese

Mountaineering Association (was he holding it upside down, we wondered?) and their two representatives stepped forward and greeted us. They had laid on transport for the one-hour drive into the city, the first of many acts which cocooned us in this land where lack of the language could have been a great bother. The rest of the team, nine of them, arrived two days later, and we were all taken under the wing on the Chinese Mountaineering Association, who provided an interpreter and a liaison officer, and made hotel and transport arrangements for us, among many other things.

Our accommodation was more than satisfactory, in large and comfortably furnished, air conditioned rooms, usually with a settee, armchairs, two or four beds, a table or desk, and always there was a big, brightly painted thermos flask of hot water, cups, and a tin of tea leaves. Though knives and forks were available in dining rooms, we mastered the use of chopsticks to tuck into course after course of fish, mutton, kebabs, duck and bamboo shoots, rice, peppers, green beans, steamed bread and lobster. There was no shortage of beer, and most meals were rounded off with melon.

What we saw in and around Peking accorded with photographs and descriptions, as if the country had been showered with traditional symbols of Chinese style: straw hats and sunflowers, pony carts of melons, sedate cyclists on three-and-a-half million seemingly identical black bicycles for a city population not greatly in excess of twice that number; brown, blue and grey trousers and jackets, but bright skirts and dresses too, paddy fields, tall, straight trees, pagodas, chopsticks, rice and noodles and hundreds of varieties of food, modern and simple four to ten storey apartment blocks, wooden scaffolding, a few packed buses, many drab green lorries, the red star, portraits of Chairman Mao, posters exhorting good behaviour and very small families, and even some advertising consumer goods such as radios and television sets. People were placid and civil, and, as everyone knows, there are lots of people there. Yet Peking had none of the teeming feel of many cities because the streets are wide and there were few cars, and though China's enormous total of about one thousand million souls amounts to one quarter of the Earth's population they do have the third biggest country in which to spread out. I've heard tales of overcrowded homes and poverty but saw no evidence of this myself, and there seemed to be no slum areas like those in India or Peru. My short stays in civilised areas were sufficient to give me only a cursory impression, however, and left me unable to comment in any depth on life in China. Prices everywhere were fixed, so there was no haggling, nor any tipping in restaurants or elsewhere, as this practice was looked upon as corrupt, and akin to what we call bribery.

Anyone who travelled from the USA or Britain to Peking without visiting the Great Wall would be regarded locally as somewhat weird, so a visit was on our itinerary. There was time, too, to visit the Imperial Palace, known commonly to Westerners as the Forbidden City because ordinary people were not formerly permitted entry.

Our progress westwards took place on two consecutive days, on two flights of about three hours each, the first in a jet and the next in a rattling twin engined prop plane, over brown desert. On the second flight the air conditioning system was simple: everyone was given a fan. Between flights at the city of Urumchi, at the airport we happened to meet some of an expedition of eleven Austrians who had attempted Muztagh Ata. Three of them had reached the top, and several had been halted by the altitude. One had become very ill and was in hospital.

The second flight brought us to ancient Kashgar city, by which time we had flown about 2,250 miles (3,620 km) from Peking back towards England; John and I had backtracked almost the width of this huge country and our companions from the USA had completed a journey almost half way round the world. We stepped from the aircraft into a hot early afternoon in a land which in some ways seemed a thousand years behind the times. Adults and children in Muslim dress rode two-wheeled carts drawn by diminutive yet strong and resigned-looking donkeys, between mud-walled houses set along irrigation ditches lined by poplar. In other ways progress had touched the place, bringing in good roads and a few motor vehicles, including tractors, and lots of bicycles, and concrete buildings.

Casual tourists were not permitted in Kashgar, so our 'rare-bird' presence created great interest among the local inhabitants. They clustered around in polite, curious, smiling hundreds whenever we stopped in the city. There was less of the uniform Chinese dress in evidence, for the Kirghiz and Uighur people there have retained traditional dress of bright skirts and blouses and headscarves for the women and more sombre trousers, jackets and shirts for men. In Kashgar, as in Urumchi, our accommodation consisted of guest house rooms inside a compound, and meals were always rich and satisfying. Bathrooms were shared with local residents: large frogs, which hopped around the floors.

From Kashgar, we set off on an early morning chartered bus ride to try our fortunes on Muztagh Ata. The gravel road soon left behind the trees, mud buildings and sunflowers, and took us out into flat desert spotted with occasional oases, before running us along parallel to and in sight of the Silk Road. This formerly important trade route stretched about 4,350 miles (7,000 km) from eastern China to the Mediterranean and was used to transport the products of silkworm cocoons to Greece before the birth of Christ.

For hours we bumped up a deep canyon road, where gangs of men and women worked to counter the ravages of sliding rubble, rockfall and river. A hundred and more miles and nine hours went by, and a huge, shallow, silted lake surrounded by sand dunes, in a broad valley. We were drowsy from the heat. Then someone shouted. 'There she is!'

Our view across flat green pastures was of a massive domed mountain with a benign appearance, but no mountain of 7,546 metres can be climbed easily, as we were to discover. For all of us, bar John, this would be the highest summit we had attempted. Soft snow and altitude would make it hard, while crevasses and bad weather and altitude sickness would be the biggest risks.

We drove on for a while and pitched camp on a meadow at 3,800 metres, in sight of Muztagh Ata, the Ice Mountain Father. The full name is probably incorrect, as it is likely that the mountain was known simply as Muztagh, or Ice Mountain. The longer name is said to have originated when an explorer asked a local resident the name of this lofty peak and was told, 'Muztagh Ata', the 'Ata', or 'Father', being appended as a term of respect to the explorer himself.

Several dozen Kirghiz people lived locally in tents and rectangular flat-roofed, mud brick houses in the vicinity of two large lakes, the Karakol Lakes. Large audiences congregated to watch us.

On the evening of our first full day at the meadow camp, a day occupied with sorting and packing food and equipment, the leader of a five-man expedition from Colorado appeared with his interpreter. They were attempting Muztagh Ata.

'Got two missing,' he said. 'They went for the summit three days ago. Should have got back the same day.'

Being unacclimatised, there was nothing we could do but offer qualified optimism and sympathy, some food and beer, before the two men went on their way in a truck flagged down on the nearby road. They would report what had happened, to the authorities. They had talked of hiring a plane for a search, and someone had voiced our scepticism about the possibility and practicality of such a proposal in this remote corner of China. Next day we met the remainder of their expedition and learned that one of the missing pair had turned up, with considerable frostbite injuries after two bivouacs. The companion who had reached the summit with him, he said, had disappeared in bad visibility on the descent, and was presumed to have fallen over a cliff or into a crevasse. They achieved two out of five on the summit and lost one of them. So much for Muztagh Ata's benign look; it was just like any other big mountain. From a diary we found later it was clear that on setting up a camp at 6,400 metres the Coloradans had not been in good shape physically, and in consequence their morale was low. Three of the five said they could not go on, and two made the questionable decision to try to climb 1,200 metres to the summit in one push. In the Alps that height gain is commonly made in a day, but there are few climbers who can manage it safely above 6,000 metres, and they should be acclimatised and feel strong before setting out.

A week later, back at home in the flat we had bought recently (a nice place that Judy loved and had waited for for a long time) someone told her about a newspaper report concerning a man who had died on Muztagh Ata. His age was put at forty-one years, which was my age, and though the name reported was not mine she had a slight nagging doubt that the name was wrong. I had always impressed on her that she should not put too much trust in newspaper versions concerned with climbing, and that it was highly improbable that any newspaper would fail to mention my lack of legs if an accident befell me. Though she knew this to be true the death report reminded her that we were undertaking a serious venture. She had three worrying weeks to face.

On 2nd August we laid out our luggage before sixteen ruminant, reeking, twin-humped Bactrian camels, which continued grazing from a kneeling position while loading went on. A wide-nostrilled, 'looking down the nose' attitude gave them a haughty appearance. After loading, they ambled a sure-footed way through areas of grass, then dusty sand, then rocky slopes, to our base camp at 4,440 metres. The beasts groaned and snorted and squeaked complaints, but went obediently where they were led; small wonder, for each had a piece of rope attached to a hole in the nose and tied to the camel in front or held by the man at the head of a three or four camel column. Capable of carrying over 300 pounds (135 kg) each, they were a valuable link in the chain intended to get us to the summit, and saved us several days of carrying.

We settled in a grassy, stony depression by a stream, at the foot of the west flank of Muztagh Ata. In a day we could have walked into the USSR. Fourteen black or black and white yaks grazed quietly there by our camp. Yak: 'Long-haired humped, grunting ox' says one dictionary descriptively. Tilman and Shipton planned to use one such animal to carry equipment and food to base camp, and Tilman extolled their virtues at some length; he even listed as an advantage the fact that the yak's short legs and rapid steps give the rider the comfortable though false impression of getting somewhere quickly! He went on to say that their particular animal must have been the exception which proved the rule, or like all mountaineers yaks have their off days, for he 'very sensibly struck and sat down at the very first hint of what was expected of him.'

After the six failed attempts on Muztagh Ata, a combined Russian and Chinese expedition made the first ascent in 1956. The second success went to the Chinese in 1960, and one of the participants in it was Mr Qui Yin-Hua, who later joined a successful Everest expedition; he was our liaison officer. Mr Qui had no toes as a result of his climb on Everest, but gave the impression that he felt he had received good value in exchange for his extremities. Since the Chinese ascent Muztagh Ata had received no more human attentions until an American ascent in 1980, when foreign climbers were permitted into the area for the first time since 1949. In 1981 two expeditions, one American and one Canadian, put members on the top, and the Austrians I mentioned had three there. No Briton had succeeded.

We must carry to Camp 1. Loads had been prepared the night before. My load, a tent, food and skis. Straightforward going on a steep slope of stones and dirt, but oh, the altitude! And the sun sucking the liquid out of us. Janet Jensen, one of the two women on the trip, carried on for a long time despite frequent vomiting, but was eventually persuaded to turn back. The rest of us dumped our loads as planned at 5,100 metres, after a climb of between three and four hours, then set about laying out flat stones in a crazy paving base for tents. With a couple of tents up, we scurried down to base to eat and relax. The early days are hard at altitude; then it gets worse as you go higher.

Next day was similar: the haul amid small five-petalled flowers like primroses, others that might have been buttercups, then the pull up loose dirt and stones. Three carries to Camp 1 were required, but vomiting and stomach pains and back pains and diarrhoea disqualified me from the third. This was worrying because we were due to go up and occupy Camp 1 that day. From there the others would make three more excursions upwards, the last of these to occupy Camp 2. Two or three days of sickness could leave me weakened, and worse, I would fall behind in our acclimatisation programme. Our interpreter, Mr Su, fell ill too with a similar ailment to mine. He was a tall, slim and remarkable man aged thirty who, wishing to visit Urumchi from his home in Hanchow, had decided to equip his bicycle with a large water container and pedal his way there. The fact that he had over 3,000 miles to cover did not deter him, and in fifty-seven days he cycled across fertile plain and desert to Urumchi. There he soon found himself employment as an English interpreter with the Chinese Mountaineering Association, and this in itself was no mean feat because, during the Cultural Revolution, he had been sentenced to 'primitive work' rather than study, and his English was largely self-taught. He had climbed his form of mountain against the odds, and we could not fail to respect this man. As well as the liaison officer and interpreter, the Chinese Mountaineering Association provided us with a cook for base camp.

Two days with hardly any food was poor preparation for what might lie ahead, but those days saw me right, and Mr Su insisted on coming with me to Camp 1 to carry my crampons, sleeping bag and water bottles. We had been going for an hour when a figure appeared on the skyline. It picked its way down the stones and turned into Don Brown, a doctor, our oldest member at the age of sixty-four, and still very fit. Within the previous few years he had climbed Aconcagua and Mt. McKinley. Don was the only other person trying the mountain on snowshoes, and he had some devastating news for me.

'It's no good, it can't be done in snowshoes.'

'Why's that?'

'You just slip back on the slopes. It's too steep and too soft.'

'Good gracious me, what a shame,' I said – or words to that effect.

I stood on the stone slope with Don just a metre above as the news sank in, and I remembered that his snowshoes covered twice the area mine did and were therefore much more efficient. The Coloradan leader's verdict had been that it was virtually impossible without skis, owing to the soft going. After getting on the expedition and receiving generous sponsorship from Sony I was going to look silly, because I had been too ambitious. Any mountain of this altitude would force failure on to a large proportion of experienced, able-bodied climbers; I had not researched the route sufficiently and had not paid enough attention to how I might get up the soft snows. Hope had been allowed to lead, where soundly based experience should have been my guide. Don had made a mistake too, or had been given the wrong guidance, had recognised this, and had reached his decision: he was going home.

My conduct was different because I wanted to salvage anything I could from this personal fiasco. I would at least carry as much as I could as high as possible, and share a little of the victory of anyone who reached our objective. So I headed up to Camp 1 and soon met another descending figure, this time a haggard Ted Mayer, with whom I had climbed Aconcagua earlier in the year. He was ill and was therefore descending to base camp. He told us that of ten people who had set out the day before from Camp 1 to Camp 2 at 5,820 metres, only six had made the full distance. The others had to leave their loads part way. (So what chance was there for me? I couldn't help wondering.) At base camp Ted became so ill he was unable to ingest even water, so Don put him on an intravenous drip.

At Camp 1 the others descended from their second carry to Camp 2. The following day they would occupy that camp, but I agreed with John that it would be premature for me to stay there because I would be gaining altitude too quickly and risking altitude sickness. After carrying next day I would have to return to sleep at Camp 1 before carrying again the next day. 'To be quite honest,' John said 'if you get to Camp 2 I don't think you'll get any further.'

He was not being unnecessarily negative. He had seen what was ahead. John had supported my case for an attempt at the mountain even in the face of someone who had failed the year before and who had on the basis of that experience maintained it was absolutely beyond me. When I first planned to climb in the Alps, John had written me a very encouraging letter, and I knew he had an open mind.

It looked bad for me, but hope was not entirely extinguished. If the snow froze hard enough during the night and I started very early and reached Camp 2, I might still be in the running. I had been ill and was less well acclimatised and the ascent of the next 730 metres had stopped four out of ten of them, including the only one on snowshoes, but if I did not make a good showing on the next carry it was clear that my hopes could be extinguished altogether.

Now I was committed to snowshoes because I had left my ski boots at base camp. Without them it was not possible to wear the skis, and I could not afford another day descending and re-ascending to and from base.

A three-quarter moon lit the chilly way and I was off two hours or more before the others. China has no time zones, just the same time throughout the whole vast country, but making an allowance of two and a half hours for our being so far west of Peking my departure was at the equivalent of 4 a.m. The early start up a rib of small, sharp rocks got me at dawn on to easy angled ice where crampons were necessary; firm snow slopes followed. There was no more rock between here and the summit. By 10 a.m. the first sliver of sunlight flashed over the mountain which stood ahead of me; the orb appeared rapidly to banish blue shadows and soften the snow. Sun, you're softening my snow. Go and put on a cloak of cloud, there's a good sun.

An hour later I was sinking to the knee and forced to resort to the snowshoes. With them strapped on all went well for a few minutes on level snow, and then came a gentle slope of thirty degrees. I went at it, but the front edges of the snowshoes broke through the crust and I floundered again at knee depth. The baskets (rounds, like those on ski sticks) on my crutches sank thirty centimetres, sixty, sometimes so deep that my hands were buried in the snow. Many a time a step up resulted in collapsed snow and I would drop back to where I had been. Don said it was impossible; for twenty minutes I fought to rise fifteen metres and I knew that at that rate I would have to give up and accept what he had said. On top of that, if I reached Camp 2 John doubted I would manage what followed. Was it worth this unequal struggle?

I stumbled on, up to the knees in snow, and dragged the big feet out, and went in up to the wrists and sank occasionally to the top of one thigh and battled to get that damned leg out and then went in to crotch level on both legs. Oh for a rock ridge or face, quite steep, so effort would be rewarded with height gain! Oh for some ice! When the crutches were laid parallel to the snow like they were skis they did not sink so deep, no more than half a metre, and that helped a little, but the altitude would not let me fight all the way up in conditions like these. I was virtually crawling much of the time and that rate of progress was out of the question, and in any case this would lead to frost-bitten fingers. It was not the sort of thing that fighting could overcome; no amount of determination would bring success, unless I risked stepping from the firm land of judgement into the mire of foolhardiness. Only a man who could walk on water had any chance here without skis. It would be grossly wrong to jeopardise the lives of the others by becoming an exhausted, frostbitten, altitude sick casualty requiring rescue, and even if rescue proved safe it would be selfish to affect adversely their chances of success.

Despair was close upon me, but had not yet seized an unbreakable hold. Try taking the slope at a gentler angle, I suggested to myself, and started on the first zig of what I hoped might be a lengthy series of zig zags. The snowshoes sank only half as deeply. Oh joy! For the time being I could carry on. Soon the slope eased off to almost level ground and the snow became firm in most places.

There was a crevassed area which could not be avoided because the crevasses came in from the right towards a rock cliff falling away for six hundred metres on the left, and I had to go up a snow ramp in between. This ramp not only sloped down towards me, but was also canted down from right to left, from crevasses towards cliff. The latter gradient was such that anyone who slipped might slide over the cliff edge. Where the ramp narrowed to thirty metres between the crevasses and the cliff, some of the skiers had been quite scared, particularly on descent.

It was a true Scylla and Charybdis. The higher one went up the right side of the ramp, the greater the crevasse danger. Reducing the crevasse problems involved keeping closer to the big drop; my choice was to keep quite low there and trust to the ice-axe pick on one crutch to brake me if I slipped. In some places it was preferable to wear crampons, for there were intermittent patches of ice or hard snow, but mostly it was so porridgy or fluffy that snowshoes reduced the possibility of breaking through into crevasses, of which there were some even low down the ramp near the cliff. Before venturing further I consciously rehearsed in my mind how I would hurl the pick into the snow or ice if I slipped: an unarrested slide would have me over the edge in five seconds. A high level of desire for the objective pushed fear, to a great extent, to the back of my mind.

Spikes on my crutches gave considerable security and as long as I kept my eyes open the crevasses did not seem to be too much of a menace. By looking up the ramp rightwards, often I could see where the wider part of the split in the ice showed, being too wide to be bridged by snow, and this gave a clue to the line. On the lower side there was sometimes evidence of the awful hole in the form of a slight concave trough in the snow. Seven or eight crevasses that were big enough to be dangerous were identified and I went further down towards the cliff to avoid them, or prodded with the crutches and found a firm place to cross, or took a big step-cum-leap across.

In fifteen minutes the snow ramp took me up to where I could rise rightwards and away from the cliff, and the crevasse hazards grew less. Having been going for seven hours I needed to get to camp 2 soon in order to leave myself enough energy for the descent. Crevasses would be less well bridged then because of the sun's work, and I did not want to go doddering down in a weary state. My pace was falling rapidly through prolonged exertion at such an altitude. Several people had said the trudge to Camp 2 was exhausting, and indeed four had not completed the distance at the first try, so I had a very real fear that I might spot the camp at such a distance that a retreat was the only way. However, I topped a rise and there were the two tents, only fifteen minutes away. I knew then a slender chance still existed that I would go for the top.

Colin and Bob, two doctors who had teamed up and climbed

together, arrived at Camp 2 shortly after me. I got the impression that they were very aware of the threat which hangs over all doctors on expeditions: that their chances might be destroyed if they had to attend to a patient over a prolonged period.

Having constructed my sledge I started down, meeting Steve McKinney, the deputy leader, then John, then Grim, Johan and Mary, toiling under huge loads in the heat of the day. Grim, whose real name was Jim Wilson, was a forty-four year old psychology and economics teacher, tall and very strong on his quite spindly legs. He proved to be a reliable and considerate companion, and his good manners caused him to draw apart if others of us became too riotous; he was PC before the term had evolved. Johan Hultin was fifty-seven years old, a runner who kept himself very fit, a wine loving pathologist who came originally from Sweden before going to live in the USA. Mary Laucks was a physics student on the way to a PhD and at twenty-six was our youngest member. She was broad shouldered and strong, but not so heavy as to prevent her being also a fast long-distance runner. The other woman in the party, Janet Jensen, was an easygoing, smiling accountant, a resident of Honolulu. She travelled extensively, was a pilot and sub-aqua diver, and was at ease with the world because she was at ease with herself.

The sledge worked quite well where the snow was steep, but would go only straight downhill, with no means of steering. This style of transport was of limited use because our route traversed a lot; straight downhill would take me over the cliff in the upper section between Camps 1 and 2. Still, I managed half a dozen exhilarating runs of up to sixty metres. I regretted not having brought up my ski boots from base, but my boats were burnt now. Even if I did not risk downhill skiing, ascent on skis and descent by sledge and on foot was looking like the best procedure for me.

At one point, as I dragged the sledge on a rope behind me across a slope, one leg went all the way into a crevasse. With the crutches I was able to prod about and find its line, and roll clear.

Janet had been ill and had not carried to Camp 2 that day, but she intended to go with me next day. At 5 a.m. it was snowing, at 6 a.m. snowing still, and the sky did not become clearer until 10 a.m. The weather was unsettled and the snow would be soft, so we waited a further day and started out at 5.45 a.m. There followed over nine disgruntled hours of thrashing a way up a snow cover much worse than on the previous journey. Despite the early start there was only one short slope where crampons could be used. The rest was just slope after slope of grunts and misery and gasping. On skis, Janet managed much better than I.

At Camp 2 we learned that Bob, Colin and Steve had set up Camp 3 at 6,400 metres the day before and returned for a day off, while John, Grim and Johan went up. The latter trio arrived back at 7.45 p.m. and one look at their drawn faces told all.

'It's very serious above here, man,' John said.

In poor visibility he had not found Camp 3 so the loads had been dumped (very near Camp 3, as it transpired) and the descent by compass had called for a lot of skill from John. There was talk of awful crevasses and steep ice, and though he did not say it I knew John felt I should not go higher.

'Looks like this may be as high as I go,' I offered, to make it easier for him.

'It would help to have someone in support here.'

I hardly needed to ask my next question.

'You think I shouldn't go any further?'

'Yes, it's serious.'

There was no argument. I had said all along that I would stop if we thought it wise. I could still help by getting breakfast and melting snow to fill water bottles for the six who had elected to go on, Bob, Colin, Johan, Grim, Steve and John. And it might prove useful to have someone rested and standing by at Camp 2, as John had suggested, in case someone was ill or injured.

So I 'mother henned' a few hours away next day, watched the lucky ones go, and wished I was going too. At the same time I knew if I went higher the soft snow would probably defeat me.

Mary had a bad headache, but her appetite had not failed. She and Janet planned to descend the next day, but their plans were about to be influenced by a third party; in the early evening Ted arrived, glazed-eyed.

'Oh, God, that was tough!' he said in a breaking voice, as he slumped into a tent. 'Janet, can you undo my laces?'

He had been unable to eat for three days and had had his fluids via an intravenous drip, so it was not surprising that he had found it hard between 1 and 2.

'You're not aiming to go higher, are you?' I asked him.

'I'm gonna do it!'

'We'll see. Right now I don't think you should.'

'I know when to turn back.'

'I think that time's come.'

Janet joined in and we tried to impress on Ted that he had been ill and was behind in acclimatisation, that he would have to cross crevasses alone, that we would not know if he met up with the others or not, that Camp 3 was not easily found, that there might be no tracks to follow because of the wind filling them in, that if he became ill some if not all of the others might have to descend with him, and that John had said Ted should not climb any higher. Throughout all this Ted was unbending in his resolution to carry on. He was certainly not short on determination.

Next day when I enquired how he was Ted said, 'I feel great. This will be a rest day. The altimeter shows bad weather.'

We all got together in one tent for a pow wow. Janet, Mary and I repeated our concern about Ted climbing but he said he was going and why didn't we help by carrying part of his load for him? We said we would not do anything to encourage him and the debate heated up. Mary began to take on an angry, hawk like appearance and to me looked like she was going to give Ted a nasty pecking. Mary and Janet wanted to descend but Janet suggested they might wait one more day in case Ted got ill and needed to be helped down. He had hardly eaten, and vomited during the day. Janet's consideration for Ted was all the more admirable because she had herself vomited and brought up blood during the night. I favoured her going down that day, but she made her decision and stayed, as did Mary. In any case the wind got up.

'I am frightened of the steep bit above the cliff,' Janet confided to me. 'I keep thinking about it, especially at night.'

When you are not well the character of any mountain changes for the worse in your eyes. Muztagh Ata, though in truth neutral, now appeared nasty to Janet.

'I can rope you down,' I said. 'No problem.'

'It's amusing,' Janet said. 'Here you have two helpless females and a sick man and you have to guide them down.'

'Helpless' was a bit strong, but as the day wore on Mary's condition gave greater cause for concern because her headache continued despite sleep and aspirin. That was a bad sign, and her appetite deteriorated.

After Ted had vomited I asked him again if he was going down the next day.

'I'll decide in the morning.'

Though he insisted he would climb, Ted didn't eat supper, and looked grey and ill when I took him a drink.

The night was very windy and I grew concerned that the opportunity for descent had not been grasped at the right time the day before, when there had been no doubt everyone could get along on their own two feet.

Anyone who became worse through the altitude could deteriorate very rapidly towards a critical condition. But Ted's presence had complicated the issue.

Friday the 13th dawned.

'Have you got an oven in there?' Ted shouted to me above the wind, from his tent. It took a while for it to sink in that this was not a joke, and he meant a stove. Only rarely did he get a word wrong like that and remind us of his German origins. I passed him the stove and he boiled some water for drinks and cereals. I felt better disposed towards him and asked if he was going down.

'I'm under no pressure.'

This noncommittal reply swayed my decision towards seeing Janet and Mary down first. When the wind dropped, around noon, I set off a little ahead of them, down a gently sloping snowfield. Janet and Mary were worried about icy conditions and soon removed their skis, and Mary, troubled by cold feet, hurried on ahead without a rope. I waited where the crevasses lay close to the cliff edge.

'You want a rope here, Janet?'

'I'm scared shitless.'

I took that to mean yes, set up a belay with an anchor known as a 'dead-man' (a metal plate hammered into the snow), an ice-axe and a crutch, tied the rope on her and fed it out as she descended a rope's length. After four or five more rope lengths she was on safe ground, half an hour below Camp 2. She joined Mary and they waved goodbye.

Now, what about Ted? I could not know, until I had almost completed the ascent back to Camp 2, that there was nothing to do about him. Just before that camp came into view I looked up and saw a dark figure moving slowly up a snow ridge, a hundred metres above. Ted had 'summit fever', no mistake about that.

Should I follow? I came down on the side of no, because by the time I packed he would be an hour or so ahead. Deciding what to take would be a problem because I did not know what Ted had in the way of food and fuel and stove. The snow would be soft. I didn't like the look of the weather either, with dark cloud swelling in from the south west; it would help no one if we became separated. Above all, the others planned to go for the summit in two days and we two could not acclimatise properly nor sensibly ascend nearly 1,800 metres in that time. John had had a bad, barking cough and it was quite likely that one or two of the six would be forced to descend and could report whether Ted had found Camp 3. If he had not, then someone would have to go to look for him, if enough fuel and rations remained. I would be fresh.

On Friday 13th and Saturday 14th I sat at the camp on the bottom edge of the huge, tilted snow bowl, and wondered what was going on high up the mountain. I tried to sort out in my mind how I would cope with the disappointment of my failure; if they all failed, too, it would be even worse. It was something I would have to face, though, if I kept pushing my limits on serious expeditions on mountains of this scale; to aim for the extreme of what you can achieve is to court disappointment at the same time. I could not complain about the results of previous expeditions, for on each occasion I had been successful in one way or another. Of course, I did now and then wonder if there was any twist of fate that might result in my having a shot at the summit, but it would need a miracle now.

The dead Coloradan's cassette player and some tapes had been left in one of the tents, and I played the theme music from Chariots of Fire, which finished with a resounding version of Jerusalem. 'Bring me my chariot of fire!' affected me deeply, for now there was no way I could reach the summit, save through that unforeseeable miracle. But my mood lifted, for the music had a profound effect in such high, beautiful and lonely surroundings. Now I knew better what people meant when they said sometimes that they were inspired, often in an unconnected area of life like work or health or grief, by a runner or a writer, a musician or a mountaineer. If my chance came, I felt able to draw on better reserves.

At 1 p.m. on 15th August, Steve skied rapidly down, forth and back, forth and back, steeply across the slope above camp 2. (He reckoned he did not exceed forty miles an hour!) Why would he descend? Was he ill? Had there been an accident? He drew to a halt by the tents.

'Hi, Steve. You seen Ted?'

'Yes. He missed Camp 3 and spent the night out. There was a big argument with John who said he should go down and Ted said he was going to solo it.'

Steve unfolded the story. While carrying from Camp 3 to Camp 4 they had come across Ted sleeping in the snow, two hundred metres above Camp 3. At first they had thought him to be the missing Coloradan.

'Hello, Robert,' Ted had greeted Steve.

'I'm Steve. Camp 3 is two hundred metres below here. Down there.' He pointed it out. 'You go down there and rest. We'll see you when we get back from this carry.'

'OK, Robert.'

On their return from Camp 4 Ted was still lying in the snow so he was escorted to Camp 3, where he was not made welcome. He had

176

insisted he would solo the climb if no one else would go with him and the argument with John followed. Steve had stepped in to say that as it was clear Ted was determined to climb he would wait for a day and attempt the summit with him. In opting to do this Steve showed an exceptional spirit of unselfishness, for if the weather turned bad his chance of reaching the summit could disappear. In any case Ted had not had so much time to acclimatise and might prove to be a slow companion. On top of that, as Ted's presence had strained food and fuel resources, Steve chose to descend to Camp 2 to replenish supplies while Ted rested. Steve had shown that there was more to the man than just the will, and the ability, to win.

'Conditions are firm above here,' he said to me. 'Why don't you come up to camp 3? You could carry some food and fuel for us.'

I was packed in a shade over the time it takes fast runners to cover a mile. At that stage we planned no further ahead than that I should carry to Camp 3 and stay the night there. But did this change everything? It was unlikely, for it would take a long time to climb 1800 metres at a pace which would avoid altitude sickness. But still, without being over optimistic, I once more began to allow myself to toy with the idea that there was a possibility that I might be about to reach my highest summit. Perhaps my chariot of fire had arrived.

With four bottles of fuel and plenty of food, as well as my sleeping bag and other necessities, I set off ahead of Steve, up a steep snow ramp above an awful cliff of ice. Within twenty minutes I was breaking through the snow crust to the knee. For one, two, three, four, five, six steps I sank right in. It can't be done if there's much more of this, I told myself, but it became easier. By 3 p.m. I was starting up the steep back wall of an amphitheatre of snow and ice, and an hour and a half more put me nearly at the top of a second amphitheatre. The last hundred metres made me fight and pray for firmness in place of the feathery stuff that yielded underfoot. Steve easily caught up near Camp 3 and showed me where it was, tucked away in a crevasse ten metres wide and thirty metres long, a navel in a vast snow belly. Four hours and twenty minutes to gain six hundred metres was satisfactory at that altitude.

As I crawled into the tent Steve had a surprise to reveal.

'I have to tell you now, John asked me to tell you to go down. But things have changed.'

'You did right, taking the initiative when things changed.'

'Hope John thinks so.'

As he had taken the risk of ignoring John's instructions, we concocted several slightly altered versions of what had happened. We found it difficult, however, to settle on the best version, so in the end I said I would explain everything to John when the time was right.

Earlier differences with Ted were forgotten; Steven's action poured oil on troubled waters. I had felt no ill will towards Ted, in any case, even though our judgement of what his behaviour should be did differ.

Steve and Ted planned to climb to Camp 4 next day and stay there for the night, then try for the summit. I knew it would be unwise for me to go with them, for that would mean a height rise of 1,200 metres in not much over twenty-four hours. At this altitude that would be asking for trouble. The only comfort was that I had carried up enough food and fuel to give this pair a fighting chance, but here again was the dreadful 'd', disappointment.

Climbing is a game of vicissitudes and the door I thought had closed did open a little again, for next day's weather was bad and forced everyone on the mountain to rest. If it had been fine I would have been left behind.

Our five friends at Camp 4 were not able to make their move for the summit. 'What a storm!' Grim wrote. 'Tents securely fastened to huge blocks of snow and ice. I cannot help but think how the situation could become desperate if the storm really sets in; no way one would want to move up or down.'

Throughout that day we downed hot drinks and took many a swig of water, for this would aid acclimatisation. Our aim throughout the ascent was to pass copious quantities of clear urine, and we often had someone or other announcing happily, 'My pee's clear.'

A nine and a half hour test of strength next day started easily enough on firm snow, which could be cramponed, but close to camp 4, at 7,000 metres, my happy world was transformed to one of torment as I plunged in to the knee and mid thigh. With one hundred and fifty metres still to gain I had started by trying to do forty steps without stopping, but soon it got so bad I was having to fight for one step at a time. Up to then I had been in front of or just behind Ted all the way, but now he and Steve drew far ahead on their skis. In half an hour they were at the tent on the level space hacked from a slope; I prepared myself for fifty minutes, but that time elapsed and I was still snowploughing a deep trench. There was a long, long way to go.

Five people had been skiing slowly into sight above Camp 4 for some time. They made many, many turns to descend the slope very gradually. Three of them came down further past the camp, and I was able to congratulate each in turn: John, Grim and Johan. With Bob and Colin they had made it to the summit in four hours from Camp 4. In

Grim's words, 'John's hands frostbitten; he was beat. Bob very cold – could not get camera out. Johan's camera frozen.' Now the pair of doctors occupied one tent there while the trio was on the way to the next camp to leave a tent vacant for us, the new arrivals.

'I'm sorry plans have changed without an opportunity to communicate with you,' I told John.

'Changed for the better,' he said. 'Good luck tomorrow, man.'

I looked at three exhausted men descending on their real legs, and wondered what I was doing there. Without skis, having been ill, and perhaps being behind with acclimatisation, what was I doing there? The collapsing snow was almost impossible to climb and I was gaining less than thirty metres on hour. Thirty metres an hour! I considered stopping for three or four hours to get the freeze on my side, but if I was to have a chance the next day I had to get some rest, and lots of liquid. So I went on, taking the slope in the gentlest of zig zags. I would raise the left leg and it would sink half a metre, then as soon as I lifted the right leg the left would go in even deeper, to be joined by the other one. I would pull the left one up with the assistance of the left hand and the motion would put the right one in even deeper. I would step up after dragging the right one out, but the snow would collapse and the right snowshoe would come down on top of the left, trapping it. The snow around the hole made by the legs would fall in, increasing the weight to be lifted at the next go, so I needed to pull with a hand again. I would prod with the crutches in an effort to find a firm spot, two firm spots, but as soon as I put any weight on them down I would sink and crutches and both feet too, and the weight of my pack would bend me almost double. Oh God! How could I gain nearly one hundred and fifty metres like this when it needed a rest after just one step up, when it was so hard to breathe, so hard to take one step? For every step I had to make up my mind and say, get ready, and now, go! And sometimes a step took me no higher because the snow was crushed underfoot.

This was one of the toughest days I've spent on a mountain. Forget about grades in the normal sense; grade 3 snow and ice would have been easier, even up there. People see the photographs afterwards, pictures of quite gentle slopes, and they say, 'Looks easy.' 'Fools,' you think, but no, they are right. It looks easy; no photograph can capture the agonies of altitude, and particularly of that day.

How long could I go on like this, approaching 7,000 metres? Hell, it was hard, it was hard. In a state of utter frustration I muttered and shouted, 'Poxy bloody snow!' and a dozen profane variations. I bellowed, 'I'll be up to my tits in snow!' and was amused at suddenly hearing myself shouting at the unhearing white mantle up there. I calmed down and got on with it. It would have been possible to deceive myself that I was close to the end of my tether, but experience told me I was not. There was enough 'keep-going' within me for a while.

The last hundred metres rise did not release me from its grip for over three hours. Steve had some hot food ready but I could not eat. My body shuddered with coughing and retching.

'How about tomorrow?' he asked.

'Day after,' I replied. 'I'm wiped out.'

'Can't. We'd miss our flights to Beijing.'

Our schedule was closing in.

'See how you feel tomorrow,' Steve went on. 'A night's rest can change everything.'

'Right. I recover quickly. If nothing else, this is the highest I've climbed, and I can add to that a bit.'

If I encountered snow like that just below Camp 4, I was doomed to failure. I think Ted was concerned about my holding him back, because he asked, 'Will we keep Norman in sight all the time?'

'Can't say. Depends on the terrain,' Steve replied.

'Don't worry, Ted. If I have to I'll turn back. I'm not going to get in your way.'

We settled down in a very tired state, and Ted started groaning with the cold. It had been minus 10F (-23C) at camp 3, and here it was much colder.

'To think we're all volunteers,' I said to Steve, and we giggled a bit, more than we would have done at sea level.

August 18 was Steve's twenty-ninth birthday. I wanted him to have the summit for a present, and I wanted to be there to see him get it. We were unsure about the weather at first, and made a late start at 1 p.m. Immediately above the tent I sank deep. Hell, this mountain was keeping me guessing to the end. Soon, however, I was walking a firm crust of up to five centimetres overlying powdery snow. If I sank at all it was only fifteen centimetres. Steve went ahead and I hung on to Ted's tail, within forty metres.

In two and a half hours I reckoned we were at 7,300 metres. At least I had surpassed my previous altitude best by a wide margin; yet I took little comfort from this. Perhaps within my grasp at last, perhaps not, the very capriciousness of the attempt on this summit had increased the sense of challenge, and I opened my mind rather more to the option of a bivouac if the snow conditions demanded this. The snow remained firm; if only it was like that all the way to the summit . . .

After three and a half hours of uniform, gently-angled crusty snow that looked like slabs of polystyrene, I saw that Steve had stopped two hundred metres ahead. His skis stood up in the snow. Could he be on the summit? Don't raise your hopes, I told myself. It is what it is.

He put his skis on and moved up again, and I was pleased not to have fallen victim to false hope.

The wind began to assert itself after Steve's brief halt. 'In early June on the North Col of Everest one could not experience such cold,' Tilman wrote of his mid-August attempt on Muztagh Ata.

We had been going for four hours when Steve approached a rock hump, big as a large whale, slightly to the right of the line we were taking. Two hundred metres to the left of that hump was another, well to our left. First Steve climbed the right hump, then started traversing to the other, which looked higher. Yes, I thought, that's higher. It must be the summit, and I headed for it. Ted, who was a few metres ahead, wanted the nearer hump to be the summit, simply because it was nearer, and he went that way. Within a few minutes, I had joined Steve and he was crying.

'I've just thrown the bones off,' he said.

He had been carrying some of the ashes of a thirty-seven year-old man who had died in his sleep, and whose brother had asked Steve to throw them from the summit. The successful ascent and this act together had a deep effect on us, for we were still alive, really alive.

'Well done, stormin' Norman,' Steve said.

Ted made it ten minutes later and I let out a Hee-ahh! war cry; just like a bloody American, I thought.

It was too cold for Steve to remove his mittens to operate my little camera, but though all the shots of me on the summit came out framed by wool, I treasure them.

There is a legend among the local nomadic people that an ancient city lies atop Muztagh Ata, dating back to times of peace and happiness. The city has had no contact with the rest of the world, and happiness and peace continue there, without death, cold, darkness or ageing, and fruit trees bear all year round. We felt old and cold, I can tell you, and death and darkness were not far from our thoughts, and we saw no fruit trees; yet it was true that none of the troubles of the lower earth had followed us up there, and none of them could later spoil the experience.

We returned to Camp 4 that day, and set off for Camp 2 or further down next day. However, we had descended no lower than Camp 3 when Ted had had enough for the day. We could not leave him there alone, partly because he had not been doing his share of the cooking, and it was essential that he should be encouraged to keep up his liquid intake. Steve decided, and I agreed, that it was best for him to ski down to let the others know we 'back-markers' should appear at base camp next day, and he went swiftly on his way. Since until a few weeks before he had held the world record for speed skiing at 125.7 miles per hour (201 km/hr) Steve was the man for the job. In three or four hours he would be at base camp. 'As time went on we could see Steve coming down,' it said in Grim's diary. 'And with good news – whew!!! I really was expecting the worst – I don't know why.' But for Ted and me, things were not going to be straightforward; there was a little drama in store for us.

Grim's words tell what was going on at base camp: 'What a scene here tonight. After beer and shrimp cocktail, a huge dinner with about ten dishes. Ne (the cook) had worked all day on this – chicken, peanuts, rice, potatoes and mushrooms, soup, peppers, pork and melon, plus some wine Qui had brought and served now he knew everyone was safe. And a birthday cake for Steve, which Mary and Jan and Ne had made from scratch. John at his best with mountain stories, tales, songs. All this in the middle of Asia. A setting to remember!'

The words 'everyone was safe' turned out to be premature. We were not all safe. Not yet. Not by a long way.

Throughout the night in our dome tent Ted had groaned and muttered, 'Oh, God!' I thought little of it, having heard him when he was cold at Camp 4. But this time it was not the cold which created his discomfort, but something much more serious, as I discovered in the morning.

'Norman, I'm snowblind.'

Snowblindness is a temporary, very painful condition. He was not totally without vision, but would have to be guided down.

'It may take a while but I'll get you down,' I said. 'Did you take your goggles off yesterday?'

'Yes, it was overcast.'

'Fool'

The weather was not in our favour, for we were faced with a whiteout, in which it is impossible to distinguish between the snow and the cloud. Visibility was as low as four metres. Ted wanted to wait, I preferred to avoid any delay that might cause others to come up to look for us. They had made the ascent with a few resultant minor frostbite injuries and had probably got down safely, and it was time to get away. Any attempts on their part to re-ascend to camp 2 or Camp 3 would involve a certain amount of additional risk which could be avoided if we headed down. Ted was hardly in a strong position to argue.

Once we were packed and the tent down I moved out of the crevasse into thick whiteness. We had marked the upper part of the route with wands, bamboo sticks supporting thin orange flags, and though they were spaced two or three hundred metres apart and therefore much too far apart for us to follow under prevailing conditions, they would give us reassurance every so often on our long and meandering descent of this white wilderness.

A brief gap in the cloud was enough; I drew an arrow in the snow towards the first wand below Camp 3, then waited for Ted to come towards me. He could not see well enough to pick out my tracks and spotting a wand was out of the question for him, but he could follow my vague outline if I did not get too far ahead. We reached the first wand, and the slope and memory told me which way to go to the next. There it was, and another, and another, but then the slope eased. It was essential that we maintained contact with the line of wands. Later it would become easier because John had written the compass bearing from one wand to the next on each little flag, but this had not been done on the upper section.

'We'd better sit and wait for a while in case it clears, Ted.'

Ten minutes later he said, 'It's getting better,' and it got much worse. After sitting on the slope for half an hour Ted said, 'It's getting worse, isn't it?' and the cloud cleared briefly. My head was going left, right, left, right, like it was on a swivel, and there, two hundred metres away, was a wand. I took a compass bearing before it disappeared in a cloak of white.

'Right, Ted. Two seven five degrees. Let's go.'

'Can you help me up?'

The past few days had taken their toll and his pack was heavy. Pain is tiring too. His fatigue was not serious at this stage and at our deliberately slow and cautious pace, but it would have to be borne in mind. Had I known the true cause of his tiredness I would have been more concerned; Ted had amoebic dysentery.

'I'm surprised he had the strength to accomplish what he did,' Don wrote to me. 'For he truly risked his life for that summit.' The ailment that had seized him, as it might have taken any of us, induced in him fever and fatigue, and could get worse, with abscesses on the liver and other complications.

So there I was, descending in a whiteout from 6,400 metres, with a snowblind man who had amoebic dysentery. I opted to go unroped because it was highly unlikely that Ted, on skis, would break through into a crevasse if I had gone ahead on foot without doing so. Also, if I fell into a crevasse when roped to him it was quite likely I would pull him in after me.

'I guess we feel a little like warriors just home from battle, yet there is some anxiety about the others', Grim wrote. 'Mr Qui perched on his rock, with John's binoculars, looking for signs of them. A storm brewing on the summit. I bet it's wild up there now. The mountain looks so big and majestic.'

We walked on a bearing, slid a hundred metres down a slope, walked a bit further, and reached the wand.

'We're at the wand, Ted.'

'You son of a gun! You did it!'

'I know the approximate direction so we might as well go forward on two seven five and see if we come on to the next wand. If we don't we can follow our tracks back.'

We advanced for three or four long minutes but saw no wand. Visibility was at its worst by then. Two metres away, below on a gentle slope, I could just make out a slight trough in the snow.

'Stop there, Ted. Take a rest. I think there's a crevasse in front of us.'

My eyes played tricks in the everywhere whiteness and many times put an instant mirage wand where there was none. Another break in the cloud showed us we had done right by waiting, for there really was a dangerous crevasse just in front of us. We had to detour right, where a sharp change on the line of the wands showed how others had gone around the hazard. Having followed their example we slid easily for a hundred metres, Ted on skis, me on my bottom. By then he was finding it difficult to sideslip down behind me, because he was so weak, so he removed his skis and copied my method of descent.

We struck it lucky with brief breaks in the cloud and several times I was able to get a bearing on a wand and march towards it by compass. Then we came across the first of the bearings John had marked on the little flags, and those took us close to Camp 2 and out of the cloud. Bless you, John.

Picking our way between the crevasses below camp 2 was a slow business. The ramp was much more icy than previously, and Ted was tired, but his vision seemed if anything improved, and he moved well and without any fuss. It was after 5 p.m. when John and Steve, who had been waiting anxiously, saw us from near base camp. A slide of one hundred and fifty metres on a snow covered ice slope took us on to the stony rib which led to Camp 1. Mr Su waited for us there and took charge of Ted.

I was at base camp by 8.30 p.m., an hour and a half ahead of Ted, who looked fit to drop when he arrived. I had hurried down to let John and Steve know we were all right, but having seen we were safe they had already descended to our meadow camp. Considerately, they had left us each a bottle of beer, and three camels with a driver, so we too could go down to the meadow camp that night. At 10.30 p.m. Mr Su, Ted and I clambered on board the three animals and swayed forth and back for three hours in the near dark. As we picked a way through boulders, Muztagh Ata put on a ferocious thunderstorm, telling us we had been allowed up once, and down too, but not to take any ascent for granted. With the emu-style head bobbing up and down ahead against the moonscape scenery I could sit back and reflect, and thank God for my good fortune. If John had opted for three camps instead of four I would not have made it. If Ted had not forced his way up contrary to the judgement of the rest of us, Steve would not have descended to Camp 2 for supplies and would not have encouraged me to go up; Ted's determination had helped me. If I had accepted that as Don could not get by on snowshoes I would do even worse – not an unreasonable conclusion – I might have given up. If we had had good weather on one particular day at Camp 3 I would have been left behind. If Steve had been a lesser man neither Ted nor I would have had such an opportunity for success.

At 1.30 a.m. our little caravan reached the meadow. The docs took Ted to a tent, gave him something to kill his pain, and bandaged his eyes. Just about everybody turned out to shake hands or give us a slap on the back or a hug, and fetch a beer or some tea, and our camp was a happy place. There was such pleasure to be found then simply from a mug of hot tea, and from time to relax, to relish the past few days and the friendship of our tiny band which had worked so hard towards our objective, from the time to think about the beauty of where we had been. The sense of joy and well-being! And of relief!

'Well done, Norm,' John said. 'There are not many here who could have got him down in a whiteout.'

I passed it off, saying, 'I was only trying to get myself down. Couldn't shake Ted off. Bugger kept following me,' and we laughed, but I did feel very pleased to have had something useful to do.

A bandaged and therefore sightless Ted was led on to our bus, and we drove back to Kashgar. The rest is a happy blur; a visit to a market, a department store, gentle crowds around us again; an orchard where young men and women in bright costumes danced and sang and played musical instruments for us; a banquet, a craft shop, the flight to

Urumchi, a jade factory, another three hour flight to Peking, a second banquet with officials of the Chinese Mountaineering Association. At both banquets, apart from being served course after course of tasty food, we were introduced to 'mao-tai'. Served in glasses about right for eggcups, if you like thrushes' eggs, neither the volume nor the appearance betrayed the power lying in this colourless spirit. The tradition is to call out 'Gan-bei', which as far as I could ascertain is the Chinese equivalent of 'Bottoms Up', and down the liquid dynamite in one go. We did. 'Gan-bei' followed 'Gan-bei' in rapid succession, as is the way. Leader, deputy leader, oldest gent, females and amputee received particularly attentive hospitality, i.e. constantly topped-up glasses. I have it from reliable opinion that immediately after descent from high altitude the effect of alcohol is at least doubled, so we as the 'away team' were soon wrapped in the arms of 'mao-tai' and 'Gan-bei' and proclaiming deep friendships with the people of China; those friendships were sincere. And they were reciprocated. Some of the politics of this nation were at variance with those of our individual members, but as ordinary people we were friends.

Ted's bandages were removed and his sight was back to normal. We started putting back on the weight we had lost. John had shed twenty-eight pounds in three weeks and I fourteen pounds. Almost everyone had lost several pounds, but one exception I must mention: Colin reckoned he gained three pounds. What on earth was his normal diet if he could put on three pounds while eating freeze-dried food at high altitude? John and I had both favoured being a little overweight to leave something to burn off, while the weight-watching Americans had a far more stoical approach and at each stopping point en route for Muztagh Ata had disappeared in all directions, running. Our respective performances proved nothing but the enigma of fitness for high-altitude climbing.

Soon we were saying goodbye to our climbing friends who flew to the USA before John and I left Peking. Then we were saying goodbye to our Chinese friends, and embarking on sixteen and a half hours of flying to Paris, before taking the short Paris to London hop. Home.

We had been away for five weeks and two days; if it had not been for the paperwork John had to handle in Peking we could have lopped a few days off that time; not bad, considering we had climbed a mountain of 7,546 metres.

For the first time in my climbing career I had, with John, achieved a British first, for no other Britons had succeeded in climbing Muztagh Ata. It was a climb of great quantity but little quality, but the magic of success could not be taken away. I had the ascent forever, a building block of experience, which would stand me in good stead if the urge to go even higher should seize me.

Judy had a good Civil service office job, but I had to pull my weight financially too. I had had some experience in lecturing about my climbing and from late 1982 I turned more to lectures as a source of income in fairly large dollops; lecture agencies relieved me of the need to haggle over fees. To make the lecture business work I had to obtain more slides, and it was quite a committing step to take, to enter the expensive arena of expeditions and to try at the same time to make a living from the results. Much time was spent travelling around the country by train, speaking at a library here, a public school there, at a ladies luncheon club somewhere else, at a sales conference, a literary society, a climbing club. Introductions by chairpersons, and votes of thanks, tended to be embarrassingly glowing, times to keep the eyes down, but there were funny moments too, such as the time when I stood in at short notice for someone who had died; an elderly lady paid me the weird compliment: 'I enjoyed your talk so much! I'm glad the other gentleman died.'

A new lifestyle permitted sufficient flexibility for some voluntary work, but I'm no Mother Theresa, and I found a level at which I was neither overworked nor resentful of the demands made. I had never been one to join committees unless I could see a very good reason for doing so, and once the outdoor pursuits campaign was well established there was no need for me to remain on more than two or three. Instead, working on an ad hoc basis with several projects concerned with disability suited me better than regular commitments.

For a while, partly because of the ascent of Muztagh Ata, there came upon me the deepest sense of urgency about attempting some climbs of quality, some smaller but diamond-bright routes. I had to follow more dreams to reach El Dorado. Simultaneously I began to prepare mentally for the time when, through serious injury to a wrist, an elbow, a hip, my back or through other injury or sickness or disability, my body would no longer endure the severe tests to which it was subjected; if the time came I would accept it, for I had had so much. Soon, a physical problem did loom: my left shoulder became painful when the arm on that side was moved. It hurt even to pick up a jacket. Though I joked about it (Well, at least I have one good limb left') the seriousness of the injury did not escape me, and I feared my climbing future was threatened.

'We'd better fix you up with an appointment with the sports injuries clinic,' my doctor said.

The specialist there, Dr J. G. Williams, was no stranger to me because I had contributed a chapter to a sports medicine book which he edited. Less than ten minutes after walking into his surgery I was out again, having had an injection deep into my shoulder, a hydrocortisone injection, which was a success.

Since I needed material for lectures and writing, many acquaintances reacted differently to my going on expeditions; they no longer queried either my motives or the virtue of my actions, but now viewed the wanderings as acceptable. There were those, of course, who reacted enviously, on the theme of, 'All right for some. Gadding about all over the world. Lucky devil.' But though there had been some luck and many people had helped, it boiled down to continued application more than to luck. You make the opportunities happen, rather than wait for luck, and you take risks and opt for sacrifices and apply yourself hard. I have ceased to be surprised at the number of people who tell me they have a climbing or other adventurous ambition but they have never achieved it because no one would give them the money to carry it out. I could advise them that getting there by stages and raising the finances are all part of the job and that securing the finance does not automatically bring the ambition about; anyone can dream up ambitions. Complaining that no one else will come up with the money is a feeble excuse, a sign of lack of commitment, and quite often they could afford to attempt what they had in mind provided they were prepared to make sacrifices. Though I do not mind if people lack ambitions (for there are some ambitious horrors around) I have no time for the windbags who say 'I wish I could' but always find excuses.

Immediately before climbing trips Judy and I seemed to live in different worlds inside our heads.

'I must put some more turf down in the middle of the garden,' she said one day.

'Fine. I'll need a new ice-axe for the next trip.'

'Honeysuckle would look nice on that wall.'

'Mmm. Haven't decided whether to take my helmet yet.'

'Mary's given me some nice seeds.'

'Must get some more ice screws.'

'Could you move the trellis on to that wall?'

'Yes. Oh, would you get me another tube of glacier cream tomorrow? You'll be near the shop.'

'All right. Can you put the washing in the launderette and I'll collect it on the way back?'

'Yes. The pick on one of my ice-axes is at the wrong angle.'

'I wonder if there's enough turf at the bottom of the garden that I can shift.'

It did not matter that our thoughts went about like two butterflies rarely alighting simultaneously on the same flower, for when it mattered we listened to each other. Her thoughts centred around her friends and closest relations, the little piece of garden that went with our flat, work and the people she worked with, and cooking, which she had studied for three years at teacher training college. With the exception of infrequent walking excursions we had given up taking mountain holidays together, for the preparations for even the simplest venture assumed the proportions of mounting a crusade; this was because she was not truly enthusiastic about going, and once we stopped trying to fool ourselves about this we had no more problems. She was a home bird, without a doubt.

'A lot of people really do believe that I must have deep frustrated ambitions,' she said one day. 'As if ambitions were inevitable and mine have been squashed. They assume everyone wants what they want. Couldn't be more wrong.'

In 1982 I joined as American group in Peru. We headed for Huascaran. Having been up the north summit already, I could muster little motivation for the ascent, and from what I had seen from a distance the route was far more broken and dangerous than in 1978. However, the opportunity to take photographs to replace some film stolen in 1978 was sufficient to draw me along with the others.

On a narrow moraine spine above base camp we passed the first of the mountain's victims, a small Japanese lady being carried down on the back of a local porter. We did not find our whether she was ill or injured. Then we came across five Peruvian climbers descending with a blue bundle, which they lowered ahead of them down the snow and ice, and dragged it on ropes across crevasses. A floppy leg sticking from the bundle at a funny angle, and a bare foot, were the first confirmation that this was a body. The foot, like the bloated face, was the colour of a red tan leather shoe, and the eyes were like glass. We heard it was a Canadian or American man who had died in a fall several days before.

The sight of the corpse cast a cold shadow on our spirits, and in any case my decision to go no higher than 5,300 metres had been made. The dangerous way we had taken, weaving through crevasses and broken cliffs, had provided the long-awaited pictures, and considering the risks to be faced thereafter the reward was too small to tempt me on. Then everyone else decided on retreat.

My deflated companions had been in Peru less than two weeks and though they had planned to stay three weeks they wanted no more to do with the mountains, and they all departed for the USA. The team's ardour had cooled too rapidly. There were many other relatively safe routes to try. Alone again; not short of company but lacking a climbing partner.

There was no need to worry, for on the day the others went home, Bob Braun and Glenn Albrecht invited me to climb with them. A New Zealander, Brian Weedon, asked if he could come along, so the absconded US expedition was soon replaced. Bob and Glenn were biologists in their late twenties or early thirties and both had broad climbing experience. Brian was twenty-five years old, had trained as a surveyor, and worked in New Zealand as a climbing instructor. He had not been blessed with good fortune while in Peru; he had bought a watch, which was wrapped for him and later he unfolded the paper to find a substituted bottle cap, and several low value coins, which imitated the strap. Then someone had stolen his passport, money, travellers' cheques and camera.

Brian and I took a pickup truck cum bus a few miles northwards to our rendezvous with Bob and Glenn on the main road through the Rio Santa valley. Having met them on the outskirts of the village of Paltey we flagged down another pickup truck and bargained for a rough ride of about four miles to Collon, 3,200 metres. It had been our intention to carry our rucksacks all the way from there, but a local woman approached us as we passed her mud brick dwelling and told us her husband, Modesto, had a donkey and a horse, which would take the loads from our backs for the next ten miles. At midday a deal was struck and we set off behind the two beasts, and Modesto was soon telling my companions I would not make it to base camp; I had other ideas, of course.

We passed through the most beautiful pastoral scenes one can imagine; soft shades of green and cornfield yellow, and nice browns in mellow textures of gently undulating land where streams laid down lush ribbon borders; and patches of darker colour, where mud brick, thatched dwellings and tall, dark trees and grazing cattle and sheep existed in harmony, before a backdrop of rounded, reddish-brown mountains behind us, distant white ones ahead. It was the kind of scene you can never properly describe. Though I limped painfully, trying to keep my companions in sight, I did not miss the quiet majesty of the place.

Bob, Brian and Glenn were considerate, with one or other of them always staying back far enough for me to be in touch with the party. As we approached base camp our objective started to show itself, and it was a fine looker. Tocllaraju, or Trap Mountain, is 6,034 metres and was worth going to Peru for on its own.

Modesto, forty-nine years old, father of seven children, married to a woman of forty, made a half-hearted attempt to raise his price by about five per cent, but his will was weakened at being fed copious quantities of an excellent thickened soup concocted by Glenn and Bob, and he gave up. Wearing sandals made from old car tyres, and wrapped in a good poncho, he settled down on the sandy, football pitch sized, beach where three of us slept in a tent and Brian spent the night out. During the night poor Modesto's animals departed, fortunately almost certainly downhill, but he would have to walk down now. Nibbling a few biscuits, he padded off over the sand in a resigned way.

From base camp at 4,400 metres we shared the vague path up a moraine crest with three Austrians. A little scrambling on easy cliffs, a short snow slope that called for crampons, an up-and-down walk on snow, seven hours gone by, and we were preparing to camp on a large, flat snowfield, close to the Austrians.

6.15 a.m. Cold. My mind said my body did not want to move, but I knew the secret: make a small effort, like putting on a stump sock, then you feel a bit more like putting on one leg, which leads to another stump sock and to the other leg and to a jacket, and in three or four minutes you have almost forgotten that you did not want to move. It worked. Now I wanted to go, but there were too many crevasses for me even to begin to think about going alone. I needed the others. Glenn had decided against; like a lot of people, he had had a bad night at altitude. Bob had had an upset stomach the day before, and Brian had hardly slept, but they were going.

The necessary water was melted from snow and drunk as tea, and we started. Walking on easy angled snow up a snaking route, after on hour we roped up for thirty metres where the way steepened and a crevasse waited at the bottom if we slipped. The Austrians were just ahead, and an Australian party of four, who had approached by way of a variation of our route, was some way in front of them. The south-west glacier and the north-west shoulder, which we were on by now, was the way we should follow, according to a vague description we had read. Other than that, our hastily crystallised expedition had had little time for research.

The ascent was in constant doubt because of the weather. Though not the summer period, this was Peru's dry season, and the weather had been continually good, until now. On this morning dark clouds covered mountains of similar altitude all around us, but Tocllaraju was left alone, at least for the time being. We traversed steep slopes with big crevasses running their length at the bottom, a hundred metres lower down, and moved carefully, unroped; to have belayed would have created too much delay, and we had one eye on the weather all the while.

'Probably just a walk to the top now,' Brian said at one stage, and afterwards we laughed about that.

At eleven in the morning a big decision confronted me. Little more than one hundred metres vertically below the summit the mountain reared up into a formidable last rampart and the real difficulties commenced. First there was a big bergschrund, six metres of mouth, overhanging at the top lip and of considerable depth, running the full length of the mountain's final thrust. Above the bergschrund it looked as of some giant hand had placed a forty metre high, layered, steep-sided meringue on the summit, and we had to climb the icy side which faced us. Amidst the large figures we talk of in the mountains, a hundred metres does not sound much, but it equates with the height of a twenty storey building.

The Australians were already part way up, and the Austrians had resigned in the face of such serious territory.

'How about the last bit?' Brian asked me.

The trip to Peru needed a good ascent to complete it. Tocllaraju, Trap Mountain, was that ascent, and was worth some extra risk.

A steep ramp of snow and grey ice, like a precarious stepladder, could be reached by way of a very soft snow bridge, which spanned the bergschrund; it looked the best (and only) way to tackle the gap. We roped up and set off one by one across uncertain snow. It held for Brian, held for Bob and held for me in turn. The stepladder led to an overhanging lip of snow on which we did not linger, and the rope length of sharply inclined snow that came next was firm and enjoyable. The three of us congregated on a snow platform, wide as a single bed and half as long again, beneath an ice bulge. Looking upwards, we could escape to the right of the bulge. Brian went first and soon disappeared around it. Bob went the same way, up a steep chute of ice. When I followed, the hard ice fractured under my axe, and small chunks, each like a small discus in size and shape, were dislodged.

Had we known about this icy section I would have brought a second axe, but had to make do with the pick on one of my crutches. It worked well on snow but did not penetrate ice nearly so well as a proper axe, so I had to be very careful. Crampon points and ice-axe picks bit only half an inch or less into the hardest ice, and quite often it shattered. Every move had to be made with caution; before moving a crampon I had to ensure that the other crampon and both picks were firmly planted. Arm muscles had to make up for a lack of leg strength and each move, performed as smoothly and carefully as possible, required both effort and concentration.

The ice took us up to a narrow snow ridge that plunged ahead and behind. Turning right, we climbed, then walked, in a blasting wind for two or three minutes on gradually levelling snow to the summit. A gem of a climb, on a high mountain, by accident rather than design.

Our descent was trouble free, apart from Bob dropping my camera down a crevasse. It slid sixty metres at first, almost came to a halt, and popped over the edge. Bob insisted on trying to get it back and went, roped, about thirty metres down a slope and into a dark hole, to recover the camera, which still worked. And some of the pictures already on the roll of film were the best of the trip.

Though life has been tainted here and there by people, climbing had brought in its wake friends and travel and wonderful times when emotions seemed as sweet as a human being could experience. Under the influence of a seemingly bizarre motivation we flirt with death and hope to come back alive, and sometimes climbers are said to have a death wish. That may be true of some but mostly, I think, the reverse is the case. It may at first seem anomalous, but they risk their lives to a greater or lesser extent because life is too precious to waste in appalling dreariness. Through climbing I have discovered my personal path to fulfilment, and feel extremely privileged to have done so. My appreciation of the blessings that have come my way is boundless. Sweet dreams have come true, rich memories spring back; dear God, let it go on and on and on, was all I could think in the eighties.

"A sip is the most that mortals are permitted from any goblet of delight." – Amos Bronson Alcott 1799-1888.

No, Mr Alcott, no sir! There were bigger sips yet to come, and from a bigger goblet too.

CHAPTER 7

To Africa

IN his book Walking Up and Down in the World the American mountain guide Smoke Blanchard wrote: 'For half a century I have tried to promote the idea that mountaineering is best approached as a combination of picnic and pilgrimage. Mountain picnic-pilgrimage is short on aggression and long on satisfaction.' An excellent sentiment, yet you will see that this cosy philosophy may desert any mountaineer, who, like me, determines to climb any of the fourteen mountains in the world which exceed 8,000 metres in height. Though success in achieving such targets can bring immense joy, the execution of the task may be a miserable undertaking and setting bold targets exposes you to the risk of failure and deep, gnawing disappointment. Having said that, mountaineering has been the spur which has projected me into such a wealth of 'picnic-pilgrimage' experiences, exquisite moments of aesthetic pleasures and thrills of consummated adventures, and the next, on the road of experience to a high altitude dream, was a trip to Kilimanjaro's Heim glacier, on the southern side of that colossus. Prior to my departure from a snow blanketed Heathrow Airport in February 1983 two strong gentlemen had introduced themselves to me at the bottom of the aeroplane steps.

'We were told you might require some assistance on the steps' one of them said.

'I'm hoping to climb Kilimanjaro'

But I was on the computer as 'a mountaineer who has two artificial legs' so on changing 'planes at Amsterdam, there was an electric buggy waiting. The chauffeuse looked so disappointed when told it was not needed, and said 'Please, Mr. Croucher, it is on my job-sheet', so I climbed in and glided quietly, guiltily, past old people staggering along laden with duty-free purchases and heavy cabin baggage. In the departure lounge I hopped out and went up the steps like everyone else, eyed with suspicion by my fellow travellers.

In the mid eighteen-eighties it was said of Kilimanjaro that gunpowder would not explode on its slopes, and your legs stiffened if you went there. Around about the same time two British explorers were told that the mountain was a dome of silver with a brass city on top, that fiery beings dwelt on high, and blood burst from your fingernails if you went there. Reports received shortly afterwards from missionaries that

Kilimanjaro was capped by snow were treated with scepticism, even ridicule, and David Livingstone wrote: 'The white mountains are masses of white rock somewhat like quartz.'

It had been arranged through the chairman of the Kilimanjaro Mountain Club that I would climb with a local mountain rescue ranger of the Chagga tribe, Hubert Siyanga, a twenty-nine year-old smiling, smoking, married, dark chocolate-skinned father of three who lived with his family, including his parents, in a hut beneath Kilimanjaro.

For two days he led the way on the narrow, rough and infrequently used Umbwe forest track leading towards the bottom of the glacier, on mossy ground and mud, under plumed giant fern which in this ideal environment attained a height of six metres. Creeper-decked trees fifty metres high provided a canopy shelter from the sun on the first day in this mysterious place of silence broken only by muffled hootings, tootings and buzzings, punctuated by unidentified rustlings. At times it was necessary to climb over the trunks of fallen trees a metre or more thick, and to pull ourselves up slippery mud banks by means of root handrails and banisters. The first night was spent under the tree canopy, the second in a cave big enough for four people. The track then entered a region where heath bushes, festooned in yellowish green Old Man's Beard, grew in abundance and reached three times the height of an adult human. Many bushes pointed dead, crooked, skeletal black branches at the sky. Almost as tall as the heath were giant groundsel, whose foliage resembled two to four broccoli atop large rough-barked candelabra. Standing among straw coloured tussock grass the groundsel plants, particularly when mist came down, gave an eerie feeling that we were being watched by still, silent observers from another world; two, three and four headed observers. Spooky! Once free of the forest's clawing fingers we could amble over wonderfully wild grassy heathland, encountering only one group of four people during three days.

We did not climb our glacier, largely because Hubert turned out to be carrying insufficient clothing for bad weather, leaving him vulnerable to hypothermia and frostbite, but as a lukewarm consolation we tramped along the mountain's southern flank to join the easy tourist trail at the Horombo Hut, actually a cluster of wooden buildings which for some reason was always referred to in the singular.

With climbing equipment dumped at Horombo, Hubert and I went well up the gentle red desert trail to the stone Kibo hut in five hours, and set out next day to zig zag upwards on scree to Gillman's Point (5,700 metres in altitude), on the shattered crater rim. The highest eminence, called Uhuru, would have to wait for another day, for better weather.

The easy descent was nevertheless tiring because my split, blood-caked right stump needed rest. Next day, too, it gave the same insistent message on the eight-hour trek through broom and dry grass, past copses of short trees and into snake-rooted forest, through clearings where big butterflies - blue and yellow and red - fluttered hither and thither in erratic, jerky flight. I paid for those sights and for the spiritual refreshment which mountains can bestow, I paid in pain and effort, and I have no complaints.

My interest in Africa had been awakened, though for a while Kilimanjaro was usurped by Mount Kenya, a remnant of an old volcano lying 200 miles to the north. Unlike Kilimanjaro, Mount Kenya has no easy routes of ascent. I wrote to the Mountain Club of Kenya to see if they had anyone free to climb the mountain with me; Geoff Hine, a classics teacher in Nairobi, volunteered.

Judy was able to come this time. She could not always do so, and did not always wish to be part of the two months or so which I devoted each year to expeditions. On some expeditions, the base camps are sited in desolate country on the rubble of glacial moraines, and no one in their right mind would choose to spend two or three weeks waiting in such places. Some people could understand why Judy preferred spending time with her parents or in her garden to going to Switzerland or Peru, but others were baffled, since they made judgements based not on what Judy wanted but on what they themselves would like. I had learned what she preferred.

At Nairobi's modern airport Geoff was waiting for us with his Land Rover. Whenever I think of this fit, fair-haired, medium-height young man with a small moustache, the word 'hearty' comes to mind.

After two days spent in a pleasant bungalow in Nairobi, once we had left behind the tatty, higgledy-piggledy shacks which cluster in some of the city's suburbs, we sped along the decaying, pot holed tarmac road running northwards through pretty farming country. Drivers hogged the centre of the highway, only moving over to their crumbling side of the road at the approach of oncoming traffic. Every so often the surroundings changed from pasture to bare earth and naked thorn trees, to shiny leafed coffee plantations, to pretty woods, to fields of sisal and to banana plantations on bright red soil. Bougainvillaea, poinsettia and flame trees added rare flashes of intense colour, but the mellow, patchy hues of grasses, crops and trees on the red, red hills were pleasing enough on their own. Scattered mud walled and thatched huts blended better than the corrugated iron dwellings but the latter, standing well spread out on the hills, still did not offend the landscape too badly. Now and then we shot through townships, past brick shops, garages, churches, advertisements for soft drinks and sewing machines and radios and clothing. Back in the country again, here and there charcoal burners sat beside sacks of their product at the roadside, and boys held up big fish for sale.

After a hundred miles of driving, we made arrangements to hire a man for one day, on the outskirts of Naro Moro. We collected him, James, from his home, and drove sixteen miles on a muddy but good road between bamboo and shrubs, under huge tree canopies, to what is known as the Meteorological Clearing. At 3,050 metres altitude it has a large space for parking, an official campsite and a lodge. We parked and quickly packed a rucksack and sent James on ahead because he was anxious to be down the same day. Then my spare legs were put in storage in a hut, and at 11am. we passed through a gate and followed a gently rising forest road which soon petered out.

In an hour a network of muddy brown paths, braided through mossy forest, faded out at the edge of steep marshland popularly known as the Vertical Bog. I doubt that it went above 15 degrees, but was slippery as lard and worse when heavy rain fell, running down in brown rivulets, and every so often a boot would be submerged in mire. But in most places progress was aided by grassy tussocks and sedges.

Several wet people in twos and threes and groups of up to eight descended. Some had explored part way up the bog, others had retreated from a camp at about 4,200 metres, and they, the victims of altitude, looked sick and disappointed. As the afternoon wore on the victors straggled down, returning from the top of Point Lenana, a subsidiary peak of Mount Kenya. Though 4,985 metres high this lower summit can be reached without any climbing, but as is the case with Gillman's Point and Uhuru, the altitude takes casualties. Mental faculties can deteriorate temporarily but considerably. In extremis, cerebral and pulmonary oedema can lead to death in a matter of only a few hours.

A bedraggled man of about fifty, accompanied by a porter, was wearily stumbling down when he spotted me a few metres to his right. He stopped, open-mouthed; I was using crutches.

'You intend going the whole way?' he asked in disbelief.

'Yes.'

'You know how far it is?'

'Yes.'

He shook his head, clearly thinking I would not make it, or should not try. And he must have been assuming our objective was easy Point Lenana, since that was where the majority of people headed for on this mountain. Who could blame him, for after all, I was the one who looked like a fish out of water.

We schluck, schluck, schlucked up the mud of the bog, which trickled through blond tussocks and sodden sedges, under heath so tall at four metres that it has earned the name of tree heath. Geoff intended we should gain 1,100 metres that day to the Mountain Club hut, but I had reservations about two recent arrivals from sea level going to 4,175 metres on their first day. Not long after 3 pm. I suggested that we should find a dry spot and sleep where we were. Geoff was reluctant and clearly unimpressed by my performance, but I had a staunch ally.

'I've never been so pleased to hear you suggest a bivi, cherub,' said Judy. Sleeping out was not high on her list of pleasures, but this time the altitude persuaded her.

Beneath the gently overhanging wall of an isolated rock outcrop about as high as a two storey building, we were protected from the steady drizzle which continued throughout the afternoon. James hurried down, having left his heavy load at the hut, and halted briefly to eat a few biscuits. Three Italians plodded upwards, laughing at us for stopping short of the hut. Judy and I were used to being cast in the role of the tortoise many a time, but Geoff was an embarrassed and frustrated hare.

Next day we re-encountered the three Italians, who were descending slowly. One was green and very, very sick, while his companions looked fed up; one night at altitude had taken its toll. At 4,000 metres the tussocky slopes opened out as we gained the crest of a ridge, the right boundary of the Teleki valley. The valley had all the lush beauty of the plants we had seen earlier: tussock grass, lobelia, cabbage groundsel like waist-high silvery-leaved artichokes, and giant groundsel twice as tall as any I had seen on Kilimanjaro, and what a foreground it was for Mount Kenya! Though the setting of the mountain was beautiful, Mount Kenya itself was more grand than beautiful in my eyes.

For an hour we contoured along the right side of the valley, then descended to its floor. After stepping across the Naro Moro stream we came in ten minutes of walking on grass to the Mountain Club hut, a round, wooden clad, metal building with a conical roof and eight wooden bunks in two tiers.

Visitors soon arrived. We had already seen several rock hyrax, which would stay within a few metres of the trail when we passed, but their cousins who lived near the hut were more bold, to the point of coming to the door, or even inside, for food. About the size of a rabbit, stiff furred, with a back end like a guinea pig, similar around the head to a beaver, and with hedgehoggy back legs and feet, it comes as a surprise to learn that the hyrax is a distant relative of the elephant. Judy was fascinated by them, so by then I had a welcome bivouac and forty-nine hyrax to my credit.

At about four o'clock in the afternoon three Norwegian women arrived at the hut. They planned a training walk and then an ascent of Point Lenana the day after, and on their return from the training walk they invited Judy to go with them. If they had not, Geoff and I would have gone up there with her, but the offer left us free to head for Mount Kenya. They departed at 7 am., and Geoff and I at noon, for our respective objectives. Soon, on the other side of the broad valley, I could pick out Judy and her three companions, coming down. The plod of successive feet up and down Point Lenana has led to the beating of a good trail between isolated dustbin sized boulders on gravel. Above that is a section where one walks on small boulders, and above that an easy snowfield.

'Did you make it?' I called across the valley.

'Yes.'

A welcome bivouac, forty-nine hyrax, and Point Lenana on my side. Brownie points galore!

Among even more giant and cabbage groundsel and tussock grass we made our way upwards towards the foot of the Lower Darwin glacier, where our ascent of the south face would begin. Vegetation decreased with altitude gain, and soon we were scrambling over boulders as big as pigs and cows, with short intermittent bare earth patches. Any appearance of total barrenness was nullified by a few clumps of a yellow daisy with multiple blossoms, surviving among the stones, and by yellow and green and brown lichens clinging to grey rocks.

Within an hour of our setting out, fluffy snow began to fall from a low, grey ceiling which permitted us a view only of the bottom of the glacier. 'Water congeals into flowers,' says an ancient Chinese text. 'And the flowers are always six pointed,' says another.

Geoff led us to a shelter where we were to sleep, beneath a big rock in what is known to local climbers as the Black Hole. The rock lean-to was formed by a thick, sloping boulder lying on another which was as big as a limousine, and the resultant wedge shelter had been improved with stone walls and a metal door. One had to stoop to stand at the highest part, and the roof sloped evenly from there to a rock floor. There was room for four people, so the two of us, being the only occupants, were as comfortable as we could have wished. Geoff had been here on a previous occasion, having attempted the south face and turned back, having climbed a different route from here, and having been there to help carry down an injured climber.

In view of the fresh snowfall we waited a day because of avalanche risk. Close to the Black Hole a small marble plaque stood as a memorial to three British soldiers killed nearby by an avalanche in 1965. Two British climbers with a similarly cautious approach to ours turned up around noon, out for a training walk before tackling a route which in the lower half would follow ours. One of them, Steve, was especially keen to reach Mount Kenya's summit three days later because that would be his birthday.

At 4 am. the next day a candle flickered in a half coconut shell left behind by someone else. There was no talk of postponement now. At least one long day to the summit would be followed by a short day to descend by another route. That was the plan, but the best laid plans …

After a few minutes spent clattering through stones to the foot of the truncated triangle of the Lower Darwin glacier, we were on a 40 degree snow-over-ice slope, for 200 metres or so to the top of the triangle. It took an hour to reach the apex of the triangle, and with Geoff leading we broke out to the left, up soft snow and down a little on an icy ramp beneath a vertical, brown, ice-draped cliff, to the bottom of the Hidden Couloir, a deep gash containing a smooth, steep white strip of ice a few metres wide and 50 metres long. The ice bulged here and there to 70 degrees but was generally more like 50 degrees, and that was the way we had to go. As Geoff chopped his way ahead with two ice axes he dislodged saucers of ice which clunked on my helmet; it could not be helped. The full length of rope had run out well before he reached the top of the couloir, so I joined him and led on, on ice and then on slushy snow, until the rope had all run out again. Thirty metres more of soft snow and loose rock put us on the Upper Darwin glacier, and there I began to struggle, taking at least four times as long as Geoff on the rock prow. There followed a few sections of mixed climbing: snow, rock, ice, rock, more snow and so on. The ice steps were not a problem, because our crampons bit well, and the rock was never too bad; but once more soft snow, my old enemy, took me in its grip. With his ability to step higher and less jerkily, and to keep his boot soles flat on packed snow steps, Geoff made steady progress. But for me it was the familiar story of jerky movements and slips, as if someone was grabbing at my ankles and pulling me back. Time and time again I slipped, regained the ground in part or whole, and slid down once more. The idea of picnic-pilgrimage was far from my mind.

'Fight,' I kept telling myself aloud. 'Fight! You made it in China on worse snow than this, so fight!'

Geoff climbed easily on while his partner floundered behind. Every so often I was forced to rest, gasping like a landed fish. Relatively easy snow was pushing me to my limits. But the snow belonged there and I began to question whether I did. I was not particularly worried about my safety, but I felt so inelegant, so clumsy, so out of place. Yet though there was no poetry in my movements, there was nevertheless a challenge in struggling against the odds; it would be as rewarding to crawl to the summit as to dance there, if crawling was the only way. I could not allow dissatisfaction with my style to force me to give up, for I would make very few ascents if I demanded graceful movement of myself all the time. As the afternoon came the weather turned misty grey to match my mood of unhappy resignation, and I knew we would not achieve the summit that day. An afternoon of grovelling (on my part) went by and at 6 pm. Geoff climbed out of sight behind a big outcrop of rock. Suddenly there was a scuffling sound which suggested he had fallen. I braced myself to take the shock on the rope. There was no cry, but the sound I heard was sufficient warning.

Geoff later wrote, 'Everything suddenly came adrift and my face shot past twenty feet of rock face.' The expected tug on the rope did not come. Geoff soon reappeared around the rock outcrop and called, 'Sorry about that. Really stupid thing to try. Really stupid.'

He explained that he had fallen from the rock and landed in a snow bank above a steep, rock-studded snow slope.

'How would you feel if I suggested a bivi here?' he asked.

We dug a little platform to sleep on, on a snow slope, and when the job was finished I began vomiting. Overexertion may have been the cause, though the violence of the affliction made it more likely that I had picked up a bug somewhere. This was confirmed next morning when I was weak and nauseous, and we agreed to wait another day. Had I merely been exhausted the rest would have put me right.

'Won't take long to get down from here tomorrow,' Geoff said.

'No. But I haven't abandoned the idea of carrying on.'

'How are you feeling?'

'Ghastly.'

My sickness resulted in an adventitious bonus for Geoff. I had not managed to eat anything the previous day since breakfast, and on this day consumed only two biscuits. We had allotted ourselves extra food in case of delay, and Geoff, who gave his stomach a high priority, needed no persuasion to eat my rations as well as his own. I was content with soothing, warm water. Occasionally during the day and the following frosty night I was sick again, but still felt well enough next day to go on. While my body managed another biscuit and some warm water for breakfast, Geoff wolfed down a large portion of cereal before we left.

Good scrunchy snow soon deteriorated to become almost as bad as the worst we had encountered before. On short ice sections of 60 degrees or 70 degrees, effort resulted in the reward of gained height, but evil soft snow waited between these easier stretches. On good snow I would have had to have worked hard, but now the effort was extreme.

Poor Geoff; it must have been trying for him, saddled with me. He seemed more resigned than discontented, but things improved. The route went from the top of the Upper Darwin glacier leftwards onto a rock rib, on the far side of which was the steep Diamond glacier, so named on account of its hard ice. Along with the Hidden Couloir the glacier would normally be considered the hardest part of the route, but in my case this did not apply. Hard ice; hallelujah! Now I could enjoy the mountain.

Ninety metres of flowing movement brought us to the Gate of the Mists, a col which separates Mount Kenya's twin summits, Batian and Nelion, named after two Masai tribal priests or rulers. Batian is eleven metres higher than Nelion; we headed for Nelion because there was a tiny metal hut almost on its summit, and reached it over firm rock which was a pleasure to climb. The hut was about the size of the back of a small van, a luxurious shelter for two.

So with three glaciers, the icy Hidden Couloir, some vile snow and good rock behind us, we stood on the summit at 5,188 metres. It was Steve's birthday but he and his friend Dave did not fulfil Steve's wish; they had turned back twice, once because of high wind, and then because of the snow's condition. They had heard us, then had seen us, so had been able to report to Judy that we were safe and still on the way up.

I was a strong candidate for the record for the slowest ascent of the route, I suppose, and I was still sick, tired and unable to keep food down. Once again a mountain had tested, but not over tested, had made me fight and had augmented the prize according to the severity of the fight. Quite often I have been said to be faster than able-bodied climbers, but this has rarely been so; it is enough that I can complete the distance, no matter what the pace, no matter how poor the style at times. I had been forced to fight harder than Geoff, and my reward was greater.

About reaching the summit of Mount Kenya, Eric Shipton wrote: 'Mountains have many ways of rewarding us for our pilgrimage, and often bestow their richest treasures when least expected. For my part, all disappointment, all care for the future, were drowned in the great joy of living that moment.' Those words fitted perfectly.

Now we had to get down, and the descent next day of the steep east side of the mountain was not going to be as straightforward as we thought. Geoff abseiled down from the top first, on our doubled 45 metres of rope. I followed, expecting to find him on a sizeable ledge, but the reality was frightening. Near the ends of the rope I swung beneath a small overhang on the vertical wall, to find him standing on a tiny ledge smaller in area than a postcard. He had chosen the wrong place to abseil. We stood with one boot each on the ledge while I attached myself to a short length of rope passed around a fist-sized stone jammed in a horizontal crack; I say jammed, which is not quite right, since it wobbled. Geoff was attached to a small metal nut placed, securely I hoped, in another crack. There was a drop of 20 metres beneath us, and we were so very careful as we pulled the rope down for our next abseil; dropping it would have left us in a fine pickle, for we could not possibly have climbed up or down the almost blank wall. A high proportion of mountaineering accidents result from abseiling and I was very scared. With the stone as an anchor for the rope I slid down first, seeking relief; what a lovely feeling it was as the ledge below me came nearer and nearer, and what joy when my boots made contact. It was a big ledge, four double beds or more in area, where I could move about and take photographs of Geoff. What good pictures these would be, with my companion standing on a tiny ledge beneath an overhang half way down a vertical cliff as high as an eight storey building. Geoff joined me and we followed the ledge south-westwards for several yards before performing another vertical abseil. The fine, firm spike of rock which formed an anchor for the rope took away any anxiety.

A series of abseils took us down vertical walls and steep faces and ice gullies. After a height loss of about 200 metres the nature of the descent changed for a while and we had some tricky traversing to do on snow-plastered rock. I was lowering myself by my arms down a big step when the velcro fastening on one of my jacket pockets popped open and something fell out; it bounced down the very steep rock and snow slope below, and I recognised my compact camera falling away in pieces for hundreds of metres. Amongst the bits I could see the film, spinning away for ever. So much for my pictures. This was a great loss, but the next time something fell the consequences were going to be more serious, much more serious.

Shortly after my camera disappeared I watched Geoff edging along a 75 degree slab on snowy footholds. Once he was across I followed, and had climbed about 7 metres diagonally across and up the slab and was about to pull up on its top edge to join Geoff when there was a sudden jolt, as if someone had kicked my boot. When I looked down it was to see a stockinged foot at the end of my right leg, and a boot tumbling down almost in the line my camera had taken.

This had never happened before and I could not understand how it had come about. Perhaps the footwear had stretched with use and having the weight on the toe of the boot had resulted in leverage which had caused the heel of my foot to flip out. It was fortunate that the extremity was not real and susceptible to frostbite or cutting, but then if it had been real the boot would not have come off in the first place.

'It's going to be a bit tricky standing on snow on a plastic foot, Geoff.'

I wondered out loud whether I should stop at the little shelter, the only one on the route we were descending, which happened to be a few metres away on a ledge. Geoff could abseil down and return the next day with someone else and a borrowed boot. My mind raced, playing with that idea and thinking of ways of binding a crampon to a plastic foot. I doubted whether this could be done and I was really worried about how slippery it would be on snow, let alone on ice; after all, plastic toboggans work very well. Then I began to consider what would happen if Geoff was delayed in finding a companion for the short climb back up. Also if the weather turned bad I would have a difficult time because although we had enough food to see me through a few days, Geoff had accidentally left the stove on unlit and we had very little gas for melting snow. We carried on down. After one abseil and a little climbing the sock on my right foot wore through, exposing plastic which held fairly well on rock but skidded dangerously on snow. On intermediate snowy ledges I had to be extremely careful, but on subsequent abseils, down an icy vertical wall and past a small overhang, then down some slabs, and once more down broken rock, the foot was no problem. Similarly, I found no difficulty, or no more difficulty than usual, in walking down the scree which followed, descending 100 metres to the edge of the Lewis glacier. But there things changed.

A few hundred metres away across the easy glacier was the Austrian hut at 4,790 metres, where there was room for thirty people. Many used it as a stage on the way to Point Lenana. Geoff wanted me to go to the hut, or down to the Mountain Club hut, but I was not crossing the glacier on a plastic foot. He gave the impression he thought I was fussing about nothing, but the chances of an awkward slip, a twist, and injury were high. He could cross and bring back Judy's right boot next day, following the easy Point Lenana trail. Neither of us thought about the alternative of borrowing a boot for a few minutes from someone at the Austrian hut for the three hundred metre crossing; what fools!

Exhausted, sick, relieved and utterly contented, I cleared a space and settled down in the rocks at the edge of the glacier. Though it was still afternoon there came the unbroken sleep of one who is tired and fulfilled, and while the few people at the Austrian hut were kept awake by fierce winds, I slept for thirteen hours. The need for liquid is increased with the dry air at altitude, the expenditure of energy also requires water and the extra effort demanded of me to cover a given piece of ground results in a necessarily far greater than normal water intake, if I can get it. That night, in brief awakenings, sips of water delighted my tongue and spread like a balm through my body. No one who has ventured on high mountains can thereafter take water for granted. Nor do they fail to appreciate the security of a rustic shelter or the rich taste of simple fare at the end of a long, long day. And rest, when you are tired, is one of life's greatest blessings.

Geoff arrived at 8.30am. with Judy's boot. The fact that it was very tight did not matter to me, of course. He chomped on almond biscuits and peanuts while I sipped warm lemonade; only four biscuits had passed my lips since breakfast four days before. The sickness, which might have been called a reason for retreating, transpired not to be so when put to the test, but I don't think anyone would have accused me of making excuses if I had turned back. If the snow had been firm we would probably have taken only one long day to the summit. Yet on this route, equipped and experienced as we were, with retreat as straightforward as it was, we had been able to afford the decision to go on. On a different route, on a different mountain, the decision might have been to turn back. Judgement - where to draw the line, when to go, whether to go, against the odds perhaps, but not unwisely, is so often the mountaineer's dilemma. We had performed poorly on a number of counts: our first abseil, Geoff's fall, my struggle on snow, my lost boot, and the waste of our precious gas. Yet we had done what we had set out to do, and though the ascent had not been straightforward it had been more interesting for the incidents. The weather and conditions had allowed us to slip through, but only just.

Once across the glacier we ambled down the easy trail, such a good trail I could have managed that part without the boot. But I had no regrets about waiting for it for the glacier crossing. The counterpart of the man who had questioned me on the Vertical Bog about where I was going now appeared in the form of a climber sweating and puffing under a heavy rucksack.

'You guys had a good walk?' he asked with a North American accent.

'Yes,' Geoff replied.

'Where you been?'

'Nelion,' Geoff informed him.

'Both of you?'

'Yes'

With an incredulous look at me, at my crutches, at my odd boots, the man passed silently by, and seemed more weary than before.

'You look awful, Norm,' Judy said when she met us on the trail. 'Gaunt.'

'I'm very happy.'

We turned tourist, being driven around the nearby Nairobi National Park, where giraffe, zebra, wildebeest, Sykes monkey, baboon, crocodile, eland, waterbuck, gazelle, warthog, pelican, ibis, spoonbill, crested crane and stork put in appearances before my delighted wife.

The trip was not quite at an end. Geoff, Judy and I booked a night at the Ark, a wooden building designed for the close observation of wildlife at a water hole. Geoff took his Land Rover northwards again to the Aberdare Country Club where we stopped for lunch before joining the tourist bus to the Ark, an appropriately named wooden building which did indeed look like a sloping-roofed boat which had come to rest in thick, medium height forest. At the floodlit water hole were buffalo, rhino, elephant and several other species.

'Best holiday of my life,' Judy said, and I suppressed an 'I told you so.'

I could not have known that this was not the last time she would use those words.

* * *

According to legend, a king once sent a large expedition to investigate the white top of Kilimanjaro, and all but one perished. The lone survivor, Sabaya, who was not short of imagination, carried on and came to a large door studded with iron spikes. Though the door was open he was too weak and frightened to go through, and with feet and hands permanently injured he retreated. I wanted to be on that white top, for the thought of going back to the Heim glacier had stayed with me since my first visit in 1983, and in late 1985 I started looking for a companion or two to climb with there. The response came in the form of a telephone call on New Year's Eve from a man called Richard Foley, who lived in London. He came to see me the next day, arriving eager and a full hour early, and it would have been hard to turn him down in the face of his enthusiasm to go. He had climbed in the Swiss Alps and the Pyrenees as well as in Britain, and had worked for a while as an instructor at an adventure centre. Before this he had studied for a fine arts degree, but had abandoned the course and worked as a motorcycle courier; how he survived this if he rode in the same impatient manner as he drove a car was a mystery. He had inherited a house and the proceeds from its sale accounted for the freedom he enjoyed to join this and other expeditions. He was twenty-six years old, boyish, square jawed, of average height, and looked like he might have developed his shoulders by weight training, which he denied. With only three weeks to go before our departure, Richard rang to tell me about Rob Lees, an experienced climbing friend of his who lived in Manchester. Rob wanted to go too. The team was completed by Ken Smith, a redundant steel worker turned photographer. At a Christmas party he had expressed an interest in joining the expedition to Kilimanjaro, and had sold his two motorbikes to pay his expenses on the trip. Ken would walk the easy ground to the bottom of the Heim glacier, from where he could take pictures. Had he been joining us as a climber I would have been more particular about his experience, which did not amount to much, and about his fitness. Ken was my age, forty-six, and carried a sensible amount of weight for his 190 centimetre frame. To walk at the pace I had in mind to the glacier's base would not require him to be in good physical condition, but he did promise to take plenty of exercise before we left. His first move in this direction was a game of squash, which exercised his leg muscles to such an extent that he needed the assistance of his daughter to put on his shoes and socks the next morning!

With regard to Kilimanjaro and my other objectives of 1986 I was fortunate in respect of sponsorship, which amounted to enough money to cover over half of my expenses for the year. Attitudes had changed from the early years when, for instance, a *Daily Telegraph* editor had written to me: '... nothing would induce me to provide financial assistance which might be the means of accidentally causing you personal injury or embarrassment'. In the early days doors were closed on account of my legs, presumably since my ambitions were considered dangerous and unrealistic by those whom I approached, and who could blame them? I had to achieve my ambitions by stages and over many years, and it was not until I began to climb regularly at above 6,000 metres or so that sponsors became less elusive. Sometimes I have to pay all the expenses but I suppose on average I raise about fifty per cent of the costs in sponsorship. My most fitting sponsors must have been J. E. Hanger and Co. and Ginsters Cornish Pasties, who between them paid about half my expenses for my first trip to Kilimanjaro; a no-legged Cornishman could have no more appropriate sponsors than his artificial limb maker and a manufacturer of Cornwall's traditional meat, vegetable and pastry dish.

My right shoulder had for many months been very painful, and it hurt even when I picked up a book or put on a jacket. Hydrocortisone injections, ultrasound, traction, acupuncture and manipulation all failed to give me relief, and I began to worry about my climbing future.'... characterised by pain which is exacerbated by movement, and which may provoke a remarkable degree of functional disability,' a sports medicine book advised gloomily about my condition. But five sessions of radiotherapy produced a complete recovery, shortly before we were due to depart for Tanzania.

Whenever my parents visited, or we visited them, Judy was sworn to secrecy about the shoulder, or anything else medical, in front of Father, for he had sold the farm, been a butcher for a few years, and become an osteopath. He had no training but after a few sessions with an osteopath for a back problem Father decided he himself had a gift for the work, and the word 'healer' was sometimes used. He claimed to be able to cure gangrene, gout, epilepsy, arthritis, high blood pressure, mental illness, cancer and MS, and he maintained that meningitis was not what the doctors thought it to be.

'Tidn't inflammation, can't be' – and he also let it be known he was able to improve the likelihood of conception in women. He worked on a horse or two, several dogs, and a hamster, all of which he reported got better.

'That rook should come in 'ere', he said as he looked out of the window. 'Got rheumatism by the look of it'.

Most conditions were said to be because of 'the nerve' or 'a spine full of fibre', whatever that was, and he would 'open 'em out'.

'If they keep on comin' back I'm doin' 'em good, and if they don't I've cured 'em', was his view. He kept no records at all, not even names, addresses and phone numbers. 'Top men can't do it but I put 'em right'. Mother, however, had a neck problem which Father could never 'open up'.

'You've never believed in my gift', he said to her one day, but despite the fact that they usually resorted to conventional medicine themselves, he maintained his delusional beliefs to the extent that he wanted to pass on his 'gift' to me, and train me. He would talk obsessively in intimate detail about his patients, the same few 'success' stories over and over again, at meals, anywhere, even once through a closed toilet door when I retreated behind it for some peace. He desperately wanted my approval, for after walking from John o' Groats to Land's End I was number one man. He had walked short stretches with me through towns in Cornwall, touting for business by handing out his card to any stranger who looked as if they had something physical wrong with them.

I did meet several people who said he had done them some good, but on the other side there had been great embarrassments. One female acquaintance of mine met Father because he was staying with us for a few days, and he soon offered treatment, which she accepted. What he failed to tell me when he returned to our flat afterwards was that she passed out on the floor and came to with him, as she put it, 'in a panic'. It was an embarrassing time when I asked the woman how it had gone.

'Didn't he tell you?'

The insurers of a local rugby club stated that they would void the insurance of any player who received treatment from him. And there was the case of the General. I had been asked to perform the starting ceremony of the disabled people's section of the Ten Tors trek on Dartmoor. Before the event Judy and I had a formal breakfast, involving silver service and several waiters, with a General and many other officers in the officer's mess at Okehampton Camp. Part way through two people appeared, tapping on a window behind the General.

'Who is that?' asked the General.

'My parents.'

'Better fetch them in. Set two more places.'

Father sat next to the General, who winced as he reached to pick something up. As was his habit, Father elbowed the General in the ribs and asked, 'Something wrong with your arm, boy?'

'I have a problem with a shoulder.'

'Let me 'ave a go at it. Soon put that right, that's what I do.'

'Thank you, but my personal physician is attending to the matter.'

'Ain't done much good, 'as 'ee? Come out in the car with me an' I'll put 'ee right.'

'No, really. Thank you.'

'No charge.'

'No, thank you.'

One day Father announced he had stopped eating pepper.

'Otherwise, when I lift people I break wind.'

But behind the occasional comedy there was a very serious side to what was going on, and Judy and I wished only to distance ourselves from his work.

My first meeting with Richard's friend Rob Lees was at Heathrow Airport, just before we boarded our plane. A technical illustrator aged thirty-one, he had climbed Mount Kenya and had alpine experience too. His quiet and sensible manner gave the impression of steadiness, an impression which was confirmed by his behaviour on each succeeding day of the expedition.

The excitement of being on the way to the airport, and of taking off, is matched during preparations for landing and during the landing itself; but there is little romance in the process of spending long hours in cattle class, or monkey class, as some airline staff put it, in big aeroplanes. I wondered what our frosty-faced cabin staff thought of the phoney glamorous image of flying put about by airlines.

The Kibo Hotel, at the foot of the mountain, is about 80 kilometres by road from Kilimanjaro Airport. Set in luxuriant and colourful gardens amid tall rain forest and the green and yellow leaves of surrounding hillside banana plantations, the hotel lives up to expectations. It has retained the aura of one special feature of mountain history, when decades ago white men and women, accompanied by porters with loads on their heads, set off on foot for that huge mountain whose proximity is the raison d'etre of the two storey building. A mixture of mountain memorabilia - old ice-axes, ancient maps, faded black and white photographs - and African objects like spears and animal skins, has been encroached upon by the bright, shiny stickers of safari organisations and manufacturers of boots and skis and climbing equipment, but the stickers have mostly been restricted to the bar and reception area; the hotel maintains the dignity it deserves.

The day after our arrival was a Sunday, which was spent in sorting and packing equipment and arranging for porters and a guide, who all arrived in good time the next day. From the Marangu Gate entrance to the Kilimanjaro National Park we followed our guide, Frederick, who was more of a foreman in charge of the porters than a guide, since he was not going to set foot on the glacier. Though we mingled with our porters on the forest trail, they talked almost exclusively among themselves, speaking to us only when asked a question. Yes, they had been to Kilimanjaro many times; Nicholas was fifteen; (which we later learned meant he should not have been portering), Wilson had been a porter for many years; this one had two children, that one had four. They assumed the role of servants, took on the ways of hired hands, and carried heavy loads willingly; we were just another bwana group with fat wallets. In their elation at walking up even the easiest way to Kilimanjaro's high points, many people imagine that they have a deeper relationship with guides and porters than is actually so. As is the case with holiday romances, the visitor experiences a freshness and depth of feeling which is not necessarily shared by the local resident, who has been through it all before. In the glow of success, Kilimanjaro's ascentionists sometimes react over generously, giving away clothing and boots which would cost two or three months' Tanzanian wages, and handing out tips that amount to ten times a man's pay for the five-day trip. Such generosity leads to high expectations and frequent dissatisfaction on the part both of the subsequent givers and receivers.

The porters carried loads in wooden boxes and rucksacks on their heads. Though one wore sandals, the others had boots, and their clothing, much of it clearly originating from tourists, was adequate. Whenever we wished to take pictures our porters posed proudly. Through exposure to tourists they had become accustomed to cameras, whereas in towns and villages and at the roadside many people objected most strongly to having their photographs taken. This is said to be because of the belief that the taking of pictures would rob them of their souls but, though their feelings should be respected, the tourist may find that with the exchange of a few Tanzanian shillings in the favour of the subject the danger can be averted and the soul retained.

The rutted, heavily-trodden trail emerged from thick forest into giant fern and bush country, and in under four hours we were installed in one of several Mandara huts at an altitude of 2,727 metres. The porters prepared a good stew which they served in the timbered dining room.

In the bush country above the Mandara huts next day we saw no signs of the wild dogs which are said to hunt there. Not far short of the Horombo hut, our next overnight stop, lobelia and giant groundsel appeared, reminding me of the Umbwe approach, and of the fascinating way to Mount Kenya. Though mountains always lured me, the pink roses of Kashmir, the golden plains of Peru, lush forests, lakes of emerald and turquoise, bright flowers on brilliant green pastures, these delights are as intrinsic to mountaineering as is the challenge of the sport; our crowdless arena is the most splendid in the world.

Next day, after a breakfast of porridge, boiled eggs and papaya, we dawdled from the huts at 3,761 metres and soon diverged from the tourist trail, taking in reverse the route Hubert and I had followed three years previously along the southern flank of the mountain, through sparse vegetation. Though the trail rose only gradually, Ken found it hard going, and on our occasional rest stops he sat with his forehead cupped in one hand, in what Richard described as his Rodin pose. Having seen it all before scores of times, Frederick had his eye on Ken. Richard was moving like a fit camel, and Rob seemed at home with the altitude at that stage. We saw no one else on the bouldery, dusty trail to the Karanga valley, where we camped at the end of the day at a bit under 4,250 metres.

Soon next day came our first views of the Heim glacier, framed through a gap in white cloud. Dark grey ice cliffs stood one above the other in the lower section. Stripped of any fresh snow cover the glacier was unsoftened and stark. In the prevailing light, from our angle of view, and under the conditions of the time, it certainly looked as if the route deserved its grade of 4 (the hardest climbing route on the mountain being 6). This was the same grade as the south face of Mount Kenya, but I did not expect to meet similar problems with soft snow. With any luck it would be firm snow and ice all the way.

Two hours away from our previous night's camp we stopped; this was where climbers and porters went their separate ways. Ken would spend the night with the porters in a nearby hut and come up to the bottom of the glacier next day to take pictures of us as we climbed. It was preferable for him to sleep lower down as he was still not feeling well. The porters clapped politely as our trio set off over broken ground towards the spine of a glacial moraine, and by mid afternoon we had reached the bottom of the glacier and settled down under the flysheet of my tent just as hailstones began to drum down on it. At about 4,600 metres altitude and with water running off the glacier snout only five minutes away, we were well placed for our attempt.

Richard and Rob developed headaches but neither seemed in such a bad condition as to need to descend. Rarely is there any requirement to conform to a timetable on a mountain - that is one of the beauties of the sport, which some never learn as they hare around seeing next to nothing - and with sufficient food and fuel in reserve, we waited a day to be on the safe side. This was bad news for Ken, who would miss out on his action pictures, because Frederick wanted to escort him back that day. We could not help feeling sorry for him.

5.15 am. Hot chocolate to drink. The three of us are feeling well. The glacier looms darkly above, clear of cloud. There is almost no wind. We can go. In an hour or so we had dressed, eaten, packed, and set off unroped on the lower ice slopes. Within a few minutes I felt the need to change from crutches to ice axes, and to resort to the security of the rope. Rob led a slope of blue-green ice, and I led one of snow and ice, and then though no decision was voiced, leading became Rob's job; tacit agreements are common if the team is working well. A 40 degree ice slope took him to the bottom of a vertical grey ice cliff bearded with pale blue, sharply pointed icicles up to the size of telegraph poles. These and successive chandeliered ice cliffs, though spectacular and pretty, presented a threat in the unlikely event of the icicles breaking off. Rob went out of sight to the left of the cliff. We listened to the thunk, thunk of his axes biting into ice and soon, by the length of rope which had run out, we could judge that he had climbed around and above that first ice cliff. Richard followed, then I, on a 60 degree ice step followed by an easy snow ramp running rightwards above the cliff.

By 10.30 am. the sun was full on us, as ever softening the snow, and melting the ice to release small stones, allowing them to skip and buzz past, sometimes several stones in a minute. Occasionally one would crack us on the helmet and bounce on its way. Judging by the litter on the snow ledges the missiles were mostly small, though a few, just lying there but bigger than cricket balls, made us feel uncomfortable.

An ice cave which was big enough for us to sit side-by-side with our feet on the 45 degree ice slope we had just come up gave welcome shelter for a brief break. Thus far none of the ice had been steeper than 60 degrees, since we had been able to find a way around the steep cliffs.

After the feeling of relative security which the cave offered, I followed in third position behind Richard. The buzzing stones, the risk of avalanche from softened snow, and the possibility of bad weather made me uneasy. In the afternoon the blue sky rapidly turned pale charcoal; an air of seriousness hung over the mountain when the sunlight left. But for the time being at least we were fortunate that there was almost no wind; that same day on one of Kilimanjaro's lower summits a German was blown to his death from a ridge. It was hard to believe that the wind had raged just a few miles away, while we experienced only the gentlest of puffs.

Ice slope followed ice slope, and we moved leftwards and upwards across snowfields above a massive ice cliff. And there we were faced by a choice. Ahead loomed a near vertical ice cliff, and below us was another. We had the option of moving further leftward and upward on soft snow, but soft snow above big ice cliffs is never an attractive prospect; the solid cliff ahead was more inviting on balance. So Rob chose that way, thus committing us, again with our unspoken agreement, to following him for thirty metres. He rose on steep, greyish-white ice hung every so often at short vertical steps with thin, man high icicles.

Before long I was about fifteen metres up that section, below which the Heim glacier tumbled in successive cliffs and slopes for 300 metres. For a short way, perhaps three metres, the ice was vertical, but the picks of my axes and the spikes of my crampons went in well, and I was soon over that little difficulty. So far so good. Within minutes there was a similar problem, but this time composed of snow as well as ice, and the sun had been doing its softening work on the snow for several hours. Sinking my axes in as well as I could I stepped up, the first step on good ice, the second also. Whamming the axes in higher I raised my right foot to kick into soft snow and brittle ice; the crampon spikes went in, but not crisply, not securely. There was no alternative but to risk it. As I lifted my left leg the snow and ice supporting the right foot collapsed and I fell off.

'I'm off!' a high pitched voice warned Rob. I am told that a high pitch makes the voice travel better, but I hit the note involuntarily. The red rope stretched; I had no idea how securely Rob was placed as he held it, for anchoring oneself to snow can be a tricky business. I was aware of a huge drop below me.

I dropped only a couple of metres on the stretching rope, and a second try at the step took me up to comparatively easy snow. With all the difficulties behind us we rose 180 metres more on a snow ramp and began looking for a spot to halt for the night. Richard had his eye on a place above in an icy gully where there could have been a good platform; as it transpired the next day there was not, but we had no way of telling from below. Rob favoured a prow of snow a hundred metres to our left as we looked up the mountain, and I liked the look of the twenty degree snow slope we were on. A boulder about the size of a small car engine entered the discussion by smashing through Rob's proposed campsite even as we looked at it and wondered how well-protected it was from rockfall. No one said anything, but clearly only two options remained. Our choice was settled by Rob saying he was tired, and we stayed where we were and dug a platform for the tent.

On the second day, the ground to the summit was easy: an ice gully 120 metres long, an icy ridge, two narrow crevasses to jump, then just slopes of snow and ice. There was still a little risk if we slipped, for we moved unroped, cautiously; that way we could go at a pace which suited each individual, and on this day I was the slowest by far.

'I've never been so tired in my life,' Rob gasped as we toiled upward. And our monotonous plod in mist up the Southern Icefield he summed up well in one word: repetitive. But when the mist rose in the afternoon ten thousand baby suns winked sparkling smiles from the ice back to the great mother in the south-west, turning the slope to mother-of-pearl. We reached Uhuru, the true summit, where we entered our names in the book left in a large metal box for the signatures of the successful. While Richard and Rob descended the tourist trail to the Kibo hut, I chose to spend the night on the summit at 5,896 metres to take photographs of the African dawn, but failed to wake up until 9.30 am.

The descent, and usual ascent for that matter, can best be described as a potter, on an obvious stony trail. Trekkers frequently exaggerate the difficulties, making Kilimanjaro one of the greatest 'Mount Bullshits' in the world. Frederick and Ken had waited at Horombo and for the short day's walk out to the Marangu gate Frederick carried Ken's rucksack and Ken carried mine. We were back down in the heat, where my stumps were inclined to be damaged more rapidly. Any assistance with load carrying was greatly appreciated.

'Mein Gott! You got up Uhuru!' a sturdy middle-aged woman said to me after Ken had told her that his friend on crutches had reached Kilimanjaro's highest point. 'Mein Gott!'

We made no mention of the Heim glacier. There were echoes here of the reactions of people beneath Mount Kenya, but though the grades of difficulty of the routes were the same on both mountains, they might have been on different planets; soft snow had made such a difference on Mount Kenya, and on Kilimanjaro my stomach had been normal. 'I was slow because my legs are artificial' seems acceptable but 'I failed because my guts were upset' sounds so feeble. Yet I can tell you that on Mt. Kenya, and on a mountain you will soon hear about, the former were less trouble than the latter.

When I arrived home Judy called her parents to tell them I was safe.

'He's brown as a berry, fit as a flea, and happy as a sandboy,' she said, summing up nicely how our trio felt, a trio who eight weeks earlier were not going anywhere, and were not even a trio.

CHAPTER 8

The Alps and Bolivia

THE ambition to climb an 8,000 metre peak had not yet taken hold. I was just drawn on by a variety of tempting adventures all over the world. As the Gatwick Express left Victoria Station a black December night sky softened in minutes to pale dawn grey. Ten hours later, after my short flight and train journey, the sky reversed the process, from the same grey to near black, as I arrived in the famous French mountain town of Chamonix. December there is the season, almost exclusively, of the fashion conscious skier.

My accommodation was a four bunk dormitory in a typically French house with shuttered windows and small iron railed balconies, these reached through French doors. Having deposited my rucksack, I left immediately, since I had an invitation to dinner that evening at the home of my prospective climbing guide, Roger Baxter-Jones, his French wife Christine, and their daughter Melanie. RBJ, as he was known to his friends, had read philosophy at an English university and had for several years lived in Chamonix, working as a mountain guide. His personality was often outgoing, though at times he appeared distant, lost in his thoughts, unhearing. In the book The Shishapangma Expedition he comes across as being prone to grumpy moods which led him to ordering people about. One expedition member mocked this tendency with cries of, 'RBJ calling water boy! RBJ calling water boy!' In the same book Doug Scott describes him as 'one of the strongest Himalayan climbers I have been with, and one of the more modest.' That Christmas Roger was two weeks short of his thirty-fifth birthday.

As a training climb we chose the Chevalier Couloir on the Petit Aiguille Vert, a mountain of about 3,500 metres which we approached by cable car next day. Powdery snow is characteristic of winter climbing in the Alps, and we were glad we had snowshoes for the hour-long trudge to the bottom of the couloir. We were the only people on our route and had seen no other climbers in the area; once you got away from the skiers, solitude was the essence of winter climbing there. And seriousness, as a result of the solitude and because of the low temperatures. After a couple of hours on 45 degree snow, up a narrow triangle between rock ribs, our training climb was over.

Soon after dark on Christmas Eve heavy snow fluttered down on Chamonix; joy for the skiers, gloom for the handful of climbers who mooned around the traditional haunt, the Bar National. Fresh snow would take time to consolidate to a fit state for climbing, and the avalanche danger would be high on most routes. Days went by and more snow fell, but then came a period without precipitation.

'We'll go tomorrow,' Roger said. 'We could try a route on the Triangle du Tacul. The ice is so steep the snow will have slid off. We can go up on the Midi cable car and start climbing early next day. There's a difficile route we could try.'

'Difficile' ranked fourth on the scale of difficulty going from one (easy) to six. It was a serious target for me in winter.

The last cable car up to the Aiguille du Midi left at 4pm. and by 5.30pm. we were settled, illegally, in a comfortable four-bunk room in the cableway station; Roger knew some of the staff there, and a bottle of wine had changed hands for a key. Otherwise we would have slept in one of the manmade tunnels which honeycomb the rock for the purpose of leading tourists to viewpoints and feeding places. Our accommodation was shared, at Roger's invitation, with two English climbers, Ken and Dave, who had their sights set on a climb quite close to where we were going.

'Been here three times in winter,' Ken said. 'Never got anything done.'

This was not an unusual story.

We rose at 4.30 am. and in a cold rock tunnel, like a small railway tunnel, tied on the rope. The tunnel end was almost completely blocked with snow, except where a small hole had been chopped through, so we crawled forward and upward through the hole for a metre or so, to emerge like rabbits in the chill dark world. Descending a snow arete by the light of head torches, we lost 270 metres, and walked on snowshoes for two hours in strengthening light, towards the face we were hoping to climb. The grey ice, touched only by faint light at first, looked grim. At a party on Christmas Day I had met a man who had suffered frostbite when caught out for a night on this mountain in November; he was waiting for his toes to be amputated two weeks later. We were nearly at the face and the snow was getting steeper. It was hard to make progress up the powder and I struggled awfully.

'Roger, I'm out of my element. Perhaps I should go back.'

'Let's just try a couple of pitches on the ice.'

For a short way the ice was at 65 degrees and then the angle eased. Roger led on to the full extent of the near 45 metres of rope. He hammered in an ice screw and clipped himself to it; this is what would hold us if I slipped, 20 centimetres of threaded metal tube as thick as my thumb. It is a method which works quite well, particularly if you use more than one, though occasionally one comes across a snapped-off ice screw, a stubby, eloquent statement of the limitations of the system; and sometimes they can be plucked out by the force of a fall. Roger had chopped out a ledge in the ice, giving us a space as big as the blade of a cricket bat to stand on side by side. It was time for me to clip into the ice screw and for him to detach himself and climb on while I paid out the rope. He tiptoed his way up the tilted ice and banged in another screw 40 metres above. At each blow from our axes the ice shattered in saucer-sized stars with thin white splinter lines radiating from their centres, but the axe picks held firm in the star centres.

'It takes three hours or more from here,' Roger said at the top of the fourth pitch. 'And at least an hour to get down the other side, and two or three hours to walk back. You want to go on?'

'Weather's good. I'm happy to go on.'

He flowed rhythmically up ice which exercised but did not stretch him, while I followed in fits and starts, close to the limit of what I could cope with physically. Lacking leg muscles, I could not wham in the crampon tips as hard or step up as steadily as I would have liked.

'Enjoying it?' he called.

'Yes.'

Picks were going in three or four centimetres and for a while I felt happy. The sixth pitch changed all that. Although at only 45 degrees the unyielding ice would hardly accept crampon tips at all. Roger led again, and when I found my crampon tips making barely a scratch I was suitably scared.

The seventh pitch was similar at first but half way up the ice became softer and more accepting of the sharp metal points.

'Bravo, you climbed that bit well, Norman.'

'I don't feel very confident.'

'I've climbed the route with someone who was a gibbering wreck on this section.'

'I'm like that inside.'

'How do you get on at high altitude?'

'Slow until we reach 5,000 metres or so. Then I'm usually somewhere around the middle of the party.'

'Depends who you're climbing with,' he said dismissively, spoiling the moment with his fair observation. I am a plodder, a marathon man, but a slow one.

The ice slope on the eighth pitch eased back, leading to an easy snow and rock ridge which ran up to the summit of Mont Blanc du Tacul. But we were not looking for a summit that day; we had completed the quality section and would ignore the plod to the high point, stopping at about 3,970 metres altitude, having gained about 450 metres from our lowest point, about 300 metres of that on ice.

We made seven or eight abseils down the steep Cherie Couloir. I remember going down some vertical rock and vertical ice and much 70-80 degree ice too, and steep snow, down, down, nearly 45 metres each time. Down towards safety, down and away from fear, down towards shelter; it would be dark soon. We were at the bottom just before dark, and a half moon lit our way back. We had 270 metres to rise on soft snow back to the cableway station and there was no way to explain adequately to Roger how hard this was. Harder than all the ice we had climbed, the low angled snow made me stagger, made me fight, made me struggle where Roger just walked.

'This is not Muztagh Ata,' he said sarcastically. For all his education and deep thinking, for all his experience as a guide, he did not understand. A feeling of resentment on my part grew; I wish we could tackle this on equal terms, Mr. Superior Bloody Roger Bloody Baxter-Bloody-Jones. Then I'd show him. Or would I? Maybe he would burn me off. So I had to accept the unique niche in which I found myself, where I did not have to compete with anyone. I liked it that way, and was pleased to have added to my C.V. one more day of experience which would soon lead on to bigger things.

Eventually, there was the rabbit hole. In we went. Even with the assistance of crutches I found it difficult to drag myself the sixty or so steps up to our accommodation, I was so drained. But, not for the first time, I comforted myself with the thought that the effort for me was greater, the challenge greater and, therefore, glory be, the reward was enormous.

Ken and Dave had retreated from a third of the way up their route and the few other climbers we met in Chamonix had failed for one reason or another. '...a few members visited the Alps for winter climbing but owing to the conditions little has been achieved' it was reported in a circular of the Alpine Club soon after. Roger's choice of route had been the key. Seven months after our Christmas 1984 climb he was killed with Jon Ryder in a climbing accident, when an ice tower collapsed on them. Their tragic deaths robbed me in two quite different ways, for in Roger's case I was denied the opportunity of making ascents with him which would have pushed me to my limits. He may not have understood my limitations, but it was my job to do that, and his to conduct matters safely as a highly skilled guide. In the other case I would miss a companion who let me use his flat in Zermatt, and with whom I could tackle easy climbs. Part of the fun of mountaineering has been the variety of personalities of climbing partners, for though the perception in some quarters may be that climbers are a rough bunch, this could not be said of these two men; they were very strong, but Roger had a deeply cerebral side, and Jon's main hobby was playing chess. Though generically linked through their sport, mountaineers are about as much alike as vegetables, with a carrot here, an onion there, a potato, a cabbage, some earthy, a few rotten. Their variety on its own was not the spice, but their vitality too. They went out and did things, they had dreams and chased them. For many people it is the dreaming which does not come readily – first, catch your dream.

Yet in my case it was is if the dream found me. It was partly a matter of luck that I went on what was at the time a rare climbing course, and acquired such a deep enthusiasm. Then came dream after dream, each one a precursor of the main dream of an 8,000 metre mountain, a dream which seemed to come from without, from external influences, from the examples of others; but I was the one who had to believe it could be done. Few others did.

I was accepted on an expedition organised by Rainier Mountaineering of Seattle, to Bolivia in 1985. I hoped to climb in the Alps and other ranges two or three times a year, and if now and then I could escape the slog of putting the expeditions together I was more than happy to do so. This does not mean that the ascents themselves are any easier, for no one does the climbing for you, and at high altitude no one has any energy left for pulling others up, but nowadays 'off the shelf' expeditions make life a lot easier for the mountaineer.

As the plane approached La Paz, the world's highest capital city at 3,630 metres, I could see in the light of a near full moon the pale bulk of Illimani, 6,463 metres. Twenty-five miles from the city, the mountain loomed over the rim of the bowl in which La Paz sits. Shapely Huayna Potosi, a little lower than Illimani, could be picked out too. These two mountains were our main targets.

We were to stay for a short while at the Hotel El Dorado, where I met the five others the next day when they arrived from the airport. A tourist courier told us that one night at the Hotel El Dorado, which was cheap to us, cost more than she earned in a month; and her earnings were high by comparison with those of the Indians. The enormous difference in the standard of living between the Indians, who constitute the majority of Bolivia's 5.6 million population, and the small percentage – I have seen figures of between five and fifteen per cent – of

European origin (the remainder being mixed blood Mestizo) is characteristic of so much of South America. Outside the cities and towns a low cash income may bear little relation to the standard of living, since barter is common. A patch of land on which to grow vegetables and to keep a few chickens and pigs ensures a certain independence and quality of life, and a herd of llamas represents great wealth. It is not a land of milk and honey, though; the low prices received for crops, and soil erosion, are common problems, and much depends on whether water is available for crops and animals. But except at the extreme where starvation hovers close all the time, rural poverty can never compare with the urban poverty of South America. Yet still the poor flock to the cities in pursuit of wealth which will elude them. Most of them finish up living in slums or in shanty towns on the city outskirts, scraping a living on the streets by selling goods or skills such as cobbling and watch repairing. A few turn to begging.

In many ways La Paz emulated Lima, with its shoeshine boys, and women wearing several petticoats which gave them the appearance of being fat, whether they were or not. And there were the same jam-packed buses, and pickups with as many as thirty people squeezed in the back, and there were ragged beggars, most of them elderly and unsupported by the state. And, again as in Lima, Spanish colonial architecture stood alongside modern office blocks which sported huge neon advertisements for cars, electrical goods and drinks, and there were statues and wide boulevards and pavements buffed smooth by passing feet, and armed policemen standing about in hotel lobbies and outside company offices.

In a heavily laden jeep, we took the road out of the bowl in which La Paz lies and soon turned right off the highway and drove for an hour across the Altiplano. For the first time we saw at close quarters the native animal which symbolises mountain South America, the llama. Though they can get a move on when necessary, they would approach the vehicle in slow, regal strides whenever we stopped. Their curiosity led them to come very close and watch steadily. They are bred in large herds for their meat and as beasts of light burdens, are related to the camel, and have distinctive ears which resemble a thick pair of parentheses. Under the inquisitive gaze of two dozen llamas, and before an indifferent donkey and two pigs, we set up our two tents a few hundred metres from some scattered mud brick, thatched farmhouses at 4,500 metres altitude.

Craig Van Hoy, the expedition leader, had made arrangements for three ponies to carry our equipment and food, and early next day a woman with a baby in a blanket on her back appeared at the tents. A boy of about twelve, a youth, a little black dog and three ponies accompanied her. I thought she might be in her late twenties but she looked to be older. The women here, as in rural Peru, seemed to go from schoolgirl to the appearance of resigned thirties very rapidly; one did not often see women who looked to be in their twenties. Was it just a hard life which took a toll? Do people age inside and outside when they realise: 'This is how my life will be ordered until I die?' When there are no more corners to look around, no more mountains to climb except the one they have climbed a thousand times, do they start to grow old because they have nothing new to hope for? I think I would.

With our inexperienced aid the woman loaded the ponies and we, with fairly light loads in our rucksacks, followed them up a rough road. Before long, at the roadside, we had hired a donkey to carry the rucksack of Cort (Courtenay) Kane, who had been sick shortly after breakfast. He and his money broker friend John Russell had spent one less night than I had in La Paz, while Craig and the two remaining members of our party - Jason Edwards and Al Bernasconi - had been at high altitude in South America for several days.

In an hour the road faded at a stream, and we continued along a narrow trail used by local people to drive their cattle to high grazing. This led in two and a half hours to a pretty lake with a diameter of about 500 metres. Skirting the lake on the right bank we set up camp on the far side, and the woman departed with her human and animal entourage.

Though at about 4,570 metres, little more than 900 metres higher than La Paz, the altitude difference was enough to affect Cort badly, and he vomited again. John had a headache, but everyone else seemed well enough. Appetite is a good clue to who is acclimatising and while Jason, who like Craig worked for Rainier Mountaineering, complimented the stew I made from fresh vegetables as 'the best meal we'll have in Bolivia', John picked at it and Cort could not eat at all.

Al said, 'May have some trouble getting to sleep.' He was snoring within three minutes and rasped quietly away most of the night. Many people have difficulty sleeping at high altitude and Cort suffered what he described as 'the worst night of my life'.

We rested for a day and, having turned in early, all of us but Cort rose half an hour after midnight. A two-thirds moon cast enough light to allow movement without the aid of torches on frozen turf, over the dried mud bed of a small lake, between boulders as big as lorries, up scree, on to a glacier snout. The moon moved in from the right to vertically overhead and we walked on our own small ink blot shadows, on long slopes. There was no great pleasure in this first climb on snows too steep to let us amble but too shallow to excite. 'A grunt', my companions called it.

We stood in sunlight on the summit of Tarija, 5,240 metres. and our eyes followed a ridge running up to the top of Alpamayo Chico, 150 metres higher. But it was early days and ambition had to be held in check, for we would have to descend the far side of Tarija to reach the other mountain. Perhaps one day there would be time to take that fine ridge to the summit of Alpamayo Chico, I thought. No, there was no perhaps about it, I would make the time. Which I did, in 1988, partly sponsored by a Cornish scrumpy cider manufacturer whose slogan, on T-shirts and bottle labels, was 'Legless But Smiling'. It was an enjoyable climb, though rather short.

On the way down the glacier John, in front of me on the rope, slipped. He failed to call out so my only warning came from a suddenly tightening rope at my waist, and there was little time to react. By ramming my spiked crutches in the snow and sitting down I was able to hold him, at the cost of two crutches bent like bows.

Next day the woman, with her baby, the boy, the youth, the black dog, two ponies and a donkey trooped in shortly after 6am. Returning the way we had come, we made our rendezvous with José, a different driver who was the proud owner of a white jeep. The roof was soon piled with our rucksacks and we were off to our next mountain, Huayna Potosi. The two hour drive on a bulldozed mine road across the Altiplano, over a high pass, and along easy-angled mountain flanks was, by the standards of South American mountain roads, not at all bad; it was a motorway by comparison with what was to come later in this expedition. At several places a vehicle going off the road might roll down long and quite steep slopes, but there were none of the big drops which wait at the edge of many a mountain road.

We drove into the Zongo valley and followed the edge of a man-made lake about 800 metres long. By the dam at the head of the lake was a guardian's home and office, and a row of long, low stone buildings with corrugated iron roofs held on with big stones, two of which buildings we rented for the night. I presume the rooms had been built for construction workers on the dam building project. Though the guardian's house and the row in which we had our rooms were the only buildings around, the road outside was graced with two streetlights.

Cocoa, canned peaches and biscuits made a palatable high energy breakfast. Our planned height rise of 760 metres would not seem much on lower mountains, but when you start at 4,700 metres with a load on your back you know you are not in for an easy day. It began with a walk across the top of the dam, on a wall 100 metres long and one metre wide. On the right it dropped as much as 18 metres to rock, while on the left the turquoise water lapped to the very top, and slopped gently over. From the end of the dam a rough path led up a long moraine crest and broke through a big cliff by way of a gully of broken rocks. A Bolivian and an American who had set out just ahead of us descended, one of them having been badly affected by the altitude. No one else attempted the mountain while we were there.

We stepped on to snow and, roped together in threes, spent the first three hours of the afternoon weaving between crevasses. The first 40 degree slope of powdery snow made my heart sink as we went in to knee depth and our steps collapsed, causing us to slide backwards, and the loads felt as if they had doubled in weight. But there were few soft sections, and those were short. Between crevasses, over crevasses, along the lips of crevasses where depths looked like green bottle glass and which could swallow fifty elephants, we puffed like steam engines.

Our night's camp was sited on a vast snow plateau. When we settled in our tents, Cort looked ill, and John was drained. The two were friends from a long time back and one had first suggested the trip to the other. Cort was more likely the instigator, since his wife's opinion was, 'Dumb bastard'll do anythin',' when she came home from work one day to find him way above their house, trying out a microlite aircraft for the first time.

'Hell,' John said, 'Ah kin be as miserable as this at home. Could have a better vacation stayin' at work. How're you feelin', Cort?'

'Ah've had better days.'

'Yu gonna go fur the summit tomorrow?'

'Ah don' know.'

'If yu wanna stay behin', Ah'm happy to stay here with yu.'

'I'm gonna have trouble sleeping,' Al said, and passed out for the night.

Cort and John did join us the next day, Cort on a rope with Jason and Al, and John with Craig and me. With our backs free of heavy loads, and the weather fine, we left an hour before dawn and by the time we started up a steep ridge of snow the daylight had come. The ridge swept up, curving to our right in a smooth and graceful crescent, raising us 60 metres.

As we topped 5,790 metres everyone was struggling in the thin air, but none so hard as Cort.

'Ah'm havin' to dig real deep to keep goin',' he gasped. 'Compared with this a marathon's nuthin'. Nuthin' compared to this.'

Thirty-one years old, slim, fit, daring and determined, a long-distance runner and a three-day equestrian eventer, as well as a participant in several other sports, Cort now looked dreadful, but he would not give up.

At noon we began the haul on to the summit ridge, a long series of cornice scollops. A little distance below the final fragile summit at 6,080 metres we stopped, for it is acceptable not to stand on the highest point of snow if, as cornices do, the summit is likely to break off and take the summiteer to his death. ('Alex went to within 20 metres of the far west summit but retreated, not wanting to ride a collapsing cornice down the northern flanks.' - Doug Scott, The Shishapangma Expedition.)

Back in La Paz, Al and I waited in the hotel lobby. The drill was the same as usual: shower and change, then meet up for a meal. John stepped out of the lift.

'Cort an' Ah are goin' home,' he said. 'We've told Craig and Jason and we don't want it discussed over lunch.'

'Hell man, you sure?' Al asked.

'We've done what we came to do. Ah've never bin this high an' Ah wanted to know what it was like. Ah've found out.'

'You're acclimatised now,' I said. 'Ready for Illimani.'

'We've made our decision.'

Since his divorce a few years before, John had looked after his nine year old son and had said, 'It's hard for him to understand why his Daddy goes away for two weeks. And Ah didn't come all the way down here to go home in a bag.' This underlined how fortunate I was not to have to take the feelings of offspring into account, for though Judy and I were by no means ascetic in bed we felt no need to respond to the primitive urge to pass on our genes. There were those who said it was selfish not to have children, while others argued the opposite, that procreation was self-interest. I'll not waste my time on that, but will say we were fortunate to have choices we took consciously, including not taking on a mortgage until we had a large deposit for a flat so that our outgoings were low; this gave the freedom to live to follow dreams rather than just to exist. It was not a question of luck; we made sacrifices in some areas and benefited in others as a consequence. I think Cort's thoughts were centred on his second wife, whom he had recently married, and his job; he had a very responsible post with an organisation which raised funds for war veterans by trading through a chain of shops and a mail order business.

Lunch was a friendly: 'here's my address; and if you're ever in my town you got a place to stay buddy' sort of affair, but as a celebration it was subdued. Normally we would have been looking forward as well as backward, to Illimani as well as back on Huayna Potosi and Tarija, but it did not feel right to look forward with too much relish to something Cort and John would not share. Mind you, it was their choice.

Their retirement was a mixed blessing, for though it meant we were not such a strong party if one of our number required rescue, we had finished up with a more strongly motivated team. Craig, aged twenty-seven, and Jason, one year his junior, were both very fit as a result of their active lives with Rainier Mountaineering. Neither of these well mannered young men was going to give up easily on a professional engagement, and Al had his eyes firmly set on Illimani because the summit was 300 metres higher than any he had reached before; Huayna Potosi was about 90 metres below his previous best and he regarded it only as a training stage on the way to Illimani's top. He had the altitude bug, whereas at that stage I had not caught it.

'I'm a tough old sucker,' he said several times, and I had no doubts about the self-motivation of this forty-nine year old man who worked with neglected children.

Next day, José, our driver, had to obtain police permission to approach the hotel through one of the city's endemic road blocks; a demonstration against the government was expected. We loaded up hurriedly, bade hasty farewells to John and Cort, and drove eastwards on tarmac streets and cobblestones through the select residential area of the city. Soon we came into idyllic farm country, where the elements were the same as throughout much of rural South America: barley, maize, cabbage, lettuce, potato and onion crops in patches, donkeys, ponies, cattle, chickens, sheep, pigs, all wandering and eating, poplar and eucalyptus trees, grasses, broom, cactus in paddle and sausage shapes, mud brick buildings with thatched roofs, mud ovens like conical beehives, a stream here, bushes of bright flowers there, occasionally a whitewashed church with a tower standing on a hill. Every bit of landscape was unique, every soft scene a picture in itself, and if I could paint this is where I would do it.

By noon, after two hours on the serpentine road, we were about half way towards the mountain; in other words, we were a mere dozen miles closer. We had been treated to countless fine panoramas and the rough road had not been as bad as we had been told; so far. The views were to remain spectacular but for the last dozen miles as the crow flies we were to begin wishing we possessed the crow's ability to fly, in order to avoid the awful road. What my friends referred to as 'white knuckle time' began soon after we had left a village. Before long we reached a place where blasting and bulldozing had gouged a single lane road across huge cliff faces, to give access to mines. The road lacked the comfort of crash barriers or even an ankle high wall; a few whitewashed stones at least would have given a little psychological reassurance, particularly where the road edge crumbled. Tiny houses and a thin string of another road far below reminded us all the while that we were a very, very long way above the valley floor to our right; certainly the drop was more than 300 metres. Mostly we were silent, though at the worst places, where the road was so narrow the jeep scraped the cliff, we laughed a bit, nervously.

'It's in the hands of the driver and God,' Al pronounced resignedly.

Soon the way was so overgrown with bushes, higher than the jeep, that it seemed that at any moment we would drive into somebody's back yard and come to a complete halt. In ten minutes, in a clearing by a typical mud farmhouse, it looked like the end of the road. But a man there pointed to the hidden track to the side of his house, and said it was a good road and would take us where we wanted to go. We were to discover that opinions on what constituted a good road could be debated. The bushes thinned and shrank, and for the most part the meandering road up gently sloping pastures induced little fear. We began to think, at least to hope, that the danger was over. But as we tilted and bumped on a rocky, wet section, with loose mud partly blocking the road to the left and a horrifying drop to the right, our thoughts turned to the heavy weight of rucksacks on the roof.

Suddenly a strange voice squeaked from the back of the vehicle: 'I wanna get out!'

It was Jason. We laughed at him playing about, but soon realised he was not joking. ('I've never heard that voice come out of my mouth before,' he said later.) He looked like the man who has seen the chicken-sized killer bees heading his way.

'I wanna get out!'

He had risen from his seat and was attempting to climb into the front to desert the vehicle. We bucked and juddered along for a further two or three minutes to where the road had again been torn from a loose cliff, from which rocks had fallen onto the road. The road edge, to our left this time, had collapsed, so José halted, opened his door and walked forward to examine the obstacles. Jason was into the front seat and out of the door like a greyhound from a trap. José decided it was safe to proceed, but our escapee was adamant he would not re-enter the doomed vehicle; he spent the remainder of the journey standing on the back bumper and clinging to the roof rack.

'I felt wholly justified,' he said afterwards. 'I really was terrified.'

If I thought I could have kept my feet on the bumper of the bouncing vehicle I would have considered joining him.

A full hour later we came to the stone buttresses of a wooden road bridge which had collapsed long ago. This was the reference point we had been told to look for. Despite the collapse of the bridge the road continued ahead of us because a bulldozer, or perhaps a party of labourers, had dug further into the hillside to create a piece of road wide enough to form a passing place. José was therefore able to continue driving without turning around, instead of returning by the route we had driven up. We hoped this would be a better way, though there was no telling whether the road was blocked or had collapsed somewhere, and become impassable. This was Tuesday and it had been arranged that José would return at 10am. on Saturday to pick us up. He had other clients for Sunday and the following week, so this was the only day on which he could do the job. The agreement was that if we had not returned by noon on Saturday he would return to La Paz, and would be paid in full. If we needed more days than the timetable allowed, then we would find some alternative way back to the city rather than abandon the attempt on the summit. This would mean we would have no one looking out for us if things went wrong, but in any case in a book on the Southern Cordillera Real Range by R. Pecher and W. Schmiemann the authors advise: 'The thought that in the event of an accident help could be summoned in La Paz is almost certainly an illusion. There are no rescue helicopters, and, in the past, assistance on foot has invariably come too late.'

Craig had brought along a roast chicken, so we feasted well on that and fresh vegetables. Craig's choice of food for our little group was good, since he took a wide variety of tasty things. Appetites can become dulled, capricious and very selective at high altitude, and it is wise to have available a broad selection of food. All too often those in charge of rations thoughtlessly take what they prefer; I know, for instance, a vegetarian who bought only what he wanted to eat for everyone on a two week expedition. Though the meals were reasonably tasty he was not a popular man.

We began the ascent at first light, on steep grass. Nine curious llamas watched as we passed within thirty metres of them, and continued to watch for five minutes until we topped a brow and clattered across flat stones like those which roof Alpine chalets. The sun began to thaw a stream and allowed us water for our bottles. Then for several minutes we scrambled up rust-red slabs of rock where fool's gold flashed in the sunlight. Having crossed chuckling streams edged with ice we climbed onto the back of a gritty, solidified mud-slide, as big as the upturned bottom of the biggest oil tanker in the world, and as yellow as the most golden sand. The scene was never the same for long; after the mudslide was a long, loose stone slope which gained us 120 metres of altitude, and above that we scrambled over slabs littered with stones. A long snow slope and a short rock cliff led on to the rising snowy crest of a ridge which to the left fell in steep, pale brown, broken cliffs, to the right in white slopes and grey ice. We were on the crest for an hour and a half, moving steadily upwards and feeling more at home through training on Tarija and Huayna Potosi.

A height gain of nearly 900 metres was achieved without too much suffering, and we put up our tent in a snow bowl at 5,426 metres. That left just under 1,000 metres to go. At first Al seemed affected by the altitude and stood looking vacantly into space while three of us put up the tent and started cooking. Then he said, 'Buddy, can you spare a dime for a cup of coffee?' which if we had not known him would have deepened our concern, but he only said this when he was happy and well.

Though up at 3.30 am. we waited around for some time for the cloudy sky to decide what it would do. Might it allow us to try for the summit, or at least to take our camp higher? The cloud dispersed, and at 6.30am. we scrunched across hard snow to a sharp and steeply-rising snow ridge, towards bright Venus and a boat moon. The insecurity of the snow forced us to keep to the left of the precise top of the knife-edge spine.

Bright daylight had arrived long before we had gained 120 metres up the ridge, to be faced by a steep, soft, rope length of snow split halfway up by a wide, deep crevasse. Fortunately the crevasse was bridged by snow at one point, and we crossed without difficulty, and continued up the slope to a flat area known as the Condor's Nest. This we knew to be at 5,600 metres, which left 865 metres to rise, at first only gradually, meandering between crevasses. We felt happier when the ground steepened into a broad, winding ridge; for a while our two ropes of two were reasonably safe.

All around were white cliffs, not plain, but layered by each year's snowfalls, and decades deep. There were old footprints ahead of us all the time, and, after four hours on the go, at the base of a huge slope, we came across a few pieces of unnecessary litter and the signs of a one-tent camp shovelled out. This must have been their second camp, and with loads on their backs the occupants would have taken about six hours from the lower camp, leaving them with a fairly easy last day, provided the weather held. The clear footprints, the uncovered litter and the camp space were evidence that there had been no fresh snow for days.

'Ten minutes rest here,' Craig announced.

'Buddy, can you spare a dime for a cup of coffee?'

Eat a little, drink a little, every time you stop. Ten minutes rest seemed like forty seconds. The next 350 metres or more of slope was dull, never went above 40 degrees, and had a nasty habit of being softest where it was steepest. The spectre of Mount Kenya haunted me, but I need not have worried because almost everywhere the snow was firm and just what the mountaineer would want. Do not assume, however, that it is easy to move even on the best of slopes. At 6,000 metres breathing comes to the mountaineer with such difficulty. You struggle along with lungs blasting like bellows, and that goes on for eight or ten hours in a day, with hardly a rest. The physical and mental effort required is enormous. Your lungs might be stuffed full of feathers as you struggle for each breath; the amount of oxygen reaching the muscles is insufficient to fuel them properly, and one step, just one step, calls for an effort of will. You can find a reason or excuse at any moment for giving up if you are not strongly motivated. Reason or excuse; the dividing line can be hazy when the mind and body are looking for relief. But no one in our group made any excuses. The weather was in our favour, the snow was good enough, and we were acclimatised. Mental strength was increased by being in a group because a group was stronger and safer, and because each was afraid to be seen to falter or fail. We needed little in the way of skill now, and barely more brains than a machine, but we did need willpower.

We reached a col. Looking uphill, to our right was a summit, the south and highest of Illimani's tops. A distinct snow ridge ran straight towards it. In a few minutes we would press on, but we enjoyed a fleeting rest first.

'Buddy, can you spare a dime for a cup of coffee?'

The 'tough old sucker' was feeling all right, that was clear.

Craig and I set off just ahead of Al and Jason, attaining a crest which rose only very gradually and was wide enough to allow us to walk on its very top without any difficulty, except that which resulted from the thin air. Still, a fall to the left or the right would have sent us down snow slopes and perhaps over a cliff, so we had to be careful. The ridge ran on and on, every so often putting up a bump which looked like the summit but which, when we reached it, proved to be concealing a bit more ridge, and a bit more. This must have gone on for 400 metres or more, but in seven and threequarter hours it was done. At least there was some reward for our self-imposed suffering; so much of the suffering of others seemed pointless. At 6,465 metres we followed the usual summit rituals: jacket on, click with the camera, nibble, nibble, sip, sip, click.

We enjoyed the luxury of remaining late in our sleeping bags the next day, and dawdled down to base camp in four hours. José arrived on cue, armed with three shovels and a pickaxe for road repairs and a pistol to repel anyone with hostile intentions. As we loaded the jeep he examined the bag of rubbish we had carried down for disposal in a waste bin in La Paz.

'Leave it by the roadside,' José insisted.

We did not like to leave rubbish, we explained.

'But the campesinos (peasant farmers) will like it. There are tins and plastic bags and bits of food. To them it is like treasure.'

It was his country, so we did as he said, but with reluctance.

There were a few bad spots on the alternative road, he told us, and Jason stepped up on the back bumper. Very soon we crossed two icy patches of road, scraping the roof rack on the cliff to our right because it was so narrow, and crept by a spot where a collapse above a drop of 150 metres meant the jeep only just fitted what was left of the rough way.

The road improved and Jason got in. Ten minutes on a reasonable surface passed, when José said quietly, perhaps to himself, 'Poor Jason.' That could mean only one thing: another bad section. We crawled very slowly, lurching towards the drop to our left, but it was soon over safely, and that was the last of the 'white-knuckle' bits. There was one more difficulty, but that occurred on a wide, safe corner where a stream had ravaged the road. With the assistance of an impish little man who lived nearby in a solitary hut we filled in the worst of the holes and the jeep crossed. As we boarded again José gave the man a rather paltry reward of a few nuts and raisins. We could not understand why he had been so mean.

'When we go around the corner,' José explained, 'he will take the rocks out and wait for the next jeep.'

José knew what he was talking about because he had been down this way four days before, and up it only hours earlier; this was probably the third time he had paid up for the stones to be moved!

In La Paz we parted on good terms, Al, Jason, Craig and I, with vague plans for more climbs together. We had been to such a pretty place, and had been successful, which all helped us get along.

At Heathrow Airport I went through the Nothing To Declare

channel, to be stopped by a young man in customs officer uniform. He asked me if I had anything to declare and I said no. He showed me a list of what I was allowed to bring in free of duty, and asked me again if I had anything to declare.

'No.'

'Then would you mind telling me what is in your cardboard box?'

'Artificial legs.'

'Artificial eggs? What are artificial eggs?'

I explained, was thanked courteously and was asked to proceed on my way.

Rob Lees on Heim Glacier, Kilimanjaro.

Mount Kenya, 5188 Metres.

Rock Hyrax which demanded food that was being thrown in a rubbish bin.

Barry Needle

Mount Assiniboine, Canada. A
stunning mountain.

On the way to Mount Assinboine.

Alpamayo, Peru, 5947 metres

The author on Mont Blanc du Tacul in winter.

Roger Baxter-Jones on Mont Blanc du Tacul.

French group on Broad Peak,
Pakistan.

Tarija (left) and Alpamayo Chico, Bolivia.

Near the top of Masherbrum II,
Pakistan.

Approaching the summit of
Cotopaxi, Ecuador, in very
cold weather.

Rural Scene in Nepal.

Yaks before Mount Everest.

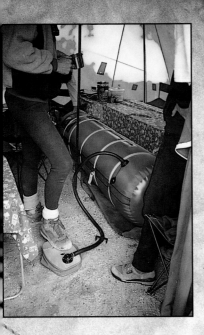

An inflated Gamow bag, which we hoped would save a life on Everest.

Harry Hakomaki approaches the North Col.

Shishapangma, Tibet.

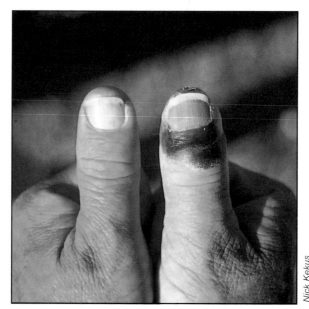

Frostbite suffered by the author on Shisapangma.

CHAPTER 9

The Canadian Rockies and Wonderful Alpamayo

A photograph of splendid Mount Assiniboine sparked my interest in the Canadian Rockies. Barry Needle, with whom I had climbed in Kashmir in 1981, liked the idea of climbing the mountain too; he was influenced by the fact that he had a close friend living in Calgary.

My limb makers performed an emergency repair on a cracked leg on the same day Barry arrived in London from Sheffield, fresh from a mountain rescue. He had been a voluntary rescue team member for over twenty years, and was an experienced, reliable and hardworking companion.

Barry's friend, John Laycock, collected us at midnight from Calgary airport, and we spent the night in his flat. The next day was devoted to buying provisions, in the graffiti-free, modern centre of this high-rise, oil-boom city. With our shopping done, Barry and I headed off along Trans-Canada Highway No. 1 in John's car. Soon, rolling hills, ranches and woods were the foreground to the marvellous white mountains straight ahead. Place names echoed the pioneering days: Elk Run, Cougar Creek, Dead Man's Flats, Bear Hill, Stony Indian Reserve, Bow River.

Less than two hours after leaving Calgary we had parked the car at a point where a rough lakeside road deteriorated to such a degree that it would not have been right to have taken John's car further. The road beside the lake led past a holiday riding ranch, and just beyond the ranch a notice warned us that we were in bear country, their country, not a place where they intrude. Both black and grizzly bears are potentially dangerous, and considering that grizzlies can weigh up to 500 kilogrammes and stand nearly two metres tall, one can appreciate why they must be treated with respect. (At birth grizzly and black cubs weigh as little as 340 grammes and 250 grammes respectively). Since many bears can run as fast as a racehorse, or in other words one and a half times as fast as the best Olympic sprinter, under many circumstances it is futile to run from a bear, and as black bears can climb well and grizzlies can reach high and are capable of pushing over or digging up quite large trees, it is advisable to avoid encounter rather than to wander about in the belief that flight is the answer. In order to avoid surprising bears, which may then feel threatened, many hikers wear a small bell to warn of their approach; bears will usually scuttle off when they hear or smell humans coming their way. Making a noise may be ineffective, though, where the thrash of a river masks the sound of a bell or conversation, and the smell of food can bring a bear from a very long distance to a camp. A safety handbook for the area says: 'Studies have revealed that human sexual activity can increase the possibility of a bear attack'. (Just how the studies were conducted is not stated!) If a bear becomes aggressive and escape is impossible, the two last resorts, fighting back or playing dead, are equally unattractive. Whether to punch and kick a creature which has big teeth and huge claws and is five to ten times your weight, or to lie still while it snuffles around and perhaps mauls you too, is a nightmarish choice.

The narrow, frequently straight, muddy (or 'mooky' as Barry put it) trail through dense, uniform conifer forest was claustrophobic, with only occasional breaks allowing a view of forested peaks. At the end of the afternoon we settled down alone in a designated campsite among tall trees. Near the regimented tent spaces were timber picnic tables and a lavatory, and wires like washing lines strung between two trees, enabling us to haul our rucksacks high up out of the reach of bears and sharp-toothed porcupines. The latter chew lavatory doors to pieces and are said to have a greater fondness for rubber and leather than a High Court judge, which accounted for several saddles and a rubber dinghy being suspended in the trees. We had encountered a few people going up and down the trail, but never met the owners of the saddles and the dinghy. The National Park is controlled in a way which makes me feel uneasy, but the alternatives are worse, much worse, when man is around. It is a pity it could not be left to nature, but this is not a realistic option in the heavily used area; by control the damage from erosion and litter is reduced to a minimum. In particular, the fifty Canadian dollar fine per item of litter left behind is an effective deterrent.

Next day's trail had more character about it, commencing with a broad, flat, open valley floor down which a crystal river snaked. Thick bushes surrounded us, but we could see above them on both sides to fine mountains, and the closed-in feeling of the day before was gone. As the trail steepened it began to weave across forested hillsides where trees stood far apart and let us see all around. Unbeknown to us this was the prelude to the visual crescendo which awaited us at Assiniboine Pass, for when we reached the crest at 2,195 metres, there was Mount Assiniboine in all its glory. It had on a clean, white lacy coat, and at the first sight of the mountain I began to mutter foolishly, 'Hey! Hey! There it is! My word! My word!' Mount Assiniboine has justly earned the title 'Matterhorn of the Rockies'.

About twenty minutes later, after we had crossed a flat meadow and climbed through the forest, the spectacle became even more splendid, for the whitish emerald Magog Lake came suddenly into the foreground at the foot of the mountain.

'There is no more beautiful lake in the Rockies than Lake Magog and Mount Assiniboine towering over it.'
- Frank Smythe, *The Canadian Rockies.*

Our campsite was at another orderly place under the mountain, and close to the lake, and next day we set out for the Hind hut, from which the mountain could be attempted the following morning. On our way there two local climbers descending from the hut advised us against attempting the route, because ice was making the climb too dangerous. A park ranger who had made four failed attempts on Mount Assiniboine had already advised us similarly. Considering the area around Calgary had received its heaviest rainfall for seventy years the day after we arrived there, we could understand that there might be problems. But, unwilling to accept that we should turn back yet, we continued in a half-hearted way towards the hut on narrow, exposed ledges strewn with stones. But deep down we knew we would turn back; always listen to the locals. So we did not climb our beautiful mountain, but instead trekked over Wonder Pass, above two more magnificent lakes named Marvel and Gloria; the pass and the lakes deserve their grand names.

The balance between ambition and caution had been weighed, and there had been no sensible option left but to turn back. The wisdom of that decision was underlined the day I arrived back home, to find that one of my climbing acquaintances and a companion had disappeared on a mountain in Pakistan several weeks earlier; they were presumed dead. The man I knew had always been an ambitious climber, and on this occasion had refused to turn back when the six-man expedition was depleted in numbers to only two, through injury and sickness. On a big and isolated mountain this was a risky thing to do. In an obituary my friend Dave Parsons wrote: '... he was probably one of the most dedicated and single-minded people that I ever met,' and '...it was always very difficult to influence him when he put his mind to something. Mountaineering was not just a hobby, it was a way of life, a driving force which he neither could, or wanted to, give up.'

Dave went on to quote Eric Shipton: 'There are few treasures of more lasting worth than the experience of a way of life that is in itself satisfying,' but added his own words: 'Standing in the church, in front of their families, friends and workmates, people who knew them well, was more difficult, as only a few there really knew them in the sport for which they gave their lives.'

Friends and family cannot be expected to understand fully, for they are the ones who pay the price if things go badly wrong. Our capsizes send waves of horror and distress sweeping again and again over those who love us; but to give up is to die in another way.

There is a timber lodge, Mount Assiniboine Lodge, situated at 2,195 metres on the edge of Lake Magog. At that time it was run by Sepp and Barbara Renner; Sepp was a Swiss mountain guide. As soon as I returned home I wrote to see if he would climb with me the next year.

'I am available to accompanie you on your climb to Assiniboine,' he replied. 'I prefare the week, as weekends tend to be to busy on the mountain.'

Applied to mountains, 'busy' is relative. Five or six people would be considered a crowd on Mount Assiniboine, fifteen a horde; how unlike the popular climbs in the European Alps, where one might see a hundred people on the same route.

A year after Barry and I had been to Canada, I set out again for Mount Assiniboine. John Laycock picked me up at Calgary airport. A draughtsman, temporarily unemployed, he was free to join us on Mount Assiniboine.

'Conditions on the mountain are good,' he informed me. 'I rang Sepp and he said he was certain this was true because he was sitting on the summit at the time, speaking through a radio telephone.'

John wanted to run up to the hut without a rucksack and this allowed me the excuse of travelling up by helicopter, with both our rucksacks. So, early on a sunny Sunday afternoon I and five other passengers boarded a small yellow helicopter standing in a car park not far from where Barry and I had left John's car a year before. It took off over big blue and green lakes and soared close to huge grey cliffs to rise over Wonder Pass. This way of viewing the wilderness may be frowned on by mountaineering purists, yet the panorama of lakes, forests, pastures and mountains was breathtaking. At times we seemed to float high and motionless, as if we sat in a transparent blister, while the wild, wild country slid quickly by beneath and around. But whenever we came close to a cliff or the ground, we were in no doubt it was we who were racing in less than ten minutes to the lodge.

Sepp met us at the landing spot fifty metres from the lodge, and helped to unload the luggage of the passengers who, for the most part, would spend between two days and a week on easy hikes in the area. He insisted that John and I should stay at the lodge without charge, instead of camping. Sepp and I had met only briefly the year before, so this arrangement gave us a better opportunity to get to know one another.

'I have my own Matterhorn in my back garden,' he said with a glint in his eye, and you could tell he loved the mountain and its splendid setting.

'My enthusiasm for this spot has no limits,' wrote Erling Strom, in Pioneers on Skis. 'Assiniboine itself, the most perfectly shaped mountain in the world, dominates the picture... Its shape is more nearly perfect than the Matterhorn and the foreground, with Lake Magog in the center, is much prettier than that of the Matterhorn.'

Erling Strom was responsible for setting up Mount Assiniboine Lodge and its attendant guest cabins. He overstates his case just a little; in the beautiful baby contest the mountain was his baby. And there are many alternative viewpoints for the Matterhorn, with a variety of interesting and pretty foregrounds on offer. But still, Mount Assiniboine is very special, the magnificent monarch with its emeralds at its feet - Sunburst Lake, Cerulean Lake, Gog and Magog Lakes, Elizabeth Lake, and the tiny Moose Bath, whose name always conjured up in my mind a cartoon picture of a moose with a loofah, sitting in the water, scrubbing its back.

John arrived at the Lodge on cue, having taken three hours from the valley. He mentioned to Barbara that he might come up on his mountain bike the next time.

'When you do, don't forget to hang it from a branch at night,' Barbara advised, 'so the porcupines don't eat your tyres.'

Next day was fine; so let's see what the mountain will serve us. Forty minutes were enough to walk through a larch forest to the far end of Magog Lake. After we had slogged up scree for several minutes, Sepp stopped.

'Here I put on my brain bucket,' he said, taking his helmet from his rucksack. 'The cliffs above are loose.'

John and I followed suit, and soon, at Sepp's suggestion, I tied on the red rope. The first part of the way was familiar, on stone strewn horizontal ledges and steep scree slopes which took us across and up, right to left across the vast black cliff at Assiniboine's hem. An easy half day ended with a long boulder field and a longer snowfield, and a gently angled slope up a promontory like a low stack of crazy paving stones, where stood the hut. The single storey, wooden framed, aluminium sheathed Gothic arch shelter was painted bright blue and looked much like an upturned boat, but very much out of place at 2,710 metres unless you believe the story of the Ark. The building housed chairs, a bench, a table, cooking utensils, cups, plates and cutlery; two tiers of bunks gave room for a dozen people to sleep on foam mattresses.

In pale dawn light we found the lower black flanks of Mount Assiniboine to be woefully loose, yet one could forgive this beautiful mountain. Loose rock soon gave way to steep, black, firm rock which allowed us to climb more easily, but in a short while the way deteriorated again to the brittle, pale brown limestone which forms much of the mountain's north ridge.

A near perpendicular 30-metre cliff known as the Red Band cuts across the whole of the north face, like a red layer in a pyramidal cake. Our route lay up the left of that face, and the Red Band was unavoidable. At close quarters the rock was not just red, but displayed bright yellow lichen too. The red, the bright yellow, the pure white snow patches, the clear blue sky above, and the emerald lakes below - what moments those were. There was colour, and there were abundant holds for one such as I, who had wondered long how the going might be at that point. By 11 am. the Red Band was beneath us. When we stopped for a rest Sepp took out his radio telephone to report our progress to Barbara.

'How's it going, Sepp?'

'We're above the Red Band.' His voice was bouyant.

The north face fell steeply to the right of our ridge, while the east face plunged vertically on the left. After half an hour of airy climbing on steep steps we were confronted by the Yellow Band, which formed another distinctly coloured step in the ridge. Like its red counterpart, the Yellow Band was not as difficult as I had thought it might be.

'Now we come to some serious mountaineering,' Sepp announced at the top of the second band. We moved rightwards on to the north face, where Sepp led the way up a short 60 degree ice slope followed by a wide, vertical, ice filled crack as high as two men, and a similar but ice free crack.

The angle of the rock eased, and I was soon moving on crutches up loose rock to the mountain's north summit, which is not the highest point. It took a few minutes more on a sharp ridge of black rock and wind-blown snow to Mount Assiniboine's real summit at 3,618 metres. There we filled in our names in a little book kept rolled in a piece of metal tubing and left on the top. About ten parties had been to the summit that year.

'I like this mountain because I can see my house from here,' Sepp said. We all liked this mountain. Our descent to the Lodge was uneventful and blessed with the good humour which comes easily to contented people. John and I were again put up as guests of the Lodge, and not only did Barbie and Sepp refuse to accept payment, but Sepp insisted he had undertaken the climb as a friend, not as a paid guide.

'This was one of the most rewarding climbs I have done,' he said. 'That is worth more than money.'

This climb was another brick in the wall of experience, but I had no idea at the time just how high that wall was to become; there were bigger bricks to come.

Back in Calgary an English veterinary surgeon and mountaineer, Carl, invited John and me around for dinner with him and his girlfriend. We had a nice celebration, though once more we were reminded that ours is a hazardous sport; Carl had attempted Mount Assiniboine in 1978 but had turned back when one of his companions had fallen and disappeared down the east face. Sepp had said about one person died on the mountain each year in recent times; that seemed a high death rate for a mountain which saw perhaps ten or fifteen ascents a year by a total of thirty to forty people. I have never climbed in blissful ignorance of the consequences, but such a toll made me think.

There was worse to come, for when I rang Judy it was to learn that Julie Tullis, Alan Rouse, John Smolich and ten other people had died recently on K2, the second highest mountain in the world.

Alan Rouse, whom I had first met in Peru in 1978, died at the same high camp as Julie, weak, dehydrated and alone, when those five who were still alive and able to move attempted to get down. Of the five who made the descent a Polish woman disappeared on the way, and two Austrians collapsed from exhaustion and associated high altitude problems, and probably perished through hypothermia. The two survivors suffered bad frostbite injuries which resulted in amputated fingers and toe joints. Alan had done much of the donkey work of breaking the trail through the snow to the summit of K2, and, typically, he had given shelter to others in his tent, even though this resulted in him having to sleep with his head and shoulders outside the tent. Such actions weaken a man at high altitude; had he been more selfish he might have survived. He had invited me to let him know if I wanted a climbing companion sometime, and I fully intended taking up his offer. I wish I had earlier.

The total of thirteen deaths in one year on K2 was made up of casualties from several separate incidents, and in one of these an avalanche killed John Smolich, with whom I had climbed in Argentina, in 1982. He was a pleasant and considerate companion; in fact, Julie, Alan and John were three of the nicest climbers I have met. Forty-seven years old, thirty-four and thirty-six respectively, they died early, but they blossomed wonderfully before they died. Perhaps one should not ask for more for oneself, but what of those left behind?

In May 1986 Judy and I were away again, to the Julian Alps of Yugoslavia, on a walking trip which was also training for me for an expedition. From the start, we were made to feel very welcome by the chamber of commerce and the tourist association in Kranjska Gora, who took us out to dinner at a lakeside restaurant.

We based ourselves for three nights in the Erjaceva hut at 1,515 metres and walked the hills and forests each day. The hut guardian, a thin Jack Sprat of a man, and his fittingly large wife, were very hospitable and gave us several little gifts: pin badges and wooden pendants of the hut, postcards of the area in autumn colours, a bunch of flowers for Judy, and even a photograph of their wedding.

We trod papery dry leaves amid the glorious spring flowers which abound there, hellebore by the hundred, kingcups at stream edges, pastures dotted with violet, gentian and crocus, and forest floors of celandine, pulmonaria, coltsfoot and wood anemones. Overhead, beech trees had upon them small fresh leaves of brilliant green which in sunlight turned to lime. The remains of exceptionally heavy snows blocked the approaches to all but a few peaks, but we were content to be among the mountains rather than on them, to walk rather than climb. Perhaps that's how it will be when I grow old.

In early 1986, I was asked to advise four members of the London Mountaineering Club on their forthcoming expedition to the Peruvian Andes. Which mountain should they try, they wanted to know? 'Alpamayo', I said. 'Whatever you do, try Alpamayo; it is so beautiful.' They made Alpamayo their major objective, and I envied them. Then they asked if I would like to go too. I jumped at the opportunity and soon was bound for Peru.

As when I went to Bolivia, I planned to arrive a few days ahead of the others in order to acclimatise, but at first a delay loomed at Madrid airport, for a connecting flight had been overbooked. Five of us, strangers until then, decided we would carry more weight as a group, so became an expedition for a while, and succeeded in pressing ourselves on board, into first class seats, complete with the champagne and grovelling which accompany that class of travel.

Grubby Lima, under a grey sky, seemed little changed from my first visit in 1978, except that most of the suburban shantytowns were no longer there, and vehicles were much less battered than before. The pavements were in the same state of disrepair, and huge hoardings still advertised Coca Cola, Pepsi Cola, Inca Cola and Japanese electrical goods and cars. The overwhelming feeling of people, people everywhere does not change, nor does the contrast between ostentatious affluence and poverty in dress and housing.

From Lima it was a nine-hour bus journey to the city of Huaraz on a good road which twisted and turned and rose through farm country. Once there, I learned that a large party of Italians, seventeen in all, had failed on Alpamayo recently. Without knowing them or their experience, I could judge little from this, so was not unduly concerned.

Three acclimatisation days passed, but my partners did not arrive in Huaraz on the appointed day, nor the next, and no news of them came. Still, I could not complain about the city in which I was forced to wait, and my friends arrived one afternoon, three days late, having been delayed in Caracas; and their bus had broken down for three lengthy periods on the way from Lima. I led them from the street where their bus journey terminated, to the Hostal Colomba, one of the best hostels in Huaraz. Entering through huge brass studded wooden gates, guests step into a large courtyard containing a fountain, vines, palm trees, cacti and rose bushes, and scores of potted plants on stands and suspended in baskets. Around the courtyard are several occupied bird cages, and the walls are painted with murals of country scenes. At one side of the courtyard is an ornate chapel with seats for twenty people. Some of the rooms look out on the courtyard, while other accommodation consists of bungalows set between avenues of trees. For US$2 a night (about £1.40 at the time) we had clean beds in clean rooms, and clean toilets.

At breakfast Chris Rhodes, our most fluent Spanish speaker, cast doubt upon his linguistic abilities by ordering an orange juice sandwich, but thereafter we came to rely on him as our interpreter. He was thirty-eight years old, a social worker turned sociology lecturer, was generally quietly spoken and level headed, but was inclined on occasions to heated outbursts. Chris's solicitor girlfriend, Annabel Yarrow, one year his junior, possessed similar views to her boyfriend, and with their occasionally bristly temperaments, they seemed a pair well matched. The remaining members of the team, Paul Allum and Gary Weston, were easy going men, and I felt there would be no difficulty in discussing strategies with that duo.

We spent three days making arrangements and buying supplies. Between us we had brought four rucksacks and two kit-bags of equipment and rations - plus a box of spare legs - which contrasted with the fifty-six crates of the Franco-Belgian expedition which first climbed Alpamayo in 1951.

My old friend Pepe Espinoza, hotel owner and entrepreneur, put us in touch with his colleague, Alfonso, who arranged for us minibus transport, donkeys and a camp guard. There had been robberies from hikers and climbers on the trail we would take (even Chris accepted this, though he naively wished to believe it different) so hiring a guard was a sensible precaution rather than a damning condemnation of all Peruvians.

On the morning of our departure for Alpamayo, Alfonso arrived at the hostel in the minibus, in company with the guard and a journalist who did not speak English. While the vehicle was being loaded Alfonso interpreted for the man.

'He asks if it is correct your legs are artificial.'

'Yes.'

'They are amputated below the knees?'

'Yes.'

'He asks if you have piles.'

'Piles?'

'Yes. Piles.'

I could not understand the relevance of the question. 'You sure he said 'piles', Alfonso?'

'Yes.'

The reporter tried to help. 'Bionico?' he asked.

Ah, that was it! The Spanish for battery was 'pila', and he wanted to know if I was battery operated!

'No. Tell him, no batteries.'

We departed around noon, on a journey like one I had made before, down the colourful Rio Santa valley. Small red and brown ploughed fields, the usual patches of mixed crops, large tracts of grassy, uncultivated land, tall and straight poplar, eucalyptus, acacia, brilliant yellow broom, cacti in many shapes, bamboo, wandering animals and adobe houses lined this lovely place. Here man lives in harmony with nature, nature which is respected. The earth is known as Pachamama, Mother Earth, and offerings are made to her, often in the form of alcohol sprinkled about. And before using a plough the farmer asks the pardon and permission of Pachamama.

Chris and Paul ordered guinea pig for their meal at our lunch stop. From the kitchen there came a squeal followed by a thud, then the hiss and crackle of frying, and a few minutes later two plates were produced, each bearing a golden brown half body, served with fried potatoes. Those of us who felt sorry for the guinea pig tucked in without conscience to our chicken and made only half joking comments about the sort of people who would eat their pets.

By the end of the afternoon the minibus had taken a rough but adequate road past foothill farms, past rolling pastures, prickly pear and barrel cactus, to the little village of Cashapampa at an altitude of 2,900 metres. Here a couple of small stores sold soap, bread, cakes, biscuits, confectionery, beer and meals to travellers and local populace alike; the latter were mostly farmers and their families. They lived in a small cluster of mud brick single and double storey houses beside the road and around a dusty square, and in other hillside houses scattered through the surrounding small fields and forests of poplar and eucalyptus. The air of peace permeating this sunny mountain village made me think of warm summer Sundays on English farms thirty years ago. On a mixed farm there was work to be done on Sundays, but there was more time to do it, less rush, less bother. That was how the pace felt at Cashapampa, beside the road, in the stores, in the fields; people had time.

Alfonso had arranged a night's stay for us in a simple whitewashed, red-tiled, single storey, one room building which housed four beds; it was satisfactorily clean, and must formerly have been an ordinary family home. He then confirmed our booking of six donkeys with a local man, and returned in the minibus to Huaraz, leaving us in the charge of our camp guard, Maximiliano. Since he was only about 150 centimetres tall and slightly built, it was his presence as a Peruvian we were relying on as a deterrent, rather than his stature.

Our donkey loading the next day was witnessed by an audience of a score of women and children. The donkey driver Hilario, and Maximiliano (or Maximo, as he was commonly known) were practised at the job, and we were soon on our way in a little crocodile of animals and people, following the right bank of a gigantic gorge, the Santa Cruz, on a steep narrow path edged by briar, pampas grass, short trees, bushes and cacti. Higher up, where the angle of the path lessened, the gorge was broad, and grazed by cattle which chewed their cud and eyed us as we passed by. They showed no hostility, but I did meet a German who was knocked into a cactus bush by a bull; he and his wife spent many hours picking five centimetres long spines from his flesh.

Apart from the cows and bulls, small herds of goats wandered the gorge, and after rising gradually for some hours we came across a black pig no bigger than a cat, at 3,800 metres. He trotted seemingly purposefully up the grassy valley, a grunting bundle of muscle moving quickly on short legs. At first I wondered if it might be lost, but after half a mile we came across an isolated little farmhouse behind stone walls, and the tiny pig ran home. That was the last habitation we saw.

Our campsite for the night, on the bank of a big, reed fringed lake was a pleasant spot at about 4,000 metres altitude. Paul and Gary looked well, while Chris was a bit pale. Annabel's pallor was no different from when she was at sea level. One might have judged from her lack of colour and thinness that she would not manage well at high altitude, but there was no real basis for that judgement; only time would tell. Many a man built like a gorilla has failed on high, while beanpoles have carried on, to underline the enigma of performance at great altitude.

We left early next day to continue our way up the gorge, along the right bank of a milky turquoise lake, the Laguna Jatuncocha, which I reckoned to be nearly one and a half kilometres long and about half as wide. Though we were headed for a climb, this gorge was worth walking for its own sake, among blue flowered, shoulder high bushes and twisted trees five times as high and covered in peeling, red bark like paper, under a clear blue sky, with a gentle breeze rippling the lovely lake, beneath huge, steep, grey, vegetated cliffs. We could only hope that the event of climbing the mountain would be as fine as the approach to it.

On the grassy plain which followed we weaved through more blue flowered bushes and more twisted trees. Then a stiff pull up a thin, zig zagging black earth trail led to undulating grassland and dried marsh and on through man high mauve lupins to a wood of those same twisted trees, and grassy spaces; this was the place which is used as the Alpamayo base camp. About ten tents stood already among the trees, most of them belonging to climbers. As yet we were not in a position to have a good view of the mountain. Alpamayo showed no pretty face, only a stern back.

Our four tents were soon erected; Annabel shared with Chris, Gary with Paul, while Maximo and I each occupied a diminutive shelter. We were by then at 4,400 metres. Chris and Annabel had been slow to arrive; the former announced he was suffering from diarrhoea and the latter was suffering a bad earache. Chris ate nothing but had no headache or difficulty with speech or breathing. But next morning neither he nor Annabel ate, and she vomited. It was clear she should descend, a realisation which, after a few tears from Annabel, was put into action immediately, with everyone bustling about to sort out food, fuel, a stove and personal belongings for her and Chris. They made a forlorn sight, following Paul and Gary, who acted as porters, across marshland and out of sight.

Paul and Gary returned in the afternoon, having left the sick couple to descend further down the easy trail. They confessed to having joked on the way back, 'Well, that's got rid of two of them. Only Croucher to go.'

246

We had eight days left. Perhaps after a couple of days to recover they could come up and climb the mountain. We, on the other hand, had time to spare, so when Gary suggested a rest day Paul and I fell in with the idea.

When the time came to move, Maximo insisted on carrying my rucksack to the edge of the glacier which we had to ascend. Two and a half hours saw three of us there, but Gary was nowhere to be seen. Maximo went back to base camp, and half an hour later there was still no sign of Gary.

'Well, that got rid of him,' we joked, and Paul went down to look for him. While I waited, eleven people descended in groups; only four had succeeded on Alpamayo.

Paul came into view again more than an hour after he had first reached the glacier; he was carrying Gary's rucksack, while the owner trailed behind, having been slowed by the altitude. Though we had gained less than 450 metres it seemed unwise to go higher that day; it was even on the cards that Gary would need to descend. So the tent was put up on a flat space on the moraine rubble. Many people opt to camp there for a night rather than risk becoming ill, and at the time there were three people camped nearby, Japanese men from Tokyo.

Paul's willingness to work was one of his great strengths on a mountain. When there was a job to be done, be it erecting a tent, fetching water, or cooking a meal, Paul was always ready to lend a hand, and at high altitude such mundane chores are essential to survival. He was tall and strongly built, twenty-seven years old, amenable, a quantity surveyor, and in Gary's opinion 'the safest person I've climbed with'. Gary was a year older, a data system editor who had studied English at university. He had a good sense of humour, and did not take offence when it was suggested that we had hired Maximo to make Gary feel better, because he was a little taller than our guard. Unlike Paul, Gary had no enthusiasm for routine tasks; but his idleness on this day could be forgiven since he felt unwell. We choose our objectives at sea-level, thinking optimistically that we will go from A to B on day one, B to C on day two, C to D on day three, but perhaps one or another person in a group feels unable to keep to a schedule, perhaps the weather dictates, perhaps dangerous avalanche conditions force a change of plan. Whatever the reason, mountain itineraries need to be flexible.

Come morning, cool and clear, Gary was fit to continue upwards. A plod on snow slopes, over a few small crevasses, up a short ramp of 40 degree ice followed by steep snow, took us in five hours to our next camp, on a col between Alpamayo and another great mountain,

Kitaraju. I found it difficult to estimate our altitude but thought 5,500 metres to be quite close to the mark; we were within striking distance of the summit and, given good health, fine weather, and an acceptable level of danger from avalanches, we could set out the next day. All the time, cloud denied us a view of our objective.

The three Japanese had erected their tent near where we would camp, and came over to give us some refreshing slices of orange. An empty tent close by belonged to a party of Columbians who were attempting Alpamayo, they explained.

Gary found a new source of energy and spent a lot of time shovelling out a level tent platform on the icy col, and he persuaded Paul to assist. The outcome was that though we started one of our stoves, between us we neglected the most important work of melting sufficient snow and ice; it can take several hours to melt enough to rehydrate a party from the day's efforts, and to prepare for the next day the necessary water, which would be kept from freezing overnight by placing water bottles inside occupied sleeping bags. When he had finished his excavations Gary flopped down with a headache, and did no more work. Perhaps one can only understand what he felt like if one has been to such altitudes and experienced the leaden tiredness which can seize you; allowances had to be made. Next time, it could be any one of us.

'We can't go on tomorrow unless we melt a lot more water,' I said as dusk approached.

'We spent too much time digging,' Paul admitted.

When darkness fell at about 7 pm. the outside temperature dropped so low that the normally more efficient of our two stoves barely made headway, even though protected from the wind in a snow pit. The risk of taking it inside the tent was too high, since occasionally it flared up. We had to face facts: we could not go on up the next day. And if the weather broke within fifteen to twenty hours it could cost us the ascent.

No one returned to the empty tent near ours during the night, and next morning we were to learn why. When we looked out at 7 am. the cloud had cleared, and there before us was our incomparable mountain; the completely white south-west face, our proposed route of ascent, soared splendidly above. Fluted by the gouging action of avalanches, it was even steeper than I had expected.

'Alpamayo, like the rarest works of art, created in us the feeling of perfection... Never have we seen a mountain with such pure lines or such perfect proportions,' reported the people who made the first ascent.

The scene was given scale by three minute figures on the summit; they were the Columbians who had quit the tent close to ours the previous morning, had climbed the south-west face, and had been forced to spend the night on the summit with the temperature at about -20 degrees C. Without sleeping bags or a stove.

One of the Japanese was mildly affected by snow blindness and stayed in their tent most of the day, while his two companions went off to climb Kitaraju. Throughout several of the twelve hours they were away our stoves purred away, and we ate and drank well. Gary still suffered from a headache, but his appetite was reasonable. I had one worry about taking a rest: time was running out for me. There was currently in Huaraz an annual festival which attracted thousands of tourists, and at the end of the week-long event there was always a scramble for seats on buses to Lima, and many people became stranded in the city for days each year. I had ordered a pony for the descent from base camp in order to reach Cashapampa in one day rather than two, then hurry from there to Huaraz to book a seat on a bus which would take me to Lima in time for my flight home. I could afford only one more day of inactivity before having to abandon the ascent; the month I had allowed in Peru had seemed ridiculously generous at the start, but various delays had eroded it to a critical stage. Paul and Gary's return flight departed two days after mine, but they could not leave me to descend the glacier alone, so, unless I could go down with someone else, their chances of success were in jeopardy too. The appearance of Annabel and Chris might introduce further favourable variables, but I had my doubts about them arriving.

The Columbians could not begin their descent from Alpamayo until 9 am. because their rope was frozen stiff and they had to wait for the sun to thaw it; frozen rope cannot be thrown down for abseils since it remains stubbornly stiff in coils like thick wire cable. When at last the sun had transformed the rope into a useful tool, the descent of the steep face took the trio five hours, and a further two hours elapsed as they made their way from the bottom of the face along the snow and upwards to the col which housed our camp. There they told us about the route, as they guzzled drinks we prepared; the bergschrund was difficult, most of the face was in good condition, and the top section, which is often called the Headwall, was very steep ice. There were aluminium snow stakes driven in at intervals, but too far apart for them to abseil from one to the next on their single rope, and that was why their descent had taken so long. We were at first concerned that this would delay us too, since we had only one rope, but the Columbians generously loaned us theirs; in that sense our delay was opportune. But their description of the Headwall, very steep and icy, made me uneasy in my stomach.

Fourteen hours later we stood in dim dawn light and looked at the outline of Alpamayo; the weather was clear and there was nothing but ourselves to prevent our going. We lost 150 metres or so down a steep slope, towards the south-west face, which had first been climbed eleven years earlier by an Italian party. Having regained the height lost from our camp, and more, we were faced by the first major obstacle, the bergschrund. This huge crevasse cut across the whole of the bottom of the face, a V-shaped trench up to 30 metres deep in places; we headed for its narrowest point, where it was partly bridged with snow which left a gap of only a metre to step across. Paul went first, stepping from the incomplete bridge on to the higher lip of the bergschrund, which for four metres was vertical ice; below him the hole was 25 metres deep. With the hole crossed and the ice surmounted, he secured himself to a snow stake on a 55 degree slope above and took in the rope as I began to follow him. Something in me said give up; something a little stronger said keep going. The vertical ice, and the hole below made me feel scared, but, puffing and blowing, I made it up to the snow slope; the angle seemed friendly then, and I felt at home.

On the avalanche gouged slope which would take us all the way to the Headwall, we fell into a routine, with Paul leading from one snow stake to another; once firmly secured to a stake he would take in two ropes simultaneously, one from Gary and one from me, as we climbed side by side. We moved up grooves which reminded me of bob sleigh runs, but which were, of course, so much steeper, and straight. We passed only one car sized rock on the face; the rest was pure snow and ice, which never went above 60 degrees, nor much below. Cloud, the colour of concrete, closed round, heightening our sense of isolation as the only people on the mountain, or on this side of it, at least.

We had climbed unhurried for seven or eight rope lengths and were nearing the Headwall. Paul, who was out of sight over a bulge of snow, called for me to climb, and for Gary to wait, since the ice was hard and we were not in sight, and one-at-a-time was the way to tackle it. I was half way to Paul when I paused for breath and, looking below me, saw that Gary had moved up some way without his rope being taken in; the rope hung slack in a long loop below him. And suddenly he slipped.

If the rope between Paul and Gary had been taken in there would have been little difficulty in arresting the fall; but Gary would accelerate before the shock came on the rope. Paul could not see Gary, could not see the long loop of slack rope, could not hear the awful sound that came to my ears as Gary's clothing and crampons and axes scraped down rough ice. Paul's snow stake anchor might hold or might not. He could be plucked, with the anchor, from his stance, could tumble and bounce after Gary, and when the rope between Paul and me went tight I could be pulled off too. We would go all the way, straight down and into the bergschrund, which is what happened, it seems likely, to two Canadians who had disappeared on the mountain two years earlier. (Though they may have been swept down by an avalanche and buried in the bergschrund.)

Gary uttered not a sound as he fell.

'Hold! Hold! Hold!' I shouted to Paul, at the same time slamming in my axes and bracing myself. 'Gary's off!'

Facing the slope, Gary slid very rapidly towards the point at which the rope would take the shock. By the time the rope started to stretch under his weight he had travelled six times his own height, and his ordeal went on as the rope stretched still further. Paul took the strain, and the snow anchor held. Gary came to rest lying on his back on one of the few little snow ledges to be found on the face. So we were safe; but Gary might be injured.

I called down, 'You all right?'

'Yes.'

'Still got your tools?'

Loss of one or both of his ice-axes would greatly hinder upward movement; he could abseil down without.

'Yes.'

Paul was still taking the strain on the rope. 'Tell Gary to find a stance,' he shouted to me.

'Gary, can you stand up on that ledge?'

This Gary did, with the slow movements of one who is dazed. His demeanour - slumped shoulders and bowed head - showed a man who wanted to rest, and perhaps to retreat.

'What's he doing?' Paul shouted.

'Resting.'

'You'd better lead through then, Norm.'

We both had the same thought: we were close to the summit and if we kept going Gary might not want to turn back. He would let us know soon enough if he did. So while he rested I climbed up to Paul.

Now it fell to me to lead the Headwall, which my mind had built up to a formidable obstacle. Reports of it varied from vertical, which it was not, to very steep. One rope-length high, it was not so much a wall as a very steep corner contained by two walls which leaned back a little from the vertical. I climbed the corner with one foot on either wall, on pitted, rough ice which held my crampons nicely. At the most the angle was about 80 degrees near the top, but the security afforded by the rough ice made it seem less. It was not so bad after all, this Headwall.

By 3 pm. we were all at the top. Gary came up last and flopped down beside a little flag left by the Columbians. He had a just reward for carrying on, and we could not have known that his troubles were not yet over. At 5,947 metres this was not the highest mountain I had climbed, but it was one of the most beautiful, without a doubt. The cloud cleared and we waved at three dots by the Japanese tent, and thought they waved back; but they were so far below we could not be sure.

When overtaken by darkness as we abseiled, we donned our headtorches and continued down, with me moving with what Paul described as 'your usual sack of potatoes style'. Well down the face, Gary somehow knocked his torch from his helmet, and it fell away out of sight. Though Paul and I lit his way as best we could it was harder for him to move without his own light, and he became very tired. My partners crossed the bergschrund ahead of me and, because they were cold, hurried down unroped. I had just crossed the gap when Paul shouted, 'Gary's fallen!'

There were a couple of big ice cliffs and several crevasses in the dark beneath us. Gary had tripped and fallen and disappeared from Paul's beam of light, down a snow slope. On his way he lost an ice-axe, his helmet, a water bottle and his camera as he tumbled down ice and snow for thirty metres, sixty metres, a hundred metres. He was again fortunate, for he missed the cliffs and crevasses, and came to rest on a gentle snow slope.

While Paul returned next day and retrieved Gary's possessions, their owner remained late in his sleeping bag. An avalanche swept the face, stopping short of Paul; we had been given the right, cold day for our ascent.

Gary was so worn out we decided not to descend to base camp until the next day. That afternoon we were joined on the col by five Polish climbers who had recently lost a companion on a mountain twenty miles away to the south-east, when she fell down an ice slope. Naturally they were very subdued, and seemed uncertain whether they wanted to climb. As individuals I think some did not, but the group had a momentum of its own, and they set off for Alpamayo.

Next day as three figures appeared on the snow col high above base camp Maximo shouted, 'There they are!'

'Japanese,' teased another guard, and they started chasing around the grassy camp, throwing sticks at each other. But Maximo was convinced, and he was right, that the trio was English.

'They are safe. I will throw three onions in the lake as we go down.' he said. I think the onions were meant as an offering of thanks to the gods.

'We didn't come up to do the climb because we didn't know where you were,' Annabel said puzzlingly, defensively, when we met. But she and Chris put up my tent and saw to it that we had plenty to eat and drink, and we were all friends as we sat around a fire and told of our little adventure. I was later very pleased that our last evening together was so convivial, for the following summer, after ending her long-standing relationship with Chris, Annabel visited the Alps with another climbing partner. There she took a short fall on her first climb, suffered head injuries, went into a coma, and died on the mountain.

'We are very sad, my husband and I and our two sons,' Annabel's mother wrote. 'Her death will make a big gap in our family. We know she was careful and experienced, but we also know that mountains are dangerous and I am sure Annabel knew it too.'

Hilario was already in camp, with a white donkey and her small, dainty hoofed grey foal, and a brown pony. When early next day I climbed on the back of the pony it moved forward about ten metres, bucked, and sat down; one feels rather silly on the back of a sitting pony at the commencement of a great journey. Once we had it standing again and I had remounted, the animal seemed content to have made a point, for it behaved well after that, perhaps because on the worst of ground – steeply uphill or downhill or bouldery – I dismounted and led it. In six hours we descended the gorge, donkey, foal, scuttling man on foot, pony with rider, in that order.

Hilario invited me to spend the night at his family's little farm in Cashapampa, and I was given a chair so I could sit in the shade in the dusty little yard which lay between the mud brick, red-tiled dwelling house and the thatched kitchen ten metres away. A calf, two sheep, several chickens, the donkey and her foal mooched about the yard while I sat in the porch and sipped beer and looked at a scene which might have been set up deliberately as a museum: wooden handled farm implements, drying sheepskins, clay pots and metal pans, ropes and leather thongs hung inside on the porch walls, above melons and empty grain sacks; and to my right as I looked out, in one corner pride of place went to an old treadle sewing machine. To my left a dozen guinea pigs chittered and squeaked in their tiny world, hemmed into a corner rectangle no bigger than a double bed by two logs; whether they stayed there by choice or whether they could have climbed over the logs, which were no thicker than my waist, I could not tell. Hilario's two pretty girls of three and five years came and played, first with my metal legs and then with my beer bottle tops, which they threw about in the dust. A man and a woman, their grandparents most likely, watched from two chairs in the shade of the kitchen, and chatted quietly to each other.

At dusk the family gathered in the kitchen to eat and, according to their custom, I as their guest was sat on my own in the place of honour – at the sewing machine. By the light of an oil lantern I ate my chips and drank sweetened milk, and with our meals over Hilario and his two girls joined me.

'Do you like music?' Hilario asked.

I said yes, and the children's faces brightened as he disappeared into the house, to return in a minute with a small, battery powered record player, which he put on the sewing machine. Placing his only record on the turntable, he turned a switch and the children's eyes were wide and happy as the tinny music of a Peruvian band drifted on the warm air of the night. The record was played three or four times, both sides, and the girls were as stimulated by this simple pleasure as rich children at an expensive circus. I do not think they will forget the day the gringo came to stay and they listened to the record player.

My bed was on the porch, near the guinea pigs, who squeaked arguments and scuttled around intermittently throughout the night. We were up early, Hilario and I, and he saw me off on the 4.30 am. bus, a typical snub-nosed South American vehicle. The gaily painted 24-seater had two sheep and two goats standing at the back and messing on the floor, chickens clucked in baskets on the laps of women, and full grain sacks lay down the aisle; it was as we are told South American buses are. Most seats were full and the vehicle groaned up the hills and bounced noisily on the roughest sections. At the main road I changed buses conveniently for Huaraz and was there by midmorning, and I managed to book a bus seat for Lima for the next day.

'My most intense happinesses have of course been among mountains.' – John Ruskin.

The Heim glacier of Kilimanjaro, Alpamayo and Assiniboine; what a year for ambitions was 1986! Someone said to me it was not good to achieve so many ambitions if none remained; but I could not agree, for though I had no immediate climbing plans, I knew the mountains would tempt me again. The challenge, the adventure, the beauty had until now been the lures, but creeping up on me was something I had not expected to grip me – the altitude ambition. Soon the dimensions of my climbing dreams were to alter radically.

254

CHAPTER 10

Broad Peak

THE inventor Thomas Edison said, 'Show me a thoroughly satisfied man and I will show you a failure.' There is some truth behind his words, but in August of 1986 I felt both satisfied and successful. Still, such emotions do not negate Edison's sentiment when viewed over a considerable period of time. Climbing satisfies me deeply, and I look back with pleasure to time well spent on peaks like Alpamayo and Assiniboine; yet, just as no piece of music can leave one content with a single hearing, so the climbing game must be played again and again. At the same time I do not entirely share the opinion of the composer Schumann, who believed that once a goal is achieved it is no longer a goal, so you aim higher and higher, making failure almost inevitable. In support of Schumann's view, it is frequently asserted that creative men and women must be driven by continual dissatisfaction with what they have achieved, or they become complacent and unproductive, but I do not see mountain ascents that way; I look back with joy as surely as forward with excitement. So, though I did not for a moment fail to appreciate the consummated ambitions of 1986, I soon grew restless to climb again, to live, live, live; fresh ambition had to grow to replace the old, as surely as new leaves come next year when the old have blown away.

I did not have long to wait for the appearance of another target, for in November 1986 Dr Mark Hallam invited me on an expedition to climb the twelfth highest mountain in the world, Broad Peak, 8,047 metres high. Though many people think of high altitude mountaineering as being confined to the Nepalese Himalaya, in fact the Karakoram range in Pakistan, where Broad Peak lies, holds many of the world's highest summits, including K2.

Mark needed a minimum of four members and at that stage only his doctor friend Jon Watt was committed to going with him. As a fourth member I suggested Richard Foley; we had spent little more than two weeks on the Kilimanjaro expedition, but few climbers can make themselves available for ten or eleven weeks at a stretch, and names had to be submitted to the Pakistani authorities, or the expedition would be cancelled.

At forty-six years of age I was by far the old man of the party: the others were in their mid-twenties. Several people took Mark to be my younger brother on account of our facial similarities.

On the last day of May 1987 we flew to Islamabad and there booked into a hotel, in a room shared with cockroaches, ants and bed bugs. A single, sometimes whirring, sometimes chuffing, ceiling fan did little to bring comfort in a room where the temperature remained at about 34°C (95° F). Room service was reliable, in that it was always very late, and the hotel staff generally ignored us except to try and refer us to a particular carpet shop, or to ask if we were Japanese.

The next stage of the long safari towards our goal was a thirty-hour minibus ride from Islamabad to the mountain town of Skardu, 750 kilometres away along the recently constructed Karakoram Highway. We were accompanied by a driver, a liaison officer, a sirdar (or porter foreman) and our cook, Abdullah Khan Bahadur. The Karakoram Highway is certainly wider than the road we had travelled to Illimani, for it can easily accommodate two-way traffic, but the word 'Highway' requires some elaboration. This spectacular and important link finds its way beneath huge overhangs across cliffs, sometimes of rock, sometimes of conglomerate mud banks which hold large football-sized and small pebbles in a surprisingly firm grip; such cliffs are more stable than they look, though streams inexorably seek weaknesses at particular points, so there are road signs identifying places where collapses of rock and earth on to the road are common: Gundlo Slide, Chillo Slide, Tatta Pani Slide, for instance, and a dozen more. At the end of each slide is another sign telling you, 'Relax. Slide area ends. Have a good drive.' That is, until the next slide, which may be five minutes down the road or may be fifty. The outer edge of the road is bounded by whitewashed stones, markers rather than a safety barrier. In some welcome sections the highway makes its way directly, tamely across a plain or along a valley bottom, but mostly one is aware that there are considerable dangers just a metre or so away as one speeds along with the mighty Indus always to one side or the other.

At about 6 am. we pulled up outside the single storey, whitewashed, three roomed house of Muhammad Iqbal, director of Baltistan Tours, in Skardu. Mark had engaged him to assist with our arrangements. Now we wanted nothing but to sleep, so we put up our tents in Muhammad's currently bare, stone walled garden, for here gardens are tied far more than in Britain to the rhythm of the rains. A few hours of welcome rest followed.

After three days spent in Skardu, buying provisions, including flour and oil for our porters, in bazaar streets which house the typical open fronted, garage-like shops, early one morning two green four-wheel drive jeeps waited to be loaded outside Muhammad's gate. Then in half a day our drivers took us through poplar avenues, busy with tractors and trailers transporting men to work in well irrigated fields, into a desert lying between barren brown mountains, with occasional oases of fields and scores of mud brick houses, to the village of Dassu, fifty miles from Skardu. On the way, schoolboys and schoolgirls held out red, pink and yellow roses as symbols of friendship, but the women who squatted in the fields turned away, covering their faces with shawls. We had been warned at the Department of Tourism, which imposed a lengthy set of regulations on expeditions, not to take pictures of women or bridges (the latter excluded for military reasons).

That afternoon, at the Dassu bungalow rest house, seventy or eighty men turned up in the hope of securing work; word had got around. But we required only forty porters, so the atmosphere was one of expectation followed by considerable disappointment at first, until the unlucky ones drifted away; they have few opportunities to earn cash. The air changed to one of excitement as loads were allocated and plastic sandals and rubber ankle boots and socks, bought in Skardu, were distributed. Our Balti porters, related to Tibetans, provided their own thin clothing in the form of the standard baggy trousers and long shirt, the shalwar-kameez, with some form of old jacket or mackintosh for the cold ends of the day. A few possessed warm clothing from earlier expeditions.

The ten day walk to Broad Peak has been described as 'gruelling' and 'the toughest trek in the world', and though the latter description is an exaggeration, I did wonder at such strength in the spindly porters' legs as they carried loads of 25 kilogrammes over loose earth, mud and boulders, and snow, on a tough approach march.

The second day lived up to the trek's reputation, when we encountered the Braldu Gorge, notorious for the deaths of several people from rockfalls onto the loose, sometimes sandy, sometimes gritty and always steep flanks. I wondered why I had not chosen another of a broad variety of sports which are available to me, as I struggled desperately for several hours with my feet and crutches sliding on the insecure terrain above the raging Braldu river. Occasionally rocks as big as large cabbages bounced down and splashed in the water, portending an incident in which I was to be involved near the end of the expedition.

At the end of every day I trailed in well behind the others, even behind the heavily laden porters. Though there were pleasant sections on good paths among irrigated cornfields, by the fourth day all the greenery was behind us, and the jumbled boulder fields of the Biafo glacier forced great effort from me under the glaring sun. The terrain changed many times over the next few days, with here a good sandy trail rising gently, there a 45 degree cliff traversed on small ledges for several hundred metres, here a huge river beach with smooth, head sized boulders scattered across the sand, there a mid-thigh deep river fifty metres wide, now a stage of indefinite trails on earth and rocky cliffs, and now boulder ridge after boulder ridge lying like huge waves across our way. We came across rubble laid thinly over the ice of the Baltoro glacier and halted at the glacier's edge to pay our respects at the graves of three porters who had died there some years earlier of what our sirdar called 'cold stomach', which was probably hypothermia. The graves were a pertinent reminder of the cost paid in porters' lives for the pleasures and ambitions of sahib mountaineers, for the porters had no other reason to venture there.

By noon of the ninth day we were at Concordia, a site famous among climbers and trekkers, where Baltoro and other glaciers meet. From there we had our first good views of K2 and of Broad Peak, throughout a restful afternoon. K2, 'the savage mountain', dominated the left side of the valley we looked up, while the triple-summitted Broad Peak held the right side.

The porters cheerfully accepted their wage of less than £5 a day each, chanted 'Live Forever', and departed hastily on the return journey. Base camp beneath Broad Peak, six small tents in quiet greens and browns, one each for the liaison officer, for our cook, and for us, and a large green mess tent in which we could stand, was established at 4,950 metres on a glacial moraine which from high above resembled an enormous brown snake with transverse white stripes of snow. Over the next few days expeditions from France, Yugoslavia, Mexico and Norway set up camps in the vicinity, all with eyes on the route we planned to tackle, the west face and north ridge of Broad Peak.

A week elapsed while we acclimatised to the altitude and waited for bad weather to clear, and then we dug two snow caves, like two small, low cellars in a snow bank, as camp 1, at about 5,900 metres. The route so far had weaved for half an hour from base camp through gleaming pyramidal towers of ice as high as a two-storey house, then up a glacier with the threat of avalanches hanging over us from ice cliffs 1,500 metres above. Easy snow slopes then led to the caves. While my three companions descended to make another carry, I remained at the caves to work at enlarging them to about the size of a two-man tent.

Richard performed best and was usually ahead of everyone else, much to Mark's annoyance, because though Richard had the least experience he was always ready and able to gallop on alone. Richard was inclined to take offence at what he perceived as Mark's authoritarian attitude. High altitude climbing strains even the best of relationships, and it would be dishonest to try to say all is always sweetness and light up there. Here we had the seeds of some conflicts of personality, but the situation was saved to some extent by Jon. Where Richard led Jon would follow, if he could, and that suited Richard, who showed no lack of determination or willingness to work at achieving the summit.

I had taken with me a child's metal beach spade, the wooden handle of which would slot inside a crutch tube to strengthen it. In his 'bull in a china shop' way Richard used the spade without the tube, inevitably causing the handle to break. He declared the idea silly, but as a matter of fact it has subsequently worked well enough. Further trouble loomed at camp 1 when Richard dropped our only snow shovel down the 40 degree slope in which we had dug our caves. The tool sped out of sight, and with it went our hopes of easily digging platforms for our tents, or excavating higher snow caves, or clearing heavy snowfalls from tents. Life did take a turn for the better when Richard set off next day and found the shovel stuck in the snow some hundreds of metres below.

On our first carry above camp 1 I made only two-thirds of the distance to camp 2, before leaving my load to be taken up later. I had awful diarrhoea; at the time I did not accept just how bad it was, and I tried unwisely to soldier on. Though I did not pull my weight, the others did nothing to discourage me from continuing, and two days later I moved up to camp 2. On the same day Mark descended to base camp having suffered severely from vomiting and diarrhoea in the night.

At various times during the next sixteen days the weather was bad, and one or more of my partners fell sick, so they spent most of the time at base camp, while I sat it out at camp 2 at 6,540 metres altitude. The wisdom of doing so was questionable, but I could not go up and down like the others partly because of the diarrhoea. The camp accommodated several tents on little stone platforms, like plantless rock garden terraces, on a sharp ridge. I was joined at various times by Yugoslavs, Mexicans, French and Norwegians, by Mark, Jon and Richard, but the weather and conditions never favoured an attempt on the summit. I could tolerate the delays, since my bowel disorder would have seriously weakened any push I made.

Two Yugoslavs pushed on against the odds, reaching nearly 7,400 metres, and another, whom we English nicknamed The Machine on account of his exceptional abilities, went even higher, but all were forced to abandon their attempts; the snow conditions rendered the climb impossible, they reported. A few days later some of the French took a chance with the weather but were beaten back by high winds and soft snow at 7,400 metres, and they followed the example of the Yugoslavs and retreated from the mountain. The following day three Mexicans launched their final attack, but one was back the same day because of cold feet (literally) and the other two came down next day having been halted at 7,000 metres by fierce winds and soft snow; one just cannot move upward for long at high altitude when sinking to the knee and deeper, no matter how determined you may be.

On 18th. July, the thirteenth day of my vigil, I was joined by my three companions. Morale had been low as reports of the conditions came from the retreating expeditions, and Mark had come to the conclusion that the avalanche risk was too high. I decided there was no need for me to descend and fetch rations and fuel because it was highly unlikely that more than two people would set out for the top; we had sufficient supplies at camp 2.

Richard clearly had Jon in mind as his partner for a summit attempt if and when the time came but Mark and I were concerned about Jon's continuing headaches, and weak voice. We need not have worried about him going upwards unwisely, for he returned from a carry to camp 3 next day, wept a little, and said, 'I can't do it.' And that was the end of it for Jon. Richard tried persuading him to stay for the night, but Jon had suffered from headaches for too long, and had made the decision to descend. Mark too had decided he had had enough, and the sight of the slopes above us had exacerbated his fears of avalanches, so Jon and Mark returned to base camp.

Richard and I were away upwards early next day, following fixed ropes left by other parties. After a short slope of 50 degrees the angles on snow and ice, and on snow thinly spread over rock, were so gentle that it is difficult to give a true impression of the suffering of the laden mountaineer, but believe me, there are no easy slopes at high altitude. And my continuing dysentery, or whatever it was, left me much weaker than normal.

On an icy slope with a crevasse echoing beneath us as we kicked our crampons in, I dug in the snow with my ice axe to find the lower lip before stepping across. Richard had trusted his luck, but I chose to be more cautious. It did not take long to explore the edge of the crevasse and step across, but my companion fidgeted and sighed. Then when I asked him if he would make the steps a little closer - my rather jerky movements are more inclined to cause snow steps to collapse the further they are apart - he complained bitterly that this was an 'implied criticism'. It was not, and I have never climbed with anyone else who took it this way.

At 6,900 metres we reached a tent and supplies dumped on the previous day's carry, and Richard wanted at first to carry on up the soft slope.

'How about it, Norm?'

'No. Not when the sun's been on it for so long.'

'Just another hundred metres?'

'Not on that slope.'

Quite soon he was forced to sit down and rest because of the altitude, and he had to accept that we should stay where we were. Early next morning we were joined by four lightly laden men who had come up that far to acclimatise for an attempt on K2. They were all very experienced in assessing avalanche risk and pronounced the slope ahead to be dangerous; one can judge to a great extent by digging a trench and examining the types of snow making up the layers. I had no grounds to disagree with such experts. The slope would remain dangerous for some days to come, and as one of the four men said, 'If this slope is bad there's more of it higher up.' There was no sensible option but to go down, either to wait for an improvement or to retreat.

'Think we ought to go down,' I said to Richard, who glowered, but said nothing. Communication between calm and well balanced people at high altitude can be difficult enough at the best of times, and the problem was well expressed by Eric Shipton in Upon That Mountain: 'Even an unconscious display of virtue can be as intolerable as any vice... efficiency as clumsiness... one is quick to resent the way one man drinks his soup or wears his hat, or the silly manner in which his beard has grown.'

Back at camp 2 I decided that I was going down to base camp.

'The avalanche danger is too great. And you don't have the experience to solo the route. You should go down too, Richard.'

'I'm staying here. I'll try to team up with the Norwegians but if you see them don't say so,' he said. 'I won't take any risks. I want to see my cat and my wife again.' (He had married Joy a month before going to Pakistan.)

'You'll be taking a big risk if you go up that snow, and you won't reach the summit. You could always blame me for making the decision, and say you couldn't allow me to go down alone.'

'If anything happens I couldn't be of much help.'

I could barely believe my ears. He was the strongest man in the team, and his physical performance was beyond reproach, but he had left his better, sea-level self behind. As in all sports, there is a great deal of difference between performance and behaviour; the latter shows the nature of the man.

I had it in mind to try again in the unlikely event that conditions improved, but fate decided otherwise, and sent me a message to that effect very soon when, next day, I started down alone. The descent was mostly on snow and down a steep ice step equipped with a fixed rope. I was unaware that the mountain was about to deliver a blow, which came when I was half way down a slope of 300 metres on snow which, having been only two hours in the sun, was not particularly dangerous. I was facing the slope, an axe in each hand and crampons on my boots, when a noise caused me to look up, a faint sound whose exact nature I cannot recall; whatever it was, it was neither loud nor distinct, but was enough to attract my attention, as almost any sound does on a mountain. And there bounding down the snow were several rocks. I believe they had come many hundreds of metres from a cliff on the left of the snowfield, and they hurtled my way, about twenty rocks of various sizes. One of fifteen kilogrammes bounced by two metres to my left and was followed by a scattered group of fist sized missiles, and before I could take any avoiding action a spinning boulder, roughly like a large cheese and weighing around four or five kilogrammes, smashed into the top of my left thigh. Pain came two or three seconds later, a sickening pain accompanied by nausea and faintness, and I clung to my axes and heard myself moan rapidly and loudly, 'Ah! Ah! Ah! Ah! Ah! Ah! Ah! Ah!' over and over again. A thought flashed through my mind - 'My femur's broken!' and I waited for the more agonising pain which would surely come if the bone was broken. All the while I groaned, 'Ah! Ah! Ah! Ah! Ah! Ah!' in a continual staccato cry, as if someone else had commandeered my voice; I don't think I could have stopped if I had tried. I waited, feeling suddenly alone. Is it broken? When a femur is broken a large volume of blood is lost into the surrounding tissue and this can result in severe shock and death. IS IT BROKEN? IS IT BROKEN? I was more worried than frightened.

In a few seconds I reckoned I had been fortunate; my femur was intact, I felt sure, and I had not been knocked off. The blow had been cushioned by a thick leather corset which helps to keep my artificial limb in place; a steel caliper which joins the corset to the leg had been in the way too. The impact had been further cushioned by a many-bladed knife in my trouser pocket; the knife was bent beyond use. Had the thigh not been so well protected I am sure the femur would have been broken.

The rock had been centimetres from my head, centimetres from my chest, from my groin, from my stomach, and clearly a blow of such severity to any other part of my body would have been very serious, and quite likely fatal. Anyone but me would have been killed, most probably. It had been a close shave. All the same the pain was bad, and I told myself to get moving to the bottom of the slope before the thigh seized up.

I could barely stand on the left leg because of the pain, but it had to be moved, so with an 'Ah!' at every other step I sweated down, still facing the slope. I could not just slide down because if I went out of control there was a real risk of shooting down a long, long gully at the base of the snow slope, to slither down steps of ice. For over half an hour I climbed thus, and then was able to slide down towards a promontory of rock where I could bivouac, free of any threat from avalanches and rockfall. The last hundred metres I crawled painfully through the snow to this safe haven. By then it was noon, and it had taken me nearly an hour to get from the point at which I had been struck.

At the bivi site, a flat space with a knee high windbreak of stones erected around it, I found a climbing helmet; it was imperative to collect snow for water, so I crawled another thirty metres to the nearest patch of snow and filled the helmet and a cooking pan I had with me. I had a stove and food, too, and found a stash of food at the bivi site, sufficient to keep me going for several days, so I was confident I could look after myself while I rested the injury. As it transpired I did not need the extra food, but it was a comfort to find it.

In the mid afternoon one of the Norwegians, a doctor who was feeling ill – ironically we encountered sick doctors at almost every turn – descended to the bivi site, and took a message to Mark that I would get down to base camp whenever I could stand long enough. Had there been no one to carry a message the situation might have been far worse. As it was, Mark came up 350 metres next day to pay a house call.

'There's a pint or two of haematoma in that thigh,' he said. I think haematoma is a doctor's fancy word for blood floating around where it should not be. 'Take painkillers and exercise it a little or if a clot ossifies it can be a bugger to treat and could leave a stiff thigh. That's not common, though. Stay here tonight and see how it goes.'

I swallowed some painkillers in preparation for the exercise, and five minutes later Mark was at the painkillers too, for a stomach pain which doubled him up. This is a funny moment, I thought, with me in my bivouac bed at 5,300 metres sharing painkillers with my doctor.
Mark became very ill when he descended and in a confused state lost his

way in the glacier towers at the bottom. Several people went out to search for him, and he was guided back to base camp. Whatever his illness was, it cleared up soon after.

Two nights at the bivi saw me fit to move down to base camp, albeit with more than usual difficulty. Jon was my watchful escort down an icy gully which had taken over as a safer alternative to the glacier we had come up, where two Frenchman had narrowly escaped death and had survived an avalanche by diving behind a rock; the blast had left them coated in snow from head to toe, like two snowmen. The new way was not without stonefall danger, and Jon was narrowly missed by several small but nevertheless dangerous ones early on. Like so much of the route on this mountain, the snow and ice rarely went above 45 degrees, and was generally much less, but my left thigh was weak, and I moved with considerable trouble.

Richard and two Norwegians reached 7,200 metres and spent the night there, and after making very little progress next day on soft snow they gave up. A second French expedition followed suit and abandoned their attempt.

Our porters arrived at base camp on time to carry everything down, but because of my thigh and bowels I was not fit to travel. So I rested for a while at the nearby K2 base camp, housed and fed by Doug Scott and an international team he was leading. The atmosphere of the base camp was infectious, deeply committed, divorced from the normal world, and dangerous. Everyone was aware of the risks, but still each reinforced the aspirations of the others.

Doug Scott and his companions had fared no better on K2 than we had on Broad Peak; nor had five other expeditions on K2. The weather and the resultant conditions precluded any ascents that year, and there was nothing we could do about it. The door was closed, and that was satisfying in one way, for there was no uncomfortable conjecturing on what might have happened had we pressed on. 'Retired hurt by a rock' sounds better than 'stopped by bad bowels' but I don't believe I could have climbed Broad Peak even if the rock had not intervened, for I was too weak. At home tests failed to identify the problem, and for several weeks I could not leave home until the pubs and their toilets were open. It was some years before the condition cleared up completely, when I took antibiotics for a different problem. Subsequent trips to high altitude have shown that my useless performance on Broad Peak was the result of illness, but for a long time I was unsure whether I was up to the 8,000 metre experience. We had failed on Broad Peak in good company, alongside determined mountaineers, many of whom had climbed very high mountains, including Mount Everest; mountaineers who agreed that this was the worst weather they had encountered in this range. Like us, they had all put in great effort for little or no reward, but so has any mountaineer at some time or other. This time the mountain said no, and we came back alive, perhaps all of us more aware of the value of the courage to fail. It is said that a common feature of millionaires is that most have failed in business at some time; the same is true of the successful mountaineer. So, though disappointed, I decided to go for another of the really big ones, partly in the hope of wiping away the disappointment with a dose of success. I would build on the experience of Broad Peak and would attempt other high mountains. From the very moment when I had decided that retreat was the only way, I was already thinking of returning to the heights. Whereas previously I had chosen mountain objectives because they looked good, now the ambition to climb one of the World's fourteen 8,000 metre peaks had seized me.

I came out by helicopter to Skardu, an eventuality for which I was insured. In Islamabad I continued to suffer badly from dysentery. My companions had departed for England so another English climber, thirty-year-old David Tarrant, looked after me, fetching drugs and soft drinks. We made plans to climb a high mountain together in Pakistan the next year. But in 1988 he and two companions were killed by an avalanche on New Zealand's Mount Cook; their bodies were not recovered. Dave's parents and girlfriend asked me to speak at a thanksgiving for his life, to put the climber's point of view; they understood what Dave was looking for, but felt that many friends and relations did not. Dave was fanatical about mountains and had been known to drive to the Alps for the weekend, missing Friday and Sunday nights' sleep in the process to climb such mountains as Mont Blanc, and then rush back to work. I did my best to explain that to us life without mountains would be very poor indeed, in the same way that one must not take the sea from a sailor. I talked about the spiritual refreshment which mountains can bring, I talked of adventure and challenge and aesthetic satisfaction, of the belief, common to many religions, that mountains are sacred places. I talked of friendship and emotions as sweet as any human being could experience, and I explained that we risked our lives because life is too precious to waste in appalling dreariness, and we sought a freedom, an excitement, as necessary to our souls as bread to our bodies. Those who had asked me to speak said it was just what they had wanted, but I was left wondering if I could ever explain why we climbed to anyone who did not already know why. To those who are devoid of a sense of adventure, is there any satisfactory explanation? Explanations sound so cliche; and perhaps it takes at least a book to explain the magic, the romance.

'For those who believe, no explanation is necessary, for those who do not believe, no explanation is possible.' - Franz Wefel.

Ang Temba on the summit of Cho Oyu.

Cho Oyu, Tibet 8201 metres.

Above Camp I on Cho Oyu.

Hard ice high on Cho Oyu.

Craig John

Encouraging beginners,
Swanage.

Torre Grande, Italian Dolomites.
Norman stands on the summit
(left).

Norman.

Norman's shows his legs! Left
and right.

A crampon.

CHAPTER 11

Ecuador and Masherbrum II

BEFORE my next 8,000 metre attempt other mountains beckoned, including Cheget Kara (3,667 metres) and Elbrus (5,642 metres) in the Caucasus; the latter is the highest mountain in Europe, and I found it to be a straightforward trudge. Next I planned to join an American expedition to climb a mountain in Pakistan well in excess of 7,000 metres, as a stage along the 8,000 metre trail. However in late April of that year came the news that the excursion had been cancelled owing to several members dropping out at short notice. They may have been influenced by a number of anxieties, including the eruption of feeling in the wake of Salman Rushdie upsetting masses of Muslims; the suggestion by an Iranian ayatollah that it would be a good idea to kill a few westerners may also have influenced some to stay at home. A bomb which blew a plane from the sky over Scotland can have done nothing to encourage North Americans to fly, particularly since threats were issued concerning further bombs. On top of that, troubles on the border between Afghanistan and Pakistan, near where we proposed to climb, must have added a further itch to the discomfort. I tease American friends that they live at ease in a country where dozens of murders occur on any day, yet at the explosion of one small bomb in Frankfurt they cancel a visit to Bradford; but in this case I could understand why they were uneasy, since Americans are not top of the pops in Pakistan.

So, no expedition, and summer on the way. Four weeks later, through a London climbing club, I made contact with one Chris Adye, who said he would climb with me in Peru. The summer seemed salvaged, but four days later a Welshman was murdered by terrorists in the mountain area of Peru which we were to visit, and several bombs were exploded there. Chris and his three companions, understandably, headed for Ecuador instead, in June. Judy and I had booked a trip to Corsica for June, so I could not join them, but Chris promised to stay on in Ecuador for the whole of July if I cared to join him. This left four weeks to organise my trip to Ecuador, two of which would be spent climbing in Corsica. In fact, I had only one day, a Saturday, before I set off for Corsica, to buy an airline ticket to Quito; this was achieved.

For this trip my Cornish scrumpy cider manufacturer and a company called Camel Hire (who hired out minibuses, not camels) had put in some sponsorship, my ticket was booked, and I had a climbing partner to meet in Quito. And soon there I was, just twenty-two miles south of the equator – the country's name comes from the word equator – in this capital city at 2,850 metres high. Now, where is my climbing partner? Chris Adye was not registered at our rendezvous point, the Gran Casino Hotel, and he had not left a message. There was no room for me at that hotel so I booked in at the nearby sister hotel, the Gran Casino International. At the former a room cost £1 a night, at the latter £2.50. The hotels were full of young people, students mainly, armed with tourist guidebooks and credit cards and travellers cheques and airline tickets and insurance documents, who travelled cheaply by bus and stayed in acceptable cheap hotels. They reminded me of how little initiative we had to show in our 'feather bedded' adventures compared with early travellers: explorers, missionaries, traders, sailors and the like. What they must have suffered! So, while I had great respect for the spirit of these young people, I felt that many failed to appreciate just how privileged and cosseted they were.

I cannot resist comparing Quito, as I have La Paz, with my first taste of South American life, which was Lima. Quito, population one and a quarter million, is not so crowded with people or traffic, but still has buses and taxis galore, is not so plagued by beggars, and is not so badly spoiled by obvious poverty; the country's oil wealth seeps down even to the lowest stratum of society. There are many close similarities with Peru's capital too: the street markets are the same, where Indian women in traditional dress squat on the pavement to sell their wares, and what they sell is no different - potatoes, tomatoes, eggs, bread, cakes, sweets, cigarettes, all manner of domestic utensils, stews kept warm over paraffin stoves, and clothing. When I bought a little bag of hot broad beans and maize a young woman tried to charge me a hundred sucres (the currency unit 'sucre' has nothing to do with sugar, but is named after a general).

'Fifty,' said a young Ecuadorian man who had purchased ahead of me. So, there were gringo prices here too. I paid fifty sucres and ate a fair sized snack for the price of a box of matches at home.

My message for Chris Adye, telling him where I was, sat for days on a noticeboard at the Gran Casino. On my fifth day in Quito I bumped into Chris as he was leaving a Turkish bath. He and his partners had climbed three mountains and then, after they went home, he had spent a few days at the coast. Though he had climbed Ecuador's second highest mountain, Cotopaxi, both on this and a previous visit, Chris fell in easily with my plan to attempt that particular volcano. Twenty-eight years old, bearded and bespectacled, he had a studious look and boyish manner; his stride was bouncy, jaunty for a tall man of twelve and a half stones. He had opted for mathematics and computer studies at Cambridge University but had failed to complete the course. He took up work as a salesman in a climbing equipment shop in London, which had not gone down well with his parents; males on his father's side of the family had by tradition joined the Royal Artillery until his father broke the succession by becoming a policeman, reaching the rank of inspector. I could imagine their bewilderment at his obsession with climbing, for he was as completely wrapped up in his sport as anyone I knew. 'I'm married to climbing,' he said (and also, 'I'm too selfish to get married,' though he did a few years later.)

A couple in their thirties walked ahead of us down a Quito pavement, hand in hand.

'In love,' I said.

'He's snowblind. She has to lead him,' Chris explained. 'They were on Cotopaxi.'

For thirty-five pence, or the price of a British Rail cup of tea at the time, we travelled by bus 80 kilometres to the town of Latacunga, in one and a half hours. With petrol at twenty pence per gallon (and sold so, in gallons rather than the usual litres of other commodities in Ecuador) road travel was very, very cheap. Chris knew the ropes and within minutes we had hired a pickup and driver, shared with three young men from a Nottingham University expedition, which took us 40 kilometres up a good trail to drop us 180 metres below the Ribas hut, a plain concrete structure built in 1971 on a rough level space at 4,800 metres, which is very close to the height of Mont Blanc. Within forty minutes we had walked an easy path on brown and grey volcanic ash and were settled in the building, which could accommodate fifty people, many of whom visited the hut in its own right, rather than attempt to climb Cotopaxi.

We set out in blasting winds, alongside two dozen Swiss, French and Canadian hopefuls, for Cotopaxi's top. About half of those who forced themselves out into the cold reached their objective but we did not, because I was happy to stop an hour short of the summit and have another go when better trained by this day's exertions; the climbing was easy but the wind was too serious for me to stick my neck out left us with a training climb and an extra day of acclimatisation in our favour, as we again pushed ourselves out into the teeth of a bitter wind which seemed all the more intimidating in the 1.30 am. darkness.

Chris and I had been joined by Jamie and Jeff, outdoor adventure instructors from Colorado.

'If it's OK with you guys we'll stick together. Be safer,' one of them suggested, and we felt more comfortable right away, wrapping around ourselves a further blanket of caution in this very cold place.

Despite a mention in our guide book of 'a problem getting on to the glacier' and of the need for snow stakes and ice screws, the route was not technically hard; not to be underestimated in harsh weather, a few crevasses around, but not hard.

'Three hundred metres to go,' said Jeff, who carried an altimeter. By 8 am. we had reached the spot where Chris and I had turned back; today I felt like a different person, or the same person in a different, fitter body. As we walked in single file through a crevassed little bowl the wind stopped us dead in our tracks, and I realised we could not continue in such conditions on the succeeding snow which the guide book described as 'quite steep'. But soon Cotopaxi's wind dropped, allowing us to press on for a while, over fluffy snow blown into regular patterns, resembling boot length, white fern fronds laid close together, as palm leaves might be put down parallel on a floor.

'I reckon we're carrying twenty pounds of ice,' Jamie shouted, referring to the layer which coated our clothing and rucksacks and rope up to an inch thick, particularly on the windward side, which was the left. We looked as if someone had been at us with an icing sugar syringe, covering us from head to foot. My crutches, an inch in diameter, had become as thick as Judy's wrist, and heavy.

The other three drew ahead and at 10 am. I joined them on the summit at 5,897 metres. Cloud precluded a view into the crater of the volcano and the wind had risen so high it was difficult to converse, even by shouting. It had not been a route which had required climbing skill, but the wind had made us fight.

'Wouldn't have done it without you guys,' Jamie said, putting into words the reassurance which came from being in a team. 'Hope you don't mind if we go down ahead of you now. Jeff's cold.'

Though he could have romped down Chris descended slowly, patiently, with me. Soon we were the only people on the huge mountain, and envious of those who could descend so quickly to the comfort of the hut.

A few days later, early one morning, I hailed a cab, driven by one Byron, who extolled the virtues of Quito as we drove to the airport; he rated it the best city in the best country in the world. That was claiming too much, but I was sorely tempted to come back for some more of those volcanoes. It is always the same; I cannot think of one country I would not visit again for its mountains.

In 1989 Judy and I were involved for the third time with an Age Concern Christmas Day party and lunch. On that third occasion I organised the event in our local cricket club for two dozen people, about half of whom were in wheelchairs; it was our most memorable Christmas Day, we agreed. This involvement with Age Concern prompted me one day to think about undertaking a second sponsored walk from John o' Groats to Land's End for Age Concern, pushing a supermarket trolley. I chose three more charities to benefit, in addition to Age Concern: Oxfam, the Royal Association for Disability and Rehabilitation (RADAR) and the Calvert Trust Adventure Centres for Disabled People.

It took me ninety-four days to walk from John o' Groats to Land's End in 1969, so I can claim a record for the longest it has taken! There were tough days on that trek when my stumps hurt a good deal, but travelling alone with my rucksack on a golf trolley I felt a great sense of independence, of self-sufficiency, as so often I do on a mountain. On my second attempt at the journey in 1990 I enjoyed the luxury of a support vehicle, a minibus which could be a mobile café by day, and a shelter for the night if necessary. It is often said that a supermarket trolley has three wheels which want to go shopping and one which prefers to go to the seaside, so I decided to have two fixed wheels at the front. With my departure date not far away a demolition contractor friend put one of his welders on the job, which was soon completed.

29th October 1990. John o' Groats. Only Judy and Willie, our driver for the first four weeks, were there with me. 10 am. and off we go! We laughed about what one newspaper reporter had asked a few days earlier: 'Norman, will you do this walk all in one go, or by stages over several days?'

Judy intended walking only a few miles each day, but stayed in my wake for the full 30 kilometres (over 18 miles) on the first day. As soon as we stopped we experienced what we called 'squeaky time', when her feet and my stumps made us go, 'Ooh! Aah! Oh!,' for several minutes. 'It'll punish your feet,' a neighbour had said. To me. The next day Judy followed me on the road, and the next, and the idea formed itself that she would walk all the way too, wearing the second-hand boots which had cost £3.50 from an Oxfam shop.

From time to time skin was rubbed from my stumps, but it was nothing to the trouble I experienced on the first walk, and Judy tolerated her few small blisters rather than discontinue the trek. We walked for days through lovely farming countryside by the sea (lots of sheep, or 'woolly pigs', as Willie called them). Then through the forested moorland hills we marched, singing as we went. The oft-predicted Scottish 'monsoon' never came, and we suffered only three days of rain in over three weeks in Scotland. Our route took us down the east coast of Scotland, then through Inverness, Pitlochry, Perth, Stirling and Cumbernauld.

To keep the expenses down we slept a dozen nights in the minibus, found cheap bed and breakfast accommodation (two to a bed for £2.25 each in one transport café!), stayed with friends, and accepted offers of free accommodation in pubs, hotels, and people's homes. At one guest house, paid for by Rotary, a Rotarian called in to welcome us.

'Been here before,' he said. 'With a crane. Came to winch a cow out of the toilet. It fell from the fields at the back and went through the roof. It was sitting on the toilet when I got there. Seat was broken.'

600 kilometres (372 miles) to Gretna. The horizontal expedition went slowly on, through Carlisle and Penrith, and over the high road of Shap.

Through Lancaster, Preston, Wigan, Warrington, Telford. In Shropshire we were warned there was snow on the way.

'Don't care if it snows. Just don't want rain,' Judy said. We had had four days of rain in forty days.

'Not likely to snow this side of Christmas,' I told her knowingly.

That night we slept in the minibus during the worst blizzard seen in Shropshire in a decade! But we earned a most beautiful day on quiet roads with breathtaking sights of trees and red berries laden with pure white snow.

Worcester, Tewkesbury, Gloucester, Bristol, Taunton. Cornwall gave us rain every day, but we were so close to the finish we did not mind. I needed only two days off because of stump injuries (eight days on the first walk). Walking was restricted to the hours of good daylight, and we took no rest days, but tramped on through Christmas and Boxing Day. Most nights we were in bed by not long after 8.30pm., in my case as much to relieve the pain as through tiredness. We finished at Land's End in violent, invigorating wind on 27th December, welcomed home by a dozen friends and relations. It had taken sixty days to cover the 1417 kilometres (880 miles).

'Best holiday I ever had,' Judy said. She must be the only person to have done the walk without intending to and the nicest thing about it was her enjoyment.

June 1991. The expedition I was to join to Kamet in India has been cancelled. It is said that the Indians with whom we were obliged by government regulations to climb our particular mountain could not afford to go. I start making phone calls; mustn't waste the summer. Little time to get something organised. Two members of the cancelled expedition are accepted to go instead to Masherbrum I in Pakistan. Perhaps I can go too? I get one of them to ask the leader, someone I had never met called David Hamilton, if I could join; I know they are still looking for members. The reply comes back that I am not welcome because I am too old. Too old, at fifty!

I see from an advertisement in a climbing magazine that Out There Trekking of Sheffield are running a trip to nearby Masherbrum II, a mountain said by the Italians who made the only ascent in 1988, to be 7,200 metres high. The leader, Mark Miller, says I can go. This will be good preparation for an attempt on an 8,000-metre mountain. The summer is salvaged.

After spending part of August training in the Alps, late in the month I departed from Heathrow for Islamabad. A full moon, mountain bright, stayed on our right beam for much of the flight, to be replaced, as I slept, by the sun. Five of us stepped out of Islamabad airport into a waiting minibus after eight hours in the air, and in minutes we were in the Hotel Shalimar. Air-conditioned; cool and clean, a haven in a hothouse. The accommodation had been arranged by Mark Miller who, as I have mentioned, was leading the expedition, and I more than anyone appreciated the coolness. Amputees, having less than the normal body surface area from which to lose heat, can suffer terribly in hot climates. In addition, the sort of legs I wear are kept in place by leather corsets around the thighs, with woollen socks inside. It's a bit like wrapping blankets around your legs in the summer heat.

Next day our gaily painted bus (or Flying Coach, as it said on the side in big letters - tempting fate on these roads) was comfortable for our party, now grown to a dozen. Mark had hired it for us alone, which was a sensible idea bearing in mind how much equipment we had and how crowded the usual buses could be.

We set off at 11.30 am. to take the same route to Baltistan's capital, Skardu, as on my first trip to Pakistan. With about a quarter, the tame quarter, of our journey behind us, our liaison officer, Abu Zafar, who was a devout Muslim, called for a halt for prayers at dusk. His God must have been looking out for him, as during the halt it was discovered that a bolt was about to drop out of the suspension, which could have resulted in serious consequences on the horror road we were about to take; it could indeed have been a Flying Coach for a short time.

Every so often we stopped at a roadside café for tea, and perhaps to risk some food as well. At one a waiter dropped a chappati on the floor on which people had spat regularly, picked it up and tried to serve it to us. We invented a skull rating system, and this was a real five skuller on a scale where five was the worst.

Unlike the moon seen from the 'plane, the near-full cheese now seemed errant, for at times it was in front, then to the left, then the right, and even behind, as we weaved up hills on hairpin bends above horrifying drops. For hours, long hours. Fatalism, based partly on the recognition that I have already had a very full life, or two lives, or more, was slender comfort now, and I believe my fears were rational, bearing in mind that the driver took only three hours sleep in a journey time of thirty-six hours.

Arriving at the 'shut for the night' K2 motel, Skardu, at 11.30pm., we camped on the sparse lawn. With a few members who had travelled ahead, we had reached our complement of fourteen plus a liaison officer and two cooks.

In the early afternoon next day we loaded three jeeps and drove for about six and a half hours. At several points on the usual rough and dangerous road, fit only for jeeps (which I would have preferred with more tread on and less splits in their tyres) we encountered police checks. Everyone out of the jeeps, fill in the book: name, passport number, nationality, occupation. And just as Dervla Murphy says she did in Where the Indus is Young, people made up names and other details. I doubt though, that under Occupation she entered, as two in our group did, 'Pope' and 'zebra'.

Hours of jeep travel left us dazed, suffering from what one of our Scots called 'jeep head'. We stopped a few hours short of our objective, the village of Hushe, and camped, completing the journey next day. The valley leading to Hushe is fringed with pretty terraced fields of corn, maize, peas in tiny pods and potatoes, and apricot, mulberry, apple, plane and poplar. Goats of various colours are common, as are chicken and cattle, which include the yak, nicely described by Dervla Murphy as having 'feet like a ballerina's and forequarters like a bison's'. Flat-roofed houses of timber and mud brick stood singly and in clusters in harmony with the countryside all the way up the valley, and in Hushe, where our jeep journey terminated.

A name sometimes applied to the 10,000 square miles of Baltistan and often to Ladakh is Little Tibet, and on the surface of it there is an air of Shangri La. But bedbugs, mud, dust, goitre, dysentery, impetigo, tuberculosis, cretinism, extreme winter cold and malnourishment, for instance, lie behind the facade, and the romantic tourist view does not stand up to close examination. However, for those such as we who merely pass through, Baltistan has real charm. We camped half a mile beyond the village in a field.

I was nauseous and weak from a bug the next day (yes again), so, though it was only a day's march from Hushe to our base camp, I opted to do it in two days. Mark allotted me a cook-cum-porter, Hakim, a smart dude by local standards in clean, casual trousers, a bright red sweater, and a round Balti hat like a pie. Most of our porters wore the long shirt and pyjama style trousers, the shalwar-kameez. They were soon out of sight ahead of Hakim and me, in a juniper forest growing on sandy ground.

'You married?' Hakim asked as we sat for a rest by a clear stream.

'Yes. Twenty-four years.'

'How many children?'

'None,' I said.

He fell silent, as much puzzled as embarrassed. He thought for a while and then asked, 'Is not possible to boom-boom without legs?'

'It's possible.'

I was glad next day to cover a loose moraine and a good trail through short bushes to reach base camp and a welcome rest. There the news was good: nine people, including two porters, had made a carry to an advanced base camp (ABC). Next day four of our men and two porters went up again, and the day after that, feeling much recovered, I headed in seven plodding hours to a grassy knoll not far short of ABC. The going was safe, over a flood plain of small boulders, and a scree covered glacier with boulders up to the size of cows, always with a way through on smaller and stable stuff. This had been followed by firm glacier ice, free of snow and so exhibiting all crevasses rather than having them lurk beneath a white mantle. The route then led to the grassy knoll. As usual I was rather sore at the end of the day, and was happy to settle down for a cold, clear night out under shooting stars with Theresa Booth, who was a solicitor, Mark's Argentinian assistant Miguel, and one of our Scots, Graham. We were a contented group, for progress of the expedition was thus far very good.

Above the grassy knoll we reached snow, and encountered a small risk from rucksack sized rocks which leapt occasionally from the cliff ahead.

'I knew you would go fast when you got to the snow, you wee shite,' said Christine, our Glaswegian medic, who was an authority on mountain medicine. She had gone up the day before with several others to occupy ABC. 'If you go faster than me I'm going to take those bloody legs off you and bury them in the snow.'

In fact I had moved rather slowly, and I was beginning to wonder whether I should again join an expedition to such a high mountain, for I was finding it a struggle to carry loads. What had not really sunk in was that once more I had a stomach problem, and was weak as a result; but on the bright side the antibiotics for this dose cleared up the Broad Peak problem too. I was not pulling my weight; but no one in this group made any complaint. On the contrary, they were most encouraging, particularly Mark and Graham.

The more Masherbrum I unfolded itself, the more I was pleased I had been rejected (perhaps for the wrong reasons) for what must have been a gruelling route, much more gruelling, I hoped, than that which faced us. I had already sent a message of good luck by porter to the pair I knew on that peak, and though my signature, Old Man Croucher, was added mockingly, there was more than a trace of irony in it, for I really was questioning whether I should venture on high peaks without a porter. Age, in conjunction with my legs, might be beginning to tell on mountains of 6,000 metres and more. But I had had such a good run I could only feel fortunate, and there would still be a place for me on many mountains; their variety would allow this, the Assiniboines and Alpamayo Chicos of the world. But still the 8,000 metre ambition would not go away.

Six dome tents of pale yellow and brown fabric on a ridge of broken stones formed ABC. There we ate well on mashed potato, noodles, chillis, salami, sweet and savoury biscuits, soups, sardines, mackerel and paté, stocking up fuel for the fray.

Progress over the next few days was rapid. Six ropes were fixed on ice at up to 50 degrees above an easy angled ice gully of 300 metres, threatened by falling rocks as big as TV sets. From the top of the ropes the route went directly across a firm snow plateau and across the back of a rising, white, icy crescent. Camp 1 was established at the high end of the crescent on 9th. September, three tents on a snow terrace above 6,000 metres. From there two days later I watched as Mark and five others, our strongest, set off for the summit at 3.15 am., up a triangular slope which rose from the camp at a steady angle, then steepened dramatically near what looked to be the top. It had all gone so well that I began to wonder if, in the words of an elderly widow friend, 'Something would come along and bend our rhubarb.'

'You coming, Norm?' Mark had asked.

'I'll wait until tomorrow. Don't want to get in the way of the faster people. It will help me acclimatise.'

A line of bobbing torchlights sparkled high up, diamonds in a dark

grey triangular background against a darker sky. Voices carried clearly.
'What's it like?'
'Try more to the left.'
'Looks all right here.'
'Follow us.'

At 5.15 am., as lights were extinguished and figures appeared boldly in the now white landscape, they seemed close to the top. But the way was blocked by a cornice, the snow overhanging by 15 degrees or more. This was tackled by Victor, one of our several strong climbers, but he fell off, without injury. So close to the summit, less than 20 metres, but the overhang was too soft to climb. We could not claim an ascent if we did not reach the true top. Then to the left they found a short, vertical wall of snow, only 3 metres, which was easily climbed, and an easy slope to the top. A whoop of victory, and another, and another confirmed a few minutes later that the job was done.

Clearly the Italian estimate of 7,200 metres was in question, for our team had reached the top in a very short time that last day.

My turn came at 2.30 am. in the chill but fortunately windless dark of the next day, in company with Graham and Anwar, our cook-cum-high altitude porter. He had leapt at the opportunity of borrowing the climbing equipment of our liaison officer, who had retreated to Skardu after one cold night spent at ABC. In Skardu he remained for treatment for an allergy.

The steady angle of firm snow suited me, and I expected to use spiked crutches almost all the way. Anwar found the going hard, and was soon pleading, 'Resting.'

'Is that a Balti word?' Graham asked. 'We don't understand it.'

It is usually assumed, mostly correctly, that those who like Anwar live high up will cope well with higher altitudes, but here was living proof that one should not make too many assumptions on that subject. After an hour we did stop for twenty minutes, to allow Ian Swarbrick, a surveyor from Sutton Coldfield, to catch up with us, since his partner, Miguel, had turned back feeling unwell. We then moved in single file on one rope, Graham, Ian, Anwar, me. Two more hours went by without too much suffering, except on Anwar's part, as the slope allowed us up, always firm and never too steep for rhythmic, steady movement.

Having followed two fixed ropes on a steep slope we arrived at the short vertical section of hard snow, a step not much higher than we could reach with our axes. Up the step, 12 metres up another friendly slope, and there we were, looking at Broad Peak, Chogolisa, K6, K7, the Gasherbrums and scores of other grand peaks. And closest of all,

Masherbrum I.

Our expedition could claim the first British ascent, only the second ascent in all, and by a new route. But such statistics mattered little. We had been there, right on top. We had been associated with such grandeur and beauty.

Theresa, Christine, another Mark (or Mark II, as he was labelled), Miguel and a Scottish oil rig man called Duncan were soon at camp 1, waiting for their attempt and hoping for good weather. Christine had had a slip in the ice gully, and was badly bruised and scraped on one arm and one thigh as a result of her slide of 30 metres down rough ice. In a letter she sent from Australia, Christine mentioned that her arm was still weak months later. This was an indication of how bad the injury was. She had every reason to turn back, but retreat was not on her mind. Christine more than anyone earned the success which came her way next day, in company with our last four other members. Everyone on top; fifteen people.

The descent began, down the crescent, across the snowfield, down the fixed ropes. Then came another incident involving Christine. Five of us sat on a promontory of snow above the gully where she had slipped, waiting for the reduction of stonefall risk in the cool of the late afternoon. Christine had, as Americans might put it, 'gone to the bathroom' a few metres away. Suddenly there was a clattering sound and we all looked up to see a bombardment of two dozen stones, large as footballs and small as walnuts and different sizes in between, bouncing our way with great speed. I shouted, 'Everyone get behind your rucksack!' and there was some rapid movement from all concerned, including Christine, who must have broken the record for a high altitude dash of fifteen metres with her knickers and breeches around her knees. Wisely, she got behind me and my rucksack, and the rocks went by to one side and the other. No one was hit, but I later learned of someone who had not been so lucky with stonefall: Chris Adye had suffered a very badly broken arm through stonefall in the Alps. Two years later the limb was still stiff, weak and painful.

As usual I was last down to base camp, two days later.

'There will be a wonderful atmosphere at base camp,' Old Man Croucher said knowingly when Theresa came out to meet him from that camp. 'Always is after a successful ascent.'

'Mark and Ewen (another Scot) have just had a fight,' she told me.

There had been a difference of opinion about the conduct of the expedition, a brief tussle, Ewen had a few stitches put in over one eye and the incident faded. Then the atmosphere was good.

'I could eat a scabby bairn between two mattresses,' Duncan said, and we tucked into chips and other delights.

Stroll down to Hushe, jeeps to Skardu, where we stayed overnight at the Sehr Hotel.

While the others travelled around the countryside, three of us - Theresa, Mark II and I - headed for Rawalpindi in two bus journeys of seven and a half and sixteen hours, with a break of two hours between them. '14 Killed As Bus Turns Turtle' read a newspaper headline concerning a recent accident on a nearby road. The second leg of the journey was so bumpy we occasionally banged our heads on the ceiling, and Mark II added 'bus bum' to 'jeep head' as a peril of Pakistani road travel. Any passengers suffering from haemorrhoids deserved special sympathy.

And how did David Hamilton and his group fare on Masherbrum I? They failed quite close to the summit. We had had a team better matched to the route, and a bit of luck as well. We had our mountain, and formed many lasting friendships among ourselves. I felt lucky to have been turned down; good fortune often comes in a negative guise. This was so even in the case of this book, which a publisher assured me they would publish. I met the managing director, who said it was just a matter of drawing up the contract, but after the meeting I said to Jude that though he was making the right noises I would not trust him until the contract was signed. 'I am thrilled that you have decided to work with us,' he wrote, and 'How glad I am to be working with you on this project.' Six months later he turned the book down mainly because his company was not experienced in publishing climbing books; took them long enough to decide that! A literary agent who expressed an interest in placing the book with a publisher similarly decided, after many months, that climbing books were not his forte. My point is that the delays provided an opportunity to amend and append a great deal, much to the benefit of the book. As when my leg broke in Argentina, it was best to think 'What can I make of this? What can be salvaged? Can it be turned around to good purpose? Be flexible and gain.' In the case of this book an extra bonus was not having to go along with that publisher's preferred title – Legless Feats!

CHAPTER 12

Mount Everest

FOR a long time I was reticent about writing this chapter, for I felt it did not belong in a 'picnic/pilgimage' book. But one way to illustrate what such a trip should be is to describe by contrast an expedition which was outside that mould. So here is an account of an expedition I would in many ways prefer not to have been involved in, one which brought me little joy.

This story begins tragically when some of the friendships born on Masherbrum II were cut off within a year. On September 28th 1992 at about 4.30pm I received a phone call from a friend of Mark Miller's girlfriend telling me that they believed he had been aboard Pakistan International Airways flight PIA 268, which had 'gone down'. A plane had crashed while attempting to land at Kathmandu. I rang PIA's London office to be told there was a passenger under the name of M. Miller on the flight, and all passengers were believed dead. The BBC news at 5.17pm said twenty-two British passengers were feared dead and at 5.32pm there was 'little hope of finding any survivors'. At 6pm this had become 'no hope of any survivors'. Christine Patterson and Mark's business partner Andy Broom were staying with us that evening and by the time they arrived at 6.30pm PIA had confirmed that Mark, and also Victor who had been on the Masherbrum II expedition, had been killed in the crash.

Mark had been particularly encouraging about my climbing and had invited me to join him in the Spring of 1993 on Shishapangma, the thirteenth highest mountain in the world. He had a rough, bullish talent for organising an expedition and driving it on to success; he was a rebel, often belligerent, and a very strong climber. His presence on an expedition could only increase my chances of success.

Seventeen days later I heard on the radio that an outdoor pursuits instructor called Graham Lipp had died in a caving accident. It seems he fell victim to hypothermia while leading a group of young people through deep water in a cave in South Wales. He was the Graham with whom I had shared the summit of Masherbrum II. It was he who, when I expressed concern at not pulling my weight in carrying loads, had said, 'Doesn't matter. Just keep going up.' And when I descended late one day after the ascent under Miguel's watchful eye, it was Graham, along with the ever considerate Duncan, who came out to see that we were all right. A few weeks later he had stayed the night in our flat in London, on the way from Scotland to his new instructor's job in South Wales.

'He was lovely,' Judy said, and when I told Ian Swarbrick of Graham's death his first words were, 'He was a gent.'

The death toll of climbing friends and acquaintances over a decade or so had reached twenty-five, though not one had died while climbing with me. Fifteen had died on the mountains, two in an air crash, two of heart attacks, one in a microlight accident, one in a paraglider crash, one in a caving accident, one in a car crash, one of cancer and one by suicide. Their deaths, the majority associated with adventure sports, did not lead me seriously to consider giving up climbing. Mountains had brought some meaning to my life, and I had to continue to seek the challenge and excitement and fulfilment to be found among them. I can only repeat what I have said earlier, that life is like a muscle, and if not exercised, it wastes. I felt sorrow for those left behind to grieve, but suffered no great sense of loss for those who had died in the saddle.

Because of Mark's death the expedition to Shishapangma was cancelled, but Andy Broom of Out There Trekking then asked if instead I would like to join an expedition he was organising, to Mount Everest. All I had to do was to raise about £12,000, the per capita amount for the attempt on the North Ridge, which is in Tibet, a country now controlled by China.

I had not sought Everest, had never seriously considered attempting that particular mountain, partly because I did not think any team would tolerate my limitations. Also, I did wonder how a double-leg amputee in his fifties could consider attempting such a route. There, people do literally lie down and die through exhaustion, or just pass away in the night because of cerebral or pulmonary oedema.

Since we were attempting the North Ridge, a less frequently climbed route which had never had a confirmed ascent by an Englishman (it is possible that Mallory and Irvine did succeed in 1924, but in the absence of any confirmation they can be credited only with a very spirited attempt), chances of success were less than if we had taken the normal route.

Thanks to Rank Xerox, my parents, Ealing Cricket Club, the Bennachie Whisky, a local pub, a few companies and several individuals, about half my expedition costs were raised in sponsorship. The Bennachie Whisky money came in memory of Graham Lipp, while the contribution from Ealing Cricket Club was the profit from a race night organised by two friends. A sponsored cycle ride from the Wheatsheaf, Ealing, to Land's End by the landlord produced the bulk of the pub sponsorship.

In preparation I spent two weeks in the Zermatt area, walking and climbing, just one of the vast aestival crowds which, along with the skiers, have put such pressure on the environment in the twenty years since I first went there. As I knew there was a hard time ahead on Everest I tried to make the training as pleasant as possible, rather than draining myself too early, and Zermatt proved ideal. Because of the ease of approach by a new cable car I shared the Breithorn, 4,165 metres with three hundred people and more.

'C'est un boulevard,' said one man as we trudged the snow trail to the top.

Though I am by nature gregarious, this was one reason why I had gone to the greater ranges, to find real wilderness, to escape the crowds for a while and find periods of peace. One recent interference by mankind I did like - the little Schwarzee Lake beneath the Matterhorn had been brought alive by the introduction of ten brown and three white ducks, and of fish, mostly tiny but some as much as 20 centimetres long. One night when the crowds had gone I slept out contentedly by the little chapel there.

As 'McDonalds' had reached the main street of Zermatt, so had 'Neighbours' come to the TV set in the lobby of the Hotel Manang in Kathmandu. This August 1993 visit was my first to Nepal's capital, which has a population of over one million people. Kathmandu is in many ways close in appearance to cities of India and Pakistan, but is essentially less hectic, distinctly Nepalese in clothing and polite manners.

'Hash? Smoke? Carpet? T-shirt? Jewellery?' Some hassling, but not like Kashmir, for instance. A relatively safe, comparatively orderly city for the developing world.

While most of the others left Kathmandu for a training trek I toured the Monkey Temple, the old city of Bhaktapur and the Patan Durbar Square, all well worth a visit. The Monkey Temple, where dogs, ducks and monkeys co-exist, with only occasional dog barking, duck scuttling and quacking, monkey screaming interludes, is symbolic of Kathmandu and of Nepal itself. The great stupa there, with huge staring eyes, is represented on postcards and in books galore, and no wonder. The buildings of Patan Durbar Square and Bhaktapur have to be seen to be believed, with one after another pagoda style temple, and houses with intricately carved wooden window and door frames.

On the second day I did some shopping for someone who had gone on the trek and suddenly found myself wondering what I was doing there, looking for cornplasters (for him, of course) on Freak Street in Kathmandu. Was this real? It was certainly a far cry from Cornwall, but nowadays reachable by anyone who puts their mind to it. Not so when I was a lad, in the days when hardly anyone flew unless they were in the armed services, or rich.

The leader of the expedition, Jon Tinker, avoided the trek too, since he had work to do in Kathmandu: organising transport, Sherpas, oxygen equipment, pulling together all the strands to bind what was quite a large group of twenty climbers, four climbing Sherpas, three more Sherpas, and four extra climbers who would join us later for part of the expedition. Jon is short, blond, good looking, stocky, cocky and quite often short tempered, or inclined to throw his toys out of the pram, as a couple of people phrased it. He has a degree in politics, has been an aid worker in Afghanistan, and had made two attempts on Everest. As this was a commercial trip run by Out There Trekking his job was to organise and lead rather than to attempt to reach the summit himself. At a meeting of the team in Sheffield shortly before we departed for Kathmandu he had said, 'My job is to get you guys to the top. I'll be the last to try for the summit.' This had prompted me to remark to Judy that time would soon tell if we had a good leader in that respect or, if he failed to stick to his word, a rat. I think 'rat' is the word I used, but it may have been something stronger. His desire to reach the summit would be understandable, but his duty and responsibility to lead, to enhance the likelihood of his clients reaching the top, was clear. Jon and his wife did not like the word 'client' but 'member' is too vague as it does not distinguish them from Jon or Jon's friends or from the Sherpas on the expedition. Customer, client - we need a word. His attitude to our expedition was ambivalent. When we talked to the sort of experienced, hard mountaineer he looked up to Jon described it as 'a dinosaur expedition, we're using oxygen and Sherpas and fixed ropes and all that crap'. Such a purist, elitist approach I could respect, but it did not sit well with a man who was leading a commercial trip. The compromise was too glaring, for in taking the money he accepted certain responsibilities. His attitude to discipline left a bit to be desired, too, as was evident in what he called his 'two walks' principle. He explained that this meant if anyone was doing anything with which he disagreed he would take them for a walk and explain the error of their ways. If their behaviour did not change, on the second walk he would break their legs and send them home. This was not the sort of leader/client relationship one expected, or am I just old-fashioned?

Jon Tinker insisted that his clients were not being guided, which would imply that they possessed the experience and skills to proceed under their own devices to the summit, and down. Clearly, this was debatable in several cases, for many lacked high altitude or extensive climbing experience.

In a twenty-six seater bus Jon, the Sherpas and I set off from Kathmandu one warm, humid morning, rising out of the traffic polluted city bowl to farm country rich with maize, rice, barley and other crops, and trees and houses making up pretty pictures in every direction. The variety of soft yellows and greens were as good as anywhere in South America, and that is saying something.

Three hours passed without incident until we came upon the first, fresh, minutes-old landslide brought on by the late monsoon rains, totally blocking the road with a thirty metre stretch of ooze and rock piles and trees, about one metre deep. Clearly the bus could go no further and the landslide would take a lot of bulldozing to clear, if a machine could be found. So we adopted the normal solution of unloading everything - a considerable amount of food and equipment for a large group for eight weeks - and carrying it across the squelchy landslide to another bus which had arrived opportunely. Our Sherpas, and local men who knew well the casual financial benefits of hanging around the nearest road landslide, soon had this done, and the second bus was hired for the next stage. We passed by more pretty pastoral scenes for about an hour and a half before encountering slide number two. Crossing the jumble of rock debris on foot in five minutes we again secured a bus and had it loaded, similarly using eager casual labour. About three miles along the road we came to slide number three, a big, quarter-mile wide, messy gouge down the mountain, fresh and still dangerous from unstable rubble hanging above on the sodden, steep slopes. This one was too dangerous to cross, and forced us and a new band of fortunate porters to climb 300 metres on reasonable, narrow paths through woodland to get above the slide, taking about two hours to transfer our goods from one side of the slippage to the other. On this section one Sherpa, Jangbu, kept a close eye on me; I could not have known that in a few weeks our 'carer' roles would be reversed.

An uninterrupted half-hour bus journey then took us to the border town of Kodari, a ribbon development on both sides of the rough road hewn from one flank of a steep sided, forested river valley. In wooden shacks and red brick buildings the traveller could find basic little restaurants and wooden stores selling toothbrushes and toothpaste, soap, cigarettes, biscuits, beer, soft drinks, bottled water, cloth and clothing, potatoes, onions, rice, eggs and meat, the last being mostly from chicken and goats. These animals wandered up and down the road, together with a few dogs, while streams of border crossers, Nepalese and Chinese people mostly, but Westerners too, passed through to catch trucks and buses in both directions.

Two days later we were reunited with our trekkers, and hearing their tales I was glad I had chosen a softies trip to Zermatt for training before going to Nepal. They had been much rained upon, had walked long stretches of muddy, slippery ground, and had been followed diligently into their tents by leeches; and, through a stupid oversight, toilet paper had been in short supply - most unsettling for a group of Westerners.

We crossed the Friendship Bridge from Nepal into Tibet with a pick-up and two larger trucks, and spent the night in the Zhangmu Hotel in the town of the same name, just over the border. The modern six storey construction had Western toilets, showers and baths, but no running water while we were there.

We were in the hands of the Chinese now, and they provided our transport, two minibuses, three lorries and a land cruiser, and our little convoy bounced its way up forested hills on a rough road zigzagging steeply out of Zhangmu. In such areas, rainfall ravages the road, carving runnels and washing the surface away, but we encountered no landslides. Soon this highway to Lhasa improved and good speed was made as we rose to the region where there is little precipitation and less resultant damage to the road. However, the looseness of the terrain and the steadily decreasing carpet of rain starved vegetation to bind it, meant stonefall occurred here and there, and we had to drive around boulders which had fallen or rolled onto the road from cliffs. The country unfolded gradually to become more open on an undulating plateau, and by then there was neither water nor stonefall to threaten the road. What a place! What barren countryside of dry boulders and stones, bare rock faces, dust and sand, 5,050 metres high at its top point, an isolated pass with not a sign of human habitation in any direction because there was no water. As we lost some height there were occasional oases where a river or stream allowed green life and permitted people to exist in small farming communities, mostly growing barley, peas and potatoes. There were cattle and horses too, in small numbers, and herds of hardy goats and sheep. But mostly it was uninhabited, pale brown and awesome, as wild as anywhere I've seen, and there was a kind of very simple beauty in this shadowed monochrome desert beneath a clear blue sky. The sight of rock ridges, worn outcrops standing alone, piles of boulders, stones which had stood untouched for centuries, produced a pleasantly strange feeling inside.

An overnight halt was made in the middle of nowhere, near the highway at the new Quomolongma Hotel, a tourist stop-off on the Kathmandu to Lhasa route. Quomolongma is the Chinese name for Mount Everest, and in that hotel guests slept at a higher altitude than most of the Alps.

Turning off the Lhasa highway, our convoy drove eight hours on a rough but adequate road the next day past and through isolated villages of ten to thirty dwellings, with horses, donkeys, cows, chickens and dogs much in evidence. Passing the famous, largely-restored Rongbuk Monastery we arrived in our base camp at about 5,150 metres. The encampment of twenty or more tents, plus a big mess tent and a kitchen tent, lay on a flat, sandy, gravelly plain closely contained by dry, brown (always those shades of brown) hills, the highest and nearest topped with a thin layer of new snow. Above and around were brown rock walls, towers, strata, scree and bouldery moraines thirty metres high. Close by were teams from Korea, Spain, India and Greece, all with their sights set on the North Ridge. From here the north face of Everest was visible, and had it not been for the knowledge that it is the highest mountain in the world it would not have attracted my eye for long. Visually it is bettered fifty times over in the Andes, many, many times in the Himalaya and the Karakorum, several dozen times in the Alps, scores of times in other ranges. I was not fired by its appearance.

Jon Tinker had done well to get this small army and its accoutrements as far as base camp with barely a hitch. His organisational skills could hardly be faulted. Now he would need those as well as leadership skills; different qualities which so far had not been tested to any extent on this expedition.

We enjoyed a varied diet and our Sherpa cooks produced tasty meals including yakburgers, tinned ham, spam, eggs, potato fritters, rice, dhal (lentils), beans and many types of dessert. The yak meat, which tasted somewhat like venison, hung in large chunks in the kitchen tent and became gradually more and more whiffy as the weeks passed, and most of us ceased to eat it, but apart from that there was no cause to complain about our food. Our 'boil-in-the-bag' rations for high altitude (obtainable from some supermarkets) were far superior to the common dehydrated high altitude packs, of which some say the pack tasted better than the contents. So, in respect of food OTT had again scored highly.

For a full week everyone acclimatised to the altitude simply by being at base camp, and by taking walks up the neighbouring hills and valleys. By the end of that period both of my stumps were bleeding a little from the exercise where patches of skin had been rubbed off. The pain I could tolerate, but I was worried about infection which might cause a stump to swell to such a size that an artificial limb would not fit; this had happened twice before.

Our two dozen hairy yaks, horned and looking a bit like their Scottish bovine brothers and sisters, and with bells ringing like alpine cattle, arrived with several drivers, who camped near us. These beasts and men would make two journeys to Advanced Base Camp over the next few days, taking two days per carry from here to that camp at 6,400 metres on the East Rongbuk Glacier.

A rucksack of medical items went missing from a tent one night (potentially a very serious theft), and though it is probable that this was stolen by a small group of trekkers camped nearby, we suspected the Tibetan yak drivers of other thefts such as a pair of boots, and one was caught in the act of stealing a large box of breakfast cereal. When a full urine bottle disappeared from outside a tent - most of us use one high up, women sometimes with the aid of a wide neck and/or a funnel, to avoid quitting a warm sleeping bag in extreme cold - we relished a mental picture of them sitting around a dung fire that night in expectation of passing the whisky.

The way began easily over a vast, dry flood plain of water-smoothed stones, turned left up a valley, and took us up a boulder covered glacier which was straightforward as such glaciers go. Above that the route was luxurious by Himalayan standards, on what is known as the Magic Highway, a whaleback of a glacier about a hundred metres wide and covered in conveniently flat stones, nature's paving stones. On both sides rose pyramidal pinnacles of white ice, huge teeth as tall as Europe's highest trees, flanking the glacial tongue.

As we slogged upwards a dozen laden yaks descended. This was only the beginning of the post monsoon climbing season, so who could be going against the upward flow of loads? It transpired to be the Greeks who, after just five days of bad weather at ABC, were going home. So, one down out of the five, and we had hardly started.

On arrival at ABC my stumps were bleeding more badly than before, largely because of the hot trudge up the Magic Highway. But at least my spare pair of legs, marked on the shins 'left' and 'right' in case I had to send someone to collect one (they are not interchangeable), had arrived safely by yak mail. I would like to have taken a bottle of brandy too for sips on the long evenings we faced, but Jon Tinker had set a limit on how much weight each person could send up as personal gear.

Our climbing Sherpa quota of four (there were Sherpa cooks as well) was sadly low for a group which started with twenty climbers.

Shortly before the expedition departure for Nepal the number of clients had risen, each adding £12,000 to the kitty, but the number of Sherpas remained unchanged. On the South Col route of Everest that year one expedition employed twelve Sherpas with fourteen climbers. Our ratio was bound to affect the likelihood of clients getting up the mountain. Jon's explanation was that OTT could not afford more Sherpas, which opened up the question of whether they had pitched the price too low: on a subsequent trip to the North Ridge, OTT planned to charge much more. Perhaps we had trusted OTT too much in respect of climbing Sherpas, not realising that the seven on the list were not all of the climbing variety. Though Jon had advised clients at our pre-expedition meeting in Sheffield not to do too much carrying, but to allow the Sherpas to establish the route, it was clear that this could not be achieved without considerable input from the clients, meaning that on closer examination the Tinker logistics did not add up.

"Ever since the first Everest attempts, most expeditions – commercial and noncommercial alike – have relied on Sherpas to carry the majority of the loads on the mountain."
- Into Thin Air. Jon Krakauer.

Now followed four weeks of activity to set up camps on the mountain. Camp 1 stood on the North Col at about 7,010 metres and was reached by a safe glacier walk to a gradually steepening wall of snow. A way had been found through this obstacle by relatively easy slopes at first, steepening in one short section to ice at 75 degrees. The Indians and Koreans had fixed ropes, secured to ice screws, to the North Col, and everyone used them repeatedly. This led the Korean leader to tell Jon that in return we should carry loads for them, but this was not agreed. The Indian leader took a different view, that the ropes were there and it would be silly to expect people not to use them - would you have someone at the bottom selling permits? - but that Jon had shown a lack of courtesy in not agreeing this beforehand. Perhaps diplomacy was not Jon's strong suit, but he was not going to be made a fool of with regard to carrying penalty loads. Apart from that the expeditions coexisted pretty amicably though largely separately, more apart than on any other expedition I have joined.

It was heartening to see that our own international mix - Australian, English, Finnish, French, Irish, Nepalese (all our Sherpas were brought in from Nepal) Polish, Russian and (later) US, worked well enough. Any problems which arose between people were the result of personality and behaviour rather than nationality, as you will learn.

Between periods of bad weather, carries were made to the North Col and higher. The Sherpas performed excellently and everyone on the expedition attained the North Col at least once. At the fixed ropes we each used a sliding clamp called a jumar to attach ourselves, and to pull up; we never climbed roped together in the usual way that climbers proceed on lower mountains, and this had the advantage that each member could move at their chosen pace. For a few of our team the North Col was enough, and several returned to base camp for a rest.

Whenever we were on the mountain we shared tents as necessary, although our one Frenchman, Thierry, did his best not to. On one occasion I came up to ABC as he descended from the North Col, and when he came into the mess tent I told him I had moved in with him. This produced an outburst of muttered, 'Merde!' and 'Sacre bleu!' and he moved his equipment out to another tent which had fallen vacant for the night.

On September 16th two of our three Australians, Jon and Brigitte Muir, moved up to stay overnight at the North Col camp, without Brigitte having fulfilled Jon Tinker's stipulation that anyone spending the night there should first have carried a load to that camp. Since the Muirs were Jon Tinker's friends, this was bound to be a bone of contention. At the same time rumblings of discontent began in certain quarters, particularly in the French quarter, about whether there was enough oxygen available: with over thirty bottles I felt we had sufficient for the few who would prove themselves capable of a summit attempt, at three bottles per person, but some did not agree.

My right stump was still bleeding but I was impatient and made my first trip, carrying a light load of gas, rations and personal gear, to the North Col on September 20th, and spent three nights there. I was prepared to stay one more night because, as I explained to Jon Tinker by radio, I thought we required someone to be there all the time to keep the two tents clear of the snow which might cause them to collapse. In my own interests (perhaps) he asked me to return to ABC because otherwise I risked burning out through being too high too long. He may have been right about that, but I still believe we should have done our best to have kept someone at the North Col, a night or two per person, all the time, to protect the tents and all that had been so laboriously taken there. These logistical considerations crop up frequently on expeditions and often there is no clear right or wrong. Perhaps equally open to debate was the suggestion that we needed another tent at the North Col so we could keep plenty of people high in periods of good weather - one tent was crammed with clothing, sleeping bags, oxygen bottles, rope, fuel cartridges and food. Jon did come round to this view, but rather late, with the result that at times when members were ready and willing to carry to the North Col and above, there was no room for them.

September 25th was my fifty-third birthday, the night of which I spent in a tent half way between ABC and base camp with two rested clients who were on their way up, while I was on my way down to recuperate. My right stump was bleeding quite badly by the time I reached BC, and I welcomed a few days' rest in relative comfort.

Four more members had arrived shortly before. Their names were printed on our expedition postcard and they shared our base camp facilities – rudimentary toilets, radio system, tents and cooks - but their objective was to get someone to the North Col to take measurements of cosmic radiation. They were to an extent a separate unit, an expedition attached to an expedition, operating under the umbrella of OTT's permission to climb the North Ridge. The leader of this group, Jon Tinker's friend Harry Taylor, was the second Briton to have climbed Everest without supplementary oxygen. By the mid nineteen nineties about sixty people had done so. With him were Nish Bruce, a Briton who was to attempt the world skydiving record the following year, Karl Henize, a sixty-six year old former US astronaut, and Brian Tilley, a paramedic whose main responsibility was to look after Karl.

On September 29th we heard by radio that the two tents at the North Col had collapsed and been badly damaged by snowfall, and on 2nd October the unoccupied camp above that, which we called camp 2, was wiped out by an avalanche. All tents had to be replaced. The collapses at the highest camp were just bad luck, because it was too high to keep people there, and in any case they could have been injured or killed by the avalanche; collapse of the North Col tents was avoidable.

Harry Taylor and his small band set off for ABC on 30th September, intending to take two or three days. The next day I followed and soon came upon Nish, descending alone towards base camp. He was not feeling well because of the altitude, and considering how recently his team had arrived it was easy to understand why.

Early October was a gloomy time, for not only had camp 2 been wiped out but also next day our doctor, Ken, decided to go home to Australia after receiving some bad news from there, and then we heard that two members of the Indian expedition had frostbite injuries and would probably lose all their fingers. Their leader decided to call it a day, leaving three expeditions. But that was not the end of the bad news, for there was much worse to come.

On the way to ABC I had come across an inadequate oblong wall of stones, full of gaps, erected by Karl, or those who had been with him, where he had bivouacked alone about 300 metres below ABC. He had left a note to say he had spent the night there; why he had written such a note I don't know. Karl had, not surprisingly, been moving very slowly, but at his age, relatively inexperienced, and so recently arrived, he should not have been left alone without someone to ensure, for instance, that he was always properly hydrated. And, having said that, was it wise to have him that high without the paramedic keeping an eye on him? Whizz-kid mountaineers are not always the best at assessing the capabilities of we lesser mortals, but there should have been someone around to escort him down. Harry had confided in me (a confidence which with the passage of time need no longer be respected) that he was concerned about Karl being so high.

'After this I'm going to do what my wife tells me and be a good companion to her,' Karl said to me shortly after I arrived at ABC. And that same day, when I asked if he was feeling all right, he said he was fine. Well, I thought, he has a paramedic looking after him, though I am not sure Brian was well himself at that stage, and two leaders in a sense, so there was no need for me to worry. I was soon to regret deeply not responding better to those faintest of alarm bells, and had I found Jon Tinker more approachable, or if I had been more assertive in this debilitating environment, events might well have taken an altogether different course.

Next morning Karl was staggering and experiencing difficulty in breathing as he entered the mess tent. There was little doubt that this was solely as a result of being so high, so the three or four of us there saw to it that Brian was summoned immediately to take a look at his charge. Doctor Ken was already at BC waiting for transport for himself and the two frost-bitten Indians. After Karl had been examined he was put in a Gamow bag, a sausage-shaped, zipped canvas bag, big enough for two average-sized people at a push, which is inflated by a foot pump similar to that used to blow up an airbed. The patient gets in (or is lifted, if necessary) and is zipped in, and he or she can then be observed through a clear plastic window which also helps to make the experience less claustrophobic. As the foot pump is operated the bag inflates to a rigid cylinder and the increased air pressure creates the effect of lowering the patient by the equivalent of perhaps 1000 metres, which aids recovery.

After two hours in the Gamow bag Karl was allowed out and put on oxygen for an hour, and then an attempt was made to get him to walk down; there are no helicopters in Tibet, so that means of rescue was out of the question. He managed only fifteen or twenty paces before he sank to his knees and lay back. Supported by two Sherpas he made a hundred metres before collapsing, then another hundred metres. Since height could be lost only very gradually and over rough terrain the option of carrying him was a last resort, and perhaps he should have been put in the Gamow bag again. I mentioned it to Harry Taylor but I could not expect him to know any better than me, and it was somehow decided to carry Karl down pick-a-back; the Sherpas, Jon Muir and our Pole Maciej undertook the exhausting task. I manned the radio at ABC, relaying messages between Doctor Ken at BC and Jon Tinker with the rescue party on a mobile radio; they could not communicate directly. Soon the news was bad; at 4pm. Jon Tinker reported, 'His blood pressure is falling and he's going into a coma.' Just ten minutes later hopes were raised when Jon reported, 'He's a bit better.' But we knew enough of the insidious nature of the pulmonary and cerebral oedema collecting in the lungs and on the brain to know that his life was still at risk. A few of the rescue party remained with Karl about 300 metres below ABC while others returned to that camp.

The next morning, 5th October, I was up early and found Jon Tinker and Harry in the mess tent.

'What news on Karl?'

'He died last night,' Jon said.

Karl was the fifth person I knew who had died on this side of the mountain. They had been there not because it is the best, but because it is the highest.

I suggested to Jon Tinker that we should bury Karl in such a way that the body could be retrieved in the event that his family wished it; it would not have been difficult to have taken the body to BC by yak, and thence by road to Lhasa or Kathmandu. I have always said I would not want any risks taken to retrieve my body, but in this case there was no risk involved, and I felt the decision should be left with the family.

'You'd open up a whole can of worms trying to dig up a body in China,' Jon Tinker said. 'And anyway, I've never known anyone wanting a body back.'

The Times, 16th December 1997: 'Relatives of four crewmen whose bodies were recovered from the trawler *Sapphire* said yesterday that the operation had been 'an answer to a prayer ... the families raised £500,000 to fund the operation. Wilma Cameron, mother of Bruce Cameron, said, 'Our prayers have been answered. We have prayed for this so that we can get our loved ones home'.'

His body could have been kept in ice, but Karl was buried beneath stones near where he had died, and quite close to where he had bivouacked.

Three times I wrote to Trudie Davis, who was in charge of family welfare at NASA's Johnson Space Centre in Houston, but received no reply. I explained that I had a book coming out which gave details of Karl's death, and I did not want Karl's family to discover them without forewarning. I said I was reluctant to open old wounds by telling the full truth but on the other hand people sometimes felt more at peace knowing just what happened to their loved ones. I asked for an opportunity to discuss matters with Ms Davis or one of the family (I was prepared to go to the U.S.A.) before deciding on the final content of the book. After no results from letters I obtained Ms Davis's telephone extension number via the Astronauts' Office (48829) and left a message on her answering machine, again with no response. I wanted to tell Karl's widow or one of his children how Karl had died, and that his body could have been (could possibly still be) recovered without risk to others.

Karl's death and the absence of any qualified medical cover (Brian went home too) highlighted just how vulnerable we were in this desolate place, particularly because of the theft of medical items. Many of us signed a document we composed ourselves recognising this lack of cover and relieving OTT of responsibility. Thierry was the only one I saw refuse to sign.

We could have run out of steam, but quite soon everyone was pulling together again spontaneously towards getting someone onto the top. The fact that the Koreans put two men on the summit on the day following Karl's burial produced a mixed reaction, in the minority of 'Damn, they've done it and we haven't', but mostly I think it spurred us on, and I was surprised at the depth of pleasure I experienced at witnessing their success. I actually saw people reaching the summit of Everest. I was very pleased for them, whereas several people felt the Korean success only underlined the fact that we still had a great deal to do if we were to succeed.

On 6th October our one Russian, George, and Bruce, a skinny, intelligent, sharp man, along with the Sherpas Nima and Jangbu, carried from the North Col to camp 2 at about 7,600 metres. On the same day, shortly before the Korean success at 12.30pm., Jon and Brigitte Muir set off for the North Col. Next day this couple and George (again) made another carry to camp 2. Brigitte was forced to hand over part of her load to the two men, thus increasing rumblings about her place in the pecking order for summit attempts. But Jon Tinker had made up his mind: Maciej (OTT's climbing leader), with Lakpa Sherpa, would try first for the summit from camp 2, then Jon Tinker and Ang Babu Sherpa, and then Jon's friends, the Muirs. Though he may not have been a fully paid-up client, no one had any objection to Maciej, with Lakpa Sherpa, having the first shot, for Maciej was a very experienced and successful high altitude mountaineer who had climbed a number of 8,000 metre peaks, including some in winter. If he broke the trail those who followed would have an easier task. He was popular and had more than pulled his weight out in front carrying loads. Lakpa had done extremely well too. The reaction to Jon Tinker's choice (made in my absence) of himself to go with one of our best Sherpas, who had already climbed this route, ranged from placid acceptance to stunned, annoyed disbelief. He and Babu would be in support, he said plausibly, but he had picked a nice slot for himself behind Maciej and Lakpa. Why not someone else with Ang Babu, one of the stronger clients, while Jon maintained control, leadership?

'I was assured the leader had no personal summit ambitions and if I had not received such assurances I would not have joined the expedition.' Kevin Bassindale, expedition member, in letter to OTT.

Was this man Tinker the one who had said his job was to lead, to see that clients ('you guys') got to the top?

'The notion that Jon (Tinker) had selfish personal ambitions is wholly inaccurate and categorically refuted.' In a letter from OTT to Kevin Bassindale.

What about our Irishman, Pat Falvey, who had gone well enough to be considered? What about the Finns, Harry and Paavo, and a couple of others who had done much better than Brigitte? About her husband's suitability there was no question; he had already climbed the South Col route of Everest and had done well on this trip. Jon Muir had earned his place to try for the summit, so the fact that he was a mate of the other Jon hardly entered into it. Or did it? Was he a fully paid-up client? Not the sort of thing Jon Tinker would discuss but there were murmurings that Brigitte and Jon Muir had not paid in full. This unconfirmed rumour fuelled mutterings about favouritism; it would have been better to have dismissed it if it were not true, though it may have been that neither Tinker nor the Muirs were aware of the rumour.

Kevin Bassendale later wrote:- 'It became immediately apparent that Brigitte Muir was not going to have to fulfil the same criteria as the rest of us when it came to selection for summit attempts. I, like most of the rest of the paying clients of OTT on that trip believe that Jon Tinker failed to honour the commitments he made to us all prior to the trip with regard to his own intentions when it came to selection of the summit parties. I believe he deprived those of his clients who were in a position to make an attempt on the summit the opportunity, in order to fulfil his own ambitions and those of his friends.'

Lakpa or Jon Muir to climb with Pat, Ang Babu with Harry - had these and other options been considered? There were other strategies which could have been employed which would have meant Jon Tinker would have kept his word. Maciej with a strong client, one or two of the other Sherpas with a client? And what of those clients who would have liked an opportunity to reach 8,000 metres - at least two of them? It was not for Jon Tinker to dictate their aspirations. Once such options were exhausted then Jon Tinker would have earned a shot at the top. I understood the temptation he faced, but his behaviour cannot be condoned for a moment. No one should be surprised if he had hoped that events might turn in such a way as to allow him an opportunity to go for the summit with honour, but the time had not arrived. Clients had carried several loads and would have to carry more to give Jon Tinker a chance for the summit, because of the lack of Sherpas.

But why did clients not object? Some, I know, had no summit ambitions, nor any desire to go back to the North Col; they would be content to be part of a successful expedition. Others thought that somehow their time would come, for we had enough oxygen for several attempts. I think few people fully appreciated at the time the implications of Jon Tinker's decision, and on top of that one does feel a sense of obedience to the leader; in fact, clients had signed a contract to the effect that 'the Member agrees to comply with all directions of the leader in every respect during the Expedition'. It smacked of the Führer attitude of early expedition leaders when put into words. We naively believed the expedition might function smoothly when the leader was knocking himself out to reach the summit; and what state would he be in on his return?

On 8th October Maciej and Sherpas Lakpa and Jangbu left the North Col and established a camp at 8,300 metres before Jangbu returned alone to the North Col, to be joined by Jon Tinker, Bruce, Pat, Thierry, the Muirs, Ang Babu and me. It had taken me six hours from ABC, which was not too bad.

That night Brigitte asked if next day she could borrow my lightweight sleeping bag. I suggested she should try it out first that night while wearing plenty of clothing because it was not adequate for normal use at very high altitude. She tried it and professed herself satisfied, so I held on to her luxurious but heavier bag and lent her mine.

Very early next morning Jon Tinker came to the tent I shared with Bruce.

'Jangbu's snowblind,' he said to me. 'You'll have to look after him. Here are the drugs.'

Did it cross Tinker's mind to take care of Jangbu himself and to control operations by radio from the North Col? He would have been a useful man to have in support at that camp and he could have operated the radio more effectively than when he was on the move, because inside a tent he could remove his mittens to operate the handset; out of doors it was risky to uncover the fingers for more than brief periods, as the two Indians had learned to their cost. It would take a better man than Jon Tinker to climb so high and simultaneously direct energies into the task of leadership. A client, or even two, could have gone with Ang Babu. Alternatively, Jon Tinker could have carried a load for them while I looked after Jangbu; that way he need not have been away from the North Col too long, and could have stayed on top of things.

Bruce, Ang Babu, Jon Tinker and the Muirs were ready for a 3am start, and then a furious argument started with Jon Muir in the tent occupied by Pat and Thierry because they were not up and ready to carry for Jon Tinker and his friends. Jon Muir seemed to feel he had a right to demand support, rather than ask for and appreciate it. Thierry was never enthusiastic about the essential chore of melting snow so by the time he and Pat were rehydrated the night before it was late, and they had missed out on sleep, and Thierry claimed a stomach problem too. Things got worse when Jon Muir demanded that Thierry should surrender the oxygen regulator valve he had kept to himself.

'I felt like punching his lights out,' said the male Muir. He was bluff, strong, wild-looking, and quite capable of doing it, but it did not come to that. I decided there and then that I would not use oxygen if I went higher; the squabble over the paraphernalia that went with it sickened me.

My caring tasks with Jangbu were light, administering eye drops and preparing drinks, and I must admit I felt quite good about looking after someone on Everest's North Col. I thought it a privilege to help someone in trouble up there, more important right then than climbing, but I knew that my chances of going higher were shrinking because I missed out on the perfect snow of that day.

At about noon we heard on the radio that Maciej and Lakpa had reached the summit about half an hour earlier. They had pioneered a new route, cutting out the famous First Step on the North Ridge. In one sense the expedition was already a success and the trail was broken; this was just when a client or two with a couple of Sherpas should have been given their chances. Now was the time for the clients, even those with only 8,000 metre aspirations, not the time for Tinker and his friends.

After telling Jangbu the news I went to Pat and Thierry's tent, to which Pat had recently returned after a carry to camp 2.

'That's great!' Pat said.

'That means we can't do it,' were Thierry's first words. 'Not enough oxygen. OTT has done everything for its own people.'

Then he muttered under his breath for some time. He was not correct about the oxygen but perhaps he did not know, as I thought everyone knew, that there were several bottles in the tent I occupied. But perhaps he meant there was not enough oxygen at camp 2, and about that he was right.

That same day Lakpa descended from the summit and took charge of Jangbu, whose sight had improved a little. Together they descended to ABC, an outstanding performance by Lakpa.

Harry and Paavo had come up to the North Col and I learned next morning that after a request by radio from the Muirs Harry had taken them some food, in the dark all the way to camp 2 and arriving at about midnight, before descending right away to the North Col. What must the temperature have been at that time? -30° C. (-22° F.) might be close to the mark, with wind chill on top of that. Harry's action confirmed in my mind that he should have been given a shot at the summit. But he and Paavo and Pat were by now disillusioned, and they had reached the conclusion that there were now not sufficient rations at the North Col to allow them to go up, and in any case they would not have a chance because the Muirs were still at camp 2, having failed to move up.

'I and two other clients were prepared to assist those three clients (Harry, Paavo and Pat).' - Kevin Bassindale.

But now we lacked the co-ordination which was required to give them a fair shot. Tinker was on his way to the summit.

On that day I set out for camp 2, loaded with food and fuel. In four hours on easy snow slopes I gained the 600 metres to find camp 2 still occupied by the Muirs. I had not found the wind too bad, and we all knew that as one climbed higher the wind soon decreased above camp 2. On the way I had met Maciej, going very slowly downhill. I was disturbed to learn that Brigitte had unthinkingly - or selfishly - given this exhausted man my lightweight sleeping bag for the night at camp 2, instead of a good Polish one left there, which she used. I had made it plain that she should use the lightweight bag only if she felt it good enough while wearing plenty of clothing; I did not expect her to fob it off on someone else and take a better one. 'I was very cold,' Maciej told me. Ironically, it was he who had supplied the Polish sleeping bag to the expedition.

The tent occupied by the Muirs had room for three, and though they were cool towards me I determined to stay the night and try to go higher; I was in no mood to be kept out by them. We were at about 7,600 metres, the highest I had been, but it did not please me greatly.

We heard by radio that Jon Tinker and Ang Babu had reached the top, the latter without oxygen, and that did not cheer me much either, though I was pleased for Ang Babu.

'Oxygen is shit,' Jon had said in Kathmandu, but changed his mind when the time came.

Then the Muirs were annoyed to hear by radio that Thierry was slowly making his way up to camp 2.

'He'll fuck up our summit bid,' Jon Muir said to his wife of Thierry. 'He'll have to go down.'

I have to admit that the tent at camp 2 would have been awfully crowded with four people in it. There was some talk later of there being another packed tent at camp 2 but I did not see one, and someone said it was ripped. I cannot remember who told me there was one - if it was the Muirs I don't know why they did not pitch it for others, if it was usable. If there was not one then they had blocked the progress of others. Jon and Brigitte did not mention another tent at that time but had there been one it would have been a difficult but not impossible job for three or four people to have pitched it in high wind; after all, the Muirs were rested. None of us suggested assisting Thierry with his load up the last stretch, but he had brought this upon himself, and the crisis which his arrival at camp 2 would have created was averted when he turned back from only a hundred metres or so below.

At about 3.30 am I started preparing drinks for the Muirs, but by 6 am they had not set out, nor had they by 7 am, nor 8 am. The wind was quite high, but as I have said before we all knew there was a band of wind that had to be battled through.

Jon Tinker descended, stopping for a few minutes. Like Maciej he was wiped out, capable only of slow descent, and certainly not in a condition to act decisively as leader. Tinker's Pecksniffian version was that he was the only one capable of being in support with Ang Babu and none of the clients were up to it. Several of them deserved an attempt, and there could be no stronger proof of that than the fact that two years later Pat, George and another client called Graham Ratcliffe all reached the summit of Everest via the North Ridge. They had shown they were capable, and in my view they were not the only ones up to that ascent; in particular Harry the Finn had earned a try.

Still the Muirs did not move. Piss or get off the pot, I kept thinking, but said nothing; there was no point. You hung around all day yesterday, but I managed in that wind, so why did you not? I could use this opportunity if you do not.

'I'd like to stay and consider going higher,' I announced to them.

'Not enough fuel,' Brigitte responded rapidly, too rapidly for good manners. I had heard there was plenty of fuel and had brought up some extra for emergencies, but I did not know who was right. In a letter Jon Tinker later claimed there had been plenty of fuel there, but it was a muddle.

The Muirs vacillated. Having given them most of the liquid melted from snow I was not sufficiently hydrated to go up immediately, and was there a stove and fuel at camp 3? If not, it would be suicide to go higher without one. I could not justify going up if they were likely to follow, since three in the small tent up there would have been too much, and they, more than I, carried Jon Tinker's approval to go up; they had a priority, though by now one for which I felt little respect. I reckoned on six hours to the next tent, a not unreasonable ambition even for me, and that would have put me at 8,300 metres. With that I would have been satisfied, though a little itchy about going higher the next day. If conditions had been satisfactory I believe, based on later experience at altitude, that I could have gone a bit higher, but my chances of reaching the summit and returning alive without oxygen would have been minute. Even with the oxygen I would have had only a slender chance of getting out and back, over the long, long North Ridge.

I felt cheated, not by the neutral mountain, but by people. About ascending the next section solo I was in two minds, feeling on the one hand that it did not offend the spirit of mountaineering, but I would hate for anyone to have felt they had to come looking for me if I disappeared. 7,600 metres high is not a place conducive to clear thinking, but I also felt life should not be squandered on this one experience; and a sense of proportion reminded me that this was only mountaineering, not an important issue of health or war or poverty or crime. My dilemma was solved by the immobile Muirs, so I descended in an easy, reluctant, two hour dawdle to the North Col. The Muirs arrived in the late afternoon, having decided that the weather might deteriorate; it looked iffy, with thin, lenticular clouds at and above the summit, though in fact it did not get worse.

At ABC next day I learned that several people had gone down to BC in disgust.

'Some of them have given me a hard time,' Jon Tinker said to me, and momentarily I felt sorry for this man. He had led an expedition which was in some senses a success, and he was the first Englishman to climb the North Ridge; but no client had reached the top and the question of whether some could have would never go away. He looked so tired and so miserable, and I would not have changed places with him, with this man who had climbed Mount Everest, for anything. Yes, I felt sorry for him, knowing the shame with which he would have to live.

'Your ascent will last forever,' I said. 'Perhaps their feelings will mellow.'

I wondered how I could bring myself to utter such words, but I suppose at the time, with this miserable man before me, I meant them, even though I wondered if I and others might have had a better chance if Mark Miller had led the expedition, as had been planned originally. Everest is not a private domain, and news of Tinker's behaviour was bound to become widely known. In performing in a manner which he must have hoped would bring him respect in the blinkered world of mountaineering, he had behaved in such a way as to risk ridicule in the world at large. Commercial expedition leaders and organisers have acquired a reputation akin to that of estate agents, who are rightly condemned if they are found to lack appropriate ethics. Jon would have to live with the debate, and one way he dealt with it, at least outwardly, was to say that criticism of his behaviour was sour grapes. Too easy to say that and to dismiss valid complaints, though to be fair not everyone was disappointed with his conduct.

'It was a good expedition, wasn't it?' Bruce said when we got home, and Chris Brown, a farmer from Yorkshire and known, naturally, as Farmer Brown, wrote to me, 'What a great trip we had on Everest.' But to know that some enjoyed the expedition did not mean that others were not bitterly disappointed, and I had a great deal of sympathy with them. Some of those who were not angered were of the 'North Col will do for me' brigade, and I think a few were happy to have been associated with a success no matter how little they had contributed to that success. Name dropping about Everest is common among trekkers and climbers alike.

Harry the Finn wrote to Andy Broom as follows: 'I am sorry to have to write you in such unpleasant matters but the thing is that me and Paavo are not pleased about the way the Everest '93 expedition was handled. Here are the things we were not happy about:

301

– At first Jon Tinker didn't have personal summit ambitions but at the end of the expedition that was the only thing he was interested in. In fact he told several members he wasn't going for the summit himself but had a back-up role and will be backing customer's summit bids. In the end he was the one everybody had to back up, took the best sherpa to make sure he had the best chances and acted as (if) the clients were there just to support him. The way Tinker handled his leadership was very unprofessional.

– We agreed that everybody who wanted to have a summit bid had to prove their capability by working up the mountain. Yet the third summit bid was handed to John and Brigitte Muir before Pat Falvey, Paavo and me. Brigitte Muir wasn't going strong at any stage and everybody knew it. Also we agreed it would be one go, no rest days on summit attempt. The Muirs started their attempt with a rest day at North Col and after that they took over the only tent we had at camp two and blocked the way for everybody else. There was four of us waiting in camp one for our turn but the Muirs didn't move up or down. All they did was ask for more food and gas. I took them the supplies we had taken for our own attempt and that was the end of our bid.

– There weren't enough sherpas for the expedition.

– On the way back we didn't stay at hotel Xomolangma which I think we had paid for. Still in Kathmandu Tinker wanted us to pay for the extra night in the hotel Manang. No big deal but something everybody was very angry about.

– As far as I am convinced the expedition was a rip-off and OTT will get a lot of bad publicity because of it. I tried to have a conversation with Jon but he wasn't too willing for it.'

And this from Ian Swarbrick, who was also a client on the trip – 'OTT are involved in a service industry and therefore by implication any expedition they are engaged in should have as its end the satisfaction and safety of each client. To hide behind the disclaimer that this was not a 'guided' expedition was to abrogate their responsibility to their clients. Incidentally, since when has the word 'client' been a dirty word in any self-respecting business involved in the service industry? Almost all of the clients on our expedition would never have sacrificed the time (10 weeks) or money to come on this trip had they known that this was the attitude that the Tinkers, in particular, were going to take. That Jon reached the summit of Everest via the long north ridge was a fine mountaineering achievement. That he did so at the expense of his strongest clients on the mountain was discreditable in my opinion. No one is perfect, and we all have selfish motives at times, but the standards expected of someone employed to provide a service are higher.'

Though in his mountaineering autobiography, *Reach For The Sky*, (yes, that is what he called it) Pat Falvey constrained himself with the teamwork theme he was attempting to promulgate, somewhat unsuccessfully, he did say, 'On his return to Advance Base Camp, Jon apologised for allowing his summit ambition to override his earlier understanding with me and the group. We decided that when his next licence for an Everest permit came through in 1995, if I wanted to return he would leave a place open on the team for me at a cost price of not greater than $15,000. This was the only way he felt he could make it up to me.' The discount offered was in the region of $10,000, so though Pat struck me as a man who might not expect nor accept favours, here was the risk of the seed of suspicion that Tinker would again show favouritism on an expedition. Pat needed Jon, and Jon's company needed the likes of strong Pat, though in other cases without the discount.

The 'understanding' Pat referred to stemmed from John's declaration at the pre-expedition meeting, through meetings in Kathmandu and at Base Camp, to a meeting at ABC on 3rd October. In Pat's words again:- 'The general consensus was that the first to go for the top would be Maciej and Lakpa and then George or myself with Angbabu, one of our most experienced Sherpas. Jon Tinker our leader, was to be at Advance Base Camp, and subsequently, the North Col co-ordinating the attempts on the summit'.

As far as teamwork is concerned, Pat's most revealing statement was, 'The mountain had thrown everything it could at us but we handled the adverse conditions well as a team. In the coming days however, this co-operative spirit would change utterly.' That was shortly before Jon Tinker put himself in the most desirable position, just behind those who broke the trail and pioneered a shorter route to the summit. As an exercise in holding a team together the expedition was not a shining example, for want of what might be called 'leadership cement'

One day at the end of the trip, when we were all assembled at BC, Jon Muir appointed himself Morale Officer,and made an embarrassing speech about how everyone should be happy because the expedition was a success. You can't tell people to be happy about something which has made them sad, and on top of everything Karl was dead; but Jon Muir and his wife had a tendency to tell others how to behave, while not displaying exemplary conduct themselves.

In August 1994 came an OTT leaflet explaining that next time on their Everest North Ridge expedition there would be one Western leader to four clients and two climbing Sherpas for every three clients. At that ratio on our trip we should have had ten climbing Sherpas, not four. Tinker had learned his lesson; too bad it was at the expense of several clients. But still the leaflet claimed a 'stunning success' in four people reaching the summit of Everest, without pointing out that they were not clients; the same leaflet crowed that the OTT 1994 expedition to Shishapangma was 'the most successful commercial expedition ever to an 8,000 metre peak' because eight clients summitted. It seems one can ignore client success when it suits. As High Magazine put it in October 1995, regarding Everest: 'Until this year not a single true client has reached the summit via the north side. Guides, yes; Sherpas, yes. Luc Jourjon from Jon Tinker's (1995) OTT Expedition was billed as the first accompanied (or guided) client to reach the top from the north side. Forty-years-old Jourjon is actually a guide and instructor... so perhaps 'client' is stretching it a bit.'

Single-mindedness I had expected, but not to the selfish extremes witnessed in some cases on Mount Everest. To win at any cost is not defensible in our daft sport, though under pressure of media and commercial considerations this philosophy seems to be creeping in throughout mountaineering and all other sports. Integrity, honour, dignity and fairness are as essential in mountaineering as courage and persistence and skill, consideration for others as much as physical strength and success, if the sport is to contribute to our society. There is a spirit I admire in mountaineering, but it was only patchily in evidence during the last two weeks of this expedition. Fair play is not inherent in the human character, any more than sportsmanship is innate; they are learned qualities which counter natural self-interest and opportunism, learned as much as anything by example.

"Our characters are the result of our conduct." – Aristotle.

"There was a time when we watched in awe, respect and pleasure those who produced winning (and even losing) performances. On and off the field of play sportsmen and sportswomen were honest, sincere, competent and determined - but not ruthless. Sport was used as a yardstick for civilised behaviour. Isn't it time, then, to reflect on what has happened to sport? I suggest we have allowed ourselves to confuse the pursuit of sporting excellence with the scramble for money or political prestige and, as a result, too many of us today condone what seems to be an irresistible compulsion for participants to behave badly."
– Michael Herd, *Evening Standard.*

I would add 'winning at all costs' to 'money' and 'political prestige'. Never have pleas for fair play been more needed than today, never has the essential message, 'We cannot all be the best but we can all do our best,' been more required in every walk of life. The whole matter leaves me saddened rather than embittered. I despair if mountaineering, albeit only a sport, but such a strong example, goes the way of low standards and cheating. We need the shame which matches that of the cheat caught in golf, rather than the shallow, ephemeral embarrassment suffered in, for instance, football. Certain ideals cannot be dismissed because they sound old-fashioned; love and honesty are old-fashioned.

On 18th October we arose at 2.30 am to pack up and save OTT paying for a night in the Quomolongma Hotel. So, following a long drive, we were sitting after dinner in the Zhangmu Hotel. I asked our Chinese interpreter if he would enquire in the kitchen whether there were any more of the crisp-like fried potatoes left; I had plenty of Chinese money and would pay for the extras for anyone who wanted them, if necessary. A plate of 'crisps' was produced and I and those around had begun to tuck in when Jon Muir came up and took the plate, saying, 'These are for everybody.' 'Hold on a minute' I said, but he pushed me aside and marched off with the plate, having made a scene which caused me to look greedy. He had taken physical advantage, and I sank to his level, for that was one of the few occasions in my life when I would have liked my legs back solely so I could give someone a good hiding. Who had given you and your wife precious liquids at 7,600 metres? Who had hogged the tent there? I did not say these things because I did not want a pointless squabble, but I felt them, and my incipient dislike of this righteous boor blossomed large in the face of his unfair and unfounded suggestion of meanness on my part in front of the whole team.

I regretted going on this OTT expedition. Of more than a score of trips to the ranges outside the European Alps, this was the worst, the one I enjoyed least. And to anyone who is contemplating joining a commercial expedition to Mount Everest, first read Into Thin Air, by Jon Krakauer, published in Britain by Macmillan. High magazine described mine as a 'notable performance', and many people said, 'Well done' on achieving a personal height record of 7,600 metres, but I experienced little sense of satisfaction. I was too frustrated for several others, who had become friends. I was too disgusted with Tinker and co., too disappointed, too saddened.

But gradually it came to me: I was freed of any desire to climb

Everest if I chose to be, free of that 'ball and chain of ambition' as another mountaineer put it. I could still attempt an 8,000 metre peak or two, without oxygen. I had thought about going on an OTT trip to Shishapangma the next year, but Jon Tinker was leading it; then I heard that Himalayan Kingdoms of Bristol were organising an expedition to that mountain and I was accepted on it. So doors were still open. Life wasn't so bad after all.

'Didn't you climb Ben Nevis or something like that?' a radio journalist asked me. Well, at least one of them was not obsessed with Everest, as if it were the only mountain in the world. There were other mountains worth climbing. To build on the experience would make sense of it all; that expedition had not been the journey but only a stage of that journey. I had learned much and would stand on the shoulders of the experience and reach a little higher, on a mountain over 8,000

Everest Postscript

In the case of high altitude mountaineering, even apparently small errors of judgement can lead to tragedy. Added to this, special favours given to some expedition members but not others may fuel resentment, leading to uncooperative behaviour and morale problems, with attendant potentially dangerous weaknesses in teamwork. Lack of candour on the part of leaders, guides and expedition organisers fans the flames still more towards tragic outcomes.

In 1999, at the age of 22 Michael Matthews climbed Mount Everest on an OTT expedition, in company with Mike Smith, a professional mountain guide. The following excerpts concerning the ascent and descent are taken from an article by David Rose in *The Mail on Sunday*, 7th May 2000, under the headline 'Why was a young man who paid £25,000 to climb Everest left to die alone at the summit?' (In fact he died a considerable way below the summit.)

"...the brochure about the proposed expedition emphasised OTT's remarkable record since 1993, with 29 successful ascents. spread over three expeditions, and no fatalities.

Michael did astonishingly little climbing in preparation. OTT agreed to provide a week's training in the Alps, where OTT guide Nick Kekus taught him the basics of mountaineering on easy local peaks and then, led by Jon Tinker, the OTT director who was to lead the Everest trip, an ascent of the 23,000 ft Aconcagua in Argentina.

Clients were told they would be joined by a mysterious 'Mr. X'. In fact he was Constantine Niarchos, heir to the Greek shipping fortune. He paid a 'substantial' premium rate to OTT and expected premium service: his own personal guide and a tent on his own, even high on the mountain. (He climbed the mountain and died two weeks later in London from a cocaine overdose.)

Dave Rodney, a forceful Canadian, was supposed to be climbing 'semi-autonomously' using OTT's facilities but making his own decisions. It was a recipe for confusion.

Rodney and Matthews said they would stay there (at Camp 2, 22,000 ft) and rest until Kekus was ready to lead the next summit bid. It was a terrible decision.

Kekus says he heard head Sherpa Lhakpa Gelu tell Matthews to turn back, (very high on the mountain). Kekus accepts he made no attempt to reinforce Gelu's suggestion.

…Smith reached camp (Camp 4, on the way down from the summit) exhausted, frostbitten and distraught. He was alone. In the thickening blizzard beneath the South Summit, he and Matthews had lost contact.

Doug Scott says the only safe way to handle them (the clients) is like dogs on a leash; to have enough staff so you never let them out of your sight.'

Almost twelve months later, his death (Michael's) is the focus of deepening controversy which may end up in the courts. Michael's father, David Matthews, believes the principal blame for his son's death lies with OTT Expeditions.

'I believe what happened, and how it happened, needs to be brought out in public.'

Tinker appears to have suffered a minor stroke (early on dining the expedition.)

'I will not be going to Everest again.' — Jon Tinker."

I feel obliged to make a few comments on this sad tale, in the hope that they will go some way towards averting similar tragedies. Firstly, the paucity of Michael's training speaks for itself. Though inexperience on its own does not preclude participation in high altitude expeditions, it can be a contributory factor working contrary to the safety and success of all concerned. Any lack of experience in a client needs to be compensated for by a recognition of the greater need for care on the part of commercial expedition organisers, leaders, guides, Sherpas, and even those other clients who are willing to give support. Also, a proper understanding is required from the clients apropos the degree of self-sufficiency which will be demanded of them. To an extent, the onus is shared, as much by the company as by the client, but companies must never lose sight of the fact that the tyro, whether diffident or cocky, probably poses and faces a larger risk, simply because he or she has not been tested physically or emotionally in the desirable real-life rehearsals. This cannot be dismissed by a contractual 'absolute prerequisite' that the client is a 'self reliant climber', as was the case in the OTT contract for the 1999 Everest expedition. Inexperience can, with appropriate support, be absorbed in small measure on some expeditions, but those who, for instance, cannot put their crampons on properly, should never be on high mountains. According to their own team member resumes, for the OTT 1993 Everest expedition OTT accepted one client with no Alpine experience at all, three with limited experience on mountains of alpine scale, and one who had achieved his highest ascent on an easy mountain of less than 5,000 metres. Clearly the level of qualifying experience was pitched low, as was the ratio of support staff to clients.

The mention of 'premium service' raises again the spectre of special favours and the resentments these can engender, as in the case of the Muirs and Pat Falvey, and 'climbing semi-autonomously' could add further pressures to the already difficult dynamics of the team.

CHAPTER 13

Shishapangma

TRAINING for Shishapangma, the thirteenth highest mountain in the world, took two forms: long walks with crutches to strengthen the upper body, and tricycle rides in the New Forest as a general fitness and thigh building exercise. Tilly the trike was bought specially for this purpose and stored in the garage of a friendly bed and breakfast hotel in Lyndhurst, which I tried to visit two days a week in summer prior to the expedition. By these means of training five hundred miles were clocked up. The New Forest is in places more hilly than many people realise, and since temperatures were frequently around 28° - 30° C. the training proved hard, and quite often painful, when skin was rubbed from my stumps. But the New Forest is an attractive place to cycle, to see what is around the next bend, so the training was always interesting. Pubs provided incentives in the form of respites in the shade, and welcome pints of shandy to make up for lost sweat. Sometimes Judy joined in on foot and it was a change to have to wait for her as I rode up and down the same stretch of road and took in side tracks and lanes, and went off to buy ice-creams. She could have hired a bicycle but preferred not to, opting for fast walking. The quieter roads and gravel tracks, ponies, donkeys, churches and villages gave her much pleasure, and we indulged ourselves with fine picnics. One spring day we cycled through a park and it was so hot I took my shirt off and pedalled along thinking that for a man in his fifties I was in good shape. A young woman sitting on a park bench thought otherwise, and quickly brought me back to earth.

'You,' she called.

'Yes?'

'Your tits are wobbling.'

The shirt went back on.

In late August at Kathmandu airport the customs form stated that I was permitted one tricycle, but Tilly had to stay at home in Lyndhurst; we were not heading for Tilly-compatible country. From the airport our group drove by private minibus to the local Summit Hotel, an attractive red brick complex with timber verandas and attentive staff. There I shared a room with Ramon Blanco, a Spanish guitar maker, resident in Venezuela, who the year before had become the oldest person to climb Mount Everest at the age of sixty. He was hurt that he had received very little sponsorship for his attempt, but had received many requests for free appearances; I felt fortunate that for the Shishapangma expedition sponsors had provided me with half the money required, which amounted to £7,000 per person.

This time the road to Kodari was clear of mudslides, so we enjoyed a straightforward ride in a thirty-seater bus to a campsite in Tatopani (Hot Water – source of such a spring), just short of Kodari and the Nepal-Tibet border. As well as going through the usual 'getting to know you' interactions of a group who were largely strangers to each other, at Tatopani several of the fifteen member team made their first acquaintance with leeches, ugly creatures, about an inch long, black, wormlike, with caterpillar movements and a fondness for the blood of any animal to which they can attach themselves. While standing I had the advantage of being less vulnerable than the others, and in any case we were not troubled as much as those on the trek the year before.

Torrential rain that night caused fears about the condition of the next section of road, but we made uninterrupted progress, through Kodari, over the Friendship Bridge, through Chinese customs at Zhangmu, to Nyalam, a town at about 3,700 metres. It is said that the name translates as 'the road to hell', but opinions about the place vary; sited in the middle of a sparsely inhabited mountainous area, an oasis of a few traditional Tibetan houses and a majority of new, functional concrete Chinese buildings, Nyalam is the social and commercial centre for people living on or near its important communicating road. Several shops, small hotels, simple restaurants and bars serve a largely local community, with we passing-through tourists in a tiny minority. We stayed in two basic hotels, and next day drove for less than an hour to a roadside acclimatisation camp at about 3,900 metres on a pasture among rolling mountains. From there some earnest walking ensued up the nearest dry, thinly vegetated hills for two days, but it made as much sense to take it easy whenever possible; it would be hard enough later, and just being there would aid acclimatisation. Anyone who was not fit had left it too late. Don Whillans, one of Britain's best high altitude mountaineers, would under the circumstances have been lying back with a bottle of Scotch in hand, looking at the people on the hills, and saying, 'Look at all those silly boogers.'

As in the previous year, we followed the Lhasa highway in our minibus and two trucks for a couple of hours, crossing the Yalung La (La means Pass) at 5,054 metres. No tea and souvenir shops here, just scores of cairns and hundreds of prayer flags, and magnificent views of high mountains. Then, turning left off the road our vehicles took a sandy track across a plain that was both sparsely vegetated and sparsely populated in consequence. It was easy; in four hours driving we were there at Shishapangma base camp, where a stone plaque like a large gravestone announced we were at 5,000 metres. Teams of Slovaks, French, Americans and Italians had arrived before us and set up a colourful tented encampment on the grassy plateau. There is something comforting as well as exciting about such gatherings, for though the clean river nearby and fine mountains beyond were wildly, gloriously attractive, this was still an extremely hard and rugged environment for anyone lacking food or shelter. Shishapangma looked complicated in shape, and grand.

In contrast with the months of sailing and arduous treks undertaken by early mountaineers to reach base camps, it had been a featherbedded approach, and retreat would likewise be easy. In a similar vein, when Capt. Scott set out for the South Pole in 1912 he had already been on the way by sea for a large part of a year before the polar journey itself could be tackled. There were no air dropped food caches for him and his men, and on arrival at the pole they did not enjoy the luxury of a permanent base to shelter in, in company of about two hundred scientists and ancillary staff. Nor were they airlifted out, but had to retrace their steps. Most modern polar walkers have done far less than half of the job by comparison; do they feel a nagging element of hollowness about their much-publicised efforts?

The Chinese authorities had instigated the building of a simple mud brick, 'holes in the floor' toilet block, men's and women's sections separate; the three holes in the men's were divided by low walls like cattle stalls, so this was a far more civilised arrangement than the often rather random toilet practices at some base camps and above. Close to the toilets, rubbish was deposited in a rectangle of walls about two metres high and as big in area as an average sitting-room. This dump was regularly scavenged by local yak herders, shepherds and goatherds, by dogs and ravens, so a form of recycling of food scraps, empty tin cans, plastic bags and bits of string went on before the remains were burnt. It was a satisfactory system provided everybody bothered to carry their rubbish to the tip; not all did, and semi-nomadic boys smashed bottles on rocks around the camp.

On the afternoon of 7th September fifteen yaks (thirteen million of the world's fourteen million yaks live in Tibet) arrived with a few drivers to carry out the first of two one-day carries to ABC. These hairy, horned beasts have the usual bovine lack of brains and are inclined to panic. Five members, including me, stayed extra time at BC, and soon

311

there were complaints about the food available. In particular, Lee, a forty-four year old American who a year earlier had reached the summit of Everest, found the rations bland, though ample (I thought the food was fine) and started talking of going home. He had a bad cold, which may have affected his taste, and was missing his family, who were in his absence overseeing the building of a new home. He soon found himself a lift out of BC on a landcruiser which had arrived to collect two people. Lee's US buddy, Paul, was naturally disappointed at his departure. He was forty-eight years of age, heavily built, and managing director of hospital care and pacemaker companies in Hong Kong.

It must be said that relationships with some of the Tibetans were not always easy, for though most were willing, hard working, good natured and took an unsophisticated interest in all we did, a significant minority were thieves. We suffered the theft of a climbing rope, our interpreter's radio, a large cheese and several other items, and some attempted thefts were thwarted by the thieves being discovered in the act. Ramon and our deputy leader, Daniel, an Argentinian, had a stormy argument about Tibetans hanging around our tents.

'You're treating them like animals,' Ramon protested when Daniel sent them away, but I think Ramon was naive. We could understand why they needed and coveted what we had, but we did their culture no favours by tolerating theft.

On 14th September Paul, Ramon and I started walking to ABC, having easily forded a fifteen metre width of the river, which nowhere came above mid calf. I had the advantage over them of not suffering from cold feet for the next hour. For Paul and Ramon it proved to be a long and tiring trek while I, as usual prepared to take the easy option if there was one, split the journey into two chunks, with a bivouac under a boulder in the loneliest, wildest of near unvegetated mountain desert. There was sufficient plant life, however, to support large numbers of pale brown hares, which hopped about showing little wariness at the presence of a human. Perhaps the Tibetans did not hunt them, which was surprising, for the pickings would have been rich.

With my arrival we were all there at 5,550 metres. ABC comprised a neat row of a dozen red tents, nearly one per person, in a long vegetated depression between two bare, bungalow high moraine ridges, with the grey kitchen tent, white mess tent, and Nepalese staff tents in a cluster at the upper end. An ample supply of water flowed from a stream and a spring, and the whole place was softened by mossy plants. By now we were so close to Shishapangma that it dominated all, a snow mountain with one face, the north, showing rock from beneath its snow veil.

Our first camp above ABC was already established in the form of four tents at 5,750 metres, beside those of the other expeditions on a stony plain which, according to my usual means of estimating such areas, was about five football pitches. Daniel and I, along with Paul, were the last to make a carry, mostly of propane and butane mix gas fuel cartridges, to this camp, which we called the depot. It was reached in three or four hours on a moraine beside some magnificent ice pinnacles to the left, reminiscent of Everest's Magic Highway. Up to twenty-five metres high, they came in a variety of closely packed teeth, some sharp, some rounded, and all glistening, mostly snow white but with green and blue ice showing through here and there. Several pinnacles stood behind the camp, that is behind as we faced the mountain, by day supplying crystal clear water in four streams. Between us and Shishapangma was a half-mile stretch of similar glacier towers and humps, but these only attaining a fifth of the height of their counterparts lower down the glacier. Between the protrusions were small ice ravines and, in the warmth of the day, streams, and this was the way we had to go. We did so next day, Daniel, Paul and I, carrying loads to camp 1. After an hour and a half Paul turned back, having crossed the glacier and started up a snow slope a little way behind the two of us. He had not been settled in his mind since Lee's departure, and a few days later Paul returned prematurely to the USA.

Daniel and I continued up the long slope until we met Ramon, three Sherpas and Nick Kekus, the leader (pronounced Keekus), coming down from camp 1. The weather was bad up there, they said, and Daniel was further persuaded to turn back on learning that one Sherpa, Pema, had fallen twenty metres into a narrow crevasse. He was fortunate not to have been injured, but he was shaken, and he went home soon. We were not going up until a rope had been fixed over that crevasse, Daniel decided.

Next day we were asked by the leader of one of two American expeditions to keep an eye out for Tod, a member who was missing while descending from camp 1 to ABC two days earlier. We began to suspect where Tod might have gone when Pema revealed that he had seen a ski stick and some sun glasses near the bottom of the crevasse into which he had fallen. (Many people use ski sticks for power and balance at high altitude). The following day three of the US team went up and one of them abseiled into the crevasse and found Tod's rucksack; of the owner there was no sign. It is likely that he had become separated from his rucksack as he fell down the crevasse and had gone into the considerable stream which swept through its bottom. Even if conscious after the fall he would not have lasted long in the near frozen water.

On the same day that Tod's rucksack was found, at ABC we watched around noon through binoculars as two Frenchmen approached the west summit of Shishapangma by way of the north ridge, which was our proposed route of ascent; they had started at 4 am. In view of recent heavy snowfall the wisdom of climbing that day was questionable since the avalanche danger was high, and it certainly must have been hard going on the fresh snow cover. We retired to the mess tent for lunch, and afterwards could not pick out the two men again. We speculated that they had reached the west summit, moving very quickly over the last bit, and were now out of sight heading for the slightly higher main summit, or they were difficult to spot among rocks, or they had been avalanched off. We watched for a long time, until dusk, but did not learn the outcome that day.

The snowfall and Tod's disappearance did nothing for the morale of the teams waiting to climb, and the Slovak and one of the two Italian expeditions went home. Whether their time had expired, I do not know.

We did not hear until the day after the incident that the two Frenchmen had indeed been caught by an avalanche and swept down a slope when about 200 metres from the west summit. They had been carried more than 300 metres but were not badly injured. However, one of them spent the night out, risking serious frostbite and death from hypothermia. One of France's prolific mountaineers, Jean Cristophe Lafaille, and his friend Dominic (or was it Dominique? I could not tell when Jean Cristophe said the name) and some Sherpas and Italians played star roles in bringing down alive on a sledge the man who had spent the night out. He was then carried pick-a-back through the pinnacles and down to BC. It was thought the casualty would lose all his fingers and half his hand on the right, and some finger joints on the left, but, as I was to learn quite soon, it can be a long time before one discovers how much of the flesh and bone will be lost as a result of frostbite.

Though a relatively easy 8,000 metre peak this one was taking its toll.

'Never again in the autumn,' Jean Cristophe said. 'It is too hard. This wind!'

He was no wimp, having made exceptional climbs at home and abroad, including descending a hard route on Annapurna alone over five days, with a broken arm. He soon came back for more.

What we called, as usual, the A team had emerged: Nick, electronic engineer Richard Forsyth from Bristol, Rae Nicholls and David Weitz from Canada, she a cello teacher, he a physicist, Derek Mitchell, a Scottish accountant whose initials spelt DRAM, Siren Greve, a Norwegian geologist, and John Fowler, English property developer. Malcolm Creasey, a British mountain guide, went well, but did not tolerate sleeping at altitude, and Daniel was as strong as anyone once he recovered from an early sickness. The Sherpas were in a different class, the A+ team. Between them all these people took on the brunt of carrying, while two plus a Sherpa had gone home and three contributed less higher up even than I, who missed out on early carries through being sick. In order to make up a bit I put a tent, known as camp Norman, on the far side of the pinnacles, cutting the journey from there (instead of the depot camp) to camp 1 by one and a quarter to one and a half hours. By doing so I could take a couple of loads to camp 1 and return in good time, saving two and a half to three hours all told, without knocking myself out; burning out is always a risk up there.

A hundred metres or so higher than camp Norman was a barrel of French food, some of which Jean Cristophe said we could take in return for his using our tents, so on 24th September Dave Callaway, a US physics professor of thirty-seven years, and Peter Gregory, a twenty-eight-year-old Australian helicopter pilot, and I forced ourselves up to camp 1 with some of these rations. The A and A+ teams had already set up and partly stocked camp 2 at 6,800 metres.

But for the altitude, the going to camp 1 could hardly have been more straightforward, just a trudge up a slope flanked on either side by magnificent snow and ice sculptures in the form of huge cliffs, draped in places by icicle chandeliers not unlike formations of candle wax on a wine bottle. On a gentle rise we had to cross the crevasse which had claimed Tod, and nearly Pema too. All that was visible at first were two body-width holes which normally we would have skirted or stepped over with care but with barely a thought about them; but now we knew their history, and they looked sinister in our eyes. It was evident that the lips of the crevasse overhung and might collapse under a person's weight, so the fixed rope, attached to long aluminium stakes hammered into the snow, was not just a comfort but an essential precaution. We all attached ourselves to the rope as we crossed.

My new weapons, huge ski baskets (rounds) made from the plastic rackets of a children's tennis game, reinforced with bamboo strips and attached to the bottoms of my crutches, proved their worth on the final soft section to our three tents on a huge plateau at 6,300 metres. Four or five more tents shared the site.

After a night of acclimatisation our trio descended to recover, and four days later I was back at camp 1 with Nick, Mal, Ramon, Dave Callaway and Peter. The A team, minus Nick, and led by Daniel, were at camp 3, prepared for a summit bid which did not transpire because of the terrible autumn winds. John had in the meantime decided to go home; four down. On his arrival home John found he had a broken rib as a result of a fall which occurred before he went to Tibet. At base camp a Chinese lorry driver had tried to charge him three hundred US dollars for a ride to the border with a departing expedition, but John and his money are not so easily parted. Instead he negotiated a lift with another driver and for a fare of thirty dollars rode hidden among the equipment of a different expedition.

Food at depot camp and above was excellent, the main courses being 'boil-in-the-bag' meals such as sausage and beans, Lancashire hot pot and stew with dumplings, complemented by soups, a wide variety of drinks, and various snacks. Though heavier than freeze-dried food, 'boil-in-the-bag' meals certainly tasted better, and don't give you wind like freeze-dried meals do. Sharing a tent with someone who has eaten the latter is like being in a small car with an elderly and excited dog; I'm sure you will know what I mean.

Those of us at camp 1 waited a day, while the A team descended for a night at camp 2 in the hope of returning to camp 3 for a summit bid. However, it was decided between Daniel and Nick that the A team should return all the way to ABC for a rest after a draining night at 7,300 metres and another at 6,800 metres. This gave Nick and we lesser mortals of the B team the opportunity to move up to camp 2, but Peter, who had been ill during the night, chose the homeward trail. Five down. All younger than me, all able-bodied.

It took me about five hours up an initially steep but gradually relenting snow slope to camp 2. The A team descended, despondent, for their chance had eluded them and they had to do it all again. Dave Callaway arrived at camp 2 last, not far behind me.

'I'm fucked,' he said, and it was perversely amusing to think that it had cost him £7,000 to join a project which had brought him to this. The following morning he too descended, never to return, leaving three of us, but that soon turned to two as Ramon turned back after an hour on the go in a fierce wind on a gently undulating plain; he was too cold, he told us later. The wind was close to what could be coped with, stopping us in our tracks now and then, and according to the A team, who had taken up to seven tough hours to reach camp 3, this was the hardest section so far. Occasionally we sank to knee depth in the snow, but mostly we were able to follow the track of hardened snow left by our A and A+ teams and several others, a kind of plank through the fluff of snow. It was seven hours of labour for me, and close-to-the-limit hard work up the last bit, only thirty degrees at the steepest, but blasted by a fierce wind it was, though not a dramatic climb, a high altitude ordeal.

Relief from extreme toil. Camp 3. Nearly 7,300 metres. Probably the effort of getting there caused the violent vomiting which I suffered several times that night, and I was fit for nothing the next day. Tuesday 4th October. The wind at 9.30 am. was bad, but not sufficiently strong to prevent a determined climber from trying for the summit. Nick wanted to go, but I was weak, nauseous and unable to. He started up alone, with my slightly reluctant approval, for it was not Nick's fault that his clients had dropped out one by one. Admittedly I might have been fit to try the next day, but I did not want to deprive him of his bid when snow conditions were fair and the weather acceptable.

Occasionally Nick was visible on the mixed snow and rock north ridge, but after 12.30pm., when he had stood out on snow near a prominent gendarme (big rock thumb) at about 7,600 metres he was no longer in view. Probably on or behind rock, and without binoculars it was in any case hard to spot someone so far away.

I prepared hot drink after hot drink from melted snow, and by mid-afternoon felt I would be up to trying the next day. Perhaps at last an 8,000 metre peak would be mine. The ambition to climb such a giant had crept up on me, a man who used to say altitude alone was not attractive. Now here I was immersed in an adventure which was continuously hard, with aesthetically satisfying interludes few and far between, and altitude the only target.

At about 4pm. Nick was visible on the snow ridge between the main and west summits, heading for the latter promontory. Judging by the time, he had probably reached the main summit, and when he returned at 5.30pm. he confirmed this.

'There was a bit of Scottish grade 3. As hard as anything I've done on Everest north-east ridge. Anyone who says it's easy is a liar. That was one of the hardest days I've had on a high mountain.'

Wednesday 5th. October. After a night at camp 3 Nick descended and I had no one with whom to climb; in any case the wind was too strong for a long ascent. The next day Jean Cristophe came up and occupied one of our three tents, and after a short rest he set out in the midmorning to climb the north ridge. He was blown over a few times and was back in two hours, defeated by the extreme wind, which gusted to 100 mph. or thereabouts.

We shared a meal in my tent that evening and he reported Daniel's anger at Nick going alone to the summit. But Nick had by no means done a full Tinker. Daniel's view was that he should have kept himself ready to go with clients, but I had (rather half heartedly) encouraged Nick to go alone because I was not fit to accompany him. Daniel was only partly right. Jean Cristophe was himself frustrated by the wind. But he had rescued someone and that was a privilege. Admittedly the rescue had drained him and had taken time, thus reducing his chances of success, but if he did no more he had done what should be done on a mountain. I would willingly have swapped places with him, for only twice in a long climbing career have I found it best to abort a summit attempt (once 50 metres from the top of an Alpine mountain) to escort down someone who was unwell.

Some of the A team were making their way up so I opted for a fourth night at 7,300 metres for a chance to climb with them. I learned by radio that the Canadians had taken eleven and a half hours from depot camp to camp 2 in one go, and were unlikely as a consequence to be able to climb the next day.

Friday 7th. October. Jean Cristophe had waited unrewarded for an abatement in the wind until after 9.30 am., then battled his way through it, frequently brought to one knee. Soon he disappeared from view on the north ridge. There had been no question of me accompanying him for he would have been much, much faster. To my great disappointment I heard by radio that Daniel and others at camp 2 might go down because of the weather; that was a measure of the conditions in which Jean Cristophe had set off. Though he was rightly worried about me being so high so long, Nick agreed I could stay in support of Jean Cristophe. The irony of being in support of someone so exceptionally able was not lost on me. Soon after, it was reported by radio that the Canadians were on the way to camp 3, and Daniel and Richard had started up an hour earlier. At noon Jean Cristophe radioed that he was close to the west summit and his feet were very cold.

I had finished the usual task of digging out our three tents from under a metre of wind-blown snow when Jean Cristophe reappeared at 2pm.

'Yes or no?' I asked.

'Yes.'

In three and a half hours he had reached the west summit, but had been unable to tackle the exposed ridge to the true summit because of the wind.

Daniel arrived before 2.30pm., with Richard not far behind. For the latter time had almost run out, as he was due to depart earlier than some of us, and tomorrow was his last opportunity for a summit bid. The Canadians had turned back and their time was up too. I felt sorry for them, and for the rest of the A team who would not have a shot at the summit. Derek was out with early signs of frostbite, which fortunately cleared up without leaving any damage. Malcolm had stormed his way up from the depot to camp 2 very fast one day, but was handicapped by his inability to sleep up there. Siren was not feeling well. They had contributed much, along with the Sherpas, Nick, Daniel and Richard, and now it looked as if only the last two, along with me, had any chance of achieving the summit; Nick had, of course, reached it already.

Daniel had feared for my physical and mental health after so many days and nights at camp 3. I had suffered no headaches but was often nauseous at night. Temperatures dropped as low as minus 12° or 13° C. at night inside the tent, the screaming wind molested it violently all the time, and as soon as the morning sun hit the shelter the rime of frost which formed from breath each night, giving a fairy grotto look, would melt and soak everything. No, it was not a pleasant place to be, but I found it within myself, just, to tolerate the discomfort, to suffer what was needed in achieving my voluntarily chosen goal. The go down and rest and come back up again option was not realistic for me. Yet tough as it was it was as nothing to men sleeping in stinking, cold, damp, muddy, rat infested dugouts in lousy clothing, while being shelled, sniped at and machine gunned.

At night I woke frequently, sometimes to regulate my temperature by putting on or taking off my hat.

'And here's one I prepared earlier,' I would say out loud every time I put the hat on. I was aware of what I was doing, heard myself speak the words, and each time wondered what the hell I was on about. Still I was rational, monitoring how I felt, looking after myself properly day and night, hydrating and feeding myself, drying my sleeping bag, carrying out an inventory of food and fuel to report to ABC, and digging out the tents from the snow whenever necessary.

Each time I used a handkerchief at night I announced 'Cloth for the world,' which made as much sense as the gibberish about the one I prepared earlier.

'When are the floorboards for the tent being delivered?' I asked of no one, again at night.

'How could you stand five nights up here?' Daniel asked. 'After one night I go grrrhh! And you eat like an ant.'

It is true I can manage on little food. I think I eat least of anyone on an expedition.

It was evident my chances of success were small because I had been so high for such a long period. A few younger people had achieved successes on big mountains after spending a long time at altitude, but they were exceptions; and, of course, they had legs. Most opted to descend and re-ascend, but I did not possess the ability to do that readily.

Saturday 8th. October. The temperature was around minus 40 , that point at which the number of degrees is the same in Celsius as it is in Fahrenheit. We were away at about 8am., Daniel, Richard and I. The wind came in gusts, toying with us, stopping us, pushing us sideways, as we crossed low angled, slabby snow which collapsed underfoot occasionally; the bully wind, I always call it. From the foot of the ridge we would stay almost entirely on snow, passing by brown rock protrusions. It was sufficiently safe to go unroped, with the snow reaching no more than 35 degrees in the lower section. I had the benefit of Daniel and Richard being ahead because their boots compacted the snow steps. On one slope of thirty metres I did need an ice-axe, with the shaft rammed in for security, but apart from that was able to use my crutches all the time.

After a couple of hours phrases began running through my head in what sounded to me like Scottish and Geordie accents. It was not a question of hearing voices, but I was thinking in accents. For instance, in Scottish, or my mind's version of it, I thought, 'Have tae stop for a drenk.' Then in Geordie, 'Ay, it's coold, man,' and back to Scottish for, 'This soft snoo is a peg.'

From one sharp snow ridge camps 1 and 2 were visible, dark dots in a huge white landscape under a clear sky. Above this we began a leftwards traverse on good snow, after four hours on the go, stopping, starting, struggling, gasping, wishing it finished. As we approached the big gendarme at 7,600 metres the thumb on my right hand was dead, the fingertips on the left also. Having stopped to examine the thumb, I quickly replaced the woollen glove and then the mitten which went over it. I had seen enough: the thumb was swollen and blistered, black with frostbite.

I gained some comfort from the fact that the frostbite was a result of bad luck rather than carelessness or bad judgement. The skin of the thumb had split some days earlier and was covered with a fabric sticking plaster; this had trapped sweat, or restricted the circulation, or both, and in my drained state frostbite was the result. In future I would carry a small tube of Superglue (or something very similar) which is commonly used to patch up splits in the skin, but it was too late on this trip; the damage was done.

'Doon,' I thought. 'Have tae go doon.'

The alternative was foolish, though as my two companions drew ahead I seriously considered whether the prize might be worth a thumb. I had met the first person ever to climb the north ridge of Everest, a Chinese man who thought the loss of his heels and toes through frostbite to be a fair sacrifice. But I was not making a first ascent, nor a climb of any great significance. If I lost a thumb, how would I hold an ice axe? And would those fingertips be lost too?

'The body is more important than the summit,' our interpreter had said.

I was not defending my nation or saving someone's life; a sense of proportion would win. Probably.

Low down of the left side of my chest I had been experiencing a dull pain for some time. On its own it would not have induced me to turn back, but it added to my fears, coloured my thoughts, and made easier the decision to retreat. As on Broad Peak the downhill option was the wise one. Apart from the avalanche danger there, I had had a stomach problem which had not been completely right for years, though at the time I had not realised how serious it was or how badly I had been affected by it. On Everest I had the fitness and energy to go higher but was prevented from doing so for reasons I have explained, and now on Shishapangma descent was the only way. Three 8,000 metre attempts and no summit. Everyone on this expedition had been given a fair shot, though many had been unlucky with the weather. I had failed, but I could not have reached the top unless I had been prepared to risk avoidable permanent injury.

7,600 metres again, equalling my previous highest. Three out of fifteen on top, and I was next in line. Not too bad, really. I had by now come to accept that a kind of failure is an inevitable item in the repertoire of the ambitious mountaineer who pushes his limits, so it did not hurt so much. Not only that, I would have another try at an 8,000 metre mountain. Already I was planning to join a Himalayan Kingdoms expedition to the sixth highest peak in the world, Cho Oyu, during the less exacting spring weather. There was, of course, some feeling of disappointment, but this was mollified by looking forward, by learning from this experience to increase the chances of success in the near future. What little disappointment there was would diminish with time, as it always did. I remembered how disappointed I had been when some exposed slide film used on the first big mountain I climbed, in Peru in 1978, had been stolen. Several years and many mountains later it does not matter at all.

Daniel and Richard had drawn further ahead, too far for me to call in the wind that I was turning back. I sat on the slope and had a drink before setting off for camp 3, feeling less despondent than I might have because I had reasons, not excuses, for going down.

'You were doing very well, Norman,' Daniel said when he and Richard returned to camp 3 shortly before dark that night, having reached the west summit. 'Why did you turn back?'

I told him about the pain in my chest and said I was drained after five nights at camp 3, all of which was true, but not the full story. Several people were soon to leave BC and I did not want Judy to hear a frostbite story which might be vague, or might grow in the telling, and cause alarm.

I believe I am right in saying that three of the group of six of which Tod had been a member reached the summit, and one out of the other US expedition of six. Several from a Korean expedition - recently arrived - succeeded too. Jean Cristophe made a solo ascent of a new route. All in all a minority of people were successful, and I must be the only one, or almost, who failed but still thought the trip rewarding. For me it felt like a satisfying draw, rather than a defeat.

This being my first direct experience of frostbite, it was a salutary lesson. At ABC the digit was examined by Dr. Mike Sinclair from the USA. We had met when he had come over from the States for Mark Miller's memorial service, and he had stayed one night with Judy and me on the way back to Heathrow Airport. It was he who arranged for a US company to send me a good lightweight rucksack for Everest. By the time it arrived out of the blue Karrimor had already donated one, so I gave the unexpected US rucksack to Jon Tinker. Dr. Mike advised me to protect the thumb and keep it clean, and there was not much that could be done. Whenever the dressings were off it became the most photographed thumb in Tibet, and Nick sent me a slide which was not at all gory, but did say, 'This is why I turned back.' So out of this small adversity we were able to salvage something positive in the form of a notable slide for lectures.

The wearying task of clearing the tents, stoves and pans and rubbish from the mountain fell mainly to Nick, Daniel and the Sherpas. Siren returned as far as camp 1 to retrieve some personal possessions, Ramon professed himself to be too exhausted to help after two nights at camp 2, and though it was not greatly painful unless knocked (I needed a painkiller only once, early on, to get to sleep) I could not risk further damage to the thumb. Everyone else had gone home. All rubbish was brought down, and the area of BC cleaned up and everything burned, so we left little trace of our passing. We had had, however, to leave camp 3 to disappear beneath the snow, because bad weather made it impossible to reach the tents there.

One day Ramon called me from my tent 'to look at some fish'. He's flipped, I thought, but there in a stream and a pool at 5,000 metres were indeed some two centimetre long fish. The highest fish in the world?

We had been away from home for two months, a short period compared with the time spent away by early Himalayan pioneers, but nevertheless quite a while for us and our loved ones. Though one can talk romantically of Tibet in the commentary of a television documentary, few westerners and few Chinese would be happy to stay there long. The romantic myth is prevalent, the reality harsh, and the Tibetans, unlike us, have to stay there and endure the dust, disease, primitive shelter, basic toilets, the cold, the poverty, the poor diet, the lack of health care and education.

'How long will it take you to get home from Kathmandu?' I asked one of the Sherpas.

'One day by bus and three days on foot.'

'Three days. A very isolated village.'

'No. But there are many tea houses on the way selling steaks and chang, and I will have lots of money.'

Someone else said it was in fact only a day's walk if you did it in one go, sober.

After a month the nail came off the thumb, and it was a further eight weeks before the necrotic black monk's cap on the tip dropped off. The dead piece looked rather like half a hazelnut shell, only black, and the remaining wound I will refrain from describing. But in a dozen more days it was healed, and I was left with one thumb only slightly shorter than the other, by less than a centimetre.

Ignore the spilt milk. The expedition had taught me much. So was it all about to come together for an 8,000 metre summit? I had been to 7,600 metres twice in recent times, and could tolerate sleeping at high altitude. The large ski baskets fixed to my crutches functioned well, as had a face mask, which reduced coughing. Throughout the Shishapangma expedition my stumps suffered no damage, probably as a result of the training on crutches and in the New Forest on Tilly. The spring weather in Tibet would be less exhausting. I had tried satisfactorily to sleep in my salopettes in a lighter than normal sleeping-bag, and I had bought a small, lightweight tent for use high up, so I could camp where it suited me, within reason. A climbing equipment supplier gave me the lightest crampons, ice-axe and climbing helmet I have come across. Would these elements now come together on Cho Oyu to bring the result I craved? 8,000 metres here we come? Yes, I'm still up for it.

CHAPTER 14

Cho Oyu

THE two months preceding departure for Cho Oyu were full and varied, just the way I like it; fallow times don't suit. I gave talks at sales conferences in Evian and Edinburgh, and one at a Women's Institute County Federation meeting, attended a trustees meeting of the Calvert Trust Adventure Centre for Disabled People at Keswick, made a hospital visit to someone who had just had a leg amputated, delivered two more Women's Institute talks and two at luncheon clubs, went to a committee meeting of the Limbless Association, appeared on an 'agony aunt' television programme concerned with disability, made a radio recording concerning the forthcoming expedition, had another Calvert Trust meeting, this time at the sister centre at Exmoor, paid a visit to Wiltshire to collect a cheque on behalf of the Limbless Association, and spoke at another sales conference. At the same time there was a long article to write for a disability magazine, a book chapter to finish and various jobs to undertake in connection with the expedition: visa, medical requirements, equipment to buy or repair, insurance. And training, on crutches or on Tilly. Could one ask for a more refreshing variety of work overlapping with other interests?

Then two days before departure disaster struck: food poisoning. You may get the impression that I am forever suffering from stomach problems, but we are talking about four incidents spread over a dozen years. We were due to fly on the last Friday in April, and after a talk in Cheshire on Wednesday evening I was taken ill. I will spare you the details, but it was not possible to travel back to London until the afternoon of the following day, so a limp rag of a man arrived back home wondering whether long distance air travel would be possible next day. And how soon would my strength be recovered? Fasting proved to be no hardship because I could not face food, and, suitably fortified with drugs - forget beta blockers, I needed drain blockers - I met the others at Gatwick airport and vomited once on the aircraft, but after a night at Kathmandu's Summit Hotel and sixty hours of fasting, felt right as rain.

The expedition leader, Martin Barnicott, or Barny as he is known, and I did not join the others for their training trek near the Nepal-Tibet border, for as usual it was wise to avoid the risk of chafing my stumps at this early stage. The roadside acclimatisation camp near Nyalam, as for Shishapangma, would have suited me better and I never found out why that option had been abandoned. Instead he and I flew over terraced farmland and forested hills for an hour and more in a twenty seat Twin Otter to the famous mountain town of Lukla. There the plane made a spectacular landing with a loud bang in a huge red-brown dust cloud, on a rough uphill slope as much like a very wide farm lane as an airstrip, bumpity, bumpity, bump and came to a halt. Bloody Nora, the pilots do this every day!

There was no hurry to go anywhere. At over 2,750 metres we were already acclimatising. Being without road traffic, Lukla possessed the languorous air of those Alpine villages where motor vehicles are banned, or where there is no access; the saying goes, 'The only wheels are prayer wheels.' The human or animal back (usually cattle rather than horse) carries everything - grain, hay, vegetables, meat, water, wood, cement, stone, babies and so on. Think of Nepal, think of walking and carrying loads on rough trails, particularly in the traditional conical wicker baskets and rectangular baby cots, suspended on the back by a strap from the forehead. Those who cannot walk, or have difficulty in doing so, truly are severely handicapped in mountain Nepal, while those who can walk have one of the most splendid places to wander, in pastures and forests dotted with lodges and tea houses. The tourist can travel light, for food and a simple bed costs very little, and porters are readily available. When you stay at a lodge you make out and total your own bill, and two US dollars a day took care of our food and accommodation.

For a week we trekked at my pace and over my chosen distance from lodge to lodge, these mostly built of flat grey stones like children's building blocks of many different sizes arranged to make walls, without any cement or mud bonding. Those constructed of timber inevitably resembled Alpine huts and chalets. It was easy to see why trekking here was so popular; compared with several other trekking areas of the world theft was uncommon (though two of our expedition group had their boots stolen from outside their tents while on their training trek), the scenery is second to none, the Nepalese are among the most friendly people in the world, the variety of food available is good, and, as I have said, the living is cheap by our standards. 'All guests are equal to Gods,' said a sign in one lodge.

Apart from the flight to and landing at Lukla a few other highlights of that week stand out in my mind, including a chat with a western surgeon who said one of his colleagues who specialised in stomach operations was so slow that he was known as the 'abdominal slowman'.

In the town of Namche Bazar the lodge at which we stayed boasted a brass plaque recording the visit of Jimmy Carter when he was President of the USA, and there was a framed photograph of the actor Robert Redford, who had also spent a night or two in the same lodge. The place was full of their young fellow countrymen, and the dining room rang with, 'Cool. Yur kidding! Oh Wow! Cumftaball. Real! Gross! Like weird! You guys. Oh rilly! Tok to me. Y'all. Like sure. Yea. Visitation (for visit). Yup. Physically challenged. Hang out. Downscaled' and a variety of other words and phrases which illustrated how far our languages are diverging.

Acclimatisation achieved; never below 2,700 metres, nor much above 3,300 metres. Returning to Kathmandu by a Russian helicopter which carried about the same number of passengers as the Twin Otter, we met our Sherpas at the Summit Hotel and next day enjoyed a trouble-free bus drive in less than six hours to Tatopani. This being the dry season, the road was in good condition and free of slides.

Reunited with our tent-burgled trekkers next morning, we crossed the Friendship Bridge and drove the zigzag road to the Chinese control. This half hour journey was made in a local truck on the bumpy, dusty road. The liaison officer and interpreter waited with a mini bus and a truck to take us along the familiar road as for Shishapangma and Everest, to Nyalam, where several of us stayed in a big hotel room with good beds on an earth floor, and a toilet - just a corner outside where two walls met - that was revolting beyond decent description. I can sympathise with the Buddhist monk who said that one of the advantages of death was, 'No more need to go to toilet.' Peter Wilson, a dermatologist from Grimsby, chose to sleep with his waterproofs on, including the hood pulled up, on the grounds that 'It would look funny if a dermatologist came back with a skin rash.'

After an overnight stop at a town called Tingri we turned off the road which leads to Everest; Cho Oyu is just under thirty kilometres west of Everest. Unlike Everest and Shishapangma it does not have a base camp accessible by road, so following a two hour ride we set up camp two days walk from Cho Oyu's hem, and waited for our yaks at the same altitude as the top of Mont Blanc.

This road head camp allowed a good view of the target, a largely snow covered mass, except very high up, where much rock was exposed. Like Everest, had we not known its altitude, it would not have drawn us strongly. The name Cho Oyu is thought to mean 'Goddess of the Turquoise' or perhaps 'Deity' rather than 'Goddess', or even, ironically, 'Demon'. 'Yu' means turquoise and the 'O' may have been added through a European mishearing and misrecording the word.

Because of its great altitude it was chosen in 1952 for a pre-expedition attempt by some of the subsequently successful Everest team. They failed on Cho Oyu but in the process gathered valuable scientific data which contributed to the success the following year. The mountain was first climbed by an Austrian team in 1954, and had a second ascent in 1958. On that occasion someone died, perhaps of pneumonia or heart failure, relatively low down below before camp 1. The next year a Sherpa was killed in an avalanche and two climbers died there in 1964. Nevertheless, Cho Oyu is not considered to be a particularly dangerous mountain, for the risks from crevasses, avalanches and stonefall are not great. What risks there are come mostly from the lack of oxygen and the bad weather associated with such altitude, and there are icy sections and some easy angled but loose rock high up, where falls are possible, particularly during descent.

Our sole American, Sean, had arrived in Kathmandu last, and had not been on an acclimatisation trek, so he sensibly joined me for my slow three day walk to base camp, starting out two days after the majority of the party and our fourteen yaks. Sean was thirty-nine years old, married with one daughter, and self-employed as a civil engineer in Reno. His voice reminded me of Clint Eastwood. Since he regularly ran hundred mile (160 kilometre) races in times ranging from thirteen to seventeen hours depending on the terrain, his fitness was not in doubt, but that alone is not enough to equip one for high altitude.

It was typical of this considerate man that he carried much more than me, allowing me an easy approach to base camp. Following a shallow, broad river crossing we enjoyed a wild walk on a plain of stones, on sandy, thinly grassed stream banks, on sparsely vegetated dusty ground, and over bouldery territory which must have made the yaks wish they had stayed at home. Three decaying yak corpses on that section gave no clue as to the cause of death, but broken legs or exhaustion seemed likely. The trail has for decades been heavily used by traders on the way to Nepal over the Nangpa La. Long processions of up to forty yaks and nearly as many people tramped in both directions every day, yet quite recently a TV documentary had tried to portray this as a 'secret' pass over which Tibetans escaped from the Chinese. 'It's good TV' has become an excuse for condoning lies in certain circles, and many media people are prepared to lie as much as the worst of used car salesmen. Integrity is seen as something quaint.

A few Americans arrived back down at their base camp tents at 5,700 metres to the whooping of their many companions. They had reached the summit a day or two earlier using supplementary oxygen.

We had no oxygen except one cylinder for emergency use.

'Why you guys not using oxygen?' one of them asked me.

'Because it's more sporting that way,' I said, adding, half joking, 'You see, we're British.'

'You're not using oxygen because you're stupid.'

You may be right sir, I thought, because at least in my case the use of oxygen could be seen as permissible. But experiences on Everest had turned me against its use.

Barny and our English born Australian resident, Paul Walters, and two Sherpas, had had a close shave with an avalanche the day before, on the way to camp 1. In a huge amphitheatre a cliff suddenly shed a mass of ice and snow with the usual accompanying roar. As a billowing white wall fifty metres wide spewed towards them they beat a hasty retreat back down the rough trail they had just come up, leaving their rucksacks. Scattering behind boulders for shelter they watched a gigantic cloud of snow and ice chunks race their way, and were soon engulfed. When it settled all were coated with snow from head to toe, but unhurt, except for Barny, who had exacerbated a knee injury in his flight. He suffered from a torn cartilage and would need an operation to put his knee right.

Between base camp and camp 1 was a tent we called the interim camp, a silver dome (reflective, therefore cool in the heat) standing in a stone wilderness of glacial moraine on the edge of fantastic ice pinnacles; no lichens, no mosses, no grasses, no wildlife but birds, just now and then a fly or a butterfly, and a little grey mouse which lived by the tent. After two days at base camp I spent a night alone at interim camp before tackling a stone slope up to camp 1. Unpleasant thoughts and words flowed out towards the 300 metre slope in its lower section because I slipped frequently on loose stones, so frequently, in fact, that the embarrassing prospect of having to give up loomed big and ugly even before reaching camp 1. With each slip rocks could be dislodged, exposing anyone who came up behind to unreasonable risk, and I was expending so much energy to make each few steps that I was not certain I could complete the distance; much of the time I was on my knees. My immobile feet could not be angled to the best advantage, and after a short while I sat on the slope experiencing a mixture of futile anger and resentment, and disappointment. However, twenty metres to the right as I looked upwards were what looked like a set of zigzags. Crossing to them on my knees, I found quite a good trail; guess who had been trying to get up the steep way which people slid down?

'Sick bastard hill,' was Paul's label for the slope as he passed by three hours later, just short of camp 1. By then I felt better about the slope, and grateful towards the people who, to use the American term, had 'punched in' the trail before us.

Camp 1, five reddish brown dome tents on a snow col, 6,400 metres high, housed Paul, Barny on his one excursion there, with a dodgy knee, and John Longmuir, who was on his second trip to Cho Oyu, having reached about 7,900 metres a year or two before. We learned by radio that Sean was already headed for home, having felt dizzy on the way to camp 1. He was the first to be out of the running, with Barny not far behind when he tried to accompany Paul, John and three Sherpas to establish camp 2. Barny was back at camp 1 in half an hour, and descended painfully to base camp the next day. From there he controlled the expedition effectively, much of the time by radio, while he hobbled around with my spare crutch and a ski stick. For a man who had climbed Everest two years before, this was a frustrating outcome, and it robbed the team of a very strong climber, while at the same time ensuring that we had a leader who was always on top of things logistically.

The three Sherpas, with John and Paul, established camp 2 on a large plateau beneath a huge, gentle snow slope which was the way to the next camp, and John and Paul stayed there for a night at nearly 7,000 metres, having taken seven hours to reach the camp.

Meanwhile at camp 1 six people had joined me: Nettie Smith, Siren Greve, Peter Wilson, Libby and Iain Peter, (married and both professional mountain guides and he deputy leader), and David Goode, retired. At twenty-nine Libby was the youngest, with David by far the most senior at sixty-three. John and Paul were both thirty-one, Nettie and Siren in their late thirties, and Peter was forty-six.

There were a few interpersonal problems centred around people being lazy about melting snow or erecting tents when high, or being slow beyond reasonable bounds, but generally it was a co-operative and unselfish group. One incident, which should not be blown out of proportion, illustrates how difficult tented living may be at high altitude. One day at camp 1 the three women shared a tent and Siren's P-bottle leaked over the floor, something she could not help, but which wet her and Nettie's sleeping bags. Siren's mistake was in inconsiderately mopping up her side of the tent but not Nettie's, and that was the end of their previously good relationship. It's like flat-sharing, only more intense.

Camp 2 was reached by Sherpas Nima, Ang Kami and Ang Temba, by Iain, the three women, and Kit Spencer, who was a former Gurkha officer, now a trek and expedition organiser living in Kathmandu, and who celebrated his fortieth birthday while in Tibet. David and Peter accompanied them a short way, but it was becoming clear that they were not strong candidates for a summit attempt. Several people found the way to camp 2, which involved a short but very steep ice cliff (icefall) to be eight or more hours of tough going, though the three Sherpas returned the same day through camp 1 to base camp with that 'been for a walk in the park' air. All the others stayed at camp 2 overnight to acclimatise. John and Paul descended to camp 1 that day, and described to me seven hard hours of climbing the day before. Seven hours, eight hours, nine hours of demanding going for the younger and able-bodied members; the times they had required were beginning to cause me some concern, and I was in two minds whether to make an acclimatisation trip to camp 2. In the end I decided the risk of burning out was too great, and four nights at camp 1 would do the trick instead. This, my third night, was the only one on which I was alone there. Four restful days at camp 1 passed quickly enough, with a couple of books and conversation, and odd jobs like making drinks and securing the tents better in case of high winds. Thus far the plan of taking it easy whenever possible had worked out. Easy trek, three days rather than two to reach BC, one night at interim camp on the way to camp 1, missing out on the acclimatisation climb to camp 2. Avoid any unnecessary suffering; unavoidable hardships are just around the corner, you can be sure.

The Americans had departed from base camp, having been quite successful, though I could not discover any figures from them.

'Those who tried for the summit got there,' was all I could get out of two of them, as if there was some secret.

The Americans were replaced by eighteen Austrians, who had with them three Tibetan porters who carried loads to camp 1. Contrary to our fears, the porters stole nothing, and I was not alone in gradually becoming ashamed of being initially standoffish with them. They often tried begging, but that is a different matter, and were friendly.

Back alone at interim camp for three nights, I missed the companionship of the others resting at base camp, and the meals, but there was an advantage in being away from the bugs; there always seemed to be somebody who was ill and running for the 'little house on the prairie', a tall blue tent on the edge of the glacier. I had an awful cough but my stomach was in good working order.

On the third day at interim camp Iain, Libby, Paul, Siren, Nettie, John, Nima, Ang Kami and Kit passed by, the earliest at 6.30am., for camp 1. Kit was as usual later than the others, moving at his own pace

331

and stopping for a puff on his pipe, and to deliver a bottle of beer. Generally on an expedition there is no booze above base camp because it is too heavy to carry. They brought extra food and a little whisky, so that too became a relaxed and easy day, physically and mentally. Relax while you can, the storm is on its way.

My visitors confirmed what I had heard on the radio, that they would go today, Friday, to camp 1, and attempt on Saturday to reach camp 2, on Sunday to camp 3 and on Monday to the summit. One day behind would be two Sherpas, David, Peter and me with Jeff Swinney, a thirty-nine year old nuclear plant operative from Scotland, and Barny, who was now walking with a knee brace provided by the far-sighted Kit. The two summit waves were supposed to be of equal strength, though clearly they were not. Mind you, I had no objection, because being with the strongest would probably have exposed me as being slow.

My day to move up to camp 1 for a summit attempt dawned with a problem, a big problem - a stitched and riveted retaining strap had come away from my left leg. It would be too complicated to describe but worked on a similar principle to having a chain on a box lid or a door to prevent it opening too far and breaking the hinges, and the absence of the strap would greatly increase the likelihood of the leg breaking. One option was to radio for a Sherpa or anyone else who would see to it to bring up the spare from base camp. That might cost me a day, putting me behind the second wave and probably losing me a summit shot, so instead I threaded a piece of strong cord through the stitching holes to make what seemed an effective temporary repair, but only time would tell. It transpired that it was fortunate I chose the temporary repair path, for when I returned home and changed a rather creaky, overused left leg for the spare, the socket of the replacement did not fit well, probably because of the inevitable weight loss which occurs on an expedition. Had I changed the leg at interim camp the wearing-in process would have caused such trouble with broken skin that I would most likely have been brought to a halt.

David, Jeff and Peter followed in that order behind me up the 'sick bastard hill', which was not so bad on second acquaintance - if you went the right way. Barny had found after all that he was not fit for the course, and had remained at BC.

Peter, Jeff and David had had enough, and decided not to go higher next morning, so I was left to set out at 6 am. with two Sherpas to myself. Two Sherpas! A luxury indeed, and I began to think very seriously that I could get up this one. Then one of the Sherpas felt unwell and stayed in his tent, leaving just Ang Temba and me from the original party of seven.

Above camp 1 were three fixed ropes, put there by the Americans, the first and second on a quite easy-angled snow ridge. The third, on steeper ground which fell away for a great distance to the left, was the only one I felt it necessary to use. We had paid the Americans in kind with other ropes for theirs to be left behind, thus saving us the time and energy-consuming task of carrying and fixing new ropes.

After half an hour on a broad ridge above the ropes we approached what looked like the crux of the climb, a near-vertical ice cliff of perhaps fifteen metres approached by a gradually steepening snow ramp. Here I asked Ang Temba to go ahead so I could shoot the best part of a roll of film of him on the juiciest bit of the route. The fact that this section cropped up relatively low on the mountain, at about 6,400 metres, was an advantage, for such a cliff 1,000 metres higher would have been a formidable obstacle to overcome in the thin air. Even down here I knew it was going to stretch me, perhaps bar my way. The snow ramp and lower-angled ice were easy enough, but higher up, being unable to kick my crampons into the hard blue ice as well as I would have wished, it became a struggle.

'What at a more sensible altitude would be enjoyable grade 3 climbing, at this height... this particular word was never further from my mind.'
- Dave Walsh, first British ascent, *Alpine Journal, 1989.*

Fixed ropes help a great deal, but it is wise not to slip and put a sudden strain on the eight-inch (20cm.) threaded tubes which secure them at the top, for these ice screws can break or be pulled out, particularly if the sun has warmed them. And falling on ice can do as much damage as falling on rock.

Ang Temba had flowed up easily, and was out of sight at the top of the cliff. Though he was not far away, I felt really alone, and had to keep telling myself to move. It was tempting, once the crampons had bitten, to stay put. Each move brought the risk of a slip. Kick as hard as you can, axe pick whammed in the ice, move jumar up the rope, kick with the other leg, the weaker left one, no, crampon tips not in, try again, that's better, pull and step up at the same time, spread the load on arms and legs, axe in again, no! the pick not in because the ice has shattered like a star, try again, same problem, try again, keep in balance, there's nothing so hard as this on Broad Peak or Shishapangma or Everest North Ridge, right crampon slipped a little but bit in again, get that axe in! that's better, right crampon up, no, it's bounced off the ice, try again, quickly, better, but not what I'd like, no fault of the crampons, these lightweights are just what I've always needed, here's a hippo bum-sized bulge of very hard ice, like shiny, smooth, blue tinged plastic, crampons slipping, it's bulbous, pull, movements are too jerky but there's nothing else I can do lacking the required leg strength, see the two ice screws holding the rope, they look all right I suppose but I am straining them more than those who went before, pull! and get that right crampon higher, now the left, oh my! not feeling safe here, get this done and it'll be plain sailing, glad I'll do this only once, rightwards now, up a short vertical chimney of ice, can't get my crampons in, slipping, but axe and rope hold me, scrabbling with left crampon, now the right too, unreasonably scared, putting too much strain on my arms, no alternative, probably a stone and a half lighter than when I arrived in Nepal but still twelve stones with legs on (one and a half stone of that being the artificial legs) arms aching tired, axe not in properly again, get it in! No! Get it in! It's in, a good placement! Pull on rope and axe! At the top of the chimney! Get up off your knees! Done it! DONE IT! DONE IT!

Gasping like a hunted stag, rest a couple of minutes at the top of the cliff. Others had reacted in the same way - 'We slumped in an untidy heap at the top of the icefall,' wrote Dave Walsh.

The expected plain sailing did not come about. I was lulled into false complacency by another easy ten metres on a fixed rope over an ice slope of 40 degrees, then a gently rising walk on snow, to face 200 metres of what looked at first like a straightforward snow slope, but turned out to be icy in a couple of places. Feeling that the job was almost done for that day, bar a long plod, I suggested to Ang Temba that he might as well go ahead at his own pace to camp 2, which he did. I followed his rapidly ascending figure, at first on excellent snow, comfortable going, and the large ski baskets were not required. Then the plain sailing came to an end, at a six metre band of ice with a fixed rope hanging down. It was not steep, 40 degrees at the most, and my companions in the first wave probably went up with no trouble at all, walking with feet angled upwards to put most of their twenty-four (twelve per boot) crampon spikes on the ice. My rigid feet allowed only the front points, which stick out forwards, to make contact with the glistening slope. With the help of the rope and my axe I made it, but not in a confident or graceful style. Sloppy was more like it. Firm snow led to the next band of ice, equally difficult and just as frightening, and then it eased back as the slope broke up into ridges, humps, natural snow caves, hollows, short snow cliffs and ice ramps through which the route weaved. Again it seemed as if the job had been done for that day. Another fixed rope gave protection on a short and easy 60 degree snow wall, split by a half-metre-wide crevasse which had to be stepped across at mid height. The boot steps of the other people were so big it was like going up a ladder. Above that a small wall, two men high, with similar bucket steps, made me feel very happy, but there my luck ran out. On this section my crutches hung free for a minute or two suspended on a cord over my shoulders, and one of them detached itself from the small plastic hook to which it was clipped, and fell. There was a lessening in the small weight on my shoulders, warning me of what had happened, and I turned to see it go thirty metres or so. It landed beneath the 60 degree wall, right by two small flags left by the Americans to mark a largely concealed crevasse; the crutch lay only a half metre from the barely discernible edges. The knowledge that camp 2 could not be more than half an hour away influenced my decision to leave the crutch there and return next day with Ang Temba and a rope to recover it. Its proximity to the crevasse, which probably had overhanging lips, gave valid cause to wonder whether it could be retrieved; four chances out of five it could be done, and if not, the summit was slipping away from me. Even if a spare ski stick were available I would be slower and less sure without that precious second crutch. Barny needed the spare one and in any case, if I could bring myself to deprive him of it for a few days, the chances of getting it from base camp to camp 2 were remote. A Sherpa might achieve that in two days, but the only one available was sick, and there was no one else up to the job who was not already higher up the mountain.

Dog-tired as I now was, and on one crutch, I snailed up the last gentle slopes, stopping to rest every twenty steps. I had reached that point where only willpower keeps you going. The toil of high altitude climbing, especially towards the end of the day, beggars description. For those who have not trodden the snow in thin air at 7,000 metres and more, perhaps it will help to imagine what it is like to climb steep sandhills while encumbered by a sack of potatoes on your back and a brick strapped to each ankle. Every step requires a mental effort to bring it about, and there is a lack of that rhythm found in running. High up, moving the left leg, gasping, moving the right leg, gasping again, is a process more like operating a ratchet - make an effort, gain a little, make another effort, gain a little more. Though you try to maintain a continuum the result still sometimes comes down to a series of separate bursts, and often mountaineers do count their steps; fifty and I'll rest, forty-eight, forty-nine, fifty, let's add five more, fifty-one, fifty-two, fifty-three... Or you pick a rock or a hump in the snow and try to get there without stopping, and features like that are almost always further away than you thought. Endurance, stamina, are all, and were it not for the fact that all this is undertaken voluntarily, high altitude climbing would be considered a very cruel form of torture, making hard labour, at least in normal temperatures, seem a soft option by comparison. The effort, accompanied by dehydration, extremes of heat and cold, and fear too, demands an enormous depth of self-motivation which makes that required for a marathon seem little, or so I have been told by mountaineers who have run that distance. In soft snow you sink and struggle, but photographs will not look spectacular, and never really show how ghastly it can be up there.

At last our three reddish brown dome tents, beside two green Austrian shelters, were reached. Though I had taken no longer than average for our team, I felt wiped out. Still, I would recover overnight, and the way to camp 2 would not be difficult, provided that the crutch was recovered.

Next morning, at 6.15 am., without any prompting, Ang Temba took off on his own to fetch my crutch.

'Don't take any risks, Ang Temba. If necessary I'll join you with a rope. We have plenty of time today.'

At 6.30 am. Nettie arrived at the tents, on her way down to BC, having turned back at a prominent rock band half an hour above camp 3, with a pain in her chest. She had had a very bad cough for several days and was quite ill. She found the final day of the walk down to the road head to be very hard as a consequence.

Nettie kindly offered me one of her ski sticks, which we arranged for her to leave with Ang Temba if he thought that my crutch could not be retrieved by him or both of us; then she continued down. Fifteen minutes later Ang Temba was back.

'I have your pole,' he said.

Pole. Slight sinking feeling in the stomach. The ski pole or the crutch? It would make a big difference, and it was a relief to learn it was the latter.

We set off immediately for the next stage to camp 3, which had been described as straightforward. The temporary repair to the leg was holding up, I was rested, the weather was still good, the snow was firm, and I had my second crutch back.

'Four or five hours for you,' Ang Temba said, before setting off up a snow slope not much above or below 15 degrees. After just under three hours the slope eased back and a couple of ravens (or choughs - big black birds, anyway) hung steady in the air like hang gliders just ahead, so I knew it was likely that I was approaching camp 3, because the birds scavenge around the camps, then buzz off down to the valley with ease - lucky beggars. And so it was, three hours to camp 3 at 7,400 metres. Another relatively easy day.

Now could we get a sight of the others? Yes, there, and there, and there. Nearest to us, a disconsolate figure walked reluctantly down, sitting quite often, and there was something about the demeanour, and also the time, 11.30 am., which told us this person had failed. It turned out to be Ang Kami, who was closely followed by Kit, Siren, Libby and John, all looking very tired, and back too early to have summitted. They had been slow compared with the three who were now continuing to the summit, and had had to turn back for that reason. For John it was particularly disappointing because he had reached about the same altitude as he had on his previous attempt on Cho Oyu..

The usual noon radio call did not come from Iain, so none of us knew what was happening to the remaining three, Iain, Nima and Paul. While on rock they were difficult to spot, and once on the huge summit plateau they would be out of sight, though they could be seen for longer from base camp.

At 12.17 pm. according to my watch, came the call from the trio. They had just reached the top after nine hours of ascent, and would now descend to camp 2 and join those who had failed.

Nine hours. So how long for me, if the weather allowed an attempt? Eleven hours? Twelve? Thirteen? If thirteen, then getting back before dark would be in question. Doubt, doubt, doubt hung around that night, in the tent I had to myself. In another was Ang Temba - Sherpas usually take separate tents when they are available - and in the third an Austrian who I believe soloed the mountain and could not get back to camp 2. Two more Austrians at camp 3 had asked if the man could use our tent because theirs was quite small and he was back well after dark. His late return further raised my doubts. The Americans had done all right, eleven to fourteen hours round trip, but that was with oxygen. It was finely balanced, and I was determined but not overconfident; confidence goes hand in hand with realism on a mountain, unless you're pretty stupid. Added to my anxieties was that awful cough, much worse than the common high altitude cough. I clung to one positive thought, that our three summiteers would not have taken so long if they had not had to wait for others.

"Hope is a good breakfast but it is a bad supper." – Francis Bacon.

337

Hope, like indigestion, kept me awake. Elusive sleep came at about 9pm., and at about 1 am. I was making hot sweet drinks, which went down nicely with a few sweet biscuits, and by 2am. it was out into the cold, clear, windless night by the light of a head torch. According to our plan, Ang Temba would start out an hour later and catch me up. I've talked before of plans which don't work out.

The first thirty minutes involved a trudge on firm snow to a break in a rock band with a fixed rope hanging down. The lower bit on snow was easy, but higher up the ice once more made me fight. Alone, with just torchlight to show the way ahead, I felt very vulnerable, and faffed about for a long time, simply standing still at times on the 40 degree ice. I'm sure that being a double leg amputee heightened the experience. Delay wasted body heat as well as precious time, so every so often I told myself to bloody well get on with it, while really I wanted Ang Temba to be close at hand in case anything went wrong. I had seen his torchlight leave the vicinity of his tent and start up the mountain, but now there was no light. It should have been visible the whole time on the gradual initial slope we took. Had he fallen in a crevasse, or had his torch bulb gone? Had he turned back? Speculation did nothing for my confidence, and I was worried for my prospects as well as for him. If he had turned back I would have no way of knowing, but surely he would have shouted? I would have to assume he had gone down a crevasse and retreat to look for him, returning to camp 3 for a rope if necessary. This would take so much time and energy we would probably have to abandon the attempt for this day, even if he was fit to continue. Perhaps tomorrow, if the weather holds? If his bulb had gone, did he have a spare? Whatever the case, there was no point in moving up only to have to go down again. So for a short while I stood undecided on my crampon tips, preparing for the moment when commitment to retreat became inevitable. Then a few hundred metres beneath was the faintest of glows; it could only be Ang Temba. I continued slowly up, and by the time I had hauled myself to the top of the fixed rope Ang Temba was on his way up the ice.

I flopped, grateful just to lie there, until he joined me. His torch battery was running low, he explained. The spare batteries I carried did not fit his torch, but by now there was enough dawn light to allow him to carry on without. We could continue, but suddenly another factor had to be taken into consideration, which was that I could not allow him to be caught out in the dark at the end of this day. Descending with one torch between two people is difficult and sometimes dangerous. I had done so once, and did not want to repeat the exercise, particularly because we would have to abseil at one point at least lower down. It is preferable that two people do not abseil on one rope at the same time because of the strain put on the anchor, be it ice screw, piton or snow stake. So one of us might have to abseil in the dark without a torch, while the other tried to light their way from above or below.

A long yellow rope gave us handholds, up and to the right on gently angled rock, sloping upwards ahead, and downwards to the right. It was a bit loose, and overlaid with shallow snow most of the way. The route then continued for hours on similar rock slopes strewn with stones and for the most part covered in snow, and up another rock cliff as high as a two storey house but easy angled and stepped conveniently – one of nature's ladders. A fatal or injurious slip during this long traverse was a remote possibility, stonefall a small risk, and though an avalanche could have swept us down, the lack of recent snowfall reduced the likelihood of avalanche to almost nil. One snow ramp in particular bothered me, not on the way up while still frozen, but the few centimetres of snow on slabby, sloping rock would be softer and less stable in the late afternoon, and since I move my feet more like a bull than a ballerina the danger would be greater to me than to Ang Temba.

We barely stopped to rest until about 7,900 metres. Though I was coughing terribly I knew the 8,000 metre ambition was within my grasp, no matter what barriers the mountain had in our way, but whether the summit was attainable too was another matter. That last long trudge had defeated many people, and in fact we were at the bottom of a long snow slope somewhere near where three of ours had turned back.

Ang Temba asked, 'What do you want to do?' Then he added, 'I have been on many high mountains.'

These included Everest and Annapurna, and I took his second sentence to mean he was not too bothered about carrying on, perhaps because he had been told that one of my ambitions was to reach 8,000m. That was a secondary ambition now, a slight comfort, a tiny consolation, but not enough. If I had said "Let's just go to 8,000 metres", Ang Temba would have agreed.

'Go for the top,' I said.

'Weather is good.'

Leaving my rucksack behind we trudged up a long slope of perfect snow; the cover had been so good that it had still not been necessary to employ the large ski baskets. The weather remained favourable, and though gaining altitude was not easy it was just a question of willpower rather than skill. In an hour we were weaving a way up and across rock ledges littered with stones. The angles were such that I could use crutches most of the time, and rarely had to put a hand to the rock, so I would call it at the steepest a scramble rather than a rock climb. Red marker flags left by the Americans guided us through. Thanks, Yanks.

A couple of black birds hovered in a light breeze not far above and we came across damned litter: sweet, chocolate and biscuit wrappers - often indications that the summit is close because people rest there, but we knew this not to be the case. I came up to the last bit of rock a few paces behind Ang Temba, and beyond him was a snow hillock with a long bamboo pole stuck in it. Could it be the summit? Despite my knowledge that the route dragged on, my silly heart rose for a while. Closer to us, to the left, was another high spot, not quite as high as the hillock. Moving between these rises we saw another hillock with a bamboo pole, a good half an hour walk away. We said nothing, but began to hope that the end was in sight.

It was noon, the hour agreed with Iain and Barny that we would turn back. That would leave seven hours of daylight to descend what had taken ten to climb - a reasonable margin, even for me. But to go on would mean, obviously, one less hour of daylight on the descent for each extra hour of ascent. Eleven hours up would mean six hours of daylight on the way down, twelve hours up would leave five for the descent, and with only one torch that would be placing us in unacceptable danger. There was an alternative, which was to send Ang Temba down from the summit at his own best speed. No, he would not leave me. But what if I bivouacked? Then he would go down. I had no tent, sleeping bag nor bivouac bag, but I did not entirely dismiss the idea.

On the noon radio call I said I thought we were forty minutes from the summit, and no one objected to us carrying on.

'What do you want to do, Ang Temba?'

'Go on.'

If he had suggested turning back I would probably still have gone on, but we were close to that line between what was acceptable and what was not, between what was sensible and what was foolish.

If the snow had been softer our party of the day before would have walked in single file, but there had been no need to make a trail, so there they were, three distinct sets of fresh tracks leading us up the huge summit plateau of humpy snow. It was a surprise not to see more tracks leading to the true summit, but perhaps wind-blown snow had erased them; or several climbers had reached the summit plateau and called it a day. That would account for there being reluctance at revealing any figures on how many had succeeded.

As we drew near the 'top', taking over half an hour after the radio

340

call, we realised there was higher ground beyond, bumps which rose just a little higher than the one we were headed for. In the nineteenth century it was said of Kilimanjaro that if you tried to walk up it the mountain receded and the summit rose, and that summed up what seemed to be happening. Let's get this over and get down, was about all I thought, except to allow myself to believe I was about to climb an 8,000 metre peak. What a contrast with my first high altitude ascent in Peru in 1978, of which I wrote: '...a feverish elation began to fuel me for the finish. Shouts and giggles and laughs came from my mouth like it was someone else making them.

'Hey! Hey! Hey! You're going to do it! You're going to do it! You're going to do it!'

I shouted loudly, happily, mad with joy. A rush of emotion came over me, a weepy feeling that is not uncommon in such circumstances. Through my blood surged that wonderful sensation which no words can properly describe, sweet as love, warm as friendship and overwhelming.'

Not so on Cho Oyu, where the highest snows sloped very gently, which was nice in a way, but we could have done without this long, bland finish. Perhaps age meant I did not experience the same depth of feeling, or was it that the first high mountain meant so much more. With Ang Temba just ahead we reached the place where the footprints wandered around ('Mostly mine,' Paul said. 'I was ecstatic.') and the mountain fell away into Nepal. We were there just after 1pm. on 30th May 1995. 26,906 ft. Two hundred and one metres above the 8,000 metre mark, on the sixth highest mountain in the world. On the go for eleven hours. At that stage relief was a stronger emotion than the joy of success.

Two pictures of Ang Temba on my camera, two of me on mine, taken by him, two of me on his, by two lines of handkerchief sized prayer flags of various colours, red, yellow, blue, strung out between bamboo poles. Had to be Sherpas who had taken up the extra weight - Nima told me a few days later he had put up one set. There was an oxygen bottle too, probably dumped by one of the Americans too lazy to take it down. Everest can be seen from there, but as is common it was in afternoon cloud.

'Let's get down,' I said after only a brief halt. We had not even sat down for a minute.

After half an hour or so on the way down we met a lone Austrian on his weary way up.

'How long to the top?' he asked in English.

'An hour,' Ang Temba said, and the man forced himself on.

I was slow, very slow, even with the slope in our favour, and guilt at holding Ang Temba back crept insidiously over me. So I finally made my decision to bivouac, and to give him my torch. We had descended the top rock steps when I asked him to go ahead, and told him what I was going to do. He did not receive the news well.

'No. No.'

'Yes. I'll be all right.'

'No!'

'Yes. It is better. You go down as fast as you like. I am used to bivouacking.'

The Austrian passed us on the way down the long snow slope, and his rapid progress only highlighted how slowly I was going. I felt my mental faculties to be intact, and have little doubt that I could reason, but meeting the Austrian on the way down brought home to me just how much your memory can be affected at high altitude, for twenty minutes later I could not have sworn I had seen him. Though I was certain I had seen him on the way up, and Ang Temba confirmed that we had seen the man descending the snowfield too, there was just that little doubt, as if it might have been a dream. It was different from hallucinations, which are quite common up there, as was the case of one man who was convinced he saw a 20 metre tall giraffe and was fired upon by Japanese soldiers, so he threw stones at the soldiers. No, this was not the same, not a case of seeing what was not there, but one of forgetting what had happened. It was akin to something Anthony Trollope wrote in his Autobiography: 'A man does, in truth, remember that which it interests him to remember; and when we hear that memory has gone ... we should understand that the capacity for interest in the matter concerned has perished. A man will be generally very old and feeble before he forgets how much money he has.' Perhaps I resented the ease with which the Austrian descended; the poor bugger coming up the hill was a different matter and just made me feel glad to have succeeded. Or was it that by now I was degenerating mentally as well as physically?

With great reluctance Ang Temba went ahead as I had ordered. Tiredness lessened the hardship of the decision to bivouac, and the insecure nature of some of the snow lower down was potentially, as I have suggested before, a bigger danger for me than for others. By the time I reached my rucksack Ang Temba was out of sight, and got back to camp 3 well before dark, I am happy to say. I had planned to give him my torch, just in case, but in my dozy high-altitude state failed to do so. One point of the bivouac was to make the torch available, and I forgot to hand it over! But now, if the weather threatened, I could descend after a rest, and on good snow.

Settling down for the night on a gently sloping ledge cleared of stones, I laid out a small insulating pad which lives in my rucksack, then piled up rocks to keep the wind off. Without a shovel, digging a snow hole would have taken ages, and the short insulating pad was not suitable for sleeping on snow, and on top of that the sweat generated by digging would have dampened my clothing just before turning in. Thermal pants and vest, salopettes, down jacket, fleece jacket, waterproof jacket and trousers, wool gloves and mittens, and a warm hat, together with woollen stump socks, were my protection against the cold and the wind, with one luxury which no one else on the trip could have enjoyed - by taking off my legs and storing them in a plastic bin bag, I could get into my rucksack and pull it up as far as my nipples. Had I taken a tiny one for the summit day, well, the story might have had a different ending.

As we carry only the bare essentials when climbing so high, there was no food apart from a bottle of energy drink. I felt no hunger, and kept a pint from freezing by putting it inside the rucksack. That would be enough to get me back to camp 3 come dawn, where there would be all the drinks and food required before proceeding down.

On the 6pm. radio link with Barny he, naturally enough, was not happy that one of his team was sleeping without a tent, bivouac bag or sleeping bag at nearly 7,900 metres.

'I'll call again at 9 o'clock tonight,' he said.

After talking to Barny I put my legs back on and moved sixty metres lower to get away from the ridge over which any wind, if it rose, would come. So far the weather had been good around Cho Oyu. The second bivi site was much like the first, on gently-sloping rock.

The night was clear and therefore colder than under a heat-retaining cloud blanket, but I doubt the temperature fell to more than 10 or 12 below zero Celsius. The night was tolerable, with very little wind blowing, and I was asleep when I should have listened for Barny's 9pm. call. I think I had just switched myself off from the suffering, and I regretted this later, because though I was warm enough and safe, he could not have been aware of this, so did not get any sleep himself. Instead he remained listening at the radio all night. I did not know this of course, and felt ashamed that it did not occur to me to try calling once or twice during the night to put him at ease. So while I enjoyed a dreamless sleep, as far as I can remember, Barny, the Sherpas and several others were beginning to believe that I had perished (or 'karked' as Paul put it in Australian) in the Death Zone.

'I expect he'll be all right. He's Cornish,' Nettie had said.

"If your training is good enough, survival is there; if not nature claims its forfeit." – Dougal Haston.

Iain moved up from camp 1 to camp 3 overnight, a magnificent effort, particularly for someone who had been so recently to the summit, to be in the right place at the right time if help were needed. He showed an admirable sense of concern and responsibility for his unusual and bothersome client. Paul too came up trumps and carried a bottle of oxygen from base camp to camp 1, just in case. Meanwhile, I slept well in my rucksack, two Eigers high, unaware that anyone was bothered, and occasionally waking up to wonder, did I really see that Austrian on his way down?

Though I am deeply moved by annual services of remembrance, I believe nations must beware of praising only their warrior heroes, for that can leave others feeling worthless. To seek sporting risk may seem perverse but we need these ritual pressure valves, the challenges, the profound emotional rewards of sport, for without them there would be even more frustrated, unfulfilled, redundant individuals around. (Though I might agree that sport is routinely over-represented on television, leading us to become spectators rather than participants.) One thought helped to keep the whole thing in perspective - the number of feet I slept above sea level was the same as the number of Allied troops, Indian, Nepalese, British and others who in the last war ended their days in unmarked graves in Burma, after suffering terrible hardships including disease, hunger, extreme danger and awful injuries. This is but one example of scores which show that our voluntary sporting hardships are small by comparison; but such outlets are necessary in times of relative peace, for it is dangerous to suggest there is room for spirit only in war or the emergency services. I would rarely use the word courage in connection with mountaineering - for that look to the Somme, Normandy and scores of other fields of conflict, to PoW and concentration camps. Climbing may now and then demand a little bit of courage, but in an entirely different class from the outstanding bravery of, for instance, George Stronach, G.C. I will outline briefly what he did, based on an obituary in the Daily Telegraph. George was on a ship anchored in Tripoli harbour in 1943 when the vessel caught fire and her cargo of petrol and ammunition exploded. He was blown seven or eight metres along the deck and knocked unconscious. When he came to, with ammunition exploding and tracer bullets flying in all directions, he led fifteen men who thought themselves to be trapped to the safety of a lifeboat, and then, unaided, lowered another boat, and made his way towards the officers' cabins, pulling a fire hose which trickled a little water over his head to protect him from flames. After dragging a badly injured officer along the deck and putting him in the boat he had lowered, he returned to rescue the Chief Engineer, who was badly burned and had both legs broken. With him lowered into the boat, Stronach went back into the inferno, knowing that one hold, which was burning fiercely, contained five hundred tons of 1,000 lb. bombs. He carried the 3rd Radio Officer, who had a broken leg and other serious injuries, to where he could lower the casualty onto a raft which he had hailed to come alongside. He was about to abandon ship when he saw another crew member lying collapsed, so he lowered him down to the raft too, then dived overboard and swam to that raft. Using first his hands and then a piece of wood, he paddled the raft back to the ship and took off the 2nd Engineer. George had stayed for an hour and twenty minutes aboard the ship, which later blew up and sank. He spent some months recovering from a back injury sustained on the ship. This is but one of many incredible, and in some cases unwitnessed and unrecorded, true stories which could be dismissed in a work of fiction as absurd. There are countless cases of people going repeatedly over long periods into frightening situations and they all help to put mountaineering, wonderful though it might be, into perspective. There are many admirable examples of morally courageous reactions in the face of all manner of challenges, but the words 'brave' and 'courageous' and 'heroic' are devalued by overuse in sport, and in highly publicised adventure stunts carried on before the cameras, backed by big budgets and satellite communications. But the purists are in a minority compared with those who gain their vicarious thrills from the screen, and the inevitable will have to be accepted, whether uncomfortably or not. Exhibitionism is a fact of modern life, and most of the public would rather shake hands with a soap star or a famous footballer than George Stronach. How sad.

So there I slept in the open, or, to use a 19th century expression, 'At the Inn of the Morning Star.' Of a bivouac on Huascaran I wrote: '...it is one advantage of being an amputee, that body heat is retained better, and one day that could mean the difference between survival or death.' I was aware that on the first British ascent of Cho Oyu in 1988 a member who bivouacked around here suffered frostbitten hands and feet.

'Norman! Norman!' The call was loud and urgent. 7 am. Bright daylight. I awoke and sat up. Nima rushed up the rock slope and hugged me.

'You are all right?'

'I'm fine.'

He took from his rucksack a large flask of hot water, which I guzzled gratefully. Later I learned that he had been reluctant to come up from camp 3 because he thought he would be finding a corpse, but it was not until I heard the relief in Barny's voice when we made our usual 8 am. radio call that I realised the anxiety I had caused.

'How are you, Norm?'

'I'm fine.'

'No frostbite?'

'No. I'm in good shape. Not a bad night.'

'Thank God for that.'

It was about then I noticed that my waterproof jacket, which is lined with netting to trap air for insulation, was inside out. I could have been even cosier.

Nima and I descended to camp 3 in - how long? Two hours? Three? I'm not sure, but anyway, in a third of the time it would have taken before a night's rest. Then Iain took over and escorted me to camp 2, where we stayed with Sherpa Yelpe, while Ang Temba and Nima continued down to camp 1. At first Iain had wanted us all to reach camp 1, but I was too drained, and by then my left stump was rubbed raw in a small patch, and very painful - the first stump injury of the expedition. My cough was still dreadful, disturbing Yelpe and Iain during the night. Iain asked if cough sweets would help.

'I don't think so. It's my chest.'

'Perhaps a whole packet, inserted sideways in the throat?'

You might expect a red-haired Scot to be short tempered (or is it a myth?) but apart from that remark Iain could not have been more attentive or patient with his coughing, drained, slightly injured charge on the way to camp 1. On ice slopes and the ice cliff he simply lowered me on a rope, which was idle luxury compared with having to abseil. I could have managed that but unlike my able-bodied companions I found abseiling burned up quite a lot of energy to keep in control, and there was little of that to spare. My slowness on the final stretch would have provoked a lesser man to outspoken anger, but he never lost patience, and took the trouble to bring down some of the fixed ropes we had agreed to remove. It was some months later that I heard that Iain had in fact been very displeased with my decision to bivouac. Perhaps he had not fully appreciated why it was done, but if he thought a committed and very experienced mountaineer had no right to assess his own degree of acceptable risk at high altitude, then he was in the wrong business.

He should have known what he was taking on when my money was accepted, or should have asked. He should have appreciated, or would have learned, that I was prepared to accept a considerable degree of risk, as any mountaineer must, provided it was not at the expense of anyone else on the expedition. Some organisers and leaders of commercial expeditions seem prepared to take the money without fully investigating whether their clients are sufficiently experienced, temperamentally suited, and prepared to accept the parameters the companies choose. I was not going to pay £7,000 to pussy-foot about for the convenience and comfort of the organisers. High altitude mountaineering inevitably involves risk, and the degree of risk cannot be absolutely qualified because there are so many variables, including the subjective; what might be attempted on one day may feel too risky for the possible reward on another day, and one man's acceptable risk is another man's unacceptable risk. On that day on Cho Oyo I did what I was driven to do, and I had paid for the privilege in both money and effort and I knew and accepted the risk. If I had tried to descend rather than bivouac, they might well have had a body on their hands, and Ang Temba in trouble in the dark. I would be nervous in this litigious world to undertake Iain's rôle, but it was his mature, adult, voluntary decision to do what he did.

As we approached camp 1 Libby came up to give us a hug, and Kit sat at the stove singing, 'Why was he born so beautiful?' very loudly, and then they treated us to mug after mug of a variety of drinks. Kit, Libby and Iain descended to base camp that day, while I stopped at interim alone, no one to celebrate with, profoundly content. Now real joy swept over me, making my mind and body feel so good.

> "One moment may with bliss repay
> Unnumbered hours of pain." – Thomas Campbell.

On my arrival at base camp Barny produced two bottles of whisky and most of us had a fine old time, except one man and Siren, the latter who withdrew, and did not speak to me for two days; for Siren, not speaking was out of character. Because of its weight, alcoholic drink is rarely available on high, whereas sharing a bottle of wine and watching the sun go down on the peaks, before retreating to sit by a wood fire in a timber hut, can be part of the romance after a hard day in the Alps. There was no fire, no hut, at Cho Oyu's base camp, but the feeling was there. Success. Relief. Joy. And a few tots with friends. Despite the inevitable deep disappointment of several others, they shared my pleasure.

Peter thought I had a chest infection which might turn to pneumonia, so he found some drugs for me in our medical kit, and it all cleared up during the forty hours of rest we enjoyed before Barny and I limped back to the roadhead. With him on one crutch and a ski stick, and me on two crutches, we provided an interesting spectacle for the few local travellers encountered in this barren place. I don't know the Tibetan for, 'Good God, Gladys! What the hell are they doing here?' but looks said it all.

On a truck to Tingri in one and a half hours. Beer in large quantities. A Chinese meal in the evening - nice change. We could not bring ourselves, however, to follow the Sherpas in drinking beer for breakfast at dawn the next day. An early start enabled us to reach Kathmandu the same day, just beating a slide which closed the road that evening.

I can look back on Cho Oyu with supreme, personal, selfish pleasure, and I'm not ashamed of that. Cho Oyu is my equivalent of Everest. At nearly fifty-five I had waited long for this. Now all the trials of early life were wiped away by one mountain. It had been worth the struggle, and I feel no sense of loss about my legs; it is just a part of the whole picture, and my mountaineering has in consequence been more challenging. There was a reason behind the hardships. This mountain tied up a lot of life's loose ends, making sense of earlier 8,000 metre attempts. It was now a true case of 'If at first you don't succeed, try, try, try again.'

High Magazine said in a report about Cho Oyu: 'This produced the season's most outstanding ascent of the mountain and indeed one of the most outstanding ascents in Nepal/Tibet during the pre-monsoon period, when Norman Croucher reached the summit with his Sherpa companion on 30th May.' I cannot deny that for the ascent to be reported in such words in a climbing magazine brought me enormous pleasure; and those who are in the know paid me a very big compliment. We have no audience in our harsh arena, nor any medals, and little or no financial reward, and need none of these. Our rewards are in our hearts.

After Cho Oyu I lost interest in climbing very high mountains, such cold, dangerous things. Instead, attention turned to mountains like the Finsteraarhorn (4,274 metres) and Monte Rosa (4,634 metres) in Switzerland; enjoyable, tastier heights. For the latter the President of the Zermatt Guides was helpful in finding someone to climb with me. On the Finsteraarhorn the shin of my left artificial leg was cracked, probably from impact with rock or ice, so when I telephoned her at home Judy arranged with the Exeter Mobility Centre for my other left leg to be sent by air and rail in less than twenty-four hours to the hotel where I was staying in Zermatt. The leg was collected from reception, and the hotel owner surprised his dinner guests by announcing that on this night he had seen a man with three legs! Another odd incident, resulting from a squeaky foot, springs to mind, when at a shop I bought a can of oil, saying to the assistant 'I'm in a hurry to catch a bus' before squirting the liquid through a sock on to the foot, and hurrying out. Also in Switzerland, two years later, sponsored climbs of seven small mountains a little in excess of 3,000 metres, raising money for a hospice, brought great pleasure and sense of purpose. Yet I must add that I would discourage inexperienced people from venturing on mountains with admirable charitable purposes in mind, if there is a risk of over extending themselves. The Dolomites gave some good climbs too, on the Cinque Torre, for instance, and the Cadini range, small mountains with a sacred and exciting look about them. They beckon me back for more climbs and walks on the wonderful flowered pastures. And not long ago I tackled the volcano Chimborazo, which lies in Ecuador. Its altitude at 6,310 metres no longer sounded high, even to a fifty-seven year old double leg amputee. Local guide Pepe Gonzalo (known to some as Speedy Gonzalo) and I climbed a short ice slope of 45 degrees and then tramp, tramp, tramped up clean snow slopes and ridges to camp at 5,800 metres. From there it was only three and a half hours next day to the Ventimilla fore summit, and a further half hour to the true top, the Whymper summit. This was how it would be done in the future, in bite-sized chunks which could be enjoyed; most people tackle Chimborazo's final snow slopes in one long day, and a high proportion fail. This mountain really brought home how times have changed; what I would have given to have reached such an altitude twenty-five years earlier!

Despite my having experienced bronchitis, dysentery, rockfall, frostbite, a tumble now and then, horrifying river crossings (you try it on metal legs), a mule ride while wearing only one leg, awful early morning starts, a bivouac sans tent or sleeping bag at 7,900 metres, dreadful heat, poor food, soft snow and avalanches, torrential rain, leeches and mosquitoes, third world transport on mountain tracks, campsites on rocks, revolting toilets, winds strong enough to pick you up or blow you over, dripping tents and snow holes, friable ice, loose and slippery rock, sliding scree, packs of yapping dogs, the odd aggressive yak, petty theft and a mugging in Lima, the small risk presented by snakes, scorpions and bears, dehydration, the utter exhaustion of high altitude, extreme cold, thunder and lightning, quite a lot of pain and the added spice of the small but ever-present possibility of mechanical failure of a leg or two, despite all these it has on the whole been fun, and deeply satisfying.

Because of the mountains mine has been such a full life that if it were to come to an end now I would not feel cheated. The accusation could be levelled that it has been a self-indulgent life. Should one feel guilty about self-indulgence which brought joy at no cost to others? I think not. And in any case I belong in the mountains as much as anyone, and perhaps more than most.

In 1998 I suffered a minor stroke. This would mean it would be unwise to go high. Perhaps at last health would clip my wings on the mountains, but I could not complain at what I had had, and I was sure that even if the condition precluded high ascents, modest mountain heights were still within reach. Now there are more mountain memories than dreams, but above all I have no regrets. I live in gratitude for the past, and in hope for the future among mountains. I envy no man; there has been too much to rejoice in.

POSTSCRIPT

Examples can be negative

EXAMPLES of the achievements of people with disabilities may provide inspiration for others who have handicaps, but many who are disabled resent being reminded ad infinitum of the successes of those who are held up to be, by implication, in some ways superior. With few exceptions, the media tend to portray as worthy only those disabled individuals who achieve physically, and this can be insulting and distressing. Exercise through sport may be the last thing that appeals in her spare time to a one-legged or wheelchair-using mother who has two young children. While I believe opportunities for sporting participation should be as broad as is reasonably possible, it must be stressed that not all able-bodied or disabled people wish to take part, and they should not be pressured to do so. In one survey a very high proportion of people with disabilities reacted with indifference or hostility when asked if they were inspired by the double leg amputee pilot and golfer, Douglas Bader. Probably the majority of them had not met him, but many felt he had been "rammed down their throats". Indiscriminate use of exemplars may not produce the positive reactions which might innocently be expected, so the approach needs to be sensible and sensitive. If the reaction of a disabled person to the mention of an exemplar is negative, it is kindness not to press the matter any further.

Ascents by Norman Croucher

1970	Monch, Switzerland	13,447 feet	4,099metres
1970	Jungfrau, Switzerland	13,641 feet	4,158 metres
1971	Aig du Gouter, France	12,552 feet	3,817 metres
1971	Mont Blanc, France	5,770 feet	4,807 metres
1972	Eiger, Switzerland	13,024 feet	3,970 metres
1973	Wellenkuppe, Switzerland	12,804 feet	3,903 metres
1973	Unter Rothorn, Switzerland *(and again in 1974)*	10,180 feet	3,103 metres
1973	Stockhorn, Switzerland	11,587 feet	3,532 metres
1974	Matterhorn, Switzerland	14,681 feet	4,478 metres
1974	Briethorn, Switzerland	13,664 feet	4,165 metres
1974	Ober Rothorn, Switzerland *(twice, and again in 1975)*	11,204 feet	3,415 metres
1975	Egginer, Switzerland	11,043 feet	3,366 metres
1975	Jagihorn, Switzerland	10,518 feet	3,206 metres
1976	Aiguille du Midi, France	12,604 feet	3,842 metres
1976	Tete Blanche, France	11,250 feet	3,429 metres
1976	L'Index, France	8,514 feet	2,595 metres
1976	Aiguille de l'M, France	9,330 feet	2,844 metres
1978	Joderhorn, Italy	10,183feet	3,104 metres
1978	Wallanaraju Sur, Peru	16,798 feet	5,120 metres
1978	Pisco, Peru	18,871 feet	5,752 metres
1978	Huascaran, Peru	21,830 feet	6,654 metres
1980	L'Eveque, Switzerland	11,128 feet	3,392 metres
1980	La Luette, Switzerland	11,640 feet	3,548 metres
1980	Point Kurz, Switzerland	1,476 feet	3,498 metres
1981	E. Summit, Ameghino, Argentina	16,781 feet	5,115 metres
1981	White Needle, Kashmir	21,500 feet	6,553 metres
1982	Cerro Manso, Argentina	18,231 feet	5,557 metres
1982	Aconcagua, Argentina	22,834 feet	6,960 metres
1982	Muztagh Ata, China	24,757 feet	7,546 metres
1983	Gillman's Point, Kilimanjaro Tanzania	18,640 feet	5,682 metres
1983	North Face, Tour Ronde, France	12,441 feet	3,792 metres
1983	Tocllaraju, Peru	19,790 feet	6,032 metres
1984	Gabarrou Route, Mt. Blanc du Tacul, France	12,800 feet	3,970 metres
1984	Mount Kenya	17,021 feet	5,188 metres

1985	Illimani, Bolivia	21,210 feet	6,465 metres
1985	Huayna Potosi, Bolivia	19,947 feet	6,080 metres
1985	Tarija, Bolivia	17,224 feet	5,250 metres
1985	Triglav, Yugoslavia	9,393 feet	2,863 metres
1985	Spik, Yugoslavia	8,110 feet	2,472 metres
1985	Lipnica, Yugoslavia	7,933 feet	2,418 metres
1986	Alpamayo, Peru	19,511 feet	5,947 metres
1986	Assiniboine, Canada	1,770 feet	3,618 metres
1986	Nub Peak, Canada	8,999 feet	2,743 metres
1986	Heim Glacier, Kilimanjaro, Tanzania	19,344 feet	5,896 metres
1986	Broad Peak, Pakistan	*reached c.* 23,000 feet	7,000 metres
1988	Alpamayo Chico, Bolivia	17,716 feet	5,400 metres
1988	Tarija, Bolivia	17,224 feet	5,250 metres
1988	Cheget Kara, Russia	12,031 feet	3,667 metres
1988	Elbrus, Russia	18,510 feet	5,642 metres
1989	Paglia Orba, Corsica	7,388 feet	2,252 metres
1989	Monte Cinto, Corsica	8,878 feet	2,706 metres
1989	Cotopaxi, Ecuador	9,347 feet	5,897 metres
1990	Aiguille de la Tsa, Switzerland	12,034 feet	3,668 metres
1990	Aiguille des Ravines Rousses, Switzerland	10,689 feet	3,258 metres
1990	Aiguille de la Tour, France	11,621 feet	3,542 metres
1990	Ulrichshorn, Switzerland	12,877 feet	3,952 metres
1991	Aiguille de Dibona, France	10,269 feet	3,130 metres
1991	Weissmeiss, SE summit, Switzerland	12,995 feet	3,961 metres
1991	Masherbrum II, Pakistan	*c.* 22,000 feet	6,700 metres
1992	Index, France	8,514 feet	2,595 metres
1993	Breithorn, Switzerland	13,664 feet	4,165 metres
1993	Everest, Tibet	*reached* 25,000 feet	7,600 metres
1994	Shishapangma, Tibet	*reached c.* 25,000 feet	7,600 metres
1994	Unnamed peak, Tibet	13,120 feet	4,000 metres
1995	Cho Oyu, Tibet	26,906 feet	8,201 metres
1997	Finsteraarhorn,Switzerland	14,018 feet	4,273 metres
1997	Monte Rosa, Switzerland	15,203 feet	4,634 metres
1997	Chimborazo, Ecuador	20,700 feet	6,310 metres
1998	Sasso di Stria, Italy	8,127 feet	2,477 metres
1998	Laganzoui, Italy	9,199 feet	2,804 metres
1998	Torre Grande, Italy	7,746 feet	2,361 metres
1998	Torre Latina, Italy	7,415 feet	2,260 metres
1998	Cima Cadin del Refugio, Italy	7,992 feet	2,436 metres

1999	La Vierge, Switzerland	10,604 feet	3,232 metres
1999	Pt. 3086.5, Switzerland	10,126 feet	3,086.5 metres
1999	Pigne de la Le, Switzerland	11,142 feet	3,396 metres
1999	Pt. Pigne de la Le, Switzerland	10,466 feet	3,190 metres
1999	Bouquetins Ridge, Switzerland	10,964 feet	3,342 metres
1999	Kl. Allalin, Switzerland	10,072 feet	3,070 metres
1999	Unter Rothorn, Switzerland	10,180 feet	3,103 metres

ACKNOWLEDGEMENTS

As well as those thanked in the text - Sherpas in particular - I wish to acknowledge the assistance given in many forms by the following:

W Adams, Agfa-Gevaert Ltd., Air France, Air India, Airtrak, Daniel Alessio, Allcord Ltd, All the Right Signs, Alpine Club, Alpine Club Library, Amtrak, Andean Society, Anglian Fell and Rock Club, Francis Antony Ltd, Applied Chemicals Ltd., Senor Cesar Morales Arnao, M.Ashraf, Aston Containers Ltd., Atholl Arms Hotel, Sue Bailey, Bernard Aylward, Bamboo Club, Banaman, Martin Barnicott, Mr & Mrs J. Batten, BBC, Caroline Beecher, Beechnuts Curling Club, Steve Bell, the Bennachie Whisky, Michael Bentine, Berghaus Ltd, Major Michael Berry, Steve Berry, the Bibby family, Mr & Mrs Roger Biggs, Margaret Billings, Mrs A.J. Blythe, Dick Boetius, Walter Bonatti, BP Oil, Peter Brady, Peter Bramick, Marion & Bryan Breed, John Brierley, The Lord Mayor of Bristol, Bristol Evening Post, Bristol Round Table, Bristol and West Building Society, Britannia Building Society, British Mountaineering Council, Monty Brown, Buchanan Booth Agencies, Roger Buckley, Burgess Hill School, The Burgess Twins, Mr Burrell, Rob Burton, Busby's Hairdressers, Penny Buttenshaw, the Caledonian at Bonar Bridge, Mike Callahan, Callestock Cider Farm, Calvert Trusts, Mike Calvin, Brian Campbell, Canon Cameras, Caravan Ltd., Mr & Mrs Cardew, Carey & Co, John Carruthers, Cathay Pacific, Mr & Mrs Joe Chamberlain, Alok & Renee Chandola, Charities Aid Foundation, the Chimes of Dunblane, Chinese Mountaineering Association, Dr A. Clarke, Dr C. Clarke, John Cleare, Climbing Gear Ltd., Clogwyn Climbing and Safety Equipment, Cole & Hicks Estate Agents, Mr & Mrs S. Coles, Chris Collins, Collins (Norwich) Ltd., Colmans Foods, the Compass at North Petherton, Diana Corbin, Ron Corkhill, Mr & Mrs J. Cornish, Arthur Cort & Co. Ltd, Pat Cox, Mr & Mrs P. Craig, Craigrossie Hotel, Crawford Arms Hotel, Mal Creasey, Simon Crombie, Crossways Inn at Highbridge, Crown Hotels, Mr & Mrs A. Croucher, Mr & Mrs E. Croucher, Mrs M. Croucher, Jane and Peter Cullinan, Peter Cummings, Richard Cuthbertson, Mrs A. Cutliffe, CWS, Damart, Margaret Dangoor, Elwyn & Doreen Davies, Mr & Mrs N. Davies at the Dingle Hotel, Dingles (Bristol), Disabled Sports Foundation, Dixons Photographic (U.K. Ltd.), DMM Engineering Ltd, Graeme Donnan, Colette & Jimmy Donovan, Terry Duffy, Rev. Jim Duncan, Frank & Mo Dunning, Dusty at the Sutherland Arms, the Eagle and Child at Garstang, Ealing Cricket Club members, Jason Edwards, the Elizabethan Luncheon Club, Susan Elliot and Dave, Peter Ellis of REMAP, Kate Emptage, Epigas International Ltd, Phil Ershler, Pepe Espinosa, Europa Sport, Mr & Mrs F.A Evans, Exeter Mobility Centre, Farillon, Mr & Mrs R. M. Feekery, Richard Fenton, Leopold Ferjancic, Field and Trek Equipment Ltd, Alec Fish, Bryan Fitzgerald and family, Dr Fletcher, Dr K. Fowler, Fowlers of Bristol, Frenchay Hospital, David Franklin, Fuller, Smith and Turner, Gallaghers Tobacco, Jim Galt, Clive Garrett, Mike Gassner, Mick Geddes, N. Gifford, Richard Gray, Geco (UK) Ltd, Mazzone Gianni, Peggy Gilliland and Joy, Ginsters Cornish Pasties, Glenfiddich, Gloria and Mike of Southview in Lyndhurst, Glorious Twelfth, Chris Grace, Granada Business Centre, Mr & Mrs F. Green, Mrs E.

Griffiths, Mr & Mrs R. Grisdale, Group 10, June Gould, John Haig & Co. Ltd., Bill Haigh, Halifax Building Society, Mark and Susan Hallam, J.E.Hanger & Co. Ltd., Dr L.E. Halliday, J.E. Hanger & Co, Annie Harris, Harrow Marmots, Mr & Mrs G. Haslam, Ken Hayward, Mr & Mrs R. Heaviside, Mrs Dwin Hendry, HFC, Himalayan Kingdoms, E.R.Hemmings, John Hinde, Geoff Hine, Mr & Mrs R.G. Holden, Holderness Limb Centre, Honeywell Ltd., Bill Hornyak, David House, Mr & Mrs J. Hultin, John Hunt and Sandy of Sprayway Ltd, Indian Mountaineering Foundation, Intermed, Jammu and Kashmir Mountaineering and Hiking Club, J. & K. Department of Tourism, Craig John, Alan Jones, Glyn Jones, Richard Jones, T.E Jones, Wanchuck Kaloon, Tourist Officer at Kargil, Karrimor International Ltd, Lily Keen, Kellogg, Sean Kennedy and family, Ayub Khan, Kilimanjaro Mountain Club, Kingston-on-Thames Association for the Disabled, Jo and Paul Kilner, Alan Kimber, Jan and Dave Kitchen, Bruce Klepinger, KLM, Jimmy Knox, Kodak Ltd., Koflach Boots, K Shoes, Terry and Brenda Lansbury, Drs Margaret and Allan Lauder, John Leycock, Tom and Sue Leadbitter, The Leeds, Richard Lehner, Dietrich Lemke, Mr & Mrs B. Leverton, Rosemary and Ken Lewis, Lima Tours, Peter and Renee Lingard, Jo Lloyd, London and Edinburgh Trust, Gerry Lynch, Andrew and Sylvia Mackenzie, Richard Mann, Mr A.J. Mansell, James Marler, Mars, Senor Gonzales Mata, Chris Martin, Phillip Mawer, Mr & Mrs W. Maycock, Anna McDermott, Jenny McGregor, Steve McKinney, Martin McWilliams, Metropole Hotel in Brighton, Mickey and Martin, Lily and John Milton, Dr John Minors, Peter Minty, Dr P. Moffit, Denny Moorhouse, Dr George Moore, Mount Everest Foundation, Mountain Club of Kenya, Mountain Equipment Ltd., Mountain Travel, Mountain World, Mr & Mrs Mullins, Natwest Bank of Ealing, A.T.Needle, Barry Needle, Nelson's of Aintree, Mark and Susie Newman, Nicholas Laboratories, Christine Nichols, Nikon U.K. Ltd., N.R. Components, Ortho Supplies, Out There Trekking, Simon Pannell, Crompton Parkinson, Mike Parsons, David Payne, Penrose Outdoors, Pentax UK Ltd, Eric Perlman, Peruvian Andean Club, Iain and Libby Peter, Bob Pettigrew, Dr Andy Pickard, Tony Pickering, Pindisports, Plume of Feathers at Okehampton, Pocahontas Ltd., Mrs A. Pollard, Mike Porter, Mr & Mrs E.R. Powell, Joan Pralong, Prince of Orange, Mr Qui, Daniel Quiggin & Sons, Dr M. Quin, Rainier Mountaineering, RADAR, Rank Xerox, Ghulm Rasool, Les Rendell, Sepp and Barbara Renner, Kay Reynolds, Alun Richardson, Mr & Mrs Richie, Jimmy Roberts, Mr & Mrs N. Roberts, James Robertson & Sons, Roboserve Ltd., The Viscountess Rochdale CBE, JP, Roehampton Limb Centre, Rohan, Alan Rouse, Royal Geographical Society, Royal Oak at Alveley, Royal Stewart Hotel, Jon Ryder, St. Joseph's School, Horwich, Miguel Sanchez, Robert Saunders (Chigwell) Ltd., Mr & Mrs T. Savage, Gerhardt Schwartz, Myfanwy Scrivener, J.A. Sharwood, Peter Schweiger, Doug Scott, Mr & Mrs E. Shand, Graham Sharpe, Mr & Mrs D.K.Shelley, Shire Hall Communications, J.J.Silber, Peter Sillett, Gary Sillitoe, Dr Mike Sinclair, Mr D. St B. Sladen, Ian and Margaret Smillie, Irene Smith, Mary and Jim Smith, Mark Smith and Sarah, Rosie Smith, Smith and Nephew, John Smolich, Karin Snape, Sony (U.K.) Ltd., South American Explorers Club, Sovintersport, Spa Filling Station at Strathpeffer, Bill Sparkes, John, Claire, Jack and James Spedding, Sprayway Ltd., Gordon Stainforth, St Mungo's Hotel, Dr Peter Steel, Hugh Steeper & Co., Iris and David Stenner, Mr & Mrs T. Stenner,

Arnis Strapcans, Mr & Mrs T. Stringer, Mr Su, Mr & Mrs G. Tarrant, Tefal Ltd., Ang Temba, Nina Temba, Terra Nova Equipment Ltd., Mick and Jenny Thompson, Norman Thompson, Mrs J. Thorn, Thornbury Rotary Club, Mr & Mrs J. Tilston, TNT Express, Jens Toft, J.Toogood, Jean and Richard Toon, many people in Topsham, Troll Safety Equipment Ltd., John, Tina and Donald Tuach, Tunbridge Wells Camera Centre, Twickenham Travel, Wendy Twist, Ultimate Equipment Ltd., Craig Van Hoy, Hector Vietes, Viasa Airways, Ulises Vitale, Ghafoor Wahid, the Walden family, Mrs E. Warne, Warwick Productions, Sandy Watson, Rob Weight, Jackie Welham, Norma Welsh, Westcroft, Wexas International, Bill & Iris Marks and staff and customers at The Wheatsheaf, Ealing, Miss Kay Whalley, White Hart Hotel at Launceston, Wild Things (USA), Adrian Williams, Angela Williams, Brian Williams, Dr J.G.P.Williams, William IV at Hampstead, George Wilson, Winston Churchill Memorial Trust, Wintergear Ltd., Women's Section of Southfields and Central Wandsworth British Legion, Woodhead Mountain Rescue Team, S.Wooler, Rod Wooley, Mr & Mrs Roy Wood, Phillip Wren, Sir George Young, Y.H.A., Yugoslav National Tourist Office, Yousuf Zaheer, Zero Point Nine.

GLOSSARY

Abseil

To slide down a rope.

Aiguille

Steep, sharp rock peak (in French, 'needle').

Arête

A sharp rock ridge.

Belay

Noun: an anchor point which may be natural, such as a spike of rock, a tree or thick icicle, or artificial, such as a piton or nut (see nut). Verb: to make use of such an anchor or to hold the rope to safeguard a companion.

Bergschrund

A big crevasse (see crevasse) which forms between the upper snow and ice of a mountain and the glacier below.

Bivouac (bivi)

To sleep without a tent, usually in a waterproof bag.

Cairn

A pile of stones set up to mark a point such as a summit, or in a series to mark a route.

Chimney

A vertical or slanting crack of sufficient width to get your body in.

Col

A pass, saddle.

Cornice

Overhanging mass of snow, formed by wind action, shaped like a wave frozen as it breaks.

Couloir

Steep chute.

Grades

For our purposes: Britain, on rock – Easy, Moderate, Difficult, Very Difficult, Severe, Very Severe, Extreme.
The Alps – 1 to 6, 1 being the easiest. (To assist the non-climber, in

this book numbers have been substituted for the usual French Alpine grades such as 'assez difficile'.)

Harness

A climbing harness is something like a parachute harness, and made of nylon tape.

Karabiner (Krab)

A strong metal snaplink which closes on a similar principle to that of a safety pin.

Moraine

In mountaineering terms, boulder, rock and dust rubble carried down by a glacier and deposited in huge mounds.

Nut

A metal chockstone which is inserted temporarily in a crack in such a way that it will not be pulled out (we hope!) when a load is put on it. Used for belays and runners (see runners).

Pack (backpack)

A modern type of framed rucksack.

Peg

See Piton.

Pitch

Section of a climb, the length of which is often dictated by the availability of belay anchors. Usually between 20 metres and 45 metres, the upper limit being the length of the climbing rope.

Piton

A metal peg with an eye-hole, which is hammered into a crack. The use of pitons is not generally popular nowadays because insertion and removal damage the rock; nuts (see nuts) are much more common.

Runner, running belay

See first the noun version of belay. In the case of a runner the climber does not attach himself or herself to the belay, but attaches a karabiner and lets the climbing rope run free through it. The karabiner then acts rather like a simple pulley wheel.

Scree

Steep slopes of loose stones.

Second

Simply, to climb second. The word is also used as a noun to denote the second climber.

Sérac

Unstable ice cliff, ice pinnacles.

Snowshoes

The older type of snowshoe was often described as looking like a tennis racket. Modern types may be made of plastic, or metal frames with nylon strings, amongst other materials. When strapped to boots they distribute one's weight, thus reducing the depth to which the feet sink in soft snow.

Spindrift

Fine, powdery snow, often wind-blown, or sliding down a mountain.

Traverse

Noun: a horizontal section of climbing. Also a verb meaning, obviously enough, to climb a horizontal section.

Verglas

A thin layer of ice no more than a few millimetres thick, coated on rock.

Wand

A light stick, possibly bamboo, usually with a small flag, left in the snow to mark a route which is complicated and/or in case of bad weather.

INDEX

Klepinger, Bruce   124, 126, 127

Laycock, John   235, 238 – 241
Lees, Rob   211 – 216
Lipp, Graham   275 – 278, 281
Loss of legs   5, 6, 7

Masherbrum II, Pakistan   273 – 279
Matterhorn, Switzerland   35, 41, 75 – 87
Mayer, Ted   153, 168 – 186
McKinney, Steve   172 – 185
Men of the Year   59
Miller, Mark   273 – 278, 281
Mönch, Switzerland   25 – 29, 32
Mont Blanc, France   42, 43 – 58
Monte Rosa, Switzerland   348
Motivation, self motivation   123, 157, 189, 220, 221, 227, 335, 336
Muirs, Brigitte and Jon   290, 293 – 305
Muztagh Ata, China   161 – 187

Needle, Barry   141, 147, 148, 149, 235
Nun, Kashmir   137 – 150

OBE 78
Opposition to climbing, rejection   1, 3, 19, 25, 28, 41, 42, 79, 80, 208,
        273, 276, 279
OTT   273, 282, 289 – 308
Outdoor pursuits for disabled people   31, 77, 78 – 80, 187

Parsons, Dave   59 – 63, 75 – 77, 237
Peter, Iain and Libby   330, 337, 344, 346, 347
Performance/behaviour   178, 262, 296, 301, 302, 304
Perranporth, Cornwall   8, 17, 20
Petrig, Eddy   80 – 87,
Pisco, Peru   104, 105

Reasons vs. excuses   135, 149, 162, 188
Redruth Grammar School   13, 16, 17
Renner, Sepp and Barbara   238 – 241
Rock climbing, early days   1, 2
Rockfall   76, 133, 278
Ryder, John   92 – 95, 220